Software Design
A Comprehensive Guide to
Software Development Projects

Software Design
A Comprehensive Guide to Software Development Projects

Murali Chemuturi

CRC Press
Taylor & Francis Group
Boca Raton London New York

CRC Press is an imprint of the
Taylor & Francis Group, an **informa** business

A CHAPMAN & HALL BOOK

CRC Press
Taylor & Francis Group
6000 Broken Sound Parkway NW, Suite 300
Boca Raton, FL 33487-2742

© 2018 by Taylor & Francis Group, LLC
CRC Press is an imprint of Taylor & Francis Group, an Informa business

No claim to original U.S. Government works

Printed on acid-free paper

International Standard Book Number-13: 978-0-8153-8276-8 (Hardback)

Library of Congress Cataloging-in-Publication Data

Names: Chemuturi, Murali, 1950- author.
Title: Software design : a comprehensive guide to software development projects /
Murali Chemuturi.
Description: First edition. | Boca Raton, FL : CRC Press/Taylor & Francis Group, 2018. |
"A CRC title, part of the Taylor & Francis imprint, a member of the Taylor & Francis Group,
the academic division of T&F Informa plc." | Includes bibliographical references and index.
Identifiers: LCCN 2017055051| ISBN 9780815382768 (hardback : acid-free paper)
| ISBN 9781351068567 (ebook)
Subjects: LCSH: Computer software--Development.
Classification: LCC QA76.76.D47 C4795 2018 | DDC 005.1--dc 3
LC record available at https://lccn.loc.gov/2017055051

Visit the Taylor & Francis Web site at
http://www.taylorandfrancis.com

and the CRC Press Web site at
http://www.crcpress.com

This book is dedicated to my family: they are

the base and the inspiration of my life.

"We have to look without fear to the

technological transformation of economy."

Papa Francesco

Contents

Foreword

As we hurtle down one of North America's high-tech highways from Michigan to the Florida Keys, my iPhone 7 Plus has just announced, in her Australian accent, that if I maintain posted speed limits, I will complete the 1523-mile journey in 22 hours, 43 minutes. The iPhone, ever helpful, will update our ETA as I adjust velocity or decide to stop for the night—after she has offered a choice of available hotels—and keep me up to date on the latest weather and traffic while providing wireless for my passengers. For the entire journey, we'll be safely ensconced in the highest of high-tech vehicles, a rented 2018 Chevrolet Suburban with auto-*everything*, including software that helps me safely manage a few dozen business calls using my Bose noise-canceling Bluetooth earpiece. Wow.

Futurist Arthur C. Clarke once said that "any sufficiently advanced technology is indistinguishable from magic." To professionals like my good friend and colleague Murali Chemuturi, it's all about design. Design is where the magic becomes real, and where the most advanced skills and capabilities are required.

This is the second time I have been honored to write a foreword for one of Murali's excellent books on software engineering, and this one hits close to home.

As a CMMI Lead Appraiser, CMMI Instructor, and Agile Leadership coach, I have observed hundreds of technology organizations and, without a doubt, the state of design capability in our industry is sorely in need of the leadership Murali provides us in his book, the latest in a long series of excellent texts on software engineering.

Craftsmanship is all the rage in the software community these days, so much so that #craftsmanship on Twitter yields millions of hits, most of them expressing a renewed interest in the concept, first introduced in 1992 in Pete McBreen's book by the same name. This is, finally, a great awakening in software engineering, but it's not enough. While the renaissance in software craftsmanship is, at last, getting the attention it deserves, excellence in *design* is the next frontier, and it is what makes the difference between a good product and a magical technology. A great design improves quality, reduces cost, and transforms an idea into an implementable product that delights the customer and ensures that the solution will meet its intended need. Any technology leader would welcome an equally enthusiastic renaissance in software design, and this book doesn't disappoint.

The "Manifesto for Software Craftsmanship" was released in 2009, and it yielded a new, positive focus on software quality. Murali has given us a new manifesto for design that will quickly become the go-to treatise for the next generation of software engineers.

Let the "magic" begin.

Jeff Dalton
President, Broadsword Solutions Corp.
CMMI SCAMPI Lead Appraiser.
Chairman, CMMI Institute Partner Advisory Board.
Marathon, FL. 2018.

Preface

I began thinking about this book in 2014 when my last book was completed and went into publication. I began my sojourn into the world of authoring software engineering books in 2008 when I first authored a book on software estimation. Then, I authored a book on software project management, followed by a book on software quality assurance. Then, I authored another book on requirements engineering and management and a book on IT project management. With these books on software estimation, software project management, and IT project management, I covered the management aspect of producing software. When I looked at the engineering side of software development, I covered the requirements and quality assurance aspects of software development. This left two topics, namely software design and software programming.

I decided to address these two topics and began thinking about software design, marshalling my learning, experience, and observation into cohesive thinking. I began forming an outline and preparing first drafts. I took much more time for this book than with the other books, as there is more misunderstanding in the industry about this topic than the others about which I have already written. There are many, both in the industry and academia, who think that software design cannot be separated from programming. But it was so in the initial stages of manufacturing, and division of manufacturing into design and implementation of design produced better-quality goods at cheaper prices. In fact, design was bifurcated into conceptual design and detailed design (also referred to as engineering). I wish to dispel this misconception that design cannot be separated from programming; in a few progressive organizations, it is already separated. I wish to bring software design as a specialist activity to the mainstream of academia and the industry.

Thus, this book was born. I would love to have your feedback and promise to respond to your emails, normally within one business day. You can contact me at murali@chemuturi.com.

Acknowledgments

When I look back, I find that there are so many people to whom I should be grateful. Be it because of their commissions or omissions, they made me a stronger and a better person, and both directly and indirectly helped to make this book possible. It would be difficult to acknowledge everyone's contributions here, so to those whose names may not appear, I wish to thank you all just the same. I will have failed in my duty if I did not explicitly and gratefully acknowledge the persons below:

- My parents, Appa Rao and Vijaya Lakshmi, the reason for my existence, especially my father, a rustic agrarian, who by personal example taught me the virtue of hard work and the value of the aroma of perspiration from the brow.
- My family, who stood by me like a rock in times of struggle, especially my wife of 44 years, Udaya Sundari, who gave me the confidence and the belief that "I can," and my two sons, Dr. Nagendra and Vijay, who provided me the motivation to excel.
- My two uncles, Raju and Ramana, who by personal example taught me what integrity and excellence mean.

To all of you, I humbly bow my head in respect, and salute you in acknowledgment of your contribution.

Author

Murali Chemuturi is an information technology and software development subject matter expert, hands-on programmer, author, consultant, and trainer. Since 2001, he has offered consultancy on information technology and training to organizations in India and the United States through Chemuturi Consultants. Chemuturi Consultants also offers a number of products to aid project managers and software development professionals such as PMPal, a software project management tool, and EstimatorPal, FPAPal, and UCPPal, a set of software estimation tools. Chemuturi Consultants also offers a material requirements planning software product, MRPPal, to assist small to medium manufacturing organizations in efficiently managing their materials.

Prior to starting his own firm, Murali gained over 15 years of industrial experience in various engineering and manufacturing management positions. He then gained more than 30 years of information technology and software development experience. His most recent position prior to forming his firm was Vice President of Software Development at Vistaar e-Business Pvt., Ltd.

Mr. Chemuturi's undergraduate degrees and diplomas are in electrical and industrial engineering, and he holds an MBA and a postgraduate diploma in computer methods and programming. He has several years of academic experience teaching a variety of computer and IT courses such as COBOL, Fortran, BASIC, Computer Architecture, and Database Management Systems. He was inducted into the Hall of Fame by the CSI, Mumbai Chapter, in December 2016.

Mr. Chemuturi has authored three books, namely *Software Estimation: Best Practices, Tools and Techniques for Software Project Estimators*, *Mastering Software Quality Assurance: Best Practices, Tools and Techniques for Software Developers*, and *Mastering IT Project Management: Best Practices, Tools and Techniques*, published in the United States by J. Ross Publishing, Inc. He authored a book titled *Requirements Engineering and Management for Software Development Projects* published in the United States by Springer Science+Business, and co-authored another book with Thomas M. Cagley, Jr., *Mastering Software Project Management: Best Practices, Tools and Techniques*, published by J. Ross Publishing, Inc., of the United States.

Murali is a senior member of IEEE, a senior member of the Computer Society of India, and a Fellow of the Indian Institute of Industrial Engineering, and he is a well-published author in professional journals.

1

Introduction to Design

Introduction

The term *design* is not just used for product design. It is also used in the following contexts:

1. Design of a product
2. Design of a service
3. Design of a facility to manufacture a set of products or to deliver a set of services
4. Design of physical systems, such as a material handling system
5. Design of a network, such as a transportation network
6. Design of organizational processes, such as planning processes, project management processes, and so on

There are many more occasions where we use the term *design*. All of these have some common objectives to be achieved:

1. There is a set of functionalities to be achieved.
2. The functionality has to be delivered securely, safely, and efficiently.
3. The functionality has to be achieved in a cost-effective manner.
4. It must be possible to implement the design with the available technology.

Many times, a design already exists that needs to be improved to take advantage of the latest developments in technology or to gain a competitive advantage over existing designs.

In this book, we focus the discussion on the product design, and that also applies to designing a software product. But before we can move on to product design, we need to understand what a product is.

Product

We need to understand what a product is so that we can design a better/new product. Let us first look at what a product is.

The Merriam-Webster dictionary defines a product as "something produced" and as "something that is marketed or sold as a commodity."

The Oxford Dictionary defines a product as "an article or substance that is manufactured or refined for sale."

The law defines a product as "a commercially distributed good that is a tangible personal property; output or result of a fabrication, manufacturing, or a production process; and passes through a distribution channel before being consumed or used."

In all these definitions, emphasis is placed on the aspect of selling, except in the definition of law. So, we need to look up what the marketing discipline has to say about products. The field of marketing has come up with a number of definitions for a product.

One definition of product is: "a product is something of value for which a customer is willing to pay." This definition emphasizes the necessity of having a customer willing to pay. If the product cannot attract a buyer, then it is not a product. Then, the questions that crops up is, "Would a customer buy this product?" or, paraphrasing it, "Would I buy this product?" If we answer one of these questions with a "yes," the next question would be, "Which class of people would buy this product and what are their preferences?" The answers to these two questions will guide us in designing a product that will meet the preferences of the potential customers.

Another definition of a product is: "a product is something that fulfills a need or a want and has a market to sell it." This definition has two key aspects, namely fulfillment of a need or want and the existence of a market in which it can be sold.

Then, one more definition of a product is: "a product is a bundle of benefits." This definition focuses on what benefits the customer expects from the product. Obviously, the customer needs to derive some benefit from the product. The benefits may be:

1. *Functional benefit*: A car helps people go from a place to another place. A light bulb gives light. A stove helps in cooking food.

2. *Visual benefit*: The product brings beauty to a place. A painting on a wall attracts people and gives satisfaction to the owner. A good dress makes the individual appear more beautiful. A beautiful car attracts glances from onlookers.

3. *Comfort benefit*: A seat in a car makes the journey comfortable. Air conditioning in a home makes one's stay comfortable. Paved roads make the drive comfortable.

4. *Convenience benefit*: A steering wheel in a car is more convenient than a handlebar. A refrigerator is more convenient than an icebox. A laptop is more convenient than a desktop. A mouse is more convenient for using the computer than giving commands using the keyboard.

5. *Relaxation benefit*: A video game provides relaxation. Radio or a CD/DVD player in a car provides relaxation while driving. A television provides relaxation in the home.

6. *Notional benefit*: The benefit is in the feeling. A beauty cream gives you the confidence that you look more attractive. A perfume can make you feel desirable.

There are many ways of classifying products. Let us look at some classifications.

1. *Product classification based on use*: Some products are used to produce another product. A lathe machine is a product that is used to produce products or components. A coffeemaker is used to produce coffee. Some products are used to provide a service. A television is used to provide entertainment. A telephone is used to converse with people not in close vicinity. A coach (bus) is used to transport people. Some

products are used to produce products as well as to provide a service. A personal computer is used to produce software products as well as to surf the Internet.

2. *Product classification based on durability*: Some products can be used in a recurring manner again and again. Some products can be used only once. Electricity is a good example of a single-use product, as are food products and all medicines. They need to be consumed upon production and are not available for a second use. A car, on the other hand, can be used again and again.

3. *Product classification based on its finality*: Some products go directly to their customers for use. All the consumer products we use in our homes are end products. These are final products. Some products are used as components or subassemblies in other products. They are not used directly. A car seat is used as a component inside a car. It is not directly used as an end product.

4. *Product classification based on hardness*: Products are classified as hard products and soft products. All documents, books, scripts, computer software, and all types of intellectual property come under soft products. All other products, including soft toys, are hard products.

There are, of course, other classifications of products from the standpoint of the market and production processes.

Definition of Design

The word *design* can be used as a verb and as a noun. In its verb form, *design* is the process of carrying out the design, and in its noun form, *design* is the outcome of the process of design.

The Merriam-Webster dictionary gives multiple meanings for the word *design*. The most appropriate ones for our context are given as "to conceive and plan out in the mind" and "to devise for a specific function," as well as "to make a drawing, pattern, or sketch." All of these are appropriate to describe the meaning of the word *design*.

While Wikipedia does not have a section for "design" per se, it has a section for "product design." It states, "The product designer's role is to combine art, science, and technology to create new products that other people can use." This also gives the definition of design in an indirect way; thus, "Design combines art, science, and technology to create new products that other people can use."

The Industrial Designers Society of America (http://www.idsa.org/) defines industrial design as "the professional service of creating and developing concepts and specifications that optimize the function, value and appearance of products and systems for the mutual benefit of both the user and manufacturer."

I have developed a definition of design drawing upon my own experience, observation, and study: "Design is a creative process to ensure that a defined set of functionality is delivered efficiently, economically, aesthetically, securely, and safely; record that design in a manner that can be easily understood and implemented to realize the product by those fabricating/constructing/developing the product; and to ensure that the resultant product is reliable, safe, secure, flexible, maintainable, and marketable. It draws upon the knowledge base of science and engineering together with social sciences and aesthetics as well as the knowledge repository of the organization."

There could be many more definitions of the term *design*. From the above definitions, we can draw these inferences:

1. Design involves conceptualization in the mind.
2. Design involves devising a product.
3. Design involves combining art, science, and technology.
4. Design involves creating as well as developing concepts and specifications.
5. Design involves optimization of the function, value, and appearance.
6. Design involves ensuring safety and security.
7. Design involves ensuring an aesthetically pleasing appearance to the target market segment.
8. Design involves defining and ensuring the capacity of the product.
9. Design involves ensuring cost effectiveness in all aspects from conceptualization through use.
10. Design involves recording the design for others qualified to understand and manufacture/develop the product.
11. Design involves ensuring reliability in performance and delivering the defined functionality over the life of the product.

Let us look at each of these inferences.

Design involves conceptualization in the mind: It is necessary to understand what needs to be achieved and how to achieve it. First, we need to understand the functionality that is to be achieved. Then, we need to understand how to deliver that functionality. The functionality can be a single function or multiple functions. This requires that the designer be a technical person with the necessary technical skills to understand the functionality. Second, the designer needs to be a thinker, especially an original thinker, to understand how to deliver the functionality. He or she must have knowledge of alternative methods of delivering the functionality. For example, let us consider the design of matchsticks and a matchbox. To the ancients, fire was a natural force to be feared and respected. Then, they discovered that fire can be produced using friction. But someone found a business opportunity in supplying fire safely to his or her customers. This conceptualized putting inflammable material at the end of a dry stick that catches fire when scratched against a rough surface. These sticks were supplied in small bundles. Present-day matchsticks and lighters are innovations over the first fire sticks. While James Watt invented a steam engine that turned a wheel with the steam produced by a boiler, making it into a transportation vehicle involved conceptualizing a locomotive by tying together a boiler, an engine, and a set of wheels. The details were worked out later as to how much steam to produce, how to supply water to the boiler, how to convey the steam to the engine, and so on. Once it is conceptualized, it is put on paper for analysis and improvement. Conceptualizing is the first step in design.

Design involves devising a product: The process of design, in addition to understanding the desired functionality and how to deliver it, involves devising a product. Here, we need to understand what a product is. It was already dealt with in a separate section in this chapter. Let us consider our locomotive example. Once the product is conceived, the components needed for building the product are enumerated as a boiler to produce steam, an engine to convert the steam energy into motive power, a steam-conveying system from the boiler to the engine, a power transmission system to covey the motive power produced by the engine to the wheels, set of wheels to convert the power supplied by the engine into motion, and a housing to hold all these components. Now, these components are the core of the product. Then, we need ancillary components for functions such as to start the engine, stop the engine, store water, fuel the boiler, store fuel, and so on. Then, we need to devise how the operation of the product should work. Some operations are performed by the product and some operations need manual support. Then, we need to devise safety and security components. In this manner, we need to devise the complete product, including core and ancillary functions.

Design involves combining art, science, and technology: The product, when built conforming to the design, ought to be appealing to the aesthetic senses of the intended users. This necessitates that the individual carrying out the design be an artist or be able to give ideas to an artist to come up with something pleasing to the eye. The product needs to use proven principles using the scientific method if it is to function. The scientific method is based on three aspects, namely repeatability, controllability, and freedom from bias. Technology comes in handy while building the product. The designed product has to be built using the available technology. Thus, the design has to devise a product that is pleasing to the eye (art), is based on proven principles (science), and is producible (technology). The automobile is an excellent example of this combination. The shape of the car is a creation of art. Internal decoration, fittings, and trim are all designed by artists. The development of new materials and processes are a contribution of science. The development of plastics and fiber-reinforced plastics converted the car from an all-metal box to a car that has a lot of reinforced plastic, resulting in reduced weight and increased fuel efficiency. The development of new varieties of paints and painting processes resulted in long-lasting surface sheen, dust repellant, and increased scratch resistance. There are so many innovations in the automobile since its inception that combined the inventions and discoveries of science that were dovetailed into the car by the use of technology. The technology of designing the car, like computer-aided design (CAD) and analysis of the performance, reduced the design cycle time. The technology in producing the cars such as computer-aided manufacturing (CAM), computer-integrated manufacturing (CIM), and flexible manufacturing systems (FMSs) have increased the efficiency of manufacturing along with increasing quality and reducing cost. Because of the effective combination of art, science, and technology, the increase in the cost of an automobile is much less than what it would have been if these improvements had not been implemented. The reliability also increased vastly.

Design involves creating as well as developing requirements and specifications: The requirements for products are enunciated by the users or by an entrepreneur. These are raw in nature and need to be developed further. A commuter may say that he/she wants an easier method to travel from one place to another. No other requirements come from the commuter. The entrepreneur may say that money can be made if a personal transportation vehicle can be designed and sold. The entrepreneur would not say what its dimensions, the capacity, or the reliability ought to be. The designers need to develop these raw requirements further so they are at a granularity from which the product can be designed with all the core and ancillary functionalities. The ancillary functionalities will not come from any other source. The onus of developing these ancillary functions is on the designer. The designer needs to come up with various specifications for the product. These include specifications for the materials, methods, quality levels, capacity, safety, security, usability, reliability, and maintainability. The designer also needs to specify the international, national, industry, or organizational standards that the product needs to adhere to so that the product can be certified as safe and usable for the targeted customers.

Design involves optimization of the function, value, and appearance: The design cannot swing to extremes in the three aspects of function, value, and appearance. Design cannot sacrifice any of these parameters for the sake of the other two. That is where the aspect of optimization comes in. If possible, we ought to design a product that has the best in functionality, the best in value, and the best in appearance, which is ideal. More often than not, we give the best possible functionality, the best possible value, and the best possible appearance to strike a balance between these three aspects. How to optimize these three components of a product is a designer's responsibility.

Design involves ensuring safety and security: No product should be released to its intended customers without safety and security built into it. The users must be safe while using the product. The features of seat belts, air conditioning, and air bags are aimed at improving the safety of the passengers and the driver. The trunk, the bumper, and the crumple space in the car shell are features aimed at securing the contents of the car when an accident takes place. The damage is restricted to the car body, but the engine and the other vital components of the car, as well as its passengers, are isolated from the impact. Insurance provides security to anybody affected by the accident. Building a wall along a railway line is a security feature to prevent cattle and other such animals from coming onto the railway tracks and being hit by a train accidentally. Again, the onus of ensuring these features are in the product rests with the designer.

Design involves ensuring an aesthetically pleasing appearance: Along with all the other essential features, the product also must have pleasing appearance. People are not worried about the appearance of essential items, but all others must have an aesthetic appearance. If you carefully observe, you will notice that people will buy, even for essential items like food products, those that are packaged aesthetically and leave those that have less appealing packages. The technical designers may not provide this feature, and we may need someone specialized in aesthetics as part of our design team.

Design involves defining and ensuring the capacity of the product: When we design a product, we need to define a capacity for the product. For example, assuming we are designing a bus, we need to specify the number of passengers it can carry as well as the luggage that can be taken on board. A bus consists of number of component assemblies. The body must provide the correct number of passenger seats and seats for the crew, including the driver, as well as luggage space. The shock absorbers ought to withstand the shocks that rock the bus due to bad road conditions, and we ought to design the shock absorbers so that they withstand shocks in the worst known conditions. We need to design each of the component assemblies that can withstand the pressure put upon them by the load of the passengers and luggage and the dead weight of the bus components. We have to balance the capacity of each of the components such that each component has similar capacity, and that must be above the defined capacity for the product. If we say the capacity of the bus is 50 passengers, then we must take into consideration the worst conditions, like each passenger having maximum weight and bringing aboard the maximum permissible luggage, the road conditions being at the worst known, and the driver being an apprentice. Another important aspect to be kept in mind is that we should design the product at the maximum capacity possible with the technology available. In other words, a similar product designed by our competitor should not possess better capacity than our product. How should we define the capacity of our product? We should define the capacity of the product based on the weakest component in our product. If even a small component fails, the product fails. To give an example of balancing the capacity of components in a product, I will examine the 68000 microprocessor chip. It had a processing capacity of 32 bits, but the bus capacity was only 16 bits. Because of this, the capacity of the microprocessor was limited to 16 bits. While the cost of the product escalated due to the processing capacity, the throughput was limited to that of a lower-capacity 16-bit microprocessor. The customer did not benefit from the product any more than a 16-bit microprocessor. This is the kind of balance we need to achieve in our designs.

Design involves cost effectiveness: It is one thing to design a product, but it is altogether something else to design a product that is cost effective. The customer will always compare the alternatives, and most are willing to pay a premium over the nearest competitor, but not too much. Where public transport is available, all commuters will compare commuting by public transport with the commute by a car. The commuter will be willing to spend double the amount for the comfort of a car, but would not be willing to spend 10 times the amount. Unless our product improves the quality of life over the present alternative, customers will not consider our offering. Unless our offering is cost effective, customers will not spend money on our offering. If we cook our meal at home and it costs $2, a person would be willing to spend around $4 for similar food in a restaurant, but would cook the food if a restaurant costs $20 unless forced. The designer has to keep this aspect in mind while designing the product.

Design involves recording: We need to record the design so that others qualified to understand it can manufacture/construct/develop the product. In engineering disciplines other than software engineering, engineering drawings are used to document the design. Engineering drawings include drawings of plan, elevation, end view, sectional view, bills of material (BOMs), schematic drawings, connection wiring diagrams, flow diagrams, and layouts. A product is depicted using final assembly (FA) drawings, general assembly (GA) drawings, subassembly (SA) drawings, part drawings, connection wiring diagrams, and so on. Engineering drawings are used in construction, manufacturing, and electrification works—you name the engineering field, drawings are used there. In fact, engineering drawing is referred to as the language of engineers. It is by using engineering drawings that engineers and designers communicate the design to the people who build the product. The only exception is the field of software engineering. In software engineering, the practice so far has been to record the design using textual documents. The use of drawings was tried in software engineering, and methods like data flow diagrams (DFDs), entity relationship diagrams (ERDs), flow charts, and so on were used, but without much success. But whatever the method, the design is always recorded, except in small works. For example, if you call a carpenter to build an extra bathroom in your house, he/she may not prepare drawings. But in all medium and large endeavors, drawings and recording the design are mandatory.

Design involves ensuring reliability in performance delivering the defined functionality over the life of the product: We dealt with the topic of quality and reliability in Chapter 16. We designers have to ensure that the resultant product of our design functions reliably over its life cycle.

Scenarios of Design

When do we design? There are two scenarios in which we design:

1. A new product is proposed and specifications are drawn up in organizations carrying out a batch production model. I call this the product scenario.
2. A new project is acquired in organizations carrying out a made-to-order model. I call this the project scenario.

The rigor of design differs vastly between these two scenarios. In the product scenario, the rigor is much higher than in the project scenario. The product scenario is further classified into three more scenarios, namely

1. *The totally new product scenario*: When a new product that does not exist at all in the market is devised for introduction into the market, it is the totally new product scenario. Recently, we witnessed the first personal computer (PC), the first floppy disk, and the first compact disk (CD) being introduced into the market. Before they were introduced, they were not available on the market. No knowledge is available on almost all aspects of the product. This goes through the full design cycle.

2. *A product exists in the market but is a new product for the company*: Take, for example, a new company set up to manufacture cars. Now, the first car for the company is not the first car for the world. It is being manufactured and sold, if not within the country, then elsewhere. This goes through the full design cycle, but some phases are shortened, as knowledge is available on many aspects of the product.

3. *Upgrading an existing product and releasing a newer version*: Again, take the automobile example. Every two or three years, car manufacturers introduce a new model. This is an updated version of an existing vehicle, or features of two or three of their own models are combined with some new features, and the new model is released. This does not go through the full design cycle.

Now, let us look at the full design cycle.

Full Design Cycle

A full design cycle is used in introducing absolutely new products into the market. CDs are a recently launched new product. The optical disk that can be etched with information in digital form was invented. Using that invention, compact disk was developed and introduced. The locomotive was perhaps the first product that was designed from scratch in the recently recorded past. We really do not know how matchsticks and weapon systems were designed, manufactured, and sold. When the locomotive was designed, there was no existing product to borrow ideas from except chariots and carts. But most of the components were available, like the boilers, steam engine, water tanks, hearths, coal, and wheels. The designers had to adapt these to develop the design of a locomotive. There ought to be a proven core concept as a prerequisite to design a new product. When the locomotive was developed, the concept that a wheel produces friction-based motion was proven and a steam engine that can turn a wheel without an animal or a human being exerting effort was available. When the airplane was designed by the Wright brothers, an internal combustion engine to turn the wheel was available, and the concept that a propeller can produce motion, albeit in water, was proven. The Wright brothers and perhaps others tried to adapt that ship/propeller to produce motion in air as it did in water.

We move from the "known to the unknown" by borrowing ideas from other products to design our product. The airplane borrowed the propeller from ships, the locomotive borrowed boilers used in homes for heating water and wheels from carts and chariots, disk drives borrowed the shape and the read/write head from gramophone records, the locomotive being placed at the front of the train borrowed the idea from carts in which the horse is up front, and even the car engine was placed in the front position based on this precedent.

Assuming that a proven concept and most of the vital components of the products are available or can be made easily, we can begin designing the product. The following are the phases of a full design cycle.

1. *Product idea generation*: A new product idea in a running company is generated in a formal manner. Brainstorming is generally the technique used to generate ideas for a new product. The participants in a brainstorming session are usually from within the company, and sometimes experts in the field are also co-opted. They meet in an informal environment and give free reign to their imaginations. All the product ideas generated in the session are recorded and are analyzed thoroughly later on, and a few are shortlisted. These shortlisted ones are further investigated for their viability, and fewer are selected for building prototypes. They are then designed and prototypes built and tested. The successful ones are sent through the remaining design cycle. In a new company, usually the entrepreneur sets up the company to realize the product idea that he/she first envisaged. Once the product is envisaged, the design cycle begins.

2. *Conceptualization of the product*: This is the first step in the design cycle. In this phase, the details of the proposed product are dreamed up by the designers. This may involve one or more designers. The ideas of the product are presented to other designers, management personnel, and marketers in a meeting. All ideas are discussed from the angle of marketability and producibility. The product concept is usually finalized in one or more meetings. Now, a design team is assigned the job of designing the product.

3. *Record the design using rough sketch drawings*: The assigned design team prepares rough sketches. When I say rough sketches, I mean they are certainly engineering drawings but are not directly usable by the production shops in producing the components. Usually, the design team is supported by highly skilled technicians who can use these sketches coupled with face-to-face discussions with the design team and produce the prototype.

4. *Select the components from the available alternatives*: Once the sketches are ready, it is known that some components have to be built in-house and some can be purchased off the shelf. There are a variety of components available on the market from which alternatives have to be selected. The selected components are purchased from the market in small quantities adequate for the prototype.

5. *Build a prototype of the product*: The technicians supporting the design team use the sketches, the purchased components, and clarifications from the design team to build one or two prototypes and deliver them to the design team for testing.

6. *Subject the prototype to rigorous testing to verify how it is functioning*: Now, the design team subjects the prototype to rigorous testing. They test it for delivering functionality even in adverse conditions. They make changes as defects are uncovered without adhering to a change management process that is usually part of production cycle. Once all the kinks are smoothed out and the prototype is functioning in a stable manner. the prototype is presented to all stakeholders. At this stage, more stakeholders are added. The new stakeholders are the quality assurance team, production team, finance team, and maintenance personnel.

Each will look at the product from their standpoint and make suggestions for improvement.

7. *Record all defects and improve the design*: Receiving feedback from the stakeholders on the initial prototype, the design team implements the feedback into their designs and asks the technicians to build another prototype.

8. *Rebuild the next version of the prototype*: The team of technicians attached to the design team builds another prototype.

9. *Repeat steps 6, 7, and 8* until no further improvements are possible, either because there are no more defects or because the team does not have the technology or means to further improve the design.

10. *Make a decision*: Decide if the product can be launched in the market. Many times, products are released into the market with known deficiencies. In such cases, the deficiencies are explained to the customers and limitations are imposed on the product usage. For a long time, the MS-DOS operating system could not access more than 32 MB of disk space. In MS-DOS 3.0, they introduced disk partitions, and it could handle multiple partitions as separate disks, but each partition was limited to 32 MB. Now 32-bit PCs/laptops are sold with more than 4 GB of RAM knowing full well that a 32-bit processor cannot use RAM in excess of 4 GB.

11. *Value analysis*: Once a decision is made to launch the product into the market, a value analysis is carried out on all components. Value analysis is a technique that ensures that the same value is delivered at a lower cost or more value is achieved at the same cost. This will achieve cost effectiveness.

12. *Then make the make or buy decision*: This decision involves determining which components are best made in-house and which components should be either subcontracted or bought off the shelf from the open market.

13. *Bring in the engineering team*: Now, the rough sketches made for building the prototype and the information about the bought components are passed on to the engineering team to work out the details and prepare the shop drawings.

14. *Product engineering or detailed design*: Now, the engineering team works out the details of all components, subassemblies, and assemblies and prepares engineering drawings that can be used by production shops specializing in making the components and building products to national or international standards adhering to all good manufacturing practices, building quality into the product. This includes packaging all the components in the most efficient housing. The housing takes into consideration the aspects of initial assembly of components, their maintainability later on, production of heat and its dissipation, positioning of controls for human intervention, aesthetic aspects, operation, and so on. All these drawings are verified and approved by the design team.

15. *Review this design* with experts and thinkers, product builders, maintenance personnel, marketers, legal experts, management personnel, finance professionals, and any other concerned persons. The product builders will ensure that the product can indeed be built with the available manufacturing technology; the maintenance personnel will ensure that the product is maintainable; the marketing personnel will ensure that it is marketable; the finance professionals will ensure that the product can be funded; the management personnel will verify if they agree to add this product to their portfolio; and the legal personnel will ensure that all applicable statutes regarding usage, safety, and security are fully met.

16. *Implement all the feedback* and release engineering drawings: The engineering team implements the feedback in the engineering drawings, approves them, and releases them for production to the production planning and control team. From now on, any change to the drawings is subjected to strict controls and approvals. Each change request is recorded, analyzed, approved, implemented, and approved before the drawing is released to production shops.

17. *Build a usable final prototype* and subject it to tests. Using the final set of approved drawings, the production shops produce one or two prototypes and hand them over to the quality control team for testing. While building this prototype, all quality control activities are implemented. The quality control team conducts tests not just from the standpoint of functionality but also from the standpoint of applicable national or international standards and statutes. This testing brings out not only design defects but also manufacturing defects. The product will not be passed on to regular production until all defects uncovered by the quality assurance team are rectified.

18. *Implement the feedback and release the production drawings*: Now, the engineering team implements all feedback received from the quality control team, updates the engineering drawings, obtains necessary approvals, and releases the drawings for regular production. Now, the production and marketing teams take over the product, and the design cycle is completed.

This completes the design cycle. This list is by no means exhaustive. Some organizations may include a few more steps, and some may abridge the list. Now, you may think that design costs a lot of money and could cost more than what it takes to build the product. You are right. Good design is not cheap. However, the cost of design is spread over the number of products that are built with this design and it will absorbed by all the products produced and sold. So, it will be small for each of the units sold.

Part Design Cycles

Part design cycles are used when a company launches a product that is new for the company but already exists in the market. The components are known and the technology is available to build it, but the organization has to differentiate their product from others. In this case, a preliminary prototype is not necessary. Preliminary rough sketches are also not necessary. They can go to the final engineering drawings and build a final prototype, test it, and release the final drawings. In this scenario, the steps of the design cycle that are used are 11–18. In step 13, instead of using the rough sketches made earlier, the design team prepares rough sketches of the changes needed in the product and passes them on to the engineering team.

In the scenario of product upgrades, the design team uses the feedback obtained from the field, the maintenance personnel, and user complaints and analyzes it. This also considers the improvements in technology and availability of better components and better methods of building the product. For example, a lot of improvement has taken place in painting cars. Originally, cars were spray painted. Then, painting cars using static electricity for better adhesion was used. Now, the chassis of the car is dipped in electrically charged hot paint tanks. We do not know what tomorrow will bring in painting technology. Designers make use of all technological upgrades to the product design when upgrading the product. Based on the analysis of feedback and developments in technology, the design team finalizes the changes to be made to the existing product. Then, they make changes on a set of blueprints of the drawings of the existing project and pass them on to the engineering team. Then, the engineering team takes over and releases the production drawings. Steps 11–18 of the full design cycle are used in this scenario.

Project Design Cycle

Many companies are organized on the basis of project execution. They are also often referred to as made-to-order organizations. Ship building; airplane manufacture; building construction; setting up chemical, fertilizer, and pharmaceutical plants; and all other such organizations use project-based organization. Software development also uses this project-oriented approach. A project is a one-time venture. It is not repeated with an identical design, but the next project for the organization could be similar. A ship-building organization builds ships that are similar in most aspects but with a few differences. Each ship is a customized version of another. The first ship the organization builds and the 100th ship it builds could be entirely different. Each project will see some improvement over the preceding project, taking advantage of the developments in technology and the availability of better components. A ship builder or an airplane manufacturer builds different classes of ships and airplanes. In each class, the first ship or airplane goes through the full design cycle. However, it is not possible to build full-scale prototypes and test them in actual environments. They build scaled-down versions of the products and test them in simulated environments before the full-sized product is built. That way, they have a proven design in each class of the products they build.

Thus, for each project, there is a proven design, and it is an adaptation of that design to the new specifications. Therefore, the design cycle is much shortened. Only steps 14, 15, 16, and 18 of the design cycle are implemented in the design of projects. In step 18, there is no feedback to implement from the quality control team. Each product is engineered and built. The design team receives the specifications, analyzes them, draw up the changes to be implemented in the engineering drawings, and passes them on to the engineering team. Of course, the design team has the responsibility to continuously scan the environment for new developments in technology and availability of components that can be gainfully used in the products of the organization to improve productivity and quality or reduce cost and delivery times.

What We Do as Part of Design

At the ground level, what are the activities designers perform? Well, designers perform the following activities:

1. Keep themselves abreast of all technical developments in their field. They do this by subscribing to technical journals; becoming members of professional societies, like the Institute of Electrical and Electronics Engineers (IEEE) American Society

for Mechanical Engineers (ASME), or Industrial Designers Society of America (IDSA); becoming members of technical discussion groups relevant to their field; attending seminars; and so on. This helps them design better products.

2. Receive high-level specifications for the product, analyze them, and then develop detailed specifications for the product.

3. Conceptualize the product by borrowing ideas from similar or competing products. This includes analyzing various alternatives for delivering functionality and technologies to arrive at the optimum mix of ideas, technologies, methods, and functions for the product.

4. Select various components needed for the product and determine what needs to be made in house, what can be bought off the shelf from the market, and what needs to be subcontracted.

5. Coordinate the procurement of bought components as well as subcontracting the components that are selected for subcontracting.

6. Prepare high-level drawings for the product so that a prototype can be built, and help build the prototype.

7. Subject the prototype to test, and freeze the design.

8. Help the engineering team prepare detailed engineering drawings that can be used by the production shops or product builders to build the product.

9. Provide clarifications to the product builders while the product is being built.

10. Receive feedback from field and maintenance personnel and locate opportunities for product improvement.

11. When a product upgrade is approved by management, dovetail all the right feedback, technical developments, and improvement ideas generated within the team and design a better, cheaper, and more reliable new version of the product.

12. Continuously innovate and improve the designs at every iteration.

13. Test the prototypes and assist the quality control team in testing the product.

14. Define processes for effective design and continuously improve upon them in a disciplined manner. Develop various standards for quality, reliability, and performance of various components used in the product as well as the product itself.

15. Assist the marketing team in the marketing of the product to its target customers.

16. Represent the organization in various forums in seminars and with statutory authorities as required.

17. Answer any technical queries from the press and journalists regarding the performance or the product as required.

18. Assist management in all areas related to product technology and in ensuring delivery of the product to customers.

19. Any other related activity as necessary.

As we discussed so far, design is a creative mental process that includes considering alternatives, selecting the right alternatives, optimizing the selected alternatives, and devising a deliverable. The understanding of design cannot be completed without understanding what a product is and what the deliverable of design is.

What We Do Not Do as Part of Design

As part of design, we do not carry out basic or applied research. We use proven solutions. The solution must have been proven in some research lab, either our own or in a university or elsewhere. However, we try it by repeating the experiments if necessary to test the veracity of the claims, and we use it in our design, build a prototype, and test it to ensure that it fits our purpose. Sometimes, for a specific purpose, we may try more than one option to deliver the best solution but, it will not be as extensive as, say, those Thomas Alva Edison tried for inventing the light bulb.

Designers do not usually build the product or service. Actual building, fabricating, constructing, or developing the final deliverable is carried out by somebody else who specializes in building the solution conforming to the design. Of course, in the software development field, the designer and developer and, in some cases, even the tester roles are all rolled into one in many cases. However, in many cases, especially in high-volume production where the demand exceeds the supply, the designers supervise the building of a prototype for field testing to assess the efficacy of the design. In the build-to-order scenario, we cannot afford this luxury. Our design has to be perfect in the first iteration. Then, we validate our design using computer-based simulation techniques.

Designers do not test the product themselves except in the preliminary prototype. Testing is carried out in a systematic manner by the quality control team. The fact is, designers are more focused on ensuring that the functionality is delivered in the most efficient manner and are not trained in uncovering defects or defect-prone areas of the product. The quality control team is best suited for that. That is why the final prototype is tested by the quality control team.

Designers do not work out the details of the components of the product. The engineering team is the one that works out the details and prepares the engineering drawings and the process plans for use by the production shops in building the products. The software development field is an exception.

Deliverables of Design

What is the deliverable of the process of design? We have noted earlier that design is a process carried out inside the mind. What is inside an individual's mind cannot be visualized, understood, or used by others. Designers deliver the rough sketches they make to the engineering team, and the engineering team prepares the drawings. To communicate the design to solution builders so that the design can be converted into a product, we need a mechanism to capture the design. This mechanism ought to have the following characteristics:

1. It should be easy to capture as well as to understand.
2. It should capture the information accurately and comprehensively.
3. It should not take too much effort on the part of designers to comprehensively capture the information.

Now, what do we call this? In the manufacturing and the construction industries, the design and engineering activity delivers the engineering drawing and bills of material.

The engineering drawings contain the sketches and dimensions, and the bills of material contain the list of materials, including their quantities and specifications. All branches of engineering except software engineering use engineering drawings to capture the design. In fact, engineering drawings are called the language of engineers.

When we come to the software engineering field, IEEE calls this software requirements specification (SRS) and software design description (SDD). Structured systems analysis and design methodology (SSADM) calls it high-level design (HLD) and low-level design (LLD). Then, there are functional design specification (FDS) and detailed design specification (DDS). Also, there is unified modeling language (UML). Perhaps there are some more names out there in the field. We will have a further discussion about this later in the book when we discuss the aspect of capturing the software design.

For the purpose of this book, I wish to call it the design description. Having put the aspect of design in general, the deliverable of design, and the product in their proper perspectives, let us look at software design specifically in the next chapter.

Who Can Be a Designer

It is essential for the designer to be thoroughly knowledgeable in the technical domain of the product. Without this primary prerequisite, we cannot expect a good product from a person with poor knowledge of the technical domain. It is common to employ postgraduate engineers in design positions. Of course, knowledge is of greater importance than qualifications. This is a primary requirement for a person to be a designer.

The second prerequisite is an unquenchable thirst for keeping abreast of developments in the domain of the product. The developments to be kept abreast of are not just in the technical field but also in user preferences, tastes, usage patterns, and the subtle shifts taking place in social scenarios. Designers also need to keep abreast of changes in statutes affecting the product domain. There could be influencers like movie and sports stars, and designers need to watch for changes in influencers. Movie and sports stars fade away and new ones emerge frequently. Every time new stars come onto the scene, the tastes and usage patterns change and the designers have to update the product to suit the new generation.

A designer ought to be able to think through a problem and come out with a robust solution. The designer ought to take into consideration not just the functionality but also the support functionality for safety, security, maintainability, and producibility.

The designer should be able to read technical material like catalogues to identify alternatives to the components used for the product as well as component reviews and usage reports. He/she should be an avid reader, especially of technical materials that are not meant for fast-paced reading. A designer should not be easily bored reading specifications and technical descriptions. To read and assimilate technical literature is not an easy task.

In short, the designer should be technically capable, be expert in the domain of the product, have information about alternative ways of delivering the solution and the availability of components, be an avid reader, and not be one to be easily bored. Some organizations take people from either quality control or production and put them in design. It certainly makes sense, but the people who come from a certain function do develop an affinity for that discipline at the cost of others. So, it is best to grow the designers in-house. However, the first designer needs to be hired from outside!

2

Introduction to Software Product Design

Introduction to Software Design

A quote attributed to Edsger Dijkstra goes something like this: "If debugging is the process of removing software bugs, then programming must be the process of putting them in." IMHO, it is not coding that introduces bugs; it is actually the design that introduces them, especially the serious bugs. It is far easier to locate and rectify coding bugs than design errors. In a physical product, we can easily differentiate between design errors and manufacturing defects, as the design was documented. A defect is called a manufacturing defect when the manufacturing deviates from the design. By comparing the product with the drawings, we can locate manufacturing errors. In the software development industry, the design is either completely grouped with coding or not recorded properly, making it impossible to decide whether the defect can be attributed to design or to coding. Having put the term *design* in its proper perspective in Chapter 1, let us now turn our attention to the main topic of this book, software design.

IEEE uses three terms for the aspects of software design. They are design, preliminary design, and detailed design, and are used in its *Standard 610 for IEEE Standard Glossary of Software Engineering Terminology*.

IEEE defines the term *design* as "The process of defining the architecture components, interfaces, and other characteristics of a system or component."

IEEE defines the phrase *preliminary design* as "The process of analyzing design alternatives and defining the architecture, components and interfaces, and timing and sizing estimates for a system or component."

IEEE defines the phrase *detailed design* as "The process of refining and expanding the preliminary design or a system or a component to the extent that the design is sufficiently complete to be implemented."

The Capability Maturity Model Integration (CMMI©) for Development model document, Version 1.3, surprisingly did not include a definition of the term *design*. However, it included a process area named Technical Solution to arrive at a product design.

In my humble opinion, these definitions do not adequately address what the word *design* connotes. If we understand the term wrongly, our work cannot deliver the right results.

I wish to reiterate the definition of design from Chapter 1 and improve upon it for the context of software design. We noted it as "Design is a creative process to ensure that a defined set of functionalities is delivered efficiently, economically, aesthetically, securely, and safely; record that design in a manner that can be easily understood and implemented to realize the product by those fabricating/constructing/developing it; and to ensure that the resultant product is reliable, safe, secure, flexible, maintainable, and marketable. It draws upon the knowledge base of science and engineering together with social sciences and aesthetics, as well as the knowledge repository of the organization."

We can eliminate the words (fabricating/constructing) not relating to software engineering and add any missing words (ease of use) needed for the software engineering field and state the definition for software design. Allow me to restate the definition of design from the standpoint of software engineering: "Software design is a creative process to ensure that a defined set of functionality is delivered efficiently, economically, aesthetically, securely, and safely, adhering to all the applicable statutes; to record that design in a manner that can be easily understood and implemented to realize the product by those developing it; and to ensure that the resultant product is easy to use, reliable, safe, secure, flexible, maintainable, and marketable. It draws upon the knowledge base of science and engineering together with social sciences and aesthetics, as well as the knowledge repository of the organization."

Let us discuss the key terms of the above definition:

1. *Defined set of functionality*: The functionality for the proposed product ought to have been defined before the creative process—the design process is not just a process but a "creative" process. The designer ought to bring his/her creative capabilities to bear upon the product specifications at hand and devise a solution that is appropriate and better than the existing products. This creativity helps the designer in considering as many alternatives as possible before the appropriate one is selected. The designer ought to have divergent thinking and ideational fluency, the pillars of creativity. Appendix A deals with the subject of creativity in greater detail.

2. *Defined set of functionality*: The functionality for the proposed product ought to have been defined before the process of design begins. The definition comes from different sources. The customer provides a part of this definition; each of the other stakeholders provides a part of the definition; the experts like the safety and security experts, maintenance experts, marketing experts, legal experts, and so on each provide a part; then, the design team itself supplements the definition and then freezes the definition. Thus, the definition of functionality to be achieved by the proposed product is a collaborative effort championed by the design team.

3. *Delivered efficiently, economically, aesthetically, securely, and safely, adhering to all the applicable statutes*: These are the objectives of delivering the core functionality by the product. The delivery of the defined functionality for the proposed product not only needs to deliver, it also needs to deliver it while optimizing resource utilization, being cost effective, and providing a secure environment for the users and protecting them from external malicious attacks. All this needs to be delivered in adherence with the laws of the land. If the product is sold in four different countries, it must be so delivered that the laws of all four countries are adhered to, or we need to have a different version for each of the countries in which we market our product.

4. *Record the design*: The design needs to be recorded in such a way that those developing the product will be able to implement the design and develop the product with minimal reference to the designers.

5. *It draws upon the knowledge base*: The design activity has to draw upon the knowledge base of science and engineering for achieving a viable solution; mathematics provides the formulas and algorithms to design the components and predict the performance of the product; social sciences helps provide a product that is in line with user preferences; aesthetics works to provide a product that users will be happy to work with.

6. *The product is easy to use, reliable, safe, secure, flexible, maintainable, and marketable*: These are the ancillary functionality objectives for the design to build into the product while designing it. As you can see, the design has multiple ancillary objectives besides its core functionality objectives. Easy to use implies that the user will be able to use it without reading a bulky user manual, the user interfaces will be self-explanatory, and a context-sensitive help facility will be available at any point in time during usage. The safety objective implies the product is safe to use; it will not cause any damage to data, other programs, or other data or cause financial or other loss to the user or user organization. The secure objective implies that the systems and data are protected from external malicious attacks. The flexible objective implies that the user can use the product without any modification of the software to add additional features like adding a new user, a new payment plan, a new scheme, and so on. The maintainability objective implies the ability to upgrade the product from outside without having to change the source code of the core product, as well as to make it easier to change the code when essential. The marketability objective implies that the proposed product ought to comprehensively fulfill a need in the market.

I am aware that the definition and its explanation are a bit lengthy, but design is a very important activity and crucial to dictating the success or failure of the product, and in some cases the survival of the organization itself. So, any economization of the definition and understanding of the term *design* would lead to having mediocre design professionals, which would be disastrous for the organization and the software industry itself.

With this definition and explanation, we can move forward in our exploration of the subject of software design.

Present Scenario of Software Design

When we look at the present scenario of software product design in the software development industry, especially in the context of a project scenario, we have to admit that we do not accord adequate importance to this vital activity. In software in the commercial off the shelf (COTS) product development scenario, we give a little more importance to the product design. In either case, we show much more interest in the visual aspects of the product than the structural aspects. It is not farfetched to say that software design in the present day is equated with designing the screens and the reports.

In most organizations, it is difficult to find a specialist design team, let alone a robust set of design documents or drawings. Most organizations merge design with coding. The philosophy of the software industry is that the design is nothing but database design, screen design, and report design. When the activities of design and coding are merged, the individual is constrained by his/her knowledge of the programming language, especially of the advanced constructs of the language. When faced with a choice, the individual compromises design to suit programming convenience.

Another major issue with software design is the paucity of the "right" tools, conventions, and techniques to record the design. Software researchers have been trying to develop a method to fit all problems of software design. There seems to be confusion about how to capture design precisely and make it easy for coders to implement the design without reference to the designer among the industry experts. In manufacturing or construction, this confusion is absent. They use drawings that precisely record the design, and the workers can easily implement the design without any reference to the designers. When we look at parallels in engineering drawings, we see that there are different types of drawings, namely

1. Plan, elevation, end-view, and sectional views in building construction with a set of their own conventions
2. Fabrication drawings with a set of their own conventions
3. Machine drawings, again with their own set of conventions
4. Connection wiring drawings for electrical circuits
5. Schematic diagrams for electronic circuits
6. Contouring for landscapes
7. Printed circuit board (PCB) layouts
8. Landscaping layouts
9. Housing colony layouts
10. Piping/plumbing diagrams
11. Air flow diagrams
12. Process simulation diagrams

There are other varieties of drawings! Why should software designers not have different conventions for different software components and use engineering drawings to record software designs?

Another major issue in the software development arena is the lack of division of labor. Everybody does everything. It is only recently that software testing has split off into a separate specialty, and the same is true for database professionals. Otherwise, the same person performs requirements analysis and software design and then writes the code for the product, then tests it and certifies it fit for use! The realization is now slowly but surely dawning that we need to look at the work in a detailed manner and see if we can implement the concept of division of labor, which would provide not just economies but also robust and excellent quality software products. Until very recently, we received specifications for proposed software products entirely from the customer. If the customer did not specify it, we did not build it. We called them requirements, implying that anything other than "requirements" would not be included in the product. Then, we had to come to terms with the term *expectations*, meaning the unstated requirements of the customer. Our philosophy was, "Well, we are programmers and not functional specialists." The customers were grumbling, "You are supplying me the product. You ought to provide for features that would make it easier for me to use your product." Now our experts are referring to these "expectations" as "nonfunctional requirements," somewhat reluctantly accepting that it would be our (software developers) responsibility to provide not just what is specified by the customer but other features that are not specified by the customer. The saner set among us began calling them "core functionality" and "ancillary functionality" rather than functional requirements and nonfunctional requirements. *The change of terminology is a required shift in the philosophy of software development. We are shifting from "We just write a program to your specified requirements" to "We will build a robust software product that would fulfill your needs."* And software design plays a very important role in making this shift a reality.

So far, all the artifacts that were used to capture the software design were text-dominant documents. These are used mainly to obtain approvals from the managements of the customer's organization or our own. Once we obtain such approvals, we keep them aside and begin coding the programs as we see fit. There is hardly any agency to ensure conformance of our final product to the approved design document. Now, with agile philosophy of "We aim more to satisfy our customers than spend time doing documentation," design documents are hurrying to join the dinosaurs. This situation is not conducive to developing a robust, reliable, safe, and secure software product.

If cars were designed the way software is designed, there would be many more accidents, and no car would function properly unless it had been recalled a minimum of three times to correct the design/manufacturing defects! A car being recalled to fix a defect is big news, whereas release of a service pack to fix errors hardly gets a mention!

Software Products

Software products are unlike all other physical products. A software product is intangible, unlike all other products, which are tangible. Here are the key differences between a software product and other products.

1. While all other products are tangible, software products are intangible. You cannot see or touch a software product. True, you can touch the CD or DVD that contains the software, but the software itself remains intangible.

2. Producing more than one unit of all other products consumes resources like materials, time, effort, and machines. Production of the first unit of a software product consumes resources. But to make multiple copies of the same software products requires just a CD/DVD and no other resources. In some cases, it just requires an internet connection and can be downloaded!

3. All other products have wear and tear and therefore need regular maintenance just to ensure that the product delivers the usual performance. Software products are not subjected to wear and tear while they are functioning and therefore do not need maintenance just to keep delivering their usual performance.

4. Even with regular maintenance, all other products have finite lives after which it is not economical to maintain them to keep them working. A car has a life of 15–20 years, and a house usually has a life of 50–60 years. But software can work cost effectively over longer periods. Software products are replaced not because they stopped working but to upgrade them to the next generation of technology or because the business environment has changed drastically.

5. Other products have limited scope to upgrade them to shoulder more load or additional functionality. A car cannot be upgraded to a bus to be able to carry more passengers. A software product, on the other hand, can be upgraded to handle much more load than it was originally built for. The software developed in the 1970s is still working in some places after getting upgraded multiple times, including the Y2K upgrade!

6. All other products cease functioning during upgrades or breakdown maintenance. They cease delivering the usual performance. A software product can continue functioning, and the upgrade or maintenance can be effected offline. The upgraded product can then replace the existing product in a jiffy.

7. Changes in environment do not affect other products' functioning. A change in the way a road is built or a changed road would not affect the functioning of a car. But environmental changes could hamper the functioning of a software product. A new virus or a major upgrade to the OS or the network protocol can affect the software product.

8. Any change needs making and breaking in other products. This means an infusion of new materials, and the process of making the change is both visible and audible. Changes being made to a software product are neither visible nor audible. This feature is the one that makes software developers resort to making changes rather than building a robust product in the first iteration.

9. To remove design or manufacturing defects, all other products have to be recalled to the factory. Software products can be improved while they are at the customer's place.

10. Defective working of other products can cause physical injury to life and limb. A software product by itself can never cause injury to life and limb. This feature aids software developers in releasing half-baked products with less than desirable quality.

Thus, you can see that a software product is unique in nature and unlike any other physical products.

Elements of Design for a Software Product

In the initial days of commercial software development, the term *design* was not used. It was *developing programs*, similar to *developing a mathematical solution to a problem*. This was so because computer programming was carried out by mathematicians. The field of computer programming originated in the mathematics departments of universities, and it remains there. But when we began producing software to solve business problems using software and computers, the business executives who have to watch the bottom line would certainly want to know answers to questions like "How much does it cost?", "When will it be ready?", and "What do we get for the money we pay?" Governments and universities run on budgets that do not set stiff targets to be achieved. Commercial software development asks for predictability about cost, schedule, and design.

In the universities, software development research is still in the hands of mathematicians, who are content with developing a solution. Some amount of applied research was carried out in commercial organizations coming up with methodologies for achieving a modicum of predictability in the activity of software development. We have a long way to go in this aspect of software development.

People a few years earlier looked askance at us when we discussed software design, but the scenario has changed. Even so, not many are clear about the importance of software design and much less about how to go about it. Design, as noted earlier in Chapter 1, involves conceptualizing how and what to do and then capturing that in a medium for facilitating the programmers' writing of the needed code. Basically, the three main functions of design of a product are design of components, design of integrating the components, and design of organizing the components. Let us first look at the elements of software that need designing.

1. *Product structure*: What is the structure of a product? The structure in a product props up and holds all other parts of the product. For example, in a building, the columns, beams, and roofing are the elements that support all the other fittings. The arrangement of these elements is called the structure of the building. In a car, the chassis and the shell support all the other elements. This is called the structure of the car. With a robust structure, you can modify other parts of the product. The product functions in a reliable manner as long as the structure remains strong and stable. Imagine a column being broken in a building. The building may collapse altogether. Or imagine the chassis falling off in a car. The seats and the engine would fall off! Now, what are the equivalent components of software akin to a chassis in a car and columns and beams in a building? Let me enumerate them here:

    a. The database that holds the configuration data, master data, and transaction data.

    b. The library/directory/folder structure that holds all the artifacts of the software.

    c. The distribution of activities between the administrators, users, maintenance personnel, auditors, and others and the manner in which each is partitioned and separated from each other yet shares information between them.

    d. The distribution of system components, namely the web server, app server, database server, security server, and so on. The distribution of these components has a telling impact on the reliable functioning of the software.

2. *Data structure*: This refers to how we distribute all the data used by the software into independent blocks of data. Basically, application data is of two types, namely the master data and transaction data. Master data is used for reference purposes by the software and its volume does not grow every day. Transaction data is generated while performing business transactions. Its volume continues to grow with every business transaction. The master data is again classified into three varieties, namely the configuration data, the reference data, and the control data. Configuration data provides data for configuring the software product. It consists of values like the type of currency, the language for labels, screen labels, report headers, the software license information, and so on. The reference data is used while processing the data received by the system while performing business transactions. In a material management system, the material master and the vendor master are reference data; in an employee management system, the employee data is the master data; in a marketing management system, the customer data and the order data are the master data. Control data is used mostly in real-time software applications but is also used in business application software. Control data includes values of variables that are monitored, and when their values cross certain predefined threshold levels, predefined actions are triggered by the software. Perhaps, control data can also be grouped with configuration data. The only difference is in its usage. While configuration data sets the behavior of the software, control data is used to trigger actions when threshold levels are exceeded by the process. Configuration

data does not usually change at any given installation. Control data changes at any installation when the parameters change. Master data changes, but not very frequently. We have a need to carefully design the data structures, as changing the structure of data in a running application is very difficult, if not impossible. Changing the structure may require modifying all the programs.

3. *Data storage*: Data storage is very important. We store data on a secondary memory medium such as hard disk, magnetic tape, read-only memory (ROM), and so on. We store data in flat files and database tables when we need to use it in the application every day so that it is always available. We usually store the backup data on magnetic tapes, DVDs, CDs, and any other suitable medium. Some data we locate at our location and some data we store at the user's location. We need to carefully design the data storage so that our system runs efficiently and can recover quickly when a disaster strikes.

4. *Navigation*: The aspects of user navigation right from invocation of the application to accessing various facilities built into the system need to be built in an efficient manner so that the user can realize efficiencies in performing business transactions.

5. *User interface design*: The user mainly performs two types of actions in carrying out the business transactions, namely giving inputs to the system and taking outputs from the system. To enable the user to perform these two actions, the application software provides a user interface. In business applications, it is usually a screen presenting and receiving information. In mobile phones, the screen is of smaller size. We have to design the user interface so the user need not search for information locations and his or her attention is captured by the presentation so that he/she will not miss any important action. The design ought to be such that the user efficiency is increased, no important and expected action is missed, no mistakes are forced on the user, and the user feels comfortable using the interface.

6. *Output design*: The system delivers three types of outputs. They are (i) output to the screen, (ii) output on paper, and (iii) output onto external devices, either wired or wireless devices. The screen output needs to be designed to aesthetically present the information in a logical manner. Paper output needs to be designed in such a way that the presented information fits the paper and the data items can easily be distinguished from one another. Output to other devices needs to follow the protocol needed by the communication system and the receiving device.

7. *Administration*: For software products that are aimed at single users, the user and administrator roles are performed by the same person. In those applications, the administration tasks are minimal. But in multiuser applications that are web-based, administration tasks assume importance and need a separate person to handle them. These tasks include user management (add, modify, and delete users), password management, security management, system audits, troubleshooting, backup and restore, and so on. Database management is usually assigned to a specialist database administrator, but it is also an administration task. Even so, software designers need not design database administration software, as the vendor of the database management system provides such tools as part of the database management system. However, the software designer has to design system administration tools as part of the rest of the software. In some applications, which are used by a huge number of users, each of the system administration tasks may be assigned to separate individuals. All these aspects have to be designed into the software product.

8. *Security design*: By security, I mean security of the software artifacts and the data of the application. We need to design security aspects to protect software programs and application data from being accessed and tampered with by unauthorized people. Some of the security aspects have to be achieved by the operations staff, including preventing unauthorized persons from physically accessing the installations, enforcing the password policy, carefully resetting forgotten passwords, and so on. Other aspects of security, like preventing direct access to web pages bypassing the login process, preventing access from unintended locations, and some aspects of enforcing the password policy, have to be built in to the software and these have to be designed by the software designers. The important aspect of security design is to assign the access privileges of users. One way of assigning access privileges is role based and the other is user based. Role-based security privileges are automatically assigned when the role of the user is defined while creating the user. User-based privileges are assigned as specified by the management at the time of user creation. Each has its own advantages and disadvantages. We have to select the appropriate method and design the best methods for ensuring security for the programs and the application data.

9. *Safety design*: While security is for the software artifacts and data, safety is for the users and the user organizations. One can argue that because there is no physical equipment, there is absolutely no danger of sustaining physical injury for the users. Absolutely true. While it is true that there is no possibility of sustaining physical injuries, there is a possibility of nonphysical injuries. For example, when something goes wrong, the trail of all actions taken leading to the error can be easily traced in paper-based systems but not in computer-based systems unless they are explicitly designed and built. Things can always go wrong. Sometimes money is withdrawn from a bank account by unauthorized persons; sometimes information is hijacked from an organization; sometimes malicious information is distributed using an innocent person's email ID. Many such things can happen and are happening. It is not so easy to trace the trail of actions in computer-based systems. Computers do not provide an audit trail. It has to be built into the system. It will not be built into the system unless it was designed. We have the responsibility to design robust systems that provide all possible safety to users and organizations.

10. *Reliability design*: A computer is a machine and the software does not wear itself out. So, what is the reason for a working system to become unreliable? If the configuration, that is, the hardware, the system software, and the environment, remain the same, there is no reason for the application software to become unreliable. But the system software gets upgraded frequently to handle environmental challenges thrown at it by the world. As most of the applications today are internet-based, the internet keeps changing and new viruses and malware keep getting released onto the network. Discovery or development of new technologies and algorithms make it possible to develop more vicious, intelligent, and undetectable malware to be released onto the networks. Just as application software developers are learning and becoming better at security software development, hackers and malware developers are also learning and becoming better at developing malware programs. As we put up fences, they are finding ways to jump over those protective fences. It is a continuous battle. In such a scenario, as software designers, we have a responsibility to keep our software running reliably in the present and, to some extent, future environments too. As is well known, all application software uses

the facilities provided by the system software, especially the dynamic link libraries (DLLs). When the system software upgrades these DLLs, our application software may be impacted and we may have to change some code. One way to avoid this problem is not to use the system DLLs either at run time or at software development time. We will discuss this aspect in greater detail in the coming chapters. But we note here that this is a very important aspect of software design.

Design Validation or Quality Assurance of Design

I am sure people will raise eyebrows when we talk of quality assurance (QA) in software development. To talk about QA for software design, I am sure people will wonder about what I have to say. However, let me assure you that QA has a significant role in any human endeavor, especially in design. Design is a crucial activity that governs the rest of the activities. It decides if the delivered product or service is good or bad, poor or rich in quality, reliable or unreliable. Design activity can never be allowed to go without QA. In the software development industry, QA has come be understood as testing and nothing more. Testing just ensures that the artifact under testing conforms to its design. Inspection and testing activities put together are referred to as "quality control" (QC) activities. They are used to ensure that the artifact conforms to its design. QC uncovers the defects lurking in the artifact. The mechanisms that prevent defects are the standards and guidelines, checklists, formats, and templates. These defect prevention activities and defect detection activities put together are called QA activities.

Software design uses defect prevention tools like standards, guidelines, checklists, formats, and templates to carry out design activity. Then, when the design is finalized, it is subjected to quality control activities. We will see more details on this aspect in Chapter 16. Here, we note that QA is essential for ensuring a design that utilizes all available knowledge to come out with the best possible design sans preventable defects for the proposed product.

3

Approaches to Software Design

Introduction

What is an approach? The word connotes moving closer to something in a cautious manner, not making fast, jerky, and hasty movements. When the term *approach* is used in the context of problem solving, we imply that we are careful, we are not hasty, and we are thorough. How are we approaching the aspect of design in software development? Let us enumerate some of the common approaches prevalent in the software development industry in the present day. In project-oriented organizations engaged predominantly in developing software for other organizations:

1. The roles of the designer and coder are merged into one role, which is predominantly coding activity. In other words, software design is an appendage to coding activity. In these organizations, software design is understood to be screen design of laying out controls on the screen and report layouts, which is aligning column headings with column data, page totals, and grand totals.

2. The design activity is entrusted to system/business analysts. In these organizations, the design activity becomes an appendage to systems/business analysis. Again, the design activity is seen merely as screen and report design and nothing else.

3. No specialist team is earmarked to carry out software design in most organizations. Software design activity does not receive special attention from management and no resources are allocated to improve design activity by management.

4. Most organizations do not have a well-defined and continuously improved design process.

5. The industry as a whole does not have a set of proper artifacts comparable to engineering drawings to record the design in such a manner that it can be used by programmers for writing code without reference to designers. The software development industry did not form industry associations along the lines of the National Electrical Manufacturers Association (NEMA), Telecommunications Industry Association (TIA), Aerospace Industries Association (AIA), and so on. These associations not only promote industry interests but also look at the way the industry operates and produce many standards for technical activities, including design activity. Such an association does not exist in the software development field.

In product-oriented organizations, the situation is slightly better. They do focus on design activity and have standards, guidelines, checklists, formats, and templates for software design activity. But dedicating a design team is still more of an exception than the rule.

The general impression in the software development industry is that software design activity is not separable from coding activity and that the two go hand in hand.

In any organization, the individual carrying out an activity and the organization as a whole have to pull together in the right direction to make the endeavor a success. Both entities play crucial roles in the success of any endeavor. The organization defines and builds a framework and the individual utilizes that framework to carry out the work. In the past, when there were no organizations, the craftsman operated in his/her own framework. But with the advent of modern organizations, the organization sets a framework within which the individual operates. The organizational framework is both a boon and a bane. It is a boon as it facilitates a comprehensive deliverable with an assured minimum level of quality being built in. It is a bane in the sense that it constrains the individual from giving free reign to his/her imagination and creativity. All the subsequent chapters of this book focus on the individual designing the software product. In this chapter, let us look at the approaches used in organizations in performing the activity of software design.

How to go about designing software products is a matter of the philosophy of the organizational management. One view is that the activity of software design is of paramount importance and that it needs a specialist group. The other view, which is more prevalent, is that all software activity is primarily writing the code. Design is not separable from coding. The roles of the designer and the coder are just one, and that is coding. The coder designs the artifacts as necessary while writing code. Having a dedicated individual to design software is anathema and unimaginable for many software stalwarts.

The other view is that the activity of software design is entirely different from coding. This view separates the roles of software designers and software coders. This view contends that software design is a specialization just like coding and testing.

The above two views are the extreme views between which software development organizations and the industry are oscillating like a pendulum in a clock. Organizations lie between these two views. Until recently, software testing was part of coding activity, but it is now being widely recognized as a separate standalone specialty. So is design, though it lags far behind testing in the matter of gaining acceptance as a separate, unique specialty.

With this background, let us now look at the approaches adopted by the organizations to software design. Two approaches are possible:

1. Ad-hoc approach
2. Methodical or process-driven approach

Ad-Hoc Approach

In organizations using this approach, the responsibility is entrusted to a person who is, in the eyes of the organization, capable of designing software products. The individual may have experience in building software products, ensuring quality of software products, or maintaining software products. Then that individual carries out software design using his/her personal experience and knowledge. If the designer is highly experienced and has the right attitude, the product will come out well. In other words, the quality, reliability, flexibility, and all other aspects of design depend on the individual. If the organization has multiple designers, the products may come out with varying levels of quality and reliability. Each designer may use different methodologies to record the design.

Such organizations use meetings to share knowledge between designers, but they are held as required rather than on a schedule. The experience gained is not captured in a formal manner. If the tenure of people in the organization is significantly long and the attrition levels are low, the formal capturing of the experience gained is not very important, as the individuals are available within the organization. However, if the attrition levels are high, losing an experienced designer would cost the organization dearly.

Another advantage of this ad-hoc approach is that the creativity of the designers is not shackled by any standards and guidelines. They have free reign on their creativity and can utilize it to their full potential.

The ad-hoc approach is also the lowest-cost approach. There are no processes or standards to be maintained. No formal applied research needs to be conducted to dovetail the developments happening elsewhere into the organizational processes.

The flip side of the ad-hoc approach is that some aspects may be forgotten or ignored. The designers misuse their unfettered freedom and create designs that have great aesthetic appeal but may be costly and time consuming to achieve and difficult to maintain. Such designs are also difficult to upgrade to meet the changing needs of the products and changes in customer preferences.

The ad-hoc approach to design is usually used in small organizations where the owner/ entrepreneur happens to be the chief designer or would be supervising the design work closely.

We should not mistake the ad-hoc approach for a neglected approach or a bad and undesirable one. The whole onus of developing a good design rests on the shoulders of the chief designer. He or she is responsible for maintaining a knowledge base. The chief designer can maintain a set of formats, templates, and checklists to ensure comprehensiveness of the design. The key aspect of the ad-hoc approach is the dependence on individuals. Not all human beings are bad. Rather, most of them are good and dependable. So, the trick is hiring good and dependable people to ensure success of the ad-hoc approach, and many organizations adopt it and flourish. If the organization has a good chief designer and a good team of designers, the ad-hoc approach produces great products with excellent design.

Process-Driven Approach

The biggest advantage of a process-driven approach is the elimination of person dependency for the performance of the activity. It enables a novice to perform like an expert and an expert to perform with much less effort and to excel in performance. While the ad-hoc approach allows creation of heroes/heroines of performance, a process-driven approach makes every team member a hero/heroine in terms of performance. It eliminates the propensity to err. A critical team member leaving the organization for any reason, like attrition, illness, personal emergencies, and so on, would have a crippling effect on the organization using the ad-hoc approach, but it would have minimal impact on an organization using a process-driven approach. Again, scaling up the activity is very easily accomplished in a process-driven organization, whereas it is not easy in an organization using an ad-hoc approach.

The advantages of the process-driven organizational approach to software design are:

1. A process-driven approach eliminates the person dependency in software design to ensure a minimum level of robustness.

2. It helps the beginner to perform like an expert and an expert to excel.

3. This approach facilitates plowing the experience gained from software design back into the process; thus, every new design project enriches the process.

4. Everyone is equipped with the best practices in the process culled from design projects.

5. As organizational-level involvement in software design is facilitated. Organizational expertise, not only from the process but also from the senior executives, is brought to bear on the designs, leading to continued improvement in designs and, as a sequel, better products.

6. It provides uniformity of software design artifacts across the organization irrespective of the people involved, thus resulting in organizational maturity.

7. It facilitates measurement and analysis, resulting in fair performance appraisals. This makes it possible to bring about real morale improvement in the organization.

8. It brings predictability to the outcome.

9. A process-driven approach enables all-round participation and iteratively drives the organization toward excellence.

10. Recruitment of people becomes easier, as the organization has processes to guide and induct new people without much hassle.

All in all, a process-driven approach facilitates person independence and process improvement, moving toward uniformity in software designs across the organization, and organizational excellence.

Right Approach for the Organization

The software development industry is characterized more by its diversity than homogeneity in the practice of software engineering. Therefore, it is not right to attempt to prescribe one right approach.

However, the ad-hoc approach will serve well when:

1. The organization is small.

2. The number of design teams in the organization is two or three, as in the case of a small organization, and it would be easy to even out differences between practices adopted by the designers with the help of meetings. Such organizations need not have a documented process. The senior designer can act as the resolution mechanism and the point of reference to resolve differences of opinion.

3. The number of concurrent design projects in execution is one or two. With such a small number of projects, it would be easy to even out differences in project design with the help of meetings. The senior designer can act as the point of reference for dispute resolution.

Almost every organization starts small and starts with an ad-hoc approach to software design. As they grow and take on more and more software development projects, the workload increases, putting pressure on human resources. At this stage, two things can happen. One—the organization buckles under the pressure and moves toward failure and closure. Two—the organization moves toward a process-driven approach. Then, they adopt process improvement and develop processes to cover software design first and then to cover more organizational areas and a move toward a more mature process. This is just natural progression. However, it would be better if organizations would take a process-driven approach proactively when they are at the take-off stage rather than waiting for it to be forced upon them by the complexity created through sheer volume of work.

Some organizational activities are already process driven. Financial accounting is the first to adopt a rigorous process through a statute in almost every country. Strict internal controls and external verification through audits are made mandatory for any company that raises funds from the public. Further, statutory bodies act as watchdogs over organizations, as do auditors.

The human resources (HR) department was the next to adopt process-driven work. This came about as a result of ensuring fairness to candidates approaching the organization and to ensure a supply of the right human resources for the organization. In addition to recruitment, unionization of workers and statutes to ensure fair working conditions resulted in adopting a process-driven approach.

The above two departments have the main objective of ensuring fairness in addition to delivering the desired results. While it was important to deliver results in these areas, it was equally, if not more, important to deliver results exhibiting diligence and fairness.

When it comes to delivering results in software development projects, this aspect of delivering fairly was not mandated by any statute. Thus, it was optional to adopt a process-driven workflow. Therefore, many organizations frown upon any process-driven approach. Some even go to the extent of saying that the process-driven approach restricts their freedom and shackles their performance. Results at any cost and by hook or by crook are the terms one often hears in such organizations. We also often hear senior managers telling the subordinates, "I do not know (or care) how you do it, but I want it by ..." Some even go to the extent of saying that a process-driven approach stifles the creativity of the individual and adopting a process-driven approach would sound the death knell for creativity in designs.

I concur—to the extent that a process-driven approach doesn't provide an avenue for exhibiting heroics. All the same, when a success is achieved, the stakeholders are all heroes! And, continued success makes the organization a hero, and, as a sequel, all employees get the halo of a hero. That is what all organizations in pursuit of excellence strive for. The fact is that somebody who works for an organization such as IBM, Microsoft, GE, and so on, feels like a hero himself or herself and others who are jealous talk about "chips on the shoulder" of such people. Organizational success belongs to its employees.

An organization that adopts an ad-hoc approach can produce heroes, but a process-driven organization makes everyone in the organization a hero or a heroine! An organization that adopts an ad-hoc approach survives on heroics of its employees, but a process-driven organization runs like a well-oiled machine without the necessity for any heroics.

Software engineers from the beginning resisted any move toward adopting a process-driven approach. The first process-driven approach to software development was the waterfall model, and more people hate it than love it. Many other approaches, namely rapid application development (RAD), joint application development (JAD), incremental, and agile methods (eXtreme Programming [XP], Scrum, ClearCase, etc.), were developed to discredit waterfall. Some of these are forgotten, but the waterfall model is still in the race.

So much resistance to the process-driven approach! So many books have been written extolling the virtues of ad-hoc approaches to software development! Discipline will never be loved, even in the armed forces, as evidenced by the popular cartoon strip Beetle Bailey!

So, my advocacy of a process-driven approach is fraught with the prospect of stiff resistance and criticism. Still, I believe that a disciplined process-driven approach is the only approach that ensures project success—the first time and every time. It is the only approach that ensures organizational success in the short term as well as in the long term.

What Process and How Much?

Once we decide to adopt a process-driven approach, the next questions that we need to address are the type of process we wish to adopt for the organization and how deeply it would penetrate into organizational functioning.

A process-driven approach consists of:

1. Processes for carrying out the activities
2. Agencies responsible for carrying out the activities
3. Processes for ensuring that quality is built into the deliverables
4. Agencies responsible for confirming quality in deliverables
5. Processes for defining and maintaining organizational processes
6. Agencies responsible for defining and maintaining organizational processes
7. Processes for measuring and analyzing process performance
8. Agencies responsible for measurement and analysis of process performance

In short, the process-driven approach should contain defined methods for carrying out work along with checks and balances thereof.

However, in a process-driven organization, the process driving the activity is of paramount importance. If the process is poorly defined, poorly implemented, or poorly improved, the organization's performance will be poor quality. Therefore, the process must be defined by adopting the highest standards of quality and implementing the best practices culled from the industry.

A process-driven organization is characterized by a well-defined process and a dedicated group of individuals to define and improve the process in a structured manner. The following are the important features of a process driven approach:

1. A well-defined set of processes and procedures
2. Standards and guidelines implementing the best practices culled from the industry
3. Formats and templates to ensure uniformity in capturing and disseminating information
4. A comprehensive set of checklists to ensure that all activities are performed thoroughly
5. A dedicated process group containing experts in their fields to define, champion, and improve the process
6. The top management being committed to drive the organization based on a well-defined and continuously improving process

Let us discuss each of these aspects in greater detail.

Process

A process (in this context) is a comprehensive set of documents, either in hard copy or soft copy form, that defines the methods for performing a major activity in the organization. It consists of procedures, formats, templates, standards, guidelines, and checklists. Some examples of a process are project management process, design process, verification process, validation process, and measurement and analysis process (*Mastering Software Quality Assurance: Best Practices, Tools and Techniques for Software Development*, Murali Chemuturi, J. Ross Publishing, 2010).

A well-defined organizational process consists of processes, procedures, standard operating practices (SOPs), standards, guidelines, formats, templates, and checklists. All these might have been defined by internal experts or experts drawn from outside the organization. A process is formally defined, subjected to quality assurance activities, formally approved, and released for adherence in the organization. An organizational process includes processes for quality assurance, project management, audit processes, and other processes for organizational management. The design process is one among them. A robust design process consists of procedures for initiation of design work for a product, architecture design, screen design, report design, inquiry design, safety design, security design, communication design, ease-of-use design, navigation design, database design, product administration design, fault-tolerance design, and so on.

Procedures are step-by-step instructions for performing a subactivity of the process. Example procedures include project planning procedures, software estimation procedures, phase-end audit procedures, progress reporting procedures, etc.

Standards and Guidelines

Every professionally managed organization should have a set of organizational standards specifying actions, features, and so on that ensure a minimum level of quality in every activity performed in the organization. Standards are prescriptive; they specify exactly what needs to be accomplished and, wherever applicable, provide quantitative data like measurements and metrics that need to be achieved by the performance of the activity. The standards achieve the following, at a minimum:

1. They achieve uniformity of output from different people.
2. They ensure a minimum level of quality in output, even from different persons working on the activity.
3. They save the effort of individuals working on activities.
4. They guide new entrants to the organization in carrying out work efficiently.
5. The reduce the effort spent on training new entrants.
6. They are the main tool to include ancillary functionality such as safety, security, ease of use, and so on.

Some of the bodies releasing standards are the American National Standards Institution (ANSI), British Standards (BS), Joint Services Specifications (JSS), Deutsches Institut für Normung (DIN), International Organization for Standardization (ISO), International

Electrotechnical Commission (IEC), International Telecommunications Union (ITU), NEMA of USA, and so on. In recognition of their contributions to quality and general well-being, a day—October 14th—is set aside every year to celebrate World Standards Day.

When we come to the software development industry, unfortunately, we do not have an industry association like NEMA to define and release standards for use by the industry. The IEEE happens to be the only professional body to release standards for software development activities, but even they are not at the level at which other engineering standards happen to be. IEEE software engineering standards are more suggestive than prescriptive.

To the question raised by some people that standards restrict the freedom of the designers, I need to say that it is true to some extent. However, every formal process provides for waivers whereby non-adherence to a standard is allowed in a controlled manner. A higher authority considers each waiver request on its merits and grants the waiver. Standards restrict only unfettered freedom but not total freedom. Second, standards specify the minimum level needed. When we exceed the minimum level, or perform better than the standards, it is acceptable.

Guidelines are just like standards but are suggestive rather than being prescriptive. IEEE standards of software engineering are more in the nature of guidelines than in the nature of standards.

The quality of the standards and their process-based improvement are vital in determining how effective the product design will be.

Formats and Templates

These facilitate a uniform manner for capturing, recording, and presenting information. Examples of formats and templates include product specifications templates, estimation presentation templates, nonconformance report (NCR) forms, review report forms, estimation request notes, project management plan templates, etc.

Checklists

These assist the person performing an activity in carrying out the task without forgetting/ overlooking/missing any aspect and help the reviewer to ensure comprehensiveness of the artifact. The checklist contains a number of items, each with a space to place a check mark or to note "yes," "no," or "not applicable" as each point is completed or reviewed. When an activity is completed, this list should be referred to to ensure that all aspects have been addressed.

Process Group

The process-driven organization ought to have a dedicated group of professionals entrusted with the work of defining new processes, improving the existing ones, piloting such processes in sample projects, and then rolling them out for implementation across the organization. They act as the champions of the organizational process and take ownership of the organizational process assets. They act as mentors for the organizational staff in implementing and internalizing the processes defined for the organization. Most organizations dedicate one or two persons for this activity and use all others on a part-time basis. Some organizations assign this responsibility to the organizational quality assurance department. Without a dedicated process group, the organizational process and the improvement thereof would be neglected and would not have any impact on the organization.

Commitment of Top Management

For any activity to be successful in an organization, the commitment of top management is essential. It is reflected in the provision of a dedicated set of professionals to handle the activity, provision of facilities and funds, supervising the activity, and allocating their time to the activity. Top management personnel need to support software design activity as well as organizational process definition, stabilization, and improvement activities for software design activity to be carried out efficiently, producing the desired results for the organization.

Product Design and Project Design

It is relevant to discuss these two approaches to design at this point. Both take different approaches. Let us now define what a product is. A product was defined as a physical object for which a customer is willing to pay money to possess. This was the classical definition of a product. Restaurants and hotels have physical objects like food items supplied to their customers. Now, a bank provides certificates of deposits, which are on paper. They have a variety of financial plans to offer to their customers. Software companies deliver a software product on a CD or as a download from the Internet. Are they not products? Taking into consideration all such facts, the definition of a product has changed; thus, "the product is a bundle of benefits for which a customer is willing to pay." (*Management—A New Paradigm for The Twenty-First Century*, Murali Chemuturi and Vijay Chemuturi, Lulu Publishing, 2015). We discussed the aspects of software products in Chapter 2.

When it comes to the software development industry, all software development is carried out as a project that results in the delivery of a software product. Therefore, we need to distinguish what I mean when I say *product development*.

When a software project delivers a software product that is used in one location or within one single organization, we need to understand that it is classified as project development. The software design carried out for this product is referred to as project design.

When a software development project delivers a product that is expected to be sold as a commercial off-the-shelf (COTS) product to be used by any individual or organization without any modification, we need to understand that it is classified as product development. Examples of products include the Windows operating system, Microsoft Office, and many apps and utilities that we download and use without modification. Some products allow for customization using parameter files or building a software layer over the product to alter its behavior. While the design activity is similar for both scenarios, the finalization of the design differs. In the product design scenario, a prototype is built with the initial design and is subjected to tests. Based on the results of testing, more rounds of design–prototype–test–improve cycles are used before finalizing the design. In the case of project design, the activity of building a prototype to test and improve the design is not performed. The design is subjected to quality assurance activities and released for the next line of activities like coding, testing, and releasing.

I will discuss the differences between these two scenarios in the subsequent chapters where applicable to set them clearly apart.

4

Elements of Software Design

Introduction

Any human endeavor is a mix of routine work and creative effort, but the proportions are different in different activities. So it is with design and software design. Software design, like all design work, involves delivering the functionality. The first part is *how* to deliver the functionality, and the second part is *delivering* the functionality. The *how* part involves creative effort, and the *delivering* is the routine part. *Conceptualizing* is the creative part. Carrying out a detailed design and capturing the design is the *delivering* part of design work. For example, consider the functionality of transporting people from one place to another. A bicycle, a scooter, a motorcycle, a car, a bus, a train, a ship, and an airplane all deliver the same functionality. Except the ship and the airplane, they all travel on the land. Even within the car segment, there is a large variety.

To deliver functionality, we use the available technology for software development to design our product. We build a structure and arrange the components to build the product. Elements are the building blocks of software. We design a software application using the design elements available to us. In this chapter, let us discuss the elements of design and how to use them in designing our software product.

Prerequisites for Software Design: Requirements

Before we decide *how* to deliver the functionality, we ought to know *what* to deliver. The term *specifications* is used to enumerate the functionality to be delivered by the product. In most physical products, the specifications are so limited that they could fit on a single sheet of paper. When it comes to software development, the specifications are numerous, often spanning a large multipage document. I have some reservations about the need to define software specifications in volumes, but the reality is that we do fill volumes to specify the required software product. In view of their large number, the term *requirements* is used to describe the functionality specifications for a software product.

Requirements can be classified into two major classes from the functionality standpoint (*Requirements Engineering and Management for Software Development Projects*, Murali Chemuturi, Springer USA, 2013). These are:

1. Core functionality requirements
2. Ancillary functionality requirements

Core functionality requirements are the functionalities of the product without which the product is not useful for the users. These functionalities must be fulfilled and exceptions cannot be granted or resorted to during development of the product. Core functionality addresses the performance of a set of business transactions. The main purpose of software development is mainly to fulfill this core functionality.

Ancillary functionality requirements supplement core functionality. Even if the ancillary functionality is not fulfilled, the product is still usable but may cause inconvenience in the form of loss of productivity, safety, or security. One significant point to be noted here is that the customer, more often than not, may not specify this functionality and even expects the development team to take care of this ancillary functionality!

The requirements must be in place before we can begin the activity of design. The requirements ought to be defined comprehensively, and the quality of that definition must be excellent for the software product design to be of excellent quality.

We need to understand that the activity of requirements definition is collaborative. In the case of project design, the end users or customers define the core functionality. In the case of product design, the marketing department or management personnel define the core functionality. Sometimes, we may re-engineer an existing product, and in this case, we, the software designers, have to define the core functionality requirements.

But in all the above cases, the ancillary functionality needs to be defined by the software designers!

One question is pertinent here: Should all these requirements be documented? I suggest documenting both kinds of requirements. Whether the document is elaborate or brief, I leave it to your convenience, but do document it. The document will bring all the stakeholders onto the same page.

Prerequisites for Software Design: Tools, Standards, and Guidelines

In a mature organization, the following will be in place:

1. Software design process as part of the organizational process
2. Formats and templates to capture software design
3. Checklists for ensuring the comprehensiveness of the design
4. Quality assurance methodology for validating the design
5. Tools to build a quick prototype for testing the design

Of course, these are not essential to carry out the design activity, but they make the life of software designers easier while increasing their productivity and quality. It is one thing to have these in place, and it is quite another to have a robust set of tools that aids the designers in their design work. Often, these are of poor quality and place additional overhead on the design team instead of making it easier for them.

Major Branches of Software Design

In a world where many people think that software design is inseparable from coding, it is difficult to push the perception that software design has branches! Fortunately, the number of people who believe in the concept that the entire process of software development from requirements through delivery ought to be performed by a single software engineer is decreasing. Testing has been spawned as a distinct specialty and so have database design and administration. Similarly, screen design separated itself into a separate specialty. Requirements engineering is now taken off the hands of the software programmers and is being assigned to business analysts who are not programmers. I am sure that software design will also divorce itself fully from coding activity in the near future.

Let us consider the design of automobiles. The engine and transmission are designed by an automobile engineer, the chassis and the housing for all the equipment are designed by a mechanical engineer, the interiors are designed by interior designers, the electrical systems are designed by an electrical engineer, the electronics like the ignition system are designed by an electronics engineer, and the control software is designed by software engineers. I admit that I am not an expert on car design and there could be more specialties—tire design readily comes to mind. Currently, most software design is carried out by one programmer or a team of software programmers. Two activities, namely screen design and database design, have been carried out by different specialists. So, more specialization is on the way and it would be advantageous for us to understand the different branches of software design. Here are the different branches of software design:

1. *Core functionality design*: This branch focuses on how best to achieve the core functionality defined for the product. It also focuses on how to present information, how to receive inputs, how to deliver outputs, how to conduct information transformation, how to process inputs into outputs, how to store information, and so on.

2. *Ancillary functionality design*: As noted earlier, this functionality is defined by the design team or experts in the concerned areas. This branch focuses on how best to achieve safety, security, integrity, ease of use, reliability, system administration, and so on.

3. *Presentation of information*: This branch focuses on how best to present information to users. The objective is to present information in such a way that the recipients are most comfortable and to present the right information in the right manner. We have the alternatives of on-screen presentation, paper reports, SMS to a mobile, and so on. Selecting the right alternative for the purpose at hand and designing it is covered under this subject.

4. *Receiving inputs*: This branch focuses on designing inputs to the system with the objectives of making it easier for the user to enter the required information, validating each of the data items received, preventing undesirable information, and, finally, storing the information carefully.

5. *Delivering outputs*: This branch focuses on how best to deliver information output to users, including the medium, the arrangement, the grouping, control statistics, and so on. The output could be to the screen, a paper report, wireless or wired networks in electronic form, speakers, or a projector, and involves selecting the most suitable methods for delivering information to the concerned users as and when they ask. This branch also focuses on validation of all the data items delivered as output to the user to ensure their accuracy and data integrity.

We will discuss these branches in greater detail in the coming chapters. Now, let us look at the elements of software design.

Elements of Software Design

The term *element* has multiple meanings and definitions. Among the many definitions given in Merriam-Webster's Dictionary, the one most apt for this context is "a distinct part of a composite device." The word *element* is most popular for its usage in the subject of chemistry. In that context, Merriam-Webster's dictionary defines *element* as "one of the basic substances that are made of atoms of only one kind and that cannot be separated by ordinary chemical means into simpler substances." Elements are the smallest components in a composite entity. They are the basic component of which composites are made. We do not break an element down into its constituent parts.

Each field of human endeavor is made of up of several elements. Designers make use of these elements and develop products. If you take an automobile, the elements include steel sheets and steel structures like angles, channels, sections of different shapes, and so on. Elements keep growing as technology improves, downgrading composites into elements. For example, a tire is an element for an automobile designer. When automakers were making everything, including tires, rubber, thread, and steel wire were elements. But now all automakers are buying tires off the shelf, making it an element for the automobile designer. But for a tire designer, rubber, thread, and steel wire are still elements! Thus, we need to recognize that the composites of today may become elements tomorrow.

In software design, too, we have several elements. We use these elements in our software design activity. We have the following elements available for our use in software engineering:

1. *Programs*: Programs are also called functions, methods, subprograms, subroutines, agents, scripts, macros, and many other names. All these are a set of programming statements arranged in a logical order of execution that will result in processing of data and delivering the expected results. Programs are the most basic elements of software, and software design is meant to enable programmers to develop the required programs for the proposed product.

2. *Forms*: Forms are screen-based elements that facilitate presentation of information to users and receipt of inputs from the users. All other elements, including programs, are anchored to a form. The form can have the size specified by the designer. It can be smaller or larger than the physical screen on the visual display unit (VDU). When the form has the same size as the physical screen, we can view all of the form without scrolling. If the form is larger in size than the physical screen size, then we need to have scroll bars. Most screens allow both horizontal and vertical scrolling. Most programming languages provide forms that sprout scroll bars automatically. But if you are designing and developing software elements, you need to provide for the scroll bars in your element.

3. *Menus*: Menus are basically a way of presenting the various available options to the user enabling him/her to select the appropriate option to fulfill the requirement at hand. There are a variety of menu models available to choose from. Each menu option can cascade further to provide suboptions within the main options. How deep the cascading can go is a matter of choice of the designer. Normally, the main menu options are placed on a toolbar. Hovering the cursor on the option or clicking on the option displays the suboptions available for the main option. In a similar way, hovering the cursor over the suboption or clicking on the suboption opens the

next level of suboptions available for the selected suboption. The menu items can be textual, icons, or both. It has become the normal practice to give text as well as icons, especially when the product is targeted to the general public. When the end-product is targeted toward a specific customer organization, we may select text only.

4. *Dialogs*: A dialogue is a conversation between two entities. When there are more than two entities, it becomes a discussion or a meeting. In the context of software design, the dialog box is a conversation between the system and its user. We usually present two or three options, such as OK, Cancel, or Reset, and ask the user to select one. Let us not confuse chat applications with dialogs. Dialogues between two human beings can be in free form. But dialogue between a computer and its user needs to be controlled and limited to presenting and selecting options. This is usually achieved through message boxes with preprogrammed messages and options.

5. *Messages*: Messages are information passed to the user about a relevant aspect. Error messages are passed when the user makes a mistake or the system encounters a defect. Information messages are used either to confirm that some action is needed from the user or as the system confirmation that an action was executed and completed.

6. *Toolbars*: Toolbars contain icons, and each icon is anchored to a subprogram. By clicking on the icon, the concerned subprogram is executed by the computer. Usually, toolbars provide an alternative to menus. In fact, toolbars and menus are redundant. Toolbar icons enable a person who is not very literate to use the computer using the icon. Toolbars are an ease-of-use facility. The aspects of design concerned with toolbars are their location, number of icons, the picture on the icon, and other aspects like providing a tool tip (discussed later in this chapter). A picture of a floppy disk has become a default icon for saving data, as have an open envelope for opening a file, blank white paper for creating a new item, and so on.

7. *Frames*: Frames help us group related items on the screen together. This grouping will help us to either hide or display them with one single statement. Another advantage is that we can display related items together, making it easier for users to locate and enter data. Another advantage is that users can refer to the group with one phrase while reporting problems or asking for help or software upgrades.

8. *Icons*: An icon in the context of software development is a small picture, usually in the shape of a square, with a clearly visible picture that denotes some action. For example, a picture of a floppy disk denotes saving the data, a picture of an open envelope denotes opening a new artifact, and a picture of scissors denotes cutting. These are primarily used in applications that are used by less computer-literate people or by people who speak a different language. For example, Microsoft Word in English is used by some people who cannot speak/read/write English. This is made possible mainly due to icons used in the application.

9. *Data controls*: To receive or display data, there are many controls. These include the text box, combo box, list box, grid, etc. All these facilitate the input of data to the system. Of course, we can use these controls to display data to the user. We will discuss them in detail in the subsequent chapters. A text box can handle one data item at a time. A combo box can be filled with multiple values of one data item and allow the user to select only one value from those values. A list box is similar to a combo box, except that it allows selection of multiple values by the user. A combo box allows entry of a fresh value for the data item as well. A grid allows display and entry of multiple values for a set of data items that are usually a record of a

database table. We can find variants of grids that allow only display but not entry or modification of values displayed.

10. *Command buttons*: Command buttons are clickable and are usually anchored to a sub-program. Clicking on a command button activates the program to be executed. Usually they are used for sending the user inputs for validation and storing in the database. Save, Cancel, OK are good examples of command button. Of course, command buttons are also used many other purposes. The main purpose of command buttons is to initiate some desired action.

11. *Boolean choice makers*: We have radio buttons and checkboxes to receive the choices of the users. When the choices are few and only one can be selected, we use radio buttons. When the user can make multiple yes or no choices, we use checkboxes. Of course, we can use combo boxes in place of radio buttons. With radio buttons, all the choices are visible on the screen without the user doing anything. With combo boxes, the user needs to click the arrow mark on the combo box and inspect the choices available. Checkboxes are so named because each box can be checked.

12. *Tables*: Tables are used to display data in rows and columns. Each column contains homogenous data of a single attribute of the entity. A row contains all the data elements describing a single entity. Each cell can contain textual or picture data. Usually, we fill the tables with data retrieved from a file. But we can also make the cells receive data from the user.

13. *Grid*: A grid is similar to a table, but, usually, the grid is connected to a database table. A row on a grid contains the data from a single record from a table. A column contains data from a single field of the database table. A grid allows editing of data contained in its cells. The data entered in the grid are usually automatically saved when we move from record to record and also when we close the form. While it is more convenient than a simple table, it is considered risky in situations when the application is abruptly closed either due to a system crash or power outage. Of course, a good Database Management System (DBMS) package takes care of this problem using a rollback mechanism of deleting a partially entered record. It is considered a better programming practice when the insertion of a new record or modification of an existing record is achieved programmatically.

14. *Picture controls*: These enable us to place a picture on a form. The size of this control can be specified by us. The controls usually resize the picture to fit within the space provided by us. We can place multiple picture controls on the form. We have to note here that we can place pictures on a hypertext markup language (HTML) form at any place without explicitly using a picture control. We can also insert an image in a table cell.

15. *Video control*: Video control is similar to a picture control in all matters except that is automatically played at the click of the play button. It also has all the buttons to pause, stop, fast-forward, fast-rewind, mute, and a progress bar.

16. *Audio control*: Audio control is similar to video control except that there is no video. It will play only an audio file.

17. *Help*: Help is a text file with special markup that enables us to navigate to the required aspect of application help. This file is connected to the application using a link, either from a menu or a HTML link.

18. *Tool tips*: Tool tips are brief text messages attached to data controls, icons, and buttons. They are normally invisible but become visible when the cursor hovers

over the them. While all the icons are usually very easily decipherable, sometimes they are not, and sometimes the user finds it confusing. Most icon pictures are selected with the United States in mind. Therefore, users from other countries are likely to be confused about the meaning of the icon. A tool tip can bridge the gap in such scenarios. Good programming practice mandates that every control should have a tool tip. A tool tip on the control can supplement the information on the label attached to the control.

19. *Hyperlinks*: Hyperlinks consist of text marked as a link using HTML. Clicking a hyperlink connects to another web page and navigates the user to that page. The new page may replace the present web page, or it can open a new browser or a new browser tab and load the page.

20. *Setup scripts*: A setup script is a program that builds the application to be loaded on another computer. It takes all the forms, DLLs, images, and so on and makes them into one single executable file or a set of files to be copied onto a CD or DVD. When we load this setup file on a new computer and execute the file, the application will create all the necessary directories, load all files in the appropriate directories, insert a shortcut to the executable file in the Start menu, and place the application icon on the desktop and other specified places like the quick-launch menu. Of course, this comes after the application is developed as a COTS product, but as software designers, we need to design this, too.

In addition to these controls, there could be other controls. There are some companies that supply controls for open source languages like Java and its variants. We can use them in our designs.

Data

You might have noticed that I omitted one crucial component of software design. Yes, I kept it for the last. It is data. After all, the computer and the software proposed to be developed are focused on processing data. Data can be classified in multiple ways. The first classification is based on the type of data. Data are of three types, namely:

1. *Numeric data*: This data consist of numbers, and numbers can be used in computations. All data processing concerns this type of data. We even generate graphics using numeric data with the help of mathematical formulas. Of course, we need not generate graphics in our programs, as the manufacturers have developed graphic primitives and supply them along with their graphics cards. Numeric data can be used in all types of processing.

2. *Alphanumeric data*: Alphanumeric data consist of alphabets, numerals, and other printable characters. Alphanumeric data cannot be subjected to any arithmetical operations. Some people say that addition operation can be performed on alphanumeric data, but it is really concatenation of strings of characters. The only processing operation they can be subjected to is comparison of one string with another to decide whether the strings are identical and whether a set of characters are part of another string. They also can be sorted in ascending or descending order.

3. *Control data*: Control data are commands to the computer and consist of nonprintable characters. Usually, the control data consist of a combination of the "control" or "Alt" key and one or more printable characters. These are used to pass on special commands to hardware or the operating system. Sometimes we use them in our programs, too.

Another classification is based on the type of data usage. These are:

1. *Parameter data*: This data set the parameters for localizing a software product, especially a COTS product, to make it suitable for the organization in which the software is installed and is proposed to be used. Parameter data drive software behavior. for example, the language for the labels (English, French, German, etc.) of the software; another example is the currency symbol used in the software, and yet another example is the name of the organization in the reports. Large COTS products like credit card processing software, enterprise resource planning (ERP), or customer relationship management (CRM) software need large amounts of parameter data. Usually, for such software product installations, the first activity after installing the software is setting the parameters for the organization. Parameter data are set once for an organization, and are not usually changed unless a major parameter changes. The volume of data remains the same through the life of software or until an upgrade to the software is effected.

2. *Master data*: Master data are similar to parameter data but are generated through business transactions whenever a new entity joins the system. Master data are used for reference purposes when processing business transactions. They are very large in volume and change more often than parameter data. Master data drive the transactions. In CRM software, the customer data are the master data; in material management software, the material master is the master data; and in payroll software, employee data are the master data. Master data also change, but more frequently than parameter data. The volume of master data remains the same, more or less, and is likely to increase at a much slower rate than transaction data, described next.

3. *Transaction data*: Transaction data are collected when the software is used in discharging the organizational functions. Transaction data continuously grow in volume at a much faster rate than master data. Usually, transaction data are much larger than the master data and, given sufficient time, the master data volume would only be a fraction of the volume of transaction data. Most of the disk space is utilized by the transaction data, especially as time passes.

There are many subcategorizations of the above data types. Here is the subclassification of numeric data:

1. *Integer data*: Integers are whole numbers. They may be prefixed by a positive or negative sign. An integer is represented inside the computer using 2 bytes. Another subclass of integer data is the long integer, which is represented by 4 bytes inside the computer.

2. *Floating-point numbers*: These numbers are fractional numbers and have a decimal point. There are two subclasses in this type, namely single precision and double precision. A single-precision data item was represented by 4 bytes originally, but

is now represented by 8 bytes. Double precision is twice as long as the single-precision number. It was originally represented by 8 bytes, but is now represented by 16 bytes.

3. *Currency*: This type of data is mostly available in databases, and it is usually represented by 8 bytes. It is a fractional number. The distinguishing aspect of this data type is that it has only two digits after the decimal point.

4. *Dates*: A date is usually a long integer and represents a calendar date. It allows us to perform date arithmetic like adding a number to a date, subtracting a date from another date, and so on.

5. *Time*: This is also a special long integer counting time. It allows us to perform time arithmetic similar to date arithmetic, like adding a number to time or subtracting a time from another.

Another classification of data is based on the source of data or from where the data is received.

1. *Hard disk data*: These data are available on the hard disk resident within the computer. These data can be accessed within the least amount of time. These data could be stored in either flat files or database tables.

2. *Keyboard data*: These data are entered by the user using the keyboard as and when necessary or when a business transaction takes place.

3. *Internet data*: These data are received over the World Wide Web. They can come from a computer at a geographically distant location or from a nearby system. They could have been entered by a user sitting in front of a computer, or they could come from a machine, a rocket, or an airplane. This information could come on wires or through the wireless medium.

4. *Network data*: These data come from a network, either a local area or a wide area network.

5. *Mobile data*: These data come from cell phones communicating with a server for a business transaction.

6. *Machine data*: Computers are used in a variety of machines, including computer numerically controlled (CNC) machines, flexible manufacturing systems, computer integrated manufacturing systems, automobiles, washing machines, and many others. The specific requirement of this type of data is that the response time has to be maintained at predefined levels.

7. *System data*: This is another class of data that is ready for us to use. These are the data stored inside the computer and are maintained by the system. They include date, time, timestamps on files and directories (or libraries), system information, and so on. We can use these data in our programs. These data available within a computer system differ from one computer system to another depending on the operating system.

Perhaps there could be other classifications of data used within specific organizations.

When we carry out the design for a software product, we use all the elements and achieve a design adhering to the principles of design detailed in the first chapter to fulfill the requirements, both core and ancillary, defined for the product in an efficient manner.

5

Software Design Activities

Introduction

What do software designers do? Where and how do they begin design activity? What is the first step in software design? What is the deliverable of software design activity? These questions are vital for a beginner in software design activity. This chapter attempts to answer all these questions.

Software design is a set of activities. There are some predecessor activities and some successor activities to software design. We have seen what prerequisites need to be in place before software design activity can begin in Chapter 4. The successor activities to software design are coding, quality control, preparing the build, installation, creation of master data, and rolling out the system. Now, let us look at the activities performed under the banner of software design:

1. Study the core and ancillary requirements for the proposed software product.
2. Study the data to be processed by the proposed software product.
3. Study the organization to identify the roles and probable users of the system.
4. Design the data.
5. Design the common programs.
6. Design the system architecture.
7. Design the input screens.
8. Design the inquiry screens.
9. Design reports expected of the system.
10. Design the ancillary aspects of safety, security, reliability, and so on.
11. Design the installation and rollout of the system.
12. Document the design.

Now let us discuss each of these activities in detail.

Study the Core and Ancillary Functionality Requirements

The foremost prerequisite to begin software design is the study of the requirements for the proposed software product. Software designers rely completely on the documented requirements that are validated using the organizational quality assurance methodology. Requirements are classified into core functionality requirements and ancillary functionality requirements. In fact, the activity of software design is the realization of the requirements in an efficient manner.

The field of information technology has become an arena where phrases and terms are bandied about, and in some cases, a cult is also formed. The cult members begin to hurl invectives on other terms and phrases. These cults are like organized religion claiming that their methodology is supreme and denouncing all others as paths to hell. I, perhaps, could have used terms like *backlogs*, *test cases*, or other phrases, but I use the term *requirements* because it reflects what the users want in a much better manner. The term *requirements* bestows primacy to the user, while the other terms bestow primacy to the development team.

Core functionality requirements are usually defined by the users or their representatives. In a COTS product scenario, it is usually the top management with the help of the marketing department or market research specialists who define the core functionality requirements. If we do not fulfill any of the core requirements, the product is not fully functional and will leave the user dissatisfied to that extent. In many cases, it is not possible to fulfill all user requirements in the first iteration itself. The reasons could be a lack of necessary technology, the prohibitive cost of such technology, the lack of resources to fulfill such a need, or any other reason that makes the managers defer fulfillment of some requirements for future releases. Studying and understanding the core requirements is for the purpose of identifying those requirements that are planned for the current iteration of the software product. Another purpose in studying the core requirements is to ensure that we have the necessary technology and methods to achieve those requirements. One other purpose of studying the requirements is to see that the requirements are defined unambiguously. If we come across any ambiguities, we need to obtain clarification from the source and clear up the ambiguities in the definition.

The ancillary functionality requirements are essentially defined by the design team and, to some extent, management, especially in the case of security, safety, and ease of usage. The onus of defining and implementing the ancillary requirements rests squarely on the shoulders of the design team, but these should have been defined before the design activity began. Studying the ancillary requirements is for the purpose of identifying those requirements that can be implemented with the available technology and methodology. We need to separate those requirements we are not planning to meet and communicate to marketing so that the limitations can be intimated to the customers or made part of the product specifications.

The purpose of studying the requirements is to understand thoroughly what the design is expected to deliver. Once we complete the study of the requirements, we are ready with a complete understanding of the core and ancillary functionality requirements we have the necessary technology and methodology to implement. Now we are ready to begin the design of the processes that deliver the functionality.

Study the Data to Be Processed by the Proposed Software Product

In studying the data as a precursor to designing efficient and effective methods to handle it, store it, and make it available to users, we try to assess the amount of storage needed and if we really have the technology to store all the data efficiently. For example, if one of the data items is extremely long—by which I mean more than 255 characters long—we may be faced with a problem. Another problem is storing data of hyperlinks, strings containing special characters like "/", strings containing markup languages that can cause undesirable actions, or some such other rogue strings.

In studying the data, we actually look at some of the existing data, which can be in paper records or computer files or database tables. At a glance, we are looking for exceptions in sizes, as at this stage, we have yet to begin the actual design activity. We also obtain clarifications about any ambiguities present in our understanding of the data. Once we complete studying the data, we are ready to begin designing the methods of storage and the processing needs thereof.

Study the Organization to Identify the Roles and Probable Users of the System

We study the organization in which the system would be implemented. In studying the organization, we identify the major functions, traverse down the organizational branches, and identify the transactions performed by each of the information processing roles. A role may be played by one person, or, in some cases, a single person performs multiple roles. Each role may perform a single transaction or multiple transactions. In this study, we identify the present roles in the organization and the transactions performed by each of the roles. This identification assists us in designing the software based on the needs of the transactions performed by the individuals as well as defining the security roles and access privileges.

We use the organization chart and job descriptions of the people holding the positions in the organization relevant to the proposed software product. If there are any ambiguities or gaps in our understanding, we obtain clarifications to bridge the same. Once we complete the study of the organization, we have a complete understanding of the information needs of each of the roles that will be using the proposed software.

At the end of this study, we know all the transactions currently being performed. Our design may combine some transactions into one, divide some transactions to spawn multiple transactions, or even add a few new transactions altogether. Similarly, we may combine, divide, or add roles. Now we are ready to begin the design of transaction processing. Now let us look at the software design activities.

Here, we need to understand a few things about transactions. A business transaction usually consists of receiving a few inputs; carrying out some processing using the inputs coupled with past transaction data, master data, and parameter data; and then producing some outputs. One business transaction may be broken down into multiple computer transactions, including an input transaction, an output transaction, an inquiry transaction, and a processing transaction. When we talk of transactions, we actually refer to input design, output design, and processing design.

Design the System Architecture

What is the system architecture in a software product? People can easily understand when we talk about the architecture of a building or a physical product, but it is not so easy when we talk about a software product that is not visible to the physical eyes. When we use the word *structure* about a product, we refer to the methodical arrangement of components that:

1. Are often invisible from outside
2. Keep the product together
3. Prop up all the other components
4. Provide strength to the product
5. Provide safety and security to the product

We will design these aspects as the first step in the design of the proposed software product. We will discuss these aspects in the subsequent chapters.

Design the Data: Parameter Data, Database Data

This is the first concrete step we take in designing the software. As the whole purpose of the proposed software is processing data, designing the data is obviously the first step. The objectives set for the data design activity are:

1. Use the disk space efficiently by avoiding the duplication of data to the extent possible. Data redundancy is inevitable in whatever form it is stored, but our objective is to keep the redundancy to a minimum. Of course, we cannot eliminate data redundancy completely.
2. Maximize the efficiency in retrieval of data by the software programs. The very purpose of data storage is to retrieve it as necessary, process it, and deliver the outputs. The data has to be stored in such a way that the time to access and retrieve it is kept at a minimum. In our eagerness to minimize the usage of storage space, we should not sacrifice the needs of data access times.
3. In these days of multiple users accessing the applications from all over the world, access conflicts and deadlocks can easily occur. We need to design the data in such a way as to avoid deadlocks.
4. Concurrency control is an issue that is not easy to detect in normal testing. Even beta testing in the field is rarely capable of detecting concurrency control issues. This issue can be detected only in a code walk-through by an experienced quality assurance person and by specialized concurrency testing. This is basically a design and reliability issue. We have to design data storage such that concurrency control is effectively tackled.
5. Any system used over long periods needs expansion. Software is no exception. Some software-driven systems designed and developed in the 1970s are still in use today. Those days, the design options were very limited and those designers never expected their systems to last so long. The result was a massive expenditure to change the software to be capable of handling two centuries (the 19th and 20th) with two digits allocated for the year field. In some cases, they postponed this problem to 2049, which at the turn of century looked far, far away, but it doesn't look so now! So, we need to predict the future needs to the best of our ability and provide for the future needs in our designs.

During data design, we carry out the following activities:

1. Design the data storage—we store some data in the database tables, some in flat files, and some in cookies. We need to design each of these to optimize data redundancy.
2. Design the mechanisms like indexing to optimize data access times.
3. Design the security mechanisms so that hacking and damaging the data is prevented, detected, or minimized.

We will discuss all of these in the subsequent chapters.

Design the Common Programs

With applications using the Internet, there will be many programs that will be used by most of the other programs. In particular, the ancillary functionality requirements like security, safety, and integrity requirements will be commonly used by the core functionality requirement programs. It is much better to design all such routines and build a DLL that can be called by all other programs.

Let us consider the login-check functionality. Now that any application page can be directly accessed over the Internet, each web page needs to have a login-check routine to ensure that the person requesting the page is already logged into the system and hence is authorized to access the page. Every web page needs to have this check. So, it pays to write the routine once and allow all other programs to access it as required. That way, when we modify or upgrade it, we need to maintain it at one place only. Designing the common programs at the beginning and making them available as DLLs to the other programmers saves an enormous amount of time for the organization while improving the efficiency and reliability of the system as a whole.

Design the Presentation

Be it the input, inquiry, or output, most of the processing activity involves presentation. For receiving inputs, we present certain prompts and some data to the user in guiding him/her to enter the right data in the right place. In output screens, we present some data to enable the user to select the desired output and present the desired information in such a way that the user can locate and effectively use what was requested. In inquiry screens, we present prompts to guide the user in making inquiries of the system and then present the requested information. For design purposes, output and inquiry screens are identical.

Then, we also need to present the user with facilities to navigate the system between the screens. Then, because computer hardware manufacturers are providing excellent graphics and color facilities, we need to provide for aesthetics for the user to gain a competitive advantage for our product besides making it interesting for the user to use our product effectively. Therefore, we need to design the presentation of information to the users as an activity separate from input or output design.

Design the Inputs

Every software product receives data from the users. We have to design inputs in such a way that the user is required to expend as little effort as absolutely necessary, at a fast pace and with the least amount of tedium. Therefore, we design our input functionality such that typing is minimized and the data is taken in the most logical fashion and as painlessly as possible.

Design the Inquiry/Output Screens

During the batch processing era, inquiries and outputs had to be designed differently. But in the present era, they are more or less identical. In these screens, the user supplies some information based on which data is extracted, processed into information, and delivered as output either to the screen or on paper. In some cases, we deliver all the information or a summary on the screen and then deliver the rest on paper. In some cases, the output may be diverted to the Internet or to another machine, which may be a computer or some other machine.

We design the output screens in such a way that they are neatly and logically organized and the user is able to locate the desired information easily. With every output, we need to design control statistics that show the extent of information processed so the user can assess how comprehensive the delivered information was. This will ensure that the information is extracted as ordered.

Design the Ancillary Aspects of Safety and Security

All the ancillary aspects are specified and designed by the software design team. Of course, the users, the marketing team, and organizational management can also take part in these specifications. The design of these aspects deals with protecting the programs and data from external entities, protecting the user from losses, protecting the organization from outsiders who may attack the organization for wrong results or perceived losses, and so on. We carry out design for all ancillary requirements.

System Administration Design

Any application has to be administered. If it is a single-user software product, it will be administered by the user himself or herself. If it is a multiuser product, it needs someone to look after the administrative tasks of user management, backup and restore, disaster recovery management, definition of organization-specific parameters and management, units and measures, and so on. We need to design a separate module for facilitating performance of these tasks. We need to focus extra attention on the security for this module as it has the capacity to damage the entire application and data. It is an important task of the software designer.

Design the Installation and Rollout of the System

The developed software has to be installed on the specified target system at a location that is different from the one in which the software was developed. In the case of COTS products, the product may have to be installed at many places, some of which are in another cities or even in other countries offshore. So, we need to make the installation as easy as inserting a DVD or CD into its designated drive. The process of installation should not require too much intervention from the installer. It should capture as much information as possible from the environmental variables of the operating system. Presently, especially in the case of web-based products, we may have to install product components on different machines. We need to install the database on the database server and programs on the app server; we may have to load our security routines on a security server, and all these can be a single machine or multiple machines. We need to design this aspect as part of our software product design.

Document the Design

We need to document the design so that the programmers can understand our design and code the product. Documenting the design has been a bone of contention since the advent of software development. Until very recently, the roles of designer and programmer were combined into one. Many people were aghast when the topic of separating design from coding was broached. But it is changing slowly but surely. Many methodologies were developed to document the design, with SSADM, object-oriented analysis and design (OOAD), UML, rational unified process (RUP), and the IEEE software engineering standards being the most important ones. More methodologies are in the offing and, in my opinion, they will not be the last. For a small single-user software product, perhaps we can skip this step, but for the rest, we had better document the design. The onus of preparing the design documents is on the software designers.

Quality Assurance of Design

It is very important to subject the deliverable of any human endeavor to quality assurance. Human beings are prone to error. It is also true that one is blind to one's own mistakes. Therefore, it is necessary that we get our designs reviewed by a peer or a team of peers.

If it is a COTS product, we can build a prototype and subject it to testing, as its cost will be absorbed by the number of products sold. But if the resultant product will be a single-site product, we cannot build a prototype and subject it to rigorous testing, as the cost has to be absorbed by one single customer. But in both cases, review by a QA team that includes design specialists, marketing people, and domain experts to validate the design is possible.

As designers, we need to both subject our designs to QA by others and help other designers by performing the QA role on their designs. This is an important activity of software designers.

Postdesign Activities

Once the software product is designed, documented, and subjected to QA and the feedback is implemented, we complete the design activity by releasing the designs for construction. We usually perform the following activities after releasing the design documents:

1. *Support during construction*: Programmers often need clarifications on implementing the design. They may also come up with suggestions for improving the design so that the efficiency and effectiveness of the product can be improved. Sometimes, they may just ask for a clarification. Whatever it is, we need to support the programmers during development.

2. *Support in QA*: During the development of the product, the code will be subjected to various quality control activities like peer reviews and testing. We need to support the process in preparing test plans, clearing the defects uncovered in the reviews, and all such other activities.

3. *Changes*: Change is inevitable. However well we may have designed the product and whatever the quality control exercised on the design, change requests are placed on the product during its coding phase. Some of the changes originate with the customer or the marketing team, and others may originate with the programmers or the QA team. The software project manager (SPM) in charge of developing the product handles all such change requests and will ask us when the change necessitates a design modification. For each such change request, we issue a design modification request/design concession request (DMR/DCR) to all the concerned, including the construction team and the quality control team.

4. *As-built documentation*: Once the product is developed and released for use at the site, we need to update all our design documents to reflect all the changes made to our designs during the coding and QA stages. These documents will be used in maintaining and upgrading the software product during its usage.

5. *Postmortem*: We need to carry out a postmortem of the designs for every product that we released into the market. This will help us look at the best practices and pitfalls we encountered during the designing of the product. This will help us improve the process of design for future projects.

Ancillary Design Activities

While carrying out the design of a software product, we need to perform several ancillary activities. These ancillary activities support our main activity. Let us discuss them here.

Stay at the state of the art: We have a responsibility to be at the edge of technology in terms of the facilities offered by the hardware, system software, off-the-shelf components, libraries, and how others are offering their products. This will help us design the best product for our organization. We do this by reading technical journals, participating in seminars, attending product demos, participating in discussion groups or bulletin boards, and so on. We must spare time for these activities or risk being outdated.

Standards and guidelines: We need to find time to develop standards and guidelines, not only for design but also for coding and QA activities. They aid us in improving productivity all around. Work becomes simplified and easy for all concerned, and that includes us.

Code libraries: We also need to focus and build a code library of components culled from the products developed in-house or bought from professional component developers and set up a code/component library for future use. This library reduces our design effort as well as the coding effort.

Knowledge repository: A knowledge repository is vital if we desire our software designs to be robust and result in robust software products. It is the software designers who can discern what is relevant for them, bring it into the organization, and insert it into the organizational knowledge repository. While the onus of building and maintaining the knowledge repository does not rest with the software designers, they have the responsibility to identify relevant knowledge from both internal and external sources, acquire it, and arrange for it to be part of the organizational repository.

Design and development: While software designers do not conduct research and development (R&D), they certainly have to carry out design and development (D&D). R&D continues to happen either inside our organization or outside of it. This could be basic or applied research. We need to continuously scan the technological horizons in our area of specialization to capture relevant new developments in our field. Then, we have to dovetail the developments into our designs. We may need to take several actions like using new methods in a pilot product or prototype, testing the product, and assessing the efficacy of the research claims. All this has to be done, as we cannot use unproven claims of R&D in our products. Design is an activity that can predict the outcomes to be expected by building the product. D&D is an important activity of software designers.

Recruitment of designers: Software designers are not born such. We need to recruit people with information technology education who have the flair to be software designers and train them. There are various approaches to identifying potential designers. Whichever approach we may adopt, we have to take up the task of recruiting software designers for our organization. They are necessary to fill the vacancies arising out of attrition or expansion of activity. This is also an activity performed by software designers as and when necessary.

Training: Recruitment of talent is one thing and realizing people's potential is quite another. Training is an important step in converting potential talent into talented software designers. Who else can conduct this training, especially the technical part, except software designers? Software designers have to find time to perform this activity as and when it becomes necessary.

Appraising: Appraising the performance of junior designers is part of motivating them and keeping up the morale of the design team. Appraisal brings out performance and how well it compares with others or with what was expected of the individual. This measurement helps in implementing measures aimed at improving the person and the performance.

In addition to the above activities, software designers partake in many organizational initiatives. Any time a technical opinion needs expression, the organization calls on the software designer. When a new product is contemplated, the organization calls on the software designer. If any statutory authority knocks on the door, asking about the product, the software designer provides the answers. If there is a court case on the services or the product, the software designer guides the attorneys and testifies in court. What I discussed above are the core activities of the software designer. In addition to those activities, the software designer performs many activities that support the organization.

6

Data, Storage, and Retrieval

What Is Data?

Data, as defined in Chapter 1, is facts about entities. An entity can be:

1. A person.
2. A location.
3. An object.
4. A system.
5. An equipment.
6. An item of material.
7. A transaction.
8. A town.
9. It can be anything that has some attributes by which it is described!

Facts can be in figures or be descriptive. For example, a person has a name, which is descriptive in nature; has a weight, which is expressed in numbers; has an educational qualification, which is descriptive; has an income, which is described in figures; has a date of birth, which is a special type of number; and has a title, which is again descriptive. In this manner, all entities have some facts and figures associated with them.

While each entity has facts and figures about it, we are not interested in all entities. We are interested in those entities whose data needs to be stored in our computer system, processed, and reported as required.

Basic Data Types

Data is basically of two types

1. The data that human beings use
2. The data used solely by the computer and its I/O devices

As programmers, we might need to handle both types of data. Then, the data used by human beings is of two types, namely

1. *Character data*: The data that contains alphabets and perhaps numbers, too
2. *Numeric data*: The data that is expressed only in numbers

Character Data

Character data includes any character that can be input to the computer. What are characters, in the context of computers? They can be anything accepted by the computers. IBM used extended binary coded decimal interchange code (EBCDIC) codification of characters for its mainframe computers. It is an 8-bit code that allows 256 characters to be codified. Later, the American Standards Association finalized the standard for codification of characters for use in computers and called it the American Standard Code for Information Interchange (ASCII). It was originally a 7-bit code, but has been extended to 8 bits and allows 256 characters to be codified. It codifies alphabets (uppercase and lowercase), digits (0–9), and other special characters that are both humanly readable (like space, (,), [,], and so on) and not humanly readable (like the enter button, CTRL+ALT, and so on). Character data can contain those characters that are not humanly readable as well as the humanly readable characters.

How do computers treat character data? The characters that are not humanly readable provide special input to computers. They are generally used in combination with other characters to give special commands to computers. Humanly readable characters are used to denote nonquantifiable attributes of entities to be stored, retrieved, and searched in the computers. The treatment of character data depends on the definition of character data by the compiler of the programming language.

In earlier days, COBOL defined character data into two classes, namely alphabetic data and alphanumeric data. Alphabetic data allowed only alphabets and a blank space. Alphanumeric data allowed alphabets, numbers, and other humanly readable characters.

The BASIC and C languages allowed definition of a single character, which allowed any character to be input to computers.

Character data is usually defined as a string of words. A word is a contiguous set of characters. A word is separated from another by a delimiter, usually a blank space. Character data that is humanly readable is usually stored inside the computer. It is used to search for a specific item of data inside a large group. It is also used to make a logical decision based on the word or a group of words. It can also be added; that is, two words can be added (concatenated) to result in a single word. It can also be used to pick parts of words and make a new word. The only arithmetic operation possible on character data is addition. Other arithmetic operations, including multiplication, division, subtraction, and so on, are not possible on character data. True, some languages permit performance of all arithmetic operations on character data, but they do not promise reliable results or provide any practical use. Character data is generally used as:

1. *Strings*: A string can consist of multiple words. When we use strings in programs, we need to enclose the string between quotation marks (" … "). Usually, the length of a string is restricted to 255 characters, in other words, approximately one-fourth of a 1 kilobyte.

2. *Memos* or long textual matter is used to store documents or long explanations inside a database. It can contain lines in addition to words and strings, numbers, and other humanly readable special characters such as parenthesis, full stop, comma, and so on.

3. *Special strings*: Recently, this data type has come into existence. The universal resource locators (URLs) used for web site addresses and email addresses form part of this data type. These are used for navigating to a web site or sending email.

Numeric Data

Numeric data is numbers expressing the value of some attribute of an entity. As you may know, there are real numbers and imaginary numbers. Computers can handle only real numbers on their own. What is an imaginary number? The square root of any negative number is an imaginary number. However, if you can come up with a procedure for handling imaginary numbers, then the computer can handle them. If, during the execution of a program, the computer comes across an imaginary number, an error is thrown.

However, most numbers are associated with a unit. The unit of money can be dollars and cents, the unit of weight can be pounds and ounces, the unit of length can be feet and inches, and so on. The units have to be handled by the programmer. Computers cannot handle units unless programmed to do so.

Computers subject numeric data to arithmetic manipulation, and all arithmetic operations can be performed on numeric data. Numeric data is further classified into the following types:

1. *Integers*: Integers are whole numbers without any fractional part. Except in counting, the real world uses fractional numbers. Integers are used in representing age, income, addressing memory locations both in RAM as well as secondary storage, wage rates, and so on. In reality, the age of a person remains an integer just for a day, on the birthday. After that, the age has a fractional part. When integers are subjected to the arithmetic operation of division, it may result in a number with a fractional part. Some programming languages allow two types of integers, namely the short integer and the long integer. Two bytes are allocated for short integers and 4 bytes are allocated for long integers. The first bit of the integer is reserved for the sign, positive or negative, and the remaining bits are used to store the number. A short integer has a maximum value of 32,767 (2^{15}–1). A long integer has a maximum value of 2,147,483,647 (2^{31}–1). When we use integers, we ought to be sure that the number will never result in a fractional part.

2. *Real numbers*: Real numbers are those that have a fractional part. Examples are 10.5, 21.2513, 100.35213, and so on. Real numbers are stored inside the computer in a special manner. They are stored as the mantissa and the exponent along with a sign. For example, the number 100.25 is stored as (+.10025, 3). That is, the number is 0.10025 multiplied by 10^3, or 100.25. Real numbers are also referred to as floating-point numbers. Real numbers are usually stored as single-precision and double-precision numbers. The precision denotes the number of significant digits the number can store. We should be careful in using double-precision numbers, as

they take up a significant amount of RAM and storage space, twice that of a single-precision number.

   a. *Single-precision* numbers are those that are allocated a minimum of 4 bytes. Currently, most computers allocate 8 bytes to single-precision numbers. A single-precision number with 8 bytes of allocation can handle up to 20 significant digits. When the language does not explicitly specify the precision, the default precision is single.

   b. *Double-precision* numbers are those allocated a minimum of 8 bytes. Most modern computers allocate 16 bytes to double-precision numbers, especially those computers that are used in scientific and mathematical applications. Double-precision numbers with 16-byte allocations can handle up to 39 significant digits in the number.

3. *Dates*: Dates are a special category of numeric data. They contain three distinct parts, namely the date, the month, and the year. The number of days in a month depends on the month. Leap years affect the number of days in the month of February. Dates are two types, namely the short date and the long date. The short date consists of only the date, month, and year. The long date consists of time in hours, minutes, and seconds in addition to the date, month, and year. The actual storage of a date depends on the computer, but most store the date as the number of seconds from a reference date, such as 1900-01-01 00 hours 00 minutes 00 seconds. When displaying the date, they convert it to the date human beings are used to seeing.

4. *Time*: Time is also a special type of numeric data. It contains three numbers for the hour, minute, and second. The minute and second have a maximum value of 59; then, they roll over to 00. The hour has a maximum value of 24. Often, the time needs to be displayed with a suffix/prefix of AM or PM and in 12-hour or 24-hour format.

5. *Currency*: Currency is also one special number whose fractional part is restricted to 2 digits after the decimal point. Financial applications use this data type, as the number of digits after the decimal point is always two.

6. *Counters*: This data type is integers and is used to count the number of iterations a set of program statements is executed inside a program.

7. *Auto-incremented numbers*: These are used in database tables to form a primary key for the table when a data item cannot be unique in the table. We will explain the primary key in the next chapter on data storage. The feature of this data type is that it will be automatically incremented whenever a new record is inserted in the table.

   We need to note that numeric data is the main data, as the main purpose of computers is to process numeric data. Most common numeric types of data used in computers are detailed above. Some computers can have additional data types to make life easier for the programmers.

Special Data Types

There are a couple of data types that are used for special purposes in programs, especially in developing system software. These are:

1. *Arrays*: Arrays are tables of data. Usually arrays are used in solving mathematical problems in matrix algebra, moving averages, sorting, and so on. Arrays can be single-dimensional; that is, there is only one row of data with multiple columns, or two-dimensional containing both multiple rows and multiple columns. Most programming languages restrict the use of arrays to numeric data, but some programming languages do allow the use of character type data in arrays. In computers, an array is a contiguous chunk of RAM. The amount of RAM allocated to an array depends on the data type used in the array. If we declare a single-dimensional array of six integers, then the computer allocates a contiguous chunk of RAM that can accommodate six integers. If we declare a two-dimensional array, say, a 3×4 array of integers, then the computer allocates a contiguous chunk of array to accommodate 12 integers. Arrays are used in both commercial software as well as system software development. Arrays have to be declared separately like other data types, but they need the following additional information besides the name of the array:

   a. Type of data to be held by the array

   b. Dimension of the array, that is, the number of rows and columns contained in the array

2. *Pointers*: Pointers are a special type of integer data. Pointers can hold the address of any location inside the RAM. So, the size of a pointer type variable is fixed so it can hold the maximum address of any location in the RAM. Usually, the size of a pointer is 8 bytes. Using pointers, we can access any location in the RAM and manipulate its contents subject to the restrictions imposed by the operating system. Application programs are not allowed to access any RAM location, as it would violate the security of the execution environment. In application programming, pointers are used for handling arrays, especially in the C family of programming languages. In system programming, we need to handle allocation, de-allocation, and manipulation of all the RAM, and pointers are used to manipulate RAM as desired by the programmer in the development of system software.

3. *Union*: A union is a special data type used in the C family of programming languages. It allows the same amount of RAM to be addressed using different variable names as well as different data types. It is perhaps the only data type that allows storage of both numeric and character data and allows the data to be manipulated as both numeric and character data. Of course, it is incumbent on the programmers to store numeric data in a union before handling it as a numeric variable and to store character data in it before manipulating it as a character variable. This is very useful in real-time software development, as there is a premium on the amount of RAM available.

4. *Boolean*: This data has only two states, namely 0 or 1, which can be interpreted as true or false/yes or no. This is akin to a flag that is either waved or held steady. This type of data is sometimes referred to as flags. Most computers dedicate a bit for this data. But, as memory comes in chunks of bytes, 1 byte gets used for this data type. This data is used to set the state when a set of circumstances occurs. For example, as you type a document, a flag is used to denote that the document has changed. When you press the save button, this flag is checked, and if it is set to true (or false depending on the programmer), the document is saved. If you press the save button immediately after a save without changing the text in the document, this flag will

remain false (or true depending on the programmer), and the save action will not be initiated. Flags are also used to denote end-of-file conditions, the existence of further records in a database table, and so on. Boolean data types are used in all types of applications, including business and system software.

5. *Labels*: Labels are usually captions of controls placed on the screen. They contain short meaningful information explaining the nature of the control, the data expected to be input into that control, or the data displayed in that control. Of course, labels can be used in reports for column headings, report headings, captions for totals, or any other explanation for the data produced on the report. While most development platforms allow a label to have a maximum length of 255 characters, it is better to restrict the length of the label to be as short as practically possible.

6. *NULL*: This is a special data type that indicates nothing. NULL is none of the data types discussed above. Most databases set the initial value of the fields to NULL in a newly inserted record. NULL is a constant when used in programs. We can compare the value of a database field to NULL and make programming decisions. In a database field, NULL indicates that no value has been inserted in that field since the creation of that record. Even so, NULL values in database fields cause program aborts and result in critical errors of the software. Since databases allow definition of a default value, it is a good practice to define the default value for all fields of a database table while designing and creating the table. Usually, the default values we use are zero for numeric fields and blank spaces for alphanumeric fields. For date fields, we can make use of the system date or some other date.

Data Classes

Basically, there are two data classes, namely local (dynamic) and global (static). The distinction surfaces when the program contains subprograms.

Local Data: Data declared inside a subprogram is usually local data by default. That is, the value stored in a local variable is used only by the subprograms in which it is declared. It is not available to be manipulated by the main program calling the subprogram. The RAM allocated to the variable declared as local to a subprogram is released to the operating system for allocation to other programs when the execution of that subprogram ends. If we want the value stored in the variable available to the main program or other subprograms, we must declare it as a global variable. A variable declared in a subprogram is by default a local variable unless it is declared as a global variable.

Global Data: A variable declared in the main program is available to all the subprograms called by the main program for manipulation. It need not be declared as global. But if we declare a variable in a subprogram and want it to be available for manipulation by other subprograms or the main program, we need to declare it as global. A variable contained in a higher-level program is available for manipulation by a lower-level program, but the reverse is not true. A variable declared as global is not released until all the programs in the main program, including the main program, are closed. A global variable ties up RAM until all subprograms and the main program are closed. Therefore, it is better to declare variables as local to reduce the burden on RAM. If more RAM is tied up by global variables and other programs need RAM, virtual RAM has to be utilized, with all its attendant disadvantages.

Use of Data in Programs

The primary purpose of computers and computer programs is to process data. To use data inside programs, we need to declare data that is proposed to be used in the program. To tell the computer we will be using data of a certain type in the program, we declare a variable, thus:

1. A variable is a name for our reference representing the data we propose to use inside the program.
2. The rules for naming a variable differ from one programming language to another.
3. A variable is associated with a specific set of data to be used in the program.
4. Depending on the data type, the computer allocates the amount of memory (RAM) when the program is loaded for execution into the computer.
5. Whenever we use that variable in the program, it refers to the allocated RAM.
6. The allocated amount of RAM remains allocated as long as the program is under execution in the computer.
7. When the program completes execution and is removed from the RAM, the space allocated for the data will also be released for allocation to other programs.

Thus, to use data in a program, we declare variables for all the data items we propose to use in the program. Then, we keep reading data into the specified locations in the RAM and process it as long as the program is in execution.

Next, we will see how data is stored in computers for storage and usage.

Storage of Data

For processing data, we need to supply it to the computer during program execution. We can do so from the keyboard, item by item, when asked by the computer. We get a prompt on the screen and we input the data using our keyboard. This procedure is all right when we process small amounts of data and in classroom hands-on sessions, but not in the real world of business and government. We need to process large amounts of data in the real world. It is just not possible to input bulk data using our keyboards. Therefore, we need to store the data on a medium from which the computer can read at its speed.

We store data inside RAM when programs for processing the data are being executed. During program execution, only one set of data items is stored inside the RAM. Bulk data is stored on secondary memory or storage. Secondary storage is magnetic media, optical media, and solid-state memory.

In the beginning, we used to store data on punchcards. Then, we moved on to magnetic tapes and then to magnetic disks. Now, we have optical disks, which are referred to as CDs and DVDs. These optical disks use laser technology. While optical disks have made giant strides in technology, they have not yet replaced magnetic disks as the primary medium for data storage inside the computer. The cycles of read and write on optical disks have not yet achieved the reliability of magnetic disks. Second, the capacity of optical disks is not large enough to replace magnetic disks. Third, the number of times read and write can be effected on optical disks is not high enough to match magnetic disks.

Solid-state memory (flash disks, pen drives, universal serial bus [USB] drives) looks very promising and could very well replace magnetic disks as the primary medium for storing data in the coming days. It is now capable of holding data up to 250 GB, which makes it feasible to be used in personal computers to begin with. Solid-state memory is the primary reason behind having handheld computers, which are referred to as tablet computers.

Magnetic tapes were used as the primary choice for storing data until the 1970s but were superseded by magnetic disks. Since being replaced by magnetic disks, tapes were used as a backup medium to keep backups of data and programs. Even today, large-capacity magnetic tapes are used to store 70 GB or more on data cartridges, which are basically quarter-inch-wide magnetic tapes kept securely inside a cartridge.

Magnetic Disks

Magnetic disks have been the primary choice for storage of data. Magnetic disks are now hermetically sealed and mounted inside the computer to store data and supply data and programs to the computer. Magnetic disks are capable of holding terabytes (1 terabyte or TB is equal to 1000 GB) of data. The time to access any location on the disk is also the lowest other than that for the RAM. Solid-state drives are competing with magnetic disks in terms of access time but not in the capacity to hold data. Magnetic disks are now referred to as hard disks or Winchester disks. They are called hard disks to differentiate them from floppy disks. While floppy disks are made with polyester film, hard disks are made on metal platters. So, polyester film disks are referred to as floppy disks and those on metallic platters are referred to as hard disks. Though floppy disks are passé, the name hard disk remains.

The magnetic disk is cut into many tracks for holding data. Each track is then divided into a number of sectors. The first track is numbered as 0 (zero) and other tracks are numbered upward. The sector is the smallest element of the disk that is addressable. In some computers, the sector is numbered from 0 (zero) upward within the track. That is, there will be a sector numbered zero in each of the tracks. This necessitates supplying two addresses, namely the track number and the sector number, to locate data on the disk. In some computers, the sectors are numbered from zero upward without reference to the tracks. In this method, we need to supply only one address, that is, the sector number, to locate data on the disk. Presently, most computers use the latter practice of numbering the sectors. That is, the first sector of the disk is numbered 0 (zero) and the last sector has whatever number it comes to, depending on the capacity of the disk. Each sector holds one block of data. Most computers use 1 KB (1024 bytes) of data as one block or one sector.

The block is the minimum amount of space allocable to data whether we use it entirely or not. When we have more data than can be allocated in one block, the disk space is allocated in multiples of blocks.

When we format a disk to make it usable in the computer, the computer writes a table on the disk. This is referred to as the volume table of contents (VTOC), or in PCs, it is called the file allocation table (FAT) or a similar name. This table usually contains:

1. The file identification number, which usually starts at zero and is numbered upward.
2. The name of the file.
3. The identification number of the block where the first block of data of the file is stored.
4. It may contain additional information about the size of the file, the addresses of the other blocks of data of the file, the address of the last block of information, and so on.

The disk also has one more table in which the block address and file to which it is allocated are written. Initially, the allocation information will be blank, and as the disk gets filled up, the allocation information is filled in against every block.

Records

Before we move on to data files, we need to understand records. A related set of data items is one record. For example, let us assume a payroll situation. An employee has an ID, a name, his or her basic rate, number of payable hours, and other allowances and deductions. In this manner, all the employees in the organization have similar information. Now, the data is organized for each employee and for all the employees. If we assume a table, each row will contain the information of one employee, and all the rows put together will hold the information of all employees. Each row can be viewed as a record. Summarizing, we have:

1. A data file contains several records.
2. Each record contains several data items.
3. Each data item contains one specific attribute of an entity. Each data item is referred to as a field.

Data Files

Data is organized in files in computers. Why are they called files? Initially, decks of cards were used to store data. When you punched data onto the punch cards and they were bunched into a deck, it resembled a paper file with papers. Then data moved on to magnetic tapes, with each tape holding one class of data or, in other words, one file. Each tape had one file of data. Though data moved onto magnetic disks, the name, *file* stuck, as people were familiar and more comfortable with that name. Even though IBM began using the name *data set*, which I think is more appropriate to describe a set of data, *file* is definitely more popular in the computer and data processing world.

Of course, the advent of DBMSs has moved mainstream data storage from plain data files into tables of databases, but data files are still used in a significant manner. Therefore, we need to learn about data files before we move on to databases.

Traditionally, files were organized as sequential access data files, and with the introduction of magnetic disks, random access data files came into existence. Then, to combine the advantages of both file types, indexed sequential access data files were introduced. We will discuss these files in greater detail now.

Sequential Access Data Files

Initially, all data files were sequential access. That is, data had to be read record by record, one item after another, in a sequential order, and it was not possible to access any required data directly without accessing all the preceding data items. When data was on punched cards and magnetic tape, this was the only way. Before we could get to a desired card, we had to read all its preceding cards. On tape, too, the tape runs only in one direction, and to get to the desired data, we had to read the preceding data. With disks, it became possible to access any desired data directly as the disk was spinning, and it is possible to access any track and sector within almost the same amount of time. In sequential access data files, there were two kinds of organization.

1. *Variable record length sequential access data files*: In these files, the length of each record can vary. It can happen when the fields of the record have variable lengths. For example, people's names do not have the same number of characters. For example, the name John has four characters, while Harold has six characters. Similarly, the pay rate for an employee can be less than a hundred, with two digits, whereas another employee can have a pay rate more than 100, with more than three digits. When the fields have different lengths, to distinguish one field from other in the same record, a delimiter is inserted after each data item in the record. Usually, a comma, a space, or a semicolon is used to delimit one field from another in the record. The advantages are that the record length for each record and thereby the size of the file is maintained at a minimum. While this was not a great advantage during the punchcard days, it was a great advantage during the initial days of magnetic disks, as the disks did not have the large capacity that is available in the present day. The flip side was that an additional character in the form of a delimiter has to be inserted between adjacent fields in the record, increasing the overall record and file sizes.

2. *Fixed record length sequential access data files*: In these files, each field has the same length. If a specific data item has less than the allocated length, the extra length is wasted. In numeric fields, leading zeroes are inserted to pad the field to its full length, and in character fields, blank spaces are suffixed to the field as needed to pad the field to its full length. With fixed-length fields, the need for delimiters is eliminated. This was more or less the practice in the days of punchcards and magnetic tapes. With the advent of disks, variable record length sequential access files have become the norm. Still, fixed record length is used in mainframe computers even today.

Now, there is one other variant in sequential access data files, referred to as line sequential files. These are mostly used in personal computer (PC) applications. In fixed record length files, no delimiter is used between adjacent records. The record sequence is determined by counting the number of characters and dividing the count by the record length. In variable record length files, the record sequence is determined by counting the number of field delimiters and dividing the count by the number of fields in the record. It works perfectly with files on magnetic tapes, but files on disk have to use a mechanism to distinguish records from one another. They use the carriage return (ASCII character #13) character and/ or line feed (ASCII character #10) character as the record delimiter.

Sequential access data files offer the best economy in terms of disk space and are still being used. In disk-based sequential access data files, the disk space is allocated contiguously as far as possible, and the file is continued in the free blocks available on the disk. In this mechanism, a record may span two or more blocks, depending on the record length. Sequential access data files are still used in a significant way, especially in mainframe computers and where bulk data needs to be processed.

Random Access Data Files

The advent of magnetic disks made it possible to access any record in a file with almost identical access time. This has led to data being organized as random access data files. In random access data files, any record in the data file can be accessed by specifying the record number relative to the first record in the file. To facilitate random access of records in the file, a record always begins on a new block on the disk. If a record length is less than one block, the remaining space on the block is wasted. If a record spans more than one block, the remaining space in the last block is wasted. Thus, in random access data files, fragmentation of space causes wastage of disk space. Purely random access files did not last long and were quickly replaced by indexed files. Random files were very efficient in locating a specific record based on a key value such as a name or an identification number.

Indexed Sequential Access Data Files

In order to combine the advantages of random access files in the ability to quickly access any desired record and the efficient utilization of disk space by sequential access files, the industry came out with indexed access sequential data files. These are popularly referred to as indexed sequential access method (ISAM) files. In this method, an index to the records is maintained as a separate sequential access data file. This index file contains two values in each record, namely the value of the key data item and its relative location in the file. Whenever a record needs a location, the index file is first searched sequentially to locate its relative location in the main data file and then, using the relative location, the desired record is located and retrieved for use. This has greatly reduced the time for locating any desired record. The extra space needed for the index file is much less than the space wasted in the fragmentation loss of the disk blocks.

ISAM files are still used, especially in COBOL applications in IBM and other mainframe computers. These are used in bulk data processing applications. IBM names sequential access data files entry sequence data set (ESDS) and index sequential access data files key sequence data set (KSDS).

However, maintaining data files had to be accomplished through programs. The extra effort needed was significant. The data had to be entered offline, that is, on a separate data entry machine by a specialist data entry operator. The entered data needed to be perfect in every way, and 100% accuracy was desirable but rarely achieved. Correction of data was laborious. This led to errors in the results. Even if the data entry were 99.99% accurate (i.e., the error rate was 0.01%), the number of defective records in a million could be as high as 10,000! While the percentage could be low, the absolute number was unacceptably high. Organizations needed significant number of employees to handle the complaints about wrong results. Another major disadvantage with data files was that they did not facilitate being used by employees who were not expert in data processing but specialized in their domain. All transactions were carried out on paper and data was entered offline. The best computers could do was to supply management information for decision making, but could not really make a significant impact on cost reduction in organizations. To reduce the costs in organizations, transactions needed to be moved from paper to computer by allowing the end users to use computers on their own. This needed better organization of data than these data files. And that shift came in the form of databases or DBMS.

By the way, these data files are referred to as "flat files" in the current time, as the files are flat and without any of the control information that exists in the databases. In real-time applications, flat files are the only ones used to store data. In machine control applications such as the software used in cars, airplanes, rockets, and so on, flat files are used to store data. In firmware, that is, software etched onto a silicon chip, flat files are used. It is only in commercial applications that databases handle the bulk of the data, but even in them, a few flat files are used for storing application configuration information. Therefore, serious software designers need to learn and understand flat files and their organization and usage.

Database Management Systems

The main issue with having data in flat files is that it needs maintenance by programs written specifically for file maintenance. Every time the file structure changes, that is, either a new field is added or a field is eliminated, all the programs need changes, especially in the sections where the file structure is defined. To alleviate this problem, the definition of file structure was taken out of the programs and stored as a copy book, and the programs just inserted a reference to the definition. But if the file structure changed, the programs had to be recompiled and converted to executable files. If the file structure changed to add a new field for the sake of one program, all the other programs that used that file had to be recompiled even if the changed file structure did not affect them. This has not only caused organizations to spend considerable effort in program maintenance, it also caused errors whenever a program was overlooked during maintenance.

The industry worked on overcoming this problem and came out with DBMS technology. DBMS is a software package with a set of programs that facilitate:

1. Definition of file structure.
2. Maintenance of file structure, including addition, deletion, and modification of fields.

3. Entry of data into files (referred to as tables).

4. Maintenance of data, including addition/insertion of new data, deletion of existing data, and modification of existing data.

5. Ability to index tables as necessary so that indexed search capabilities are made available for programs for quick data retrieval. It also includes automatic updating of indexes as and when the data changes.

6. A language that is optimized for fast conditional data retrieval that can be called from programs. This has relieved the programmers of the hassle of coming out with the best possible routines to retrieve data efficiently and quickly.

Databases have been adopted by the industry quickly, and DBMS has become an inseparable part of present-day commercial applications and those applications that use large volumes of data. With DBMS, programmers need not define the file structure inside the program. They need not even recompile programs even if the file structure changes. Another major advantage of DBMS technology is that no programs need development for entering data. DBMS provides data entry facilities. Another major disadvantage of flat files that prevented multiple users from concurrently using the same file was overcome by DBMS. With DBMS, the entire file need not be dedicated to a program. It is adequate to lock one record to the program, and other programs are able to use the other parts of the table or the database in their applications. This facilitates online data processing by end users of the computers, and the need for specialist data entry operators was eliminated. As users are now entering the data directly, the need for data verification has also been eliminated.

DBMS facilitated storing large volumes of data, simultaneous use by multiple users, and efficient and quick data retrieval. This has facilitated moving business transactions from registers and papers to computers and paved the way for paperless offices.

Now, DBMS has four levels of organization:

1. *At the bottommost is the field or domain*: It is the smallest unit of data and holds data of one specific attribute of the entity. For example, a name is a field and holds the values of names; similarly, pay rate is a field that holds the values of pay rates for different people. A field is like a column in a two-dimensional table.

2. *At the next level is a record or tuple*: It holds the complete information for one entity. For example, in payroll data, a record contains the pay information for one employee. It contains information like the employee identification number, name, pay rate, other allowances, deductions, payable number of hours, and so on. A record consists of multiple fields. A record is akin to a row in a two-dimensional table.

3. *A table or relation*: It is related to information for an application. It consists of a number of records. In a payroll application, a master table consists of the master data of employees such as employee id, name, designation, pay rate, allowances applicable to the specific employee, normal deductions, and so on. A payroll transaction table consists of employee id, number of payable hours, other earnings during the pay period, deductions during the pay period, and so on. In this manner, there could be other tables in the payroll application.

4. *A database*: It is a collection of tables that are related together. For example, a payroll database may consist of an employee master table, transaction table, union

membership table, income tax table, and other such tables. An organization may have multiple databases such as a marketing database, material management database, finance database, personnel database, and so on.

In programs, a reference needs to be made to the database, and then all the data in the database can be used; any record can be accessed, any field can be updated, any record can be added or inserted, and any record can be deleted. In this manner, any data can be manipulated as required by the organization. DBMS technology has achieved removal of the dependency on data for programs. Now, programs and data are independent of each other and can be maintained without worrying about their impact on each other.

Currently, most commercial applications make use of databases to handle the data of applications. Databases evolved from hierarchical and network databases to relational database technology. In hierarchical databases, a relation could be set from one table to many tables. In network databases, a relation could be set from many tables to many tables. In relational databases, a relation can be set from one table to just one other table. It is a one-to-one relationship.

However, by using interface tables, we can achieve many-to-many relationships in relational technology. Relational databases utilize disk space very efficiently and hence are preferred over the other two technologies. Oracle, SQL Server, Ingress, Informix, My SQL, and Progress are examples of commercially available relational DBMS software. A standard scripting language, structured query language (SQL), was developed for data definition, retrieval, and maintenance. Programmers can call the SQL routines in their programs directly and make use of them for data maintenance and retrieval.

The design of databases and definition of tables can be performed independently of software development. Let us now examine a few basic requirements of DBMS packages so that we can effectively use them in software development.

Each table needs to have a primary key. A primary key is a field in a table in which data values are not duplicated. Each data value of the primary key is unique. Without a primary key, a table cannot be defined in a truly relational database. In some relational database systems, a combination key with the values of two or more fields can be combined to form the primary key, but most systems require one field to be defined as a primary key. In certain cases, it may not be feasible to set aside any one field as a primary key. In such cases, we usually define an additional field and fill it with auto-incrementing numbers to have a primary key.

As some perceive, a DBMS does not completely eliminate duplication and redundancy of data across multiple tables. What it really does is control the data redundancy. To set a relationship between two tables, a field must be common between those tables. It is referred to as the secondary key. While the primary key cannot have duplicate values in the table, the secondary key can have duplicate values. Incidentally, the secondary key in a table ought to be the primary key in another table with which the current table is related. A relation is set between the primary key of a table and the secondary key of a different table. A table can have only one primary key, but it can have multiple secondary keys.

The design of a database is a large enough subject to merit a book in itself. Here, I am including a brief explanation for you to understand the basics. Usually, in organizations specializing in software development, it is common to dedicate a database specialist to design the database and develop routines for efficient data manipulation, which are used by the programmers in their programs. Here are the steps in the design of the database:

1. First, compile all data items used in the application.
2. Then, divide the data items into logical groups.

3. Then, carry out a process referred to as normalization. Normalization is a systematic process of elimination of data items in logical groups and eliminating duplication of data. It is usually carried out in three stages; the third normal form has a primary key, and all other data items in the group do not have duplicates.

4. Each of the logical groups in the third normal form is defined as a separate table.

5. Most DBMS packages have in-built facilities to build indexes and set relations automatically.

Each package has different rules for naming the tables and fields as well as data types for defining data, but most DBMS packages support the data types described earlier in this chapter. All DBMS packages implement the standard SQL language with some extensions and a few adaptations of their own.

Depending on the type of application you are developing, the type of data storage and retrieval needs to be determined and used in development. This chapter introduced you to the two basic types of data storage and retrieval, namely flat files and DBMS tables. Now we are ready to look at what computer programs are.

7

Data Design

Introduction

Oftentimes, I am asked by beginners in software design about where to begin the design of a software product. While I was not so sure in the beginning what to tell them, now, I have no doubt whatsoever that the design of the data is the first step to be taken in designing a software product. As you are aware, the purpose of any computer-based system is to process data. Data goes in, is processed and stored, and a subset is given out as output at the demands of its users. So, obviously, we need to design the data first. Then, we build the system around the data. First things first: before we begin the software design activity, the requirements analysis and engineering activity should have been completed and all the information about the system to be built should already be available. It should include the data items or groups of data items that need to be processed by the proposed system. When I say design of data, what I mean is:

1. Understand the data.
2. Understand the sources of data.
3. Design the organization and storage of data.
4. Design the retrieval mechanisms for the data.
5. Design security mechanisms to protect the integrity of the stored data.

Let us discuss these in greater detail in the following sections.

Understand the Data

In Chapter 4, we had a preliminary discussion about data while discussing the elements of software design. Let us discuss the same here, but in greater detail so that we can design the data aspects of the product efficiently.

We need to classify data for the purpose of achieving a good data design into three major categories.

1. Application data
2. Parameter data
3. Security data

73

Application Data

The application that we design and build accepts some data as input and stores it through business transactions; it has some data that is more or less static, which is used for reference by the modules of the software product. It also generates some data, most of which is transient, and sends it as output. All this data is the core data and is processed by the software product we design and build. The users of the software product are involved either in inputting the data, processing it, or generating the outputs.

This data is generated mainly by the end users of the application, and some of this data could be generated by the system and database administrators.

Parameter Data

If the product is to be used at a single location by a single user, this data, in most cases, may have no place in the software product. This data is needed when the contemplated software product is a multilocation, multiuser one. This data is used by the software product at the time of its initiation. This is the data we should have hard-coded (included inside the program). This data is invisible to the end users. It is maintained by the system administrators of our product. The parameter data includes such items as:

1. Language for the presentation to the users, such as English, French, German, Italian, and so on
2. Currency symbol
3. Comma position
4. Date and time formats
5. Number of permitted users
6. Organizational details, such as
   a. Name
   b. Logo
   c. Address details
7. License number
8. Date of installation and expiry of the license
9. Product-specific parameters

The end users are not allowed to change this type of data. Only the designated system administrator for the application can carry out modification of this data, using a strict process of authorizations and approvals. Most of this data is input at the time of initial installation and commissioning activity. Later on, changes could be made by the system and database administrators.

In some cases, the processes of the application have parameters that may change over a period of time. Examples that come to mind are credit cards, insurance policies, financial applications, and so on, which use a lot of such data. All of these also use parameter data.

It is also common practice to compile all possible error messages into a file and use it in the application to achieve uniformity across the application that will be developed by multiple programmers. This is also considered a parameter file.

Security Data

This data ensures security and safety for the integrity of the application data as well as keeping the programs from being hacked. This data consists of some data that is predefined at the time of installation and commissioning of the application and some created by the application as transactions are performed by the end users. The predefined security data consists of:

1. *Security roles*: All applications have several roles with different levels of access rights for users. This data contains definitions of all such roles and the security permissions granted to each of those roles.

2. *Security rules*: All applications enforce certain rules for ensuring security. These include password changes, access rules, security alert rules, incident handling rules, and so on.

3. *Authorized locations from which the application can be accessed*: The locations from which the users can access the application. For example, the customers of an American bank should be able to access the application from anywhere within the United States and from outside the United States with certain restrictions. This data contains all such location information.

4. *Locations that are not authorized to access the application*: Access to certain or all aspects of the application is usually restricted. For example, the system administration functions cannot be accessed from any location other than where the system administrator is stationed. This data contains information about those locations from which access to the application shall be denied.

The end users are not allowed to change this type of data. Only the designated system administrator for the application can carry out modification of this data, using a strict process of authorizations and approvals.

Data Generated from Application Usage

When an application is used, transactions are performed and the data is changed. Sometimes, the transaction may be questioned regarding its authenticity and be termed illegal. To enable auditing such transactions, we need to capture certain details of the transaction that are not part of the transaction, like the time of transaction, the place from which it is performed, the change effected, and so on. The security data that is created by the processing of transactions by the application are:

1. Audit trails
2. Session details

3. Login attempts
4. Details of parameter data changes
5. Details of security data changes

This data is generated every time a transaction takes place; therefore, the volume of data generated is very large. In some cases, the volume of this data exceeds the application data. Therefore, this data has to be designed very carefully. We have to select such data items to form part of these data only when they add some value and assist investigation when a security incident takes place. Most of this data has to be automatically generated by the application. Let us discuss each of these items and their design considerations here.

Audit Trails

Audit trails are provided by most database software developers as part of database functionality. They capture the details like the name of the field whose value is changed, the date and time of its change, which user changed it, and any other useful details. Usually, a facility is provided to select the fields for which audit trails need to be captured. The database administrator can set these parameters. But, as software designers, we need to select the fields for which audit trails have to be captured. There is no point in capturing the modifications to each and every field. We need to select such fields that are relevant and vital in conducting an investigation when a security incident occurs. Here are some guidelines for selecting the fields:

1. Any addition, modification, and deletion of user profiles.
2. Password changes of any user.
3. Changes to any parameter field.
4. Transactions involving suspiciously large sums of money. We need to set a limit beyond which an audit trail is captured based on the specific situation of the organization.
5. Too-frequent transactions, as in the case of lost credit cards. We have to define what is too frequent. We can take two approaches here:
   a. Define an absolute value like more than three transactions per day.
   b. Compute a moving daily average of the previous six months and define a percentage, say 50%, over the average as the limit for triggering audit trails.
   c. Of course, we will be discussing what to do in such cases in the chapter on security design.
6. Changes to master data files, especially the modification and deletion of master data file records.
7. Any deletion of a record on which records of some other files/tables are dependent.
8. Any other application-specific information that is either deleted or modified; in some cases, even addition of a new record may have to be captured.

Session Details

It is possible to hack into applications on the Internet. Therefore, every time a new session is set up, it is important to capture the session details for future reference. We need to capture the following information for every session, even if the login attempt fails.

1. The Internet protocol (IP) address to get the place from which the session is set up. When the first hacking incident takes place, it is certain that many innocent sessions were set up prior to the incident. Each first login is preceded by just opening the web pages that do not require logins. For each successful hacking login, there would have been quite a few innocent unsuccessful login attempts. Seasoned hackers do not try to gain access by attempting too many logins in one session, as it gets detected and the screen and the IP address might be locked up. Therefore, every time a security incident happens, all these session details help the investigators locate the perpetrator. Second, it also helps us design a robust security system, as our analysis of unsuccessful attempts reveals hacking attempts before they actually happen.

2. For every successful login, the details of the user id need to be captured. It helps us ensure that the user is at the expected location. For example, if the user is usually expected to be in the United States and the login has taken place from a country like Iran, Russia, or North Korea, we can protect our application by asking for additional authentication information.

3. The date and time of the session initiation and closure need to be captured, as this enables our system to ensure that the login is at the expected time. For example, if the login was at 2 a.m. from within the country, obviously, it could be a malicious attempt. We can ask more questions to authenticate the user.

4. The type of session closure needs to be captured. A genuine user would usually properly close the session by logging off. If we receive abrupt closures without logging off successively from a specific location and user, it becomes suspicious.

5. The browser from which the session was set up helps us learn which are the common browsers through which our application is accessed. This in turn helps ensure that our application is maintained to be compatible with these browsers.

6. Any other application-specific information from the session can be captured.

Login Attempts

When there is a successful login attempt, it goes through the usual security process and its information is captured. But when a login attempt is unsuccessful, we need to capture the following information:

1. The usual session information detailed given in the preceding section.

2. The user id: if it is a nonexistent id, it could of course be an innocent spelling error by a genuine user. But if the wrong user id is used more than once, it could be a hacking attempt to discover a right user id. When we analyze a number of unsuccessful login attempts with a wrong user id, it may reveal a pattern.

3. Password: if it is a nonexistent password, it could of course be an innocent spelling error by a genuine user. But if the same wrong password is used more than once, it could be a hacking attempt to detect a right password for a specific user id. It could be that the hacker obtained a right user id and is trying to obtain the right password. When we analyze a number of unsuccessful login attempts with a wrong password but a right user id, it may reveal a pattern.

Details of Parameter Data Changes

Parameter data defines the way the application behaves and performs. Modifying the parameter data is the easiest way the hackers can affect our application. Therefore, we need to capture each and every change that is made to any of the data items in the parameter data.

Details of Security Data Changes

Security data contains vital information that controls the security of both the application and the application data. Any change made any time to the security data like security roles, permissions, and so on must be captured and stored for future reference to aid in investigations when necessary.

Now that we understand the nature of all types of data we deal with in software design, let us begin our discussion of the design considerations for each major category of data.

Design of Parameter Data

The first question we need to answer in designing parameter data is: Should we put it in flat files or database tables? While most parameter data does not change, some of it changes, and some of it can change many times. None of it will change daily, but it can change a few times a year. For example, tax rates and prices can change a few times. There can be similar data items in the parameter data. It is tempting to use database tables for parameter data, and many designers do that.

I would suggest using flat files, as they are more secure. It is argued that a flat file can be totally deleted and a new file uploaded in its place. True. But it is very difficult for a hacker to locate the file in a maze of files. To look at the contents of all files surreptitiously to locate the required file is very difficult. Second, flat files contain data only and by looking at alphabets and numerals, it is very difficult to decipher the purpose of the file in the application. All this has to be accomplished manually. Computer programs cannot automatically locate the right file. They may locate text files but not the one that the hacker is looking for. The sheer volume of work deters hackers from hacking the parameter file.

We can easily check the authenticity of flat files at the beginning of each session by checking the properties of the file. This is because to change the value of one data item or several, the whole file has to be rewritten. For database tables, we need to check the audit trail. This is because changing the value of one data item does not require rewriting the entire table. We can encrypt the flat file using our own algorithm, and it is not easy for a hacker to decipher the encryption because it is not in the public domain. To encrypt a database table, we may have to use the encryption algorithm supplied by the DBMS supplier. Then, that algorithm would be in the public domain and facilitates easy decryption.

Flat files allow different types of records. The number of fields and their types can be different from one record to the other. We can define each record as a single string of characters and then break them up into right data type items inside the program. Usually, database tables require all the records in one table to have the same structure. But this can be overcome by defining all fields as character types and then converting them inside the program. Alternatively, we can define the record as a single field with sufficient length and use the same mechanism as in the case of flat files to break it up into its constituent data items. However, flat files, when defined as pure sequential files, achieve their advantage of having varying-length records. On the other hand, database tables have records of the same length and therefore occupy more disk space than flat files.

Some computer systems like the AS/400 may not provide any facility for using flat files. They may provide a DBMS as standard information storage. In such cases, the solution is obvious and we need to use whatever is permitted by the system.

But, there are solutions to every problem and each solution brings in a new problem. So, as the adage goes, to each his own. My recommendation and vote go to flat files for storing parameter data.

Once we settle the storage system between flat files and database tables, we need to answer the question: Should we have one single parameter file/table or should we have multiple files/tables? In some applications, there will be so many parameters that the decision is obvious, and that is to use multiple tables/files. In many cases, the decision is not so obvious. If we use a single parameter file, all the data in the file will be read once and stay in the RAM for the duration of the session. Fortunately, the cost of RAM has come down significantly over the years, and gigabytes of RAM are now available. Unfortunately, the software developers of system software and application packages eat up all that RAM, leaving very little for application software. An IBM PC came out with 128 KB RAM in 1982 and the reviewers went overboard about "so much" RAM! Now, each 32-bit PC comes with 4 GB, and without any application being invoked, swapping already begins! Of course, one may argue that we can read only those data items as required by the usage. If we place all of our parameter data in one single file, the file obviously becomes large and opening, accessing, and then reading the right record consume more time. If instead we divide the parameter data into smaller files, logically associating them with modules or units of software, they can be opened and the right record accessed and read with minimum expenditure of the time resource.

Both alternatives are in use, and each alternative has its own adherents. My vote goes to multiple files/tables for parameter data. Having more files makes it tougher for a hacker to decipher what we are doing. We surely do not want to make the life of a thief or vandal any easier, do we? We wish to make it as tough as possible for the hacker.

Another aspect you need to focus on is whether to encrypt the parameter data. Encryption places an additional overhead on the programs and programmer. Every time the file is accessed, it needs to be decrypted before reading it, and it takes some time, however little it may be. But parameter data is a very important part of the application and can affect the application as a whole. So, my recommendation is to encrypt the data.

Summarizing the above discussion, here are the aspects a software designer has to focus on while designing parameter data:

1. Determine whether database tables or flat files are right for your scenario.
2. Determine if you wish to place all parameter data in one file/table or multiple files/tables.
3. Determine if you wish to encrypt the files/tables containing parameter data.

The last aspect is to design the records of the file or table. A record is a logical grouping of related data items. If the record is too lengthy, say, more than 255 characters, it becomes difficult to accommodate it on one screen and edit it. especially in the case of a flat file. Of course, we do have programs to edit data, but a data processing person will encounter the need to display the record on the screen at some time or other. So, it is better to limit the length of a record to 255 characters. If it is feasible, design the record so it can supply all parameters for a module.

Again, if it is feasible, make the parameter file have one record for each of the units in the module. That is, each unit requires one record in the parameter file and the parameter file supplies all parameters required for all the units in one module.

TABLE 7.1

Format for Capturing the Design of a Parameter File

Product Name:		Date of Design:	

Name of Parameter File: Global_pars

Module Name: All modules

Name of Data Item	Data Type	Length	Remarks
Currency_symbol	Char	1	Global
Dec_point	Char	1	Global
Language	Char	10	Global
GST_rate	Numeric	Single precision	Global
Org_name	Char	50	Global
Future_field1	Char	50	
Future_field2	Char	50	

Needless to say, the parameter files have to be online for the software to function properly. But whenever the parameters change, we capture all the changes made to the parameter file. These records can grow larger over a period of time, so consider removing the older data to be archived. We can determine the period of storage based on these two considerations:

1. The age of the data. Most organizations keep the data based on this consideration. Usually, they keep the data for a period of five years, but it differs from organization to organization.

2. The disk space occupied, If the disk space occupied is too small to cause concern, then the data is kept until the disk space causes concern. Sometimes companies may also set a time limit, such as 10 years

We document the design of the parameter file using an Excel spreadsheet. We use one Excel sheet for each parameter file/record; see Table 7.1.

Using the format in Table 7.1, we capture the design of all parameter files to be used in the application. Of course, we can add additional columns in the above format specific to our organization.

Design of Security Data

Security data, as detailed in the preceding sections, needs to be referred to frequently. Unlike parameter files, which are read once to retrieve the needed parameter data and load the program parameters, security data is frequently referred to by programs to enforce security to the application, prevent hacker intrusion, and protect the application from damage. In a single session, the security data may be referred to more than once, and not only that, the security data may be referred to by multiple sessions from multiple locations concurrently. Therefore, I suggest using database tables for storing security data.

We use multiple tables for designing security data. Let us now see how we design the table for each of the security data categories.

Security roles: There are two ways of enforcing application security. One is role-based security, in which each role has certain permissions pre-assigned by the software as

TABLE 7.2

Table Design of Security Roles Table

Role_number	Sec_role	Permission
1	Sec_Administrator	User_admin
2	Sec_Administrator	Backup_module
3	Sec_super	Backup_module

defined by the software designers. The other is permission-based security. In this method, the system administrator assigns permission to each of the users as necessary for the organization. We will be discussing this topic more in security design. In role-based security, we design a table to hold the records of a role and its corresponding permissions. The table design is shown in Table 7.2.

Security rules: In this table, each record contains a security rule and the corresponding action. This table has three fields, namely

1. Rule_id, which is a character type data field, and the width can be about 15 characters.

2. *The rule:* It is usually a numeric field containing some numeric value to be used for making decisions. Sometimes, it can be a character field, also containing a series of values. It can be split into two fields, one containing the minimum value of a range and the other containing the maximum value. It is usually a floating-point value of single precision.

3. *Remarks:* This is an optional field suggested by me. It can be used to include an explanatory statement about the use of the rule. It will help in maintenance later on. This is a character field, usually 255 characters, which is the maximum allowed for a character field. An example table containing a few example records is given in Table 7.3.

Authorized and unauthorized locations for application access: Two methods are used in the design of this data. One is to define locations from which the application is allowed to access the data. In this, the application will allow access from the locations defined in this table and deny access requests from all other locations. In the other method, we define all locations that are unauthorized to access our application, and the application will deny access if the location is in the table. This table will contain simply one field, the location's IP address. In the IP address, we usually use only the first two digits. That is, any IP address beginning with those first two digits will either be allowed or disallowed. High-security applications like a weapon launch systems or space vehicle control system will use the complete IP address. The table design is given in Table 7.4.

TABLE 7.3

Security Rules Table

Rule_id	Rule	Remarks
Pwd_change	15	Number of days before password needs change
Login_attempts	3	Number of times wrong login is permitted
Incident_phone	3143392345	Phone number to call in case of a security incident
Secalert_phone	3143392346	Phone number to alert in case of excess false login attempts

TABLE 7.4

Unauthorized Locations

Field Id	Type	Length
IP_first	Integer	3
IP_second	Integer	3
IP_third	Integer	2
IP_fourth	Integer	1
IP_country	Character	25

Design of Data Generated from Application Usage

Under this heading, we have a few distinct data classes. We need to have a separate data file/table for each of the classes. Let us look at each of them now. But first, let us discuss the appropriate storage mechanism for this class of data. By nature, this will be a large amount of data that is not frequently referred to. It is the data we collect and go back to only when we need to investigate an incident. Because the data is large in size, if we use database tables, the overhead will be very high. Of course, present-day hard disks have practically unlimited space, but, believe me, it gets filled up very quickly. So, we need to back up this data and vacate space frequently. We usually back it up and clear the space once a week, but depending the volume of transactions in the specific organization, the frequency of backing up and clearing space can be more or less frequent than one week. We need backup media in large numbers even to back up this data. So, we need to conserve space.

Audit Trails

Audit trails are a feature generally included in most professional DBMS packages. All we need to do in such cases is just turn it on once we commission the new system at the client location. Supposing we do not have such a facility in the DBMS we selected for our application, we need to design the audit trail. It is better to use flat files for audit trails, as the data generated will be huge and is not referred to in business transactions. It is used for analysis and location of information for investigation of a security incident. All such work is carried out programmatically. So, a flat file conserves space and is the best alternative for storing audit trail data. What data should we select and store in our audit trail? We need to store the following data:

1. The date of modification of data
2. The time of modification
3. The database name if we use multiple databases in our application
4. The user id that effected the modification
5. The name of the table in which the modification was effected
6. The field that was modified
7. The value in the field before the change
8. The value in the field after the modification
9. The IP address or location from which the modification was effected

We can have some more fields appropriate for the situation in the organization. If, in one transaction, multiple fields were modified, we need to have separate records for each of those modifications. All these fields are of character type data fields, and the record is of variable length to conserve space. We achieve this by using a field delimiter such as a comma.

We need to periodically back up this audit trail data and free the space so that the online disk space is not clogged up with this data. We usually set this interval as weekly and if the transaction rate is low, then we can do it once a month. It really depends on the transaction rate.

Deletion of Records from Tables

As software is used, we keep adding new records and deleting existing records. While designing software applications, one care we ought to take is that we never really remove a record from the database. What we usually do is use one field to indicate if it is active or not. We use a Boolean type field, which is set to "NO" by default. When the user deletes the record, we turn this field to "YES" to indicate that this record is marked for deletion. While processing data, we exclude all records that are marked for deletion. But the modification of this field is added to the audit trail.

Addition of Records

It is common for new records to be inserted into the table as business transactions take place. We add this information to the audit trail. In the field "Modified column," we enter "Record"; in the field "Value before modification," we enter "Blank"; and in the field "Value after modification," we enter "NEW." Of course, we also use other types of codes to capture the information about new record insertions. Whatever type of mechanism we use, we should capture information on the addition of records in the audit trail.

Session Details

We capture the details of each session that is logged into our system. This will help us detect the location from which a security incident has taken place. We capture the following details, at a minimum:

1. The IP address or location from where the session is set up
2. The date of the session
3. The time at which the login was successful
4. The time at which the logout was successful
5. The type of session termination: Either through logout, forced through timeout, or abrupt termination
6. The user id of the successful login
7. The machine (PC/laptop/mobile/tablet and so on) from which the session was set up
8. The OS of the client from which the session was set up

All these are character type fields, and we use a variable-length record flat file to capture this data. This data, too, can grow to large volumes. So, we need to periodically back up this data and free the space. We usually back up this data on a weekly basis, but other intervals are also used based on the volume of data generated.

Login Attempts

We capture this data only when the login attempt fails more than a preset limit of attempts, which is usually set to three. If the login was successful before the limit on the attempts, then the data would be captured in the session details file. But if the login attempt fails until the limit is reached, we capture this data. Of course, we lock the session and the user id from making further login attempts. This data is referred to frequently; in fact, every time a login attempt is made, this data will be searched to verify whether the location is locked out. Because of this searching, we use a database table to capture this information. We include the following data in this information:

1. The IP address or location from where the failed login attempts were made
2. The date of the failures
3. The time of failure
4. The user id and password of the three failed login attempts
5. The machine (PC/laptop/mobile/tablet and so on) from which the login was attempted
6. The OS of the client from which the login was attempted
7. A Boolean field to indicate that the lock was cleared
8. A field to capture the user id of the person unlocking the IP address
9. Date of the unlocking the IP address

As you can see, we use only one field for removal of the lock. The fact that the IP address is found in this file attests to the fact that it was once locked out. If the field indicating removal of a lock is turned on, it indicates that some authorized person investigated the incident and then cleared the lock. Until this field is turned on, we will not allow login attempts from this IP address. Since we are using a database table, we can select appropriate data types for each of these fields.

Details of Parameter Data Changes

Parameters are defined during the installation and commissioning of the system by entering the data. The changes to this data are made with strict controls and only by authorized persons. The programs used to make modifications to parameter data are kept under strict configuration control and allow access only to authorized persons. Still, the possibility, however miniscule it may be, exists to hijack the authorized credentials and modify this very important data. Therefore, we need to capture the information changes to this data. The modifications to parameter data are infrequent and few. Therefore, we can use either flat files or database tables for this purpose. We capture the following information:

1. The date of modification of data
2. The time of modification
3. The name of the parameter data file/table in which the modification was carried out
4. The user id that effected the modification

5. The data item that was modified
6. The value of the data item before the change
7. The value of the data item after the modification
8. The IP address or location from which the modification was effected

Of course, we may capture additional data items in this information than indicated above, depending on the organizational needs.

Details of Security Data Changes

Security data is defined during the installation and commissioning of the system by entering the data. The changes to this data are made with strict controls and only by authorized persons. The programs used to make modifications to security data are kept under strict configuration control and allow access only to the authorized persons. Still, the possibility exists, however miniscule it may be, to hijack the authorized credentials and modify this very important data. Therefore, we need to capture the information changes to this data. The modifications to security data are infrequent and few and are modified whenever the security scenario changes. Therefore, we can use either flat files or database tables for this purpose. We capture the following information:

1. The date of modification of data
2. The time of modification
3. The name of the security data file/table in which the modification was carried out
4. The user id that effected the modification
5. The data item that was modified
6. The value of the data item before the change
7. The value of the data item after the modification
8. The IP address or location from which the modification was effected

Of course, we may capture additional data in this information than indicated above, depending on the organizational needs.

Application Data

Application data is mainly of two categories, namely:

1. Master data
2. Transaction data

Application data needs to be stored only in a DBMS, as it is referred to very frequently and is significantly large in volume. Application data was stored in flat files during the batch-processing era. Now, in the era of end-user computing and online systems, flat files are simply obsolete. We need to use a DBMS system and database tables for storage of application data.

Master data describes the entities in the system. It will be clear when we see some examples. In an HR system, the employee is an important entity. A record in the employee master table is added when a new employee joins the organization. That record is deleted only after the employee leaves the organization, after the final settlements of that employee are made and some time has elapsed, with special approval. Similarly, in a material management system, the material master is master data. A new record is inserted in the material master table when a new material is procured. It will be retained in the master more or less permanently. Deletion of a material master record needs special approval. In a CRM system, product details form a master data table. In a hospital management system, the procedures performed by the doctors form a master data file. A procedure is deleted only when the procedure becomes obsolete and the need to refer to it for any purpose does not exist any longer. Deletion of such record needs special approval. I can give more examples of master data, but I am sure you have a proper understanding of master data. Usually, the master data is identified during the requirements analysis phase of software development. Here are some important characteristics of the master data:

1. The master describes the attributes of an entity.
2. This data is entered infrequently into the system. It is inserted only when a new entity enters the system and is authenticated.
3. This data is frequently referenced: It is referred to every time a transaction is performed involving the entity.
4. This data undergoes modifications infrequently: the master data is modified in a controlled manner and approved by specially designated individuals only when the attributes of an entity are changed.
5. Once entered, it is never deleted as long as some transactions continue to be performed referring to them. If deletion is performed, it can be in only two cases, namely
   a. Before any transactions are performed using this data, it can be deleted. Such cases arise only when it is wrongly entered initially.
   b. When the entity has completed its full life cycle and is retired from the system. Even then, the data is retained on the backups.
6. Even when a record is deleted, the data will still be retained on the backup.

Master data is usually identified by the business analysts or systems analysts during the requirements analysis stage of the software development life cycle.

Design of Master Data Table

We need to have one table for each of the entities in the system. The design of the master data table is similar for all master tables. We will have one id field and its name, description, and all other relevant details. A sample table design for a master file for an equipment master in a maintenance system is shown in Table 7.5.

TABLE 7.5

Design of Equipment Master Data Table

Field	Type	Length
Eqpt_id	Character	15
Eqpt_desc	Character	50
Eqpt_sup_id	Character	15
Eqpt_recpt_dt	Date	
Eqpt_Inst_dt	Date	
Eqpt_cost	Numeric	Single precision
Eqpt_maint_days	Numeric	Integer
Eqpt_sup_phone	Numeric	Long integer
Eqpt_amc_amt	Numeric	Single precision

Of course, the real-life record would have many more fields depending on the equipment, but I am sure you get the idea of how to design the master data table.

Transaction data is generated when business transactions are performed. For example, the payment of a premium in an insurance system is a transaction. Concluding a sale is a transaction in a CRM system. Issuing an item from the warehouse is a transaction in a material management system. Making or receiving a payment is a transaction in a financial management system. The main characteristics of transaction data are:

1. Transaction data is generated when business transactions are performed by the end users.

2. Transaction data is the record of all business transactions performed in the organization using the proposed software product.

3. Once a transaction is recorded and authenticated, it cannot be modified. Instead of modifying a transaction data record, we insert a transaction-modification record into the transaction data table.

4. No authenticated transaction data record is ever allowed to be deleted. Instead, we insert a transaction-reversal record into the transaction data table.

5. As transaction data is likely to be built up into large volumes, we free the disk space periodically, adhering to a well-defined and approved process.

Let us assume that we sold an item to a customer on credit and did not receive payment. We perform another transaction to write off the payment that was not received. Suppose we issued an item from our stock in the warehouse and the user returns it: we perform another transaction to return the item to the stock.

Design of Transaction Data

The design of each transaction table depends on the transaction and the master data tables involved. These are the important aspects to be noted in designing transaction data tables:

1. A single business transaction may refer to more than one master data file. For example, the transaction of placing a purchase order with a vendor refers to the

vendor master table and the material master table. Therefore, we provide space only for the id part for every master data record used in the transaction.

2. A single transaction may spawn more than one type of transaction data record. For example, a single purchase order on a single vendor may order more than one item. In such cases, we split the purchase order transaction into two transaction records. One record contains the details of the purchase order, and the other contains the details of the ordered items.

3. One important aspect to be noted is that we need to design the transaction record with as few fields as necessary so that the space occupied by the transaction data is minimized.

Let us look at the table design of the purchase order transaction data tables to understand the above aspects clearly. The design of a purchase order record is given in Table 7.6, and the items table is in Table 7.7.

Of course, there could be more fields in the table, depending on the organization's specific requirements. This table will include all the purchase orders raised in the organization.

The design of the item data table for the above purchase order is shown in Table 7.7.

When we present the purchase order details, either on the screen or on paper, we extract information from these two tables and present the complete purchase order. This table will contain all the items of all the purchase orders raised in the organization. We use the combination of the Po_id and the Po_item_code to retrieve the desired information.

Right now, we are using a relational database management systems (RDBMS). These require one-to-one relationships. While it is not my intention to describe the entire DBMS

TABLE 7.6

Purchase Order Record

Field	Type	Length
Po_id	Character	35
Po_dt	Date	
PO_vendor_id	Character	15
Po_delivery_dt	Date	
Eqpt_spl_condition	Character	50
Po_vendor_contact	Character	25
Po_vendor_Phone	Numeric	Long integer
Po_vendor_email	Character	50

TABLE 7.7

Item Table for Purchase Orders

Field	Type	Length
Rec_number	Long integer	Primary key
Po_id	Character	35
Po_item_code	Character	15
Po_item_price	Numeric	Single precision
Po_item_qty	Numeric	Single precision
Po_item_tax_rt	Numeric	Single precision
Po_item_Del_dt	Date	
Po_Item_spl_cond	Character	50

technology in this book, this aspect needs to be dealt with here for the purpose of designing tables. The relationships between entities are of three types, namely the one-to-one, one-to-many, and many-to-many. The RDBMS allows only one-to-one type of relationships. Taking the above example of a purchase order, each record in the purchase order table will have one vendor only. But each purchase order can have multiple items. Therefore, the relationship between the purchase order and the item is one-to-many. We achieve this by creating another table in which we enter one record for every item in the purchase order. We include the po_id along with the item_code in the record for cross-referencing purposes. As both the item_code and the po_id are likely to be duplicated, we cannot define either as the primary key to the table, and we create a primary key using the record number.

To understand many-to-many relationship, let us consider another example. We have medicines. Each medicine can be used to treat multiple diseases. Then, there are diseases. Each disease may require multiple medicines for treatment. Of course, there can be cases where a medicine can be used only for one disease and a disease needs only one medicine. But when we design a table, we need to cater to all the cases. As a doctor's assistant, the software needs to pick all medicines that can help treat a disease when the doctor inputs the disease for inquiry. Similarly, if the doctor inputs a medicine, we need to display all the diseases that can be treated with this medicine. This is a case of a many-to-many relationship. In such cases, we add another table, referred to as the "interface table." Let us design three tables for this example so we understand the concept better. Table 7.8 gives the design of the disease table, Table 7.9 gives the medicine table design, and Table 7.10 gives the interface table design.

Of course, depending on the requirements, the tables can have more fields. But the interface table will usually have only the three fields indicated above. Using this interface table, we can retrieve all the medicines for a disease or all the diseases that can be treated with a medicine.

TABLE 7.8

Disease Table

Field	Type	Length	Remarks
Disease_id	Character	20	Primary key
Disease_Desc	Character	50	
Disease_incidence	Numeric	Integer	1 = infant
			2 = child
			3 = adult
			4 = elderly

TABLE 7.9

Medicine Table

Field	Type	Length	Remarks
Med_id	Character	20	Primary key
Med_desc	Character	50	
Med_class	Numeric	Integer	1 = vitamins
			2 = antibiotics
			3 = probiotics
			4 = poisons
			and so on

TABLE 7.10

Disease-Medicine Interface Table

Field	Type	Length	Remarks
Rec_Id	Numeric	Long integer	Primary key
Disease_id	Character	20	
Med_id	Character	20	

Interface tables can be used for integrating data between any two related tables to achieve a many-to-many–type relationship when we design applications to interface with other applications besides the above example.

I did not delve deeply into the subject of normalization techniques as a tool to design a relational database. I did this on purpose. This book is not about DBMS systems. It is about software design. Data and database design are but one part of software design, albeit a vital component. To be a good and effective designer of data in software applications, one needs to be adept in DBMS technology. I implore upon you to get a good book on DBMS technology and get expertise in that area.

Design of Views

Views are a feature of DBMS software packages. Tables contain data. IBM refers to these tables as physical files (PFs). Views contain only a table structure, but do not contain data. A view is a relation between two or more tables. It shows the data on the fly whenever we access the view. It extracts data from the tables included in the relation based on the relation. IBM calls these views logical files (LFs). We can make use of these views just the way we use tables.

A view does not need to contain all fields from all the included tables. It can have, let us say, 3 out of 12 fields in the first table, 4 out of 15 fields from the second table, just 1 out of 4 fields from the third table, and so on.

How to design views or logical files is beyond the scope of this book, and I suggest that you read a good book on database management or entrust this work to a database specialist. Currently, the industry is moving toward using database specialists for designing databases, which includes designing views.

Stored Procedures

Stored procedures, triggers, or PL/SQL routines are generally short programs developed using SQL embedded with the database. Different DBMS packages use different names for this feature. When we need to make decisions and extract data from multiple tables and views do not serve our purposes, we use this feature of DBMS packages. Usually, a database specialist is entrusted with the task of developing these routines. These are embedded along with the database and can be called from within programs. They function like just like any other programs except that they only work on database tables and extract data to be supplied to the program for processing.

Design the Organization and Storage of Data

The database is located as part of the DBMS installed on the server machine. All the same, it is a good idea to put the data files of the DBMS in a different directory/folder/library. If, for any reason, the DBMS is corrupted or damaged, our data would be safe. In some DBMS systems, this is feasible, and in some this is not permitted. Where feasible, separate the data files of our database from the DBMS.

The flat files used by the application can be placed anywhere within the application directory. It would be better to place all of them in a separate directory. That way, it becomes easier to back up and restore.

We will discuss this aspect in greater detail in the chapter on architecture design.

Design the Retrieval Mechanisms for the Data

We have to retrieve data for various purposes in our application. There are two ways to achieve this retrieval: one using the programs directly interacting with the database tables and the other using the facilities provided in the DBMS to retrieve the data. In the case of flat files, we need to go only through the programs to retrieve data. But in the case of DBMS packages, they provide a facility to write programs in SQL to manipulate the data in the database tables. When we use this facility, any unforeseen problems that could come up will be handled by the DBMS efficiently. This facility to write programs in SQL is called triggers, stored procedures, queries, and so on. In programs, we call the SQL program and pass parameters like the table name, the fields to be retrieved, the filter, and so on and receive the data.

Design Security Mechanisms to Protect the Integrity of the Stored Data

Data has to be protected from hacking or damage by viruses or malicious users. Data security has three levels, namely

1. Physical level
2. Application level
3. Attacks by viruses, malware, or hacking

We will discuss these aspects in greater detail in the chapter on security design.

Data is the most important part of the application. All programs work on data, either getting it, storing it, retrieving it, processing it, or giving the desired outputs. *The entire application will be inefficient if the design of data is inefficient.* Changing the design of data after the application is rolled out is next to impossible or very difficult at the least. We use both flat files as well as database tables in our application. We have to carefully decide what data ought to go into flat files and what data goes into database tables.

8

Product Architecture Design

Introduction

What is architecture? The term *architecture* was popularized in the design of buildings. Building design deals with two subjects, namely architecture and structural engineering. Merriam-Webster's dictionary defines *architecture* in the context of building design thus: "the art and science of designing and creating buildings." Interestingly, it also offers a definition in the context of computers too: "the manner in which the components of a computer or computer system are organized and integrated." IEEE standard 610, *IEEE Standard Glossary of Software Engineering Terminology*, defines architecture as "the organizational structure of a system or a component." CMMI® for Development Version 1.3 of SEI (Software Engineering Institute, Carnegie Mellon University, USA) defines architecture as "the set of structures needed to reason about a product. These structures are comprised of elements, relations among them and properties of both." It gives another phrase, "functional architecture," and defines it as "the hierarchical arrangement of functions, their internal and external (external to the aggregation itself) functional interfaces and external physical interfaces, their respective requirements, and their design constraints."

In all these definitions, one theme is common: organization or arrangement. These definitions give us an idea of what product architecture is and allow us to move forward on the topic. However, I prefer the definition given by Merriam-Webster's dictionary in the context of computers, which is simple, concise, and to the point. I stated in the previous paragraph that in building design, there are two subjects. The structural design deals with components generally hidden from view, but these are the ones that bear the load placed on them by all the other components as well as protecting the building from external forces like earthquakes, gale winds, floods, and accidents. In the context of building construction, the columns, roof trusses, and beams are the ones that bear the brunt of attacks on the building. They hold all the ornamentation of the building and protect the building as well as its inhabitants, keeping them safe and secure. Architecture deals with the arrangements of rooms, halls, the façade, water closets, and so on so that the building looks aesthetically beautiful, is convenient for use and easy to navigate, avoids collisions between inhabitants, is easy to maintain, hides what needs to be hidden, and keeps open what needs to be open.

Such is the case with computers and software. The programs, macros, scripts, and data bear the brunt of all the attacks to keep the product and the users safe and secure. The architecture arranges the system components in such a way that the system is easy to maintain, facilitates efficient functioning of the product, hides the components that need to be hidden, facilitates easy maintenance, and keeps the product as small as possible.

As noted earlier, the three main functions of design of a product are design of components, design of integrating the components, and organizing the components. In product architecture design, we focus on organizing the components of the software product. IEEE standard 610, *IEEE Standard Glossary of Software Engineering Terminology*, defines architecture design as "the process of defining a collection of hardware and software components and their interfaces to establish a framework for the development of a computer system."

Components of a Software Product

One way of looking at the software product is from the standpoint of functionality. The other is to look at it as its physical components. From the standpoint of functionality, the components are:

1. *Modules*: A module fulfills one related set of functions of the application domain. A module may contain submodules and multiple programs, which can include forms, reports, and programs. For example, in a material management application, purchase order functionality can be a module, goods receipt can be another module, and goods issue can be another module. In the purchase order module, we achieve functionality such as raising a material procurement requisition, obtaining quotations, placing the purchase order, and so on. There could be submodules. Of course, we can make each of these submodules an independent module. How to divide the application into modules and submodules is the work of software designers.

2. *Data*: We discussed data in detail in the earlier chapters. While most of the data is in database tables, some data is in flat files, too. The location of flat files needs to be determined by us. We can place all flat files in one location or keep them in their respective modules or submodules.

From the standpoint of the physical components, they are:

1. Programs
   a. Programs that are used by multiple modules
   b. Programs used by only one module
2. HTML pages
3. Bought-out software components
4. Images
5. Flat files of data
6. Databases
7. Intermediate software packages like the web server, app server, framework, and database server

Let us discuss these two types of architecture.

Architecture Focused on Functionality

We also can refer to this as logical architecture. This can be viewed by the user only while working with the application. We achieve this by the menus we provide in our screens and the way we arrange and display information on the screens and in the reports. But first, the architecture of a product from the standpoint of functionality begins with the arrangement of modules and units within the modules. Our application itself can be divided into products independent of each other that combine together to be the application. Every application needs system administration functions and data administration functions besides the functions for processing business transactions. In a single-user desktop application, we combine all this functionality into a single product because all the functions are performed by a single individual. But in large-scale enterprise applications based on the Internet, these are performed by different individuals. Therefore, it makes sense to spawn these into separate products with different entry points and different anchor screens.

In this approach, we may break the application down into as many products as the number of functional roles we define in the application. We provide a separate entry point (login screen) for the following functions:

1. Business transaction functions
2. System administration functions
3. Data administration functions
4. Any other independent function that we may define in the application

Even though the entry point for all the business transaction roles is the same, we navigate them to different anchor screens that display the functionality appropriate for the individual logging in. Then, within that anchor screen, we provide links for all the functionality the user is authorized to access. We hide all other functionality of the application that is not allowed for the logged-in user. This way, we make it easier for the user to perform his/her transactions and we don't confuse the user with unnecessary distractions.

In any business transaction, there is a series of steps sequentially one after the other and each user has multiple business transactions to perform. If we take a cashier role, whose function is to handle cash, it will have at least two functions, namely to receive cash and issue a receipt or pay cash and take acknowledgment. In both these functions, there are two steps, namely handling cash and a receipt to be performed sequentially. The two functions of receiving and paying cash are independent of each other. In this manner, each role has multiple independent functions and each transaction has multiple steps.

While designing our applications, we need to guide the user through these transactions in a way that even a new user does not need more than rudimentary training. The practice had been to show one link for every independent function on the anchor screen for the role. For navigating the user through each business transaction, there are two methods being followed. The first one is to present a series of screens, one after the other. When the functionality of one screen is completed, the user is navigated to the next screen by clicking a button, often captioned as "Next" or a right-pointing arrow. Of course, we provide a button captioned "Previous" or a left-pointing arrow to go back to the previous screen. We may also provide numbers (1, 2, 3, 4, and so on) if there are too many screens to help the user navigate to any of the screens.

The other alternative for navigating the user through multiple screens of a business transaction is to use tabs captioned carefully to reflect the functionality achieved in the screen displayed when the tab is clicked.

In some cases, the user is navigated to the next screen on completing the functionality on the previous screen automatically without requiring the user to click a button. This needs to be used with care and in special circumstances. The processing of business transactions may have to be terminated for a host of reasons like a power outage, network outage, the user being called to attend to another more pressing activity, and so on. So, we ought to provide a facility so the user can begin the transaction where it was left off. Automatic navigation through the steps of the business transaction does not facilitate this. The user would be forced to go through all the screens all over again.

One other method is used to provide a submenu for the transaction with clickable options. On completing one step, the user opens the submenu and selects the next option to perform the next step.

Another option is to group the steps into frames and then allow the user to move from one frame to the other. We may enable the next frame once the previous frame is processed or allow the user to move to any frame without any restriction. This is suitable when there are a few steps and each needs only a few items to be processed. It depends on the nature of the functionality and the number and size of the steps to select the method of navigation from one frame to the other.

Summarizing the above discussion, the application is architected in this manner:

1. The application is divided into multiple products.
2. Each product has a different entry point.
3. In each product, we have a different anchor screen for each of the roles defined.
4. The anchor screen for each role shows the functions allowed for the user that are independent of each other.
5. If the business transaction has multiple steps that need to be performed sequentially, we need to select one of the available methods to navigate the user from one step to the next, or the reverse, and design the screens.

Architecture Focused on Physical Components

This arrangement is visible without logging in to the application. We can see it if we have access to the folder/directory/library by using the command to display the list of directories/libraries/folders. This arrangement is to be designed in such a way that it becomes easy to troubleshoot in case of malfunction and is amenable to upgrades when necessary. Each operating system has a different architecture in terms of software. In some OSs, the executable files are in a central directory, with sharable libraries in another location and other files of the application in some other location, as in the case of UNIX. In OSs such as MS Windows, all the files of the application, including the executables, are located in one folder. While designing application architecture, we need to conform to the requirements of the OS on which our application is going to reside. In either case, the executable file, the index, or default landing page needs to be located at the appropriate location. It may be the central directory housing all the executable files or the root directory of the application files.

This file, when executed, sets the path for the computer to search for other files called by the application. Now, let us look at the arrangement of other files in the application.

Basically, we arrange the folders/directories/libraries in two ways:

1. Module-wise
2. File type-wise

Of course, we can use other ways to arrange the components depending on the situation at hand.

Architecture Based on Modules

In this method, we create one main directory for each module, which will have subdirectories as necessary. For example, let us take a material management application. It can have main directories for:

1. Master data maintenance module
2. Material procurement initiation module
3. Purchase order module
4. Material receipts module
5. Material issues module
6. Inventory control module
7. Report generation module
8. And any other module necessary

In this manner, we can create the main directories. Then, each main directory can have one or more subdirectories based on the needs of the application. For example, in the material procurement initiation module, we may have subdirectories for:

1. Material procurement requisition submodule
2. Soliciting quotes from vendors
3. Vendor selection
4. Authorizations

In this manner, we create subdirectories as necessitated by our application. In the bottommost directory, we place the files pertaining to that directory. In this arrangement, we can easily locate the required file for troubleshooting as and when it becomes necessary.

The advantage of this type of file arrangement is that it is easy to locate the required file quickly and easily. The disadvantage of this type of arrangement is the dilemma of files common to more than one module. Of course, we can create another main directory with the name of common files and place the common files in that directory, or place the files in individual directories and call them from those directories. Another disadvantage is encountered after the software has gone into production while replacing the existing file with an upgraded version of the file. We need to search all the directories to locate the file and then replace it. File replacements are a frequent occurrence, and this could turn out to be a major concern. If the file is placed at a wrong location, it could impact the proper functioning of the application.

Architecture Based on File Types

In this arrangement, we create directories based on the types of files. We have one directory for each file type. Each such directory can have subdirectories if the file type has subtypes, as in the case of pictures, which can be pictures, drawings, logos, icons, buttons, and so on. In this arrangement, we may have directories for:

1. HTML files
2. Picture files
3. DLLs
4. Executables/binaries
5. Data files (flat files)
6. Bought-out components
7. Report files
8. Temporary files
9. Any other files as necessitated by the application

As noted above, we can have subdirectories for each of these directories as necessary. For example, the Pictures directory can have subdirectories for:

1. JPEGs
2. Drawing files
3. Logo files
4. Icon files
5. Button files
6. Any other files

Of course, the way the physical components are arranged in real life varies vastly from one application to another. Is there one best way, as some of us would like to ask, to arrange the physical components that has only advantages sans any downsides? I am afraid there is no such method available. Designers use a hybrid of functional arrangement and file type arrangement. While designing the arrangement of physical components, we have to keep in mind these aspects:

1. The arrangement makes it easier to locate the file to troubleshoot it.
2. The arrangement is amenable to the easy maintenance of the configuration register after the software goes into production.

3. The arrangement makes it easier to replace existing files with upgraded versions during the production operations of the software.

4. The arrangement fosters security of the application.

Security Aspects of Arrangement of Physical Components

Now, if we arrange the files in such a way that it is easy to locate any required file very quickly, will it not be so for a hacker who accesses our directories? The word *hacking* itself connotes causing indiscriminate damage. While we cannot stop the hacker from causing damage, we do not have any obligation to make his/her life easier in locating the files to damage. The more chaotic the arrangement, the more difficult it would be to locate the desired component. But it would be difficult for the configuration managers as well.

Therefore, it would be wise to camouflage the arrangement so that it will be difficult for the untrained person but meaningful to the trained person. We can codify the names of the directories and use them in place of long, meaningful names. The shorter the names, the more difficult it is to decipher what is contained in it. IBM follows a convention of using 8 characters to name a file or library. They have been using it for a long time very successfully. I agree that it is not user friendly, but architecture and configuration management are activities that are not left to untrained users. These are professionals who know the art and science of their professions. Therefore, I advocate using shorter codified names for folders and software artifacts to ensure security for the physical components of the software application.

Location of the Application

In the present day, the technology allows us to locate the application across multiple computer systems at geographically disparate locations. Of course, we can locate the entire application on a single machine too. But using the facility to locate the application on different machines is advantageous from the standpoint of security. Even if the hacker gets hold of one machine, the other parts of the application are safely out of reach for the hacker. In order to hack the entire application, the hacker would have to break into multiple machines with different login credentials. It has become standard practice to locate the database on one machine and the application on another.

In the previous sections, we discussed dividing the application into independent products for system administration functions, business transaction processing functions, data administration functions, and any other situation-specific functions like investigation functions. It would be better if we could place the product for business transaction processing functions on a separate computer system and others on a different server. The products for carrying out system administration, data administration functions, perform vital functions and can cause significant damage to the entire application when hackers break into those functions. Hackers can easily discover the details of the server housing the product for business transaction processing functions, as most of the users perform their work by logging into that server. We make a demo version of the product for processing the business functions to enable prospective clients to try out our application. Hackers usually hack into that product when successful. But there is no need to publicize the details of other functionality products.

Of course, when our application is offered as software as a service (SaaS), we have to provide the details of system administration and other functionality, but only to clients. Even in that case, there would be one or two people performing those functions, while there would be many individuals performing business transaction functions.

While it is easier and tempting to design the application as a single product and house it on a single machine, it is better to design the product into multiple products and house them on different servers. Of course, it would be costlier, as additional machines need to be bought and maintained, but it provides additional security and protects us from loss of data, saving us much more year after year as well as providing us with uninterrupted operation of our application, helping us perform many more business transactions and earn more revenue.

9

Security and Safety Design

Introduction

When we think of security, what readily comes to mind are the fortresses built and lived in by the kings of yesterday. Their concerns were threefold: prevention of enemy forces from breaking in, the ability to fight enemy soldiers from a position of advantage to repel them, and an escape door in case the enemy troops could not be beaten back. Their first two concerns, preventing outsiders from entering without proper authorization and minimizing the damage an intruder can do, are both shared by us while designing software applications. How did fortress designers achieve their objective of preventing enemy troops from breaking in? They designed and built tall, robust walls that inhibited the enemy from trying to break in or scale the walls. They also dug moats around the fortress and filled them with water and carnivorous water animals like alligators. But that left the door, which is definitely not as robust as the walls. The door was the weakest point in the entry system to the fortress. It had to allow easy access to regular visitors to enter the fortress and yet shut the enemy out in those once-in-a-lifetime events of invasion. Fortresses had a strong trap door that also functioned as the bridge across the moat.

We all know that fortresses have been broken into by scaling the walls by throwing hooks onto the walls and climbing them in the face of boiling oil being poured down. Present-day hackers are as determined as the enemy soldiers of yore. Now, there is only a fear of prosecution if and only if they are caught. There is no fear of being scalded immediately by boiling oil. If the hacker is from a country with which your country has not signed an extradition treaty, then the hacker is fearless.

In today's scenario, banks face a similar situation. They have to be secure enough to deter and prevent bandits from looting the bank vaults, yet pleasant and easy enough to motivate customers to walk in and conduct business. Banks build an easily accessible business area but build strong rooms with special security measures and allow only authorized persons to access the strong rooms in which all their assets are stored.

We also know that bank vaults have been broken into and money and such other valuables stolen, even if such events are rare. Now let us look at what security is and how to achieve the objectives of ensuring security for our applications.

Security is protecting the data and software artifacts from external attacks and malicious internal attacks. Security has to be provided physically and logically. Physical security consists of securing the premises where the servers are located and preventing unauthorized persons from physically accessing the machines. Logical security involves preventing unauthorized access over the Internet or over the internal networks. Security has to allow authorized users access without much pain and prevent all unauthorized accesses. One aspect of security is to ensure that the application puts up all fences necessary to prevent unauthorized access. The second aspect of security is operations. Operations have to ensure that all the designed security features function fully and without any interruption. It is operations that define new users and modify their access rights. They must be diligent.

What do we mean by security in practical terms? Here are the three aspects:

1. *Attack prevention*: The first aspect of security is to prevent attacks from both external and internal sources. We need to design and build in measures that do not allow any unauthorized person into our system.

2. *Incident handling*: However securely we may build our systems, attempts to attack and penetrate our systems do happen. One of Murphy's laws says, "It is impossible to make anything foolproof because fools are so ingenious," and rightly so! Hackers will find a way to penetrate our system. So, irrespective of our robust design and development, we need to acknowledge the possibility of successful attacks and be prepared to handle such incidents. We need to design our systems so that we detect penetration, contain the hacker, minimize the damage, and then assist investigation to bring the culprit to justice.

3. *Investigation and catching the culprit*: We need to design our system such that we capture data changes and user activity so that we can supply useful and actionable data to the investigators to assist them in locating the culprit and catching that individual.

We will examine these aspects in this chapter.

Security and Safety

More often than not, these two terms are used together. Security is for the application and safety is for the user. To understand the distinction better, let us consider the example of an automobile. When we say security, it is to prevent the vehicle from being stolen. We design features like electronic locks for the doors, a special key for the door, a special key for the ignition switch, and an alarm when the wrong key is used for either the door or the ignition. Passenger safety is ensured by air bags and collision safety features.

In the same manner, we secure our application and data from being damaged or stolen by unauthorized users and provide safety to the users by keeping incidents from affecting authorized users.

Purpose of Security in Application

The application security we design has three purposes:

1. To prevent damage by preventing unauthorized access to the application data and programs
2. To assist investigation when a security incident takes place
3. To make it painless for authorized users to access and use the system

Unauthorized users have to be kept out of the system. Unauthorized users are not accountable for their actions to our organization. Sometimes, unauthorized users can be from within our organization, too, but mostly, they are outsiders to our organization. Unauthorized users have no business being there accessing our system. But we cannot prevent unauthorized users from trying to access our application. What we can do is to prevent them from gaining access to our data. We have to design our application in such a way that our application is an impregnable fortress.

In spite of all the care we take to secure our application, security incidents, rare though they may be, do take place. When such an unfortunate incident takes place, our design must be such that the perpetrators can be traced through the actions they performed. Our application must be designed to gather as much relevant information as possible and provide it to the investigators so they can locate and apprehend the perpetrator. This aspect takes significant effort in designing the application.

In our eagerness to keep out unauthorized users, we should not make it unpleasant for genuine authorized users. Some airports have gone overboard in their security measures so that passengers are discouraged from traveling by air, resulting in losses and closure of profitably operating airlines. We should not follow this example. I have seen some computer-based systems using a Captcha picture that is practically unreadable. Most users go away when confronted with such an obstacle.

In the security of our applications, we have to achieve all three above-mentioned purposes. Now, let us discuss how to achieve these purposes.

Who Is Responsible for Security?

Security falls within the ancillary functionality requirements. Therefore, the onus is on the designers to define the requirements of security, and it is to be designed by the software designers. We should not expect the end users or their management to define security requirements. We have to define how to achieve security based on the usage information and the expected user profile provided by the end users and their management in the requirements analysis document.

Security for an application is to be ensured at two levels, namely the software level during its design and development and by operations while the application is in production and being used by the end users in achieving the business goals of the organization. Neither can be neglected. But the focus of this book is in designing the software, so we will focus our discussion on designing software that takes care of the security that can be enforced by the software. Of course, we will also specify the procedures to be implemented by the operations staff to ensure security of the application during production.

Assets to Be Secured

What are the components of our system that need to be secured in order to ensure that our application functions securely? The entire system has to be secure for our application to be secure. Some of these components are out of scope for software designers. Still, we need to consider those assets while designing security for our proposed software application. Let us look at the components now.

1. *Hardware*: Unless the hardware is secure, the software cannot be secure. When we say hardware, system software, especially the OS, is included in the term. Mainframe and supercomputer hardware and OSs have excellent security features built into them. We can rest assured that they do not allow hackers a chance to hack into the system. We only need to build secure software. In single-user (such as windows) OSs, the hardware and the OS both may not be able to effectively prevent hackers from entering. That means it is not adequate to build secure software, we also need to build additional components in our software to plug the loopholes in the hardware.

2. *DBMS*: In the present day, DBMS is more or less a mandatory asset for most business applications. Most applications make use of a DBMS that is available off the shelf. These range from almost free to very high priced. Needless to emphasize, an almost-free DBMS will not have excellent security built into it. In such cases, we need to build a higher level of security into our application.

3. *Data*: With the exception of systems like AS/400, which do not have a flat file system, most other systems do allow flat files, and most applications use flat files as parameter files at the least. The more flat files we use, the more security we need built into our system.

4. *Programs*: While programs protect the other assets, they cannot protect themselves from being replaced with weaker programs or outright malicious ones. So, we need to build the product architecture in a secure way so that the programs cannot be easily accessed or replaced.

5. *Scripts*: Scripts are also programs and have to be secured just like other programs.

6. *Cookies*: These are small data files stored on the computer of the end user for storing user preferences. It is easy to modify cookies because they are almost unsecured. We need to ensure that the configuration is not changed before accessing and making use of them.

There could be other system-specific components, and we need to consider all such components while designing software applications.

Impact of the Type of Application on the Security Design

All developed applications are not alike. They are classified on the basis of user profiles. Here is one classification:

1. *A single-user desktop or laptop application:* This type of application does not need too much thought for designing security. The OS of a single-user application enforces minimal security based on a simple password. In most cases, whoever can log in to the computer can access all the applications available for the user. The prevention of hacking attacks from the Internet is handled by the antimalware

utility installed on the computer. We need to protect applications using a simple user id and password, along with a Captcha code or a biometric included in our application to allow entry into our application.

2. *A limited multiuser application to be used within one organization at one location:* Certain applications are used strictly in one organization at one location in a building or a campus by the employees of the organization. We can be a little lax on the design of security aspects, as all are authorized users paid by the organization. However, we need to design security aspects to assist investigation when a security incident takes place because of an internal malicious attack.

3. *A limited multiuser application to be used within one organization but at multiple geographically disparate locations:* These types of applications are primarily for internal use of an organization but from different geographical locations. The different geographical locations may be marketing offices, sales outlets, or manufacturing hubs. Users are employees of the organization and there are no users external to the organization. If we design aspects of assisting postincident investigations, it will suffice.

4. *A multiuser application in the public domain but to be used within one country:* Certain applications, especially in the domain of government, expected to be used within one country fall into this category. We need to ensure that people from other countries cannot log in to the application. Since this is in the public domain, though restricted to one country, we need to design all aspects of security in the application.

5. A multiuser application in the public domain that is expected to be used from anywhere in the world. The focus of this book is this type of application. All aspects of full security have to be designed and built in for this category of applications.

Components of Security

The security that we design into our software application needs to have the following components:

1. Prevention of intrusion into the system—This component deals with preventing intruders into the system.
2. Detection of intruders and minimization of the damage due to intrusion.
3. Measures to assist investigation.
4. Data security.

Designing Prevention of Intrusion

Our website will contain information pages and application pages. The information pages are aimed at providing information to our prospective clients and are generally static pages with links to other information pages. These can be allowed access without any restriction. Of course, there may be some pages that provide information for our clients only. Such pages need to have restricted entry.

Then, we have our application pages that allow access to users authorized to access the application. In this category of users, we have internal and external users. Internal users work as employees in our organization and access the pages of the application relevant to them. The external users are those who are not employees of our organization and are authorized to access our application by being our clients or complimentary users. The external users may be of various categories such as paid users, complimentary users, guest users, statutory users, and so on. Each has different purposes and should be allowed to access pages that are relevant to them and not any other pages.

Now, the main mechanism for software applications in the commercial domain is the login page. For high-security applications, we can use biometrics to authenticate the user. But for commercial applications, it would be a luxury and the users may not be able to afford to use biometric devices to provide the application with authentication information. So, let us focus on the login page design. As we understand that the users can be of different categories, it is better to design and develop different login pages. Of course, all the login pages can share some routines so that they need not be recoded.

It has been the practice to capture just two pieces of information from the user, namely the user id and the password. The user id is visible as the user types it in, but the password is camouflaged by displaying an asterisk character for every character typed by the user in the password box. Recently it has become a practice to display a Captcha picture and ask the user to read and type those characters in a separate box. Of course, in high-security applications, it is the practice to attach a fingerprint reader to the workstation and read the fingerprint during the login process. How many pieces of information should we ask of our user? It depends on the type of user, and we will discuss this aspect in the following sections.

First, let us look at the design of a general user who performs business transactions using the application. This category of users does not perform any administrative functions such as changing application parameters, user management, changing programs, and so on. This category of users forms the bulk of the users. They would like to get into the application with a minimum of hassle, do their work, and log out. Their login process should be simple, with a minimum number of boxes to be filled in.

1. If the users are internal, we may include user id, password, and a biometric input. Now, you may ask, why do we need user id and password when we are capturing the biometric? Obviously, from the biometric itself, we can derive the user id and password and retrieve the accurate user profile! We need to ensure that the user is the right one by counterchecking the supplied user id, password, and biometric. It is an additional check. Reality shows us instances of faking biometrics, too. So, by asking all three, we are minimizing the chances of a malicious hacker intruding into our system.

2. Then, we also have applications like banking operations, wherein the ordinary internal users have the opportunity to cause alarming damage to the organization. Even though these types of ordinary users do not perform any application administration, we need to ensure that only the right user logs in to the system. Therefore, in addition to the login and password, a biometric may be asked of the user. Then, we need to capture the terminal information from which the login

is attempted and ensure that the person is logging in with not only the right credentials but also from the right place.

3. Then, we have ordinary users who log in to our application to book a ticket for a journey, a movie, a concert, or some such ticket. We may just ask for user id and password. We can ask, and some are already asking, for the entry of a Captcha code. A Captcha code can only authenticate whether the entity logging in is a human being and eliminate bots from logging in. So, in my humble opinion, user id and password will suffice in such cases unless we wish to make sure that only human beings are logging in.

4. Then, we may have ordinary users who are high-net-worth individuals and transact thousands of dollar amounts on our application. For such people, we need to provide a higher level of security, as they are more likely to be hacked. A biometric entry along with user id and password has to be used to ensure the right person is logging in. Such people may access our application from any location in the world; therefore, authenticating with the help of the IP address may not be useful. However, we may capture the IP addresses from which login is not expected and check for such addresses. Another alternative is to make use of a one-time password (OTP) through a mobile phone whenever a login attempt is made from an unexpected IP address.

5. Then, we have a class of ordinary users who log in to access special content available on the web site. This class is used in libraries and special-content-offering web sites. For this category of users, a simple user id and password are adequate.

6. We can use screen-based keyboards to eliminate the possibility of keystroke capture software tools capturing the passwords and passing them on to mischief mongers.

Now, let us look at administrative users. Administrative users are those who can impact the application by setting or modifying the application parameters, managing users and their privileges, adding/modifying/deleting code artifacts, and so on. There can be one to four levels of such users with different privileges. Now, let us discuss how to authenticate their login.

1. First, the login page for such users must be a different one from the login page of the ordinary users. The login page used by ordinary users should not have the ability to access administrative functions. There should be no link to an administrative login on the information web pages. The administrative user is not expected to be a novice and he/she ought to know how to access the administrative functions login page.

2. We should not allow administrative functions to be performed from any terminal or IP address. We must restrict the login to the designated terminal within the organization. But if that is resisted by the users, we need to add a biometric to authenticate these users. We cannot allow them to log in with just a user id and password, as the havoc that can be caused by these users is unimaginable.

3. Configuration managers are that class of administrative users who add or replace code artifacts in the website from which our application is launched. These functions must be limited to internal terminals to log in and perform configuration management functions.

There could be other categories of users depending on the application. For example, in war management applications, rocket launching applications, airplane piloting applications, and so on, the functions are critical. We have to use authentication mechanisms appropriate to the situation, including biometrics, physical locations, and IP addresses in addition to a user id and password. We should also check for the device from which such functions are performed.

The login functionality ought to perform the following functions;

1. Present a screen designed to capture the credentials that need to be captured.

2. Present an onscreen keyboard in case using the normal keyboard usage is considered risky.

3. Capture the information and store the following details in the designated table:

    a. User id

    b. Password

    c. IP address

    d. Login time

    e. Terminal or device id from which login is attempted

    f. Status of login: failed or succeeded

    g. Logout time when logged out

    h. If idle for a certain amount of time, after which the session is locked out, then the status of locked session: locked or active

    i. Any other situation-specific data that is considered necessary for the security of the application

4. Store the user credentials after authentication in session variables so that all other application page access attempts can refer to them and allow access to the user.

5. When the session is idle:

    a. Lock out the session when idle for a lower threshold limit of idle time.

    b. Log out when the session is idle for a longer threshold of idle time.

    c. The threshold limits of idle time for session locking or logging out need to be defined in a database table, and these should be used to determine if the idle time warrants session locking or logging out.

An effective login page and functionality prevent hackers from entering the system. But then, to protect our application comprehensively from unauthorized intruders, we need to monitor the system and contain them. Let us now see how to design a security system to do exactly that.

Designing Intruder Detection and Minimizing Damage Thereof

We have seen or heard of instances where an unauthorized person intruded into an application and caused damage to the data and code artifacts. Here, too, we have to keep a balance between ease of use or user-friendliness and security. Most multiuser and multitasking operating systems follow user profile–based security. That is, a user is granted privileges to create, read, modify, and delete (often referred to as CRUD rights) based on the needs of the user. Then, these systems also provide one user with uninhibited access to all rights over all artifacts of the system. Some operating systems define certain security roles with differing rights but also provide one superuser or system administrator with unhindered access to all artifacts with all rights. But if we are not building an operating system, we need not follow that example. However, in my experience and observation, most application developers follow the model of one superuser who has all the rights over all the artifacts of the application, including database and code artifacts.

This is detrimental to security, in my humble opinion. If we take the example of a manufacturing organization, the organizational security staff would not be allowed entry inside the factory. They guard the premises. Security inside the plant is the responsibility of the executives holding senior positions. If they feel it is necessary, they call the organizational security department for assistance. In the case of a country's security, too, security agencies share the responsibility among them and do not overstep their authority. The army protects the country from external invasions. The police ensure security within the county or state. The Federal Bureau of Investigation or an agency holding similar authority and responsibility ensures security only in cases that involve one or more states. In my humble opinion, software application designers ought to emulate this model.

I advocate role-based security and elimination of the role of superuser. I suggest the following roles, and if you feel it is necessary or your organization is short of people, you may combine some roles into one.

1. *Database administrator*: This role manages the database. It backs up the database and restores as necessary. It repairs the database when it is damaged. It also creates the database roles as necessitated by the application and manages their privileges. Most DBMS packages allow unhindered access to the administrator to all database artifacts with all rights. If there is a way, however, this role may be prevented from changing data in the tables in raw mode. Data in the tables needs to be managed only through the application programs.

2. *Configuration manager*: This role maintains the code artifacts. It allows the code artifacts to be checked out of the library using a strict authorization process and then checks them in again when they are modified, also after a diligent authorization process. In particular, the check-in of the artifacts has to conform to a rigorous process and must be audited periodically. This role should not be allowed to change the artifacts all by itself, and the process of checking in or checking out ought to be handled programmatically and not in a manual manner.

3. *User management*: This role adds new users, grants access rights to users, modifies the access rights of users, deletes users from the system, temporarily blocks user access to the application, clears the lock placed on user access, and resets passwords when required. This role is not permitted to carry out any other functions of the application. Of course, and needless to say, all these activities should be carried out programmatically and not manually.

4. *Parameter definition*: Most large-scale applications necessitate setting parameters in the application. Modern software programming prohibits hardcoding any values into programs, which in turn necessitates defining parameter files, either in database tables or flat files. These have to be entered initially and they may need modification when the environment changes. We may carry out bulk data entry

in the beginning to quickly ramp up the application for rolling out, but parameter changes are effected by this role. They should be carried out programmatically.

5. *Master data file maintenance*: We discussed this kind of data in Chapter 7 on data design. There will be additions, modifications, or deletions to the data items in these tables. This role carries out those functions programmatically.

6. *Transaction processing roles*: These are the roles that make use of the application software and carry out business transactions. These will be several roles, depending on the application. We have to define roles with different access rights based on their functional responsibility. For example, in a material management scenario, the roles of the store executive and purchase executive ought to have different access rights. The store executive handles receipts and issues, while the purchase executive handles inquiries and purchase orders. In an insurance scenario, one handles issuance of policies and another settles claims. Each role should be limited to such access rights that are essential to that role and should be blocked from accessing other parts of the application.

7. *Transaction authorization roles*: When we handle business transactions on a computer system, these roles are enabled to make decisions. The roles of transaction processing and authorization are generally merged into one role. But there are situations when a separate role of authorization is necessary. In financial roles, when making payments of large sums, a separate authorization is mandatory. Similarly, when placing a purchase order committing the organization for a large amount of money, a separate authorization is desirable. Therefore, most applications need some transaction authorization roles. We have to define these roles as necessary to authorize transactions. Obviously, there will be several authorization roles in the application, depending on the organization.

8. *Report extraction roles*: There will be roles in the organization that access the application for extracting the information necessary to perform their functions. The senior management is one good example of such a role. Senior management does not perform business transactions but needs information for making decisions. These roles have to be restricted to extracting reports from the application and are not allowed to perform any other function.

9. *Inquiry roles*: There are many roles that extract information from our application. Usually, these roles are external to our organization. For example, statutory authorities are interested in inquiring about the payments transacted by us, especially those that exceed a preset limit. Here, let me differentiate between reports and inquiry. Inquiry is for one piece of information at a time with or without mathematical processing. Reports are the generation of multiple types of information for multiple entities.

By defining roles and limiting their access rights, the intruders would be restricted to the privileges of that specific role and would not be able to destroy the entire application as a whole. If we allow access privileges to individual entities, those in senior management with all privileges may be tempted to facilitate an intruder in damaging the application and data. Again, we should eliminate the superuser role that would have unhindered access to all artifacts of the application.

Then, there is the tendency to group some of these roles into one. This is for basically two reasons. The first is that none of the administrative roles like user management, database administrator, and configuration manager would have a full workload for all eight hours of the day around the year. True enough. I would suggest assigning these roles to different persons, not on a full-time basis but on a part-time basis along with other assignments. The second reason is that it is easier in the coding of the application. Coding is a onetime activity, and but usage and risk are recurring. As software designers, we need to minimize risk during operations and make the application secure. Still, there are many software designers who advocate and argue passionately against role-based security and favor assignment of access rights to users.

By defining roles and limiting access privileges, we can do our best to minimize the damage an intruder can cause to our application. By separating transaction processing and authorization roles, we limit the damage that the intruder can do in addition to making it difficult for the intruder.

We can make use of OTPs as an additional mechanism to limit the damage and prevent the intruder from committing damage. For large-value transactions or transactions that can change parameters or critical master data items like changing passwords and such other critical application data, we can send an OTP and ask the user to input the same before proceeding with the transaction. This will be especially useful in credit card misuse. When the number of transactions exceeds a modal value per day, we can use the OTP mechanism to prevent further misuse. We can make use of the OTP mechanism to further prevent intruders into our system in this manner. We capture the login information whenever a user logs into the system. At that time, the login process needs to check if that is the normal time for the user to log in. We can do this by:

1. When we define a new user id, we need to capture the normal working hours of the user. Then, we can make use of this information to see if the user is an authentic one or an intruder.

2. When capturing the normal working hours of the user or when the user specifies 0 to 24 hours as normal working hours, as in the case of users external to our organization and in applications such as ticket booking, we need to compute a modal value and make use of the OTP to authenticate the user when the usage crosses that modal value.

3. We can also check the IP address from which the user is attempting to log in and see if it is one that has been used by the same user in the past. If it was never used, then we may make use of the OTP mechanism to authenticate the user.

We do as much to contain the damage perpetrated by the intruder using role-based security. But how do we detect an intruder? Obviously, the intruder used the right credentials to intrude into the system. (S)he would be prevented from entering the system otherwise! We can detect that an intruder entered the system by monitoring the activity of the logged-in users. We can monitor the user activity in this manner:

1. When the user attempts to access functionality that is not allowed for that role more than a preset limit of times, we may lock the user out and make it necessary for the user manager to clear the block.

2. When the user attempts to perform functions just below the threshold level for requiring authorization, especially involving money, more than once or a preset threshold limit of attempts, we may block the transactions and raise alerts.

3. When the user tries to delete in bulk or delete items serially, we can use the OTP mechanism to once again authenticate the user before proceeding with the transaction.

4. Any other suspicious activity performed by the user needs to raise an alert. Of course, these entail additional programming and make the application costlier. Therefore, these can be used in highly secure applications. What is a suspicious activity? It can be defined as an activity that violates the security privileges or exceeds amounts outside the authority of the user or an action that was not performed in last six months (or another such limit defined based on the situation of the organization).

The information for monitoring ought to be available in the audit trails of the database and can be made use of for detecting an intruder. Once an intruder is detected, we need to raise an alert. It is best to alert system administrators by messages during working hours and by shutting down the system during nonworking hours and sending Short Message Services (SMSs) to the mobile phones of individuals concerned with the security of the system. While it may be possible to alert statutory security agencies like the police, I would suggest that it is a decision to be made by organizational management. Of course, there are exceptions when security agencies can be alerted by the application.

Designing Measures to Assist Investigation

We discussed the design of audit trails in Chapter 7 on data design. This is a measure to assist investigation in the event of a security incident. It gives us the information of who did what, especially about changes of data in database tables. Flat files, which are heavily used for storing parameter data, do not have built-in facilities for audit trails, so we need to design audit trails for flat files. We need to design a table to hold the audit trail data of flat files and then include routines to capture audit trail data into that table whenever the data in the flat files is modified. The design of an audit trail is given in Chapter 7 on data design.

Then, we have to design security-related information extraction artifacts. Usually, we design reports that can be viewed on screen as well as printed out. We use report-generation software tools and design the reports. We need to design many reports for the purpose of assisting the investigators. Here are some examples of such reports:

1. *The history of a data item modification for a specified period:* This includes information like the item description, value of the item at the beginning of the selected period, each modification with the date, the details of the user who effected the modification, the value before and after modification, and any more details that are situation specific.

2. *The login activity of a specific user for a selected period:* This includes details like the date and time of login, the IP address of each login, the amount of time online, the functionality accessed, and any other details specific to the situation.

3. *The list of users on a specific date:* This includes details like the user ids, their names, the times of their logins and logouts and any other details specific to the situation for the given date.

4. *Details of a specific transaction:* This includes details like the user id and name of the user who carried out the transaction, the function performed, the data items affected, the receiving party in cases of transmission of information or money, and such other details as required by the organization.

5. *Traces of user activity:* A trace is a contiguous series of actions performed either by a user or a data item by all users. This report is for a specified period. When a user trace is selected, we need to present all logins, including failed login attempts, the IP addresses for each login attempt, the actions performed by the user, all the data items affected by such action, the before and after values of the data items changed, and any other relevant details as applicable to the organization. This report is in the chronological order of login attempts. When a data item is selected, we need to present the data, including each change of the user who changed the value, the value before and after the change, the date and time of change, the IP address of the user, and so on.

6. *Trace of an entity that entered the system from birth until death:* This report is often referred to as an end-to-end or birth-to-death report. This report traces all the modifications the entity has undergone from the first time it entered the system to the last time the entity is deleted from the system. In an insurance system, this can be a policy or a customer. In a payroll scenario, it can be an employee. It enumerates all the transformations the entity underwent in the system.

7. *Details of policy violations:* Policy violations take place in an organization, sometimes with a waiver granted by an appropriate authority and sometimes without any authorization, either due to urgency, frivolously, or maliciously. This report helps the investigators if there indeed was a violation, and during audits, it brings to light how diligently the employees are adhering to the defined and approved processes. We design the report to scour all policy violations, match them with the authorizations, and then present a comprehensive report or an exception report.

8. *Details of activity from suspicious sources:* Suspicious sources are the IP addresses that are not expected to originate login attempts. Even if all the login attempts from a suspected source were blocked, it would still be useful to understand if unauthorized individuals are trying to hack into our system. If there are rare occurrences, these could be accidental errors. But if there is a pattern from locations in close proximity to each other, we can safely infer that someone is making a deliberate effort to hack into our system, and we can strengthen our fortifications.

9. *Details of activity from a range of IP addresses:* This report includes all the login attempts from a specified country, state, and county. This tells the investigators if any deliberate hacking efforts were put in from a suspected source. This report helps investigators narrow down the search for the perpetrators of the security incident. The range can be from a country to a state to a county to a single IP address to progressively narrow down the suspects.

The data necessary for generation of these reports can be found mostly in the audit trails built into the DBMS or the audit trails designed by us. For flat files, we need to design audit trails.

Designing Security Implementation

We have seen that we have to design programs to perform various checks to prevent intruders from accessing our application. Obviously, our application will have a number of pages, and every time a page is loaded, it will have to perform a variety of security checks:

1. Checking to ensure that the user is indeed logged in after diligent authentication of credentials
2. Redirecting the user to the login page if the user was not logged in or the session expired
3. Checking to see that the session had not been idle for more than the permitted threshold level
4. Checking to see that the user has access rights to the requested application page
5. Checking to see that the request is coming from an expected IP address
6. If there is any policy violation, redirecting to the appropriate page to ensure that the violation was properly authorized
7. Raising all types of alerts whenever necessary
8. Handling any other situation-specific checks to ensure whatever is necessary

There is no point in rewriting all the code at the beginning of every page.

The software development kit (SDK) supplied by the development platform supplier contains certain callable routines to perform some of these operations. But we need to write code to call these routines and supply the parameters required by the routine. These are usually supplied in the form of DLL. We need to develop some more routines in addition to the routines included in the DLLs supplied by the development platform supplier. We may need to use the functionality provided by the supplier of the development platform, but in most cases, we have to develop some routines.

In the present scenario, at least in the majority of the cases, the software design is grouped with the coding activity. Therefore, more often than not, the software developers begin writing the required security routines for every page individually. This results not only in duplication of effort but also adversely affects the effectiveness of security. This is one reason for most hacking successes. It is a good practice to think through the application's security needs, evaluate the security functionality provided by the supplier of the SDK, determine the common routines additionally needed by our application, and then develop all these routines and build a DLL for the coders to make use of in every page. I would go one step further and say even if the need for an additional security routine was uncovered at the time of writing the code for a specific page, it is better to include it in the DLL rather than including it in the page load functionality.

It is a best practice to include security checking routines as the first step in the routine of loading the page. Only when the security checks allow should the page loading functionality be called. For checking, all the routines ought to be called from a common location such as a DLL rather than passing execution control to a subroutine within the page code. Each development platform provides facilities to build DLLs, and we can make use of those facilities and build the required DLLs. I would also advocate building a separate DLL for security routines and other DLLs as required for developing routines common to many application pages.

Designing Data Security

Data is the most important part of the application and needs the utmost security if our application is to be secure and serve the organization effectively. As we saw in the earlier sections and chapters, data is basically placed in two types of data storage. One is in the database of a DBMS and the other is in flat files. Let us now discuss how to ensure security while designing our applications.

Database Security

Fortunately for us, all suppliers of DBMSs provide security at various levels for the DBMSs they supply. Of course, setting the security permissions for the users is the responsibility of the database administrator where the application is rolled out. But, as software designers, we have the responsibility to design and communicate security settings, as it is very difficult to draw the line between software design and operations when apportioning blame for a security breach. We can design a script that sets security permissions if we are using role-based security in our application.

The first measure I suggest is to disable the default administrator role defined by the supplier and replace it with an organization-specific user id and a strong password. The default id of the administrator would be known to all the experts in that specific DBMS, and that can be too many people to protect our data from. If we disable such a default administrator id, the prospective intruders not only have to find the user id but also its password. Thus, we double their effort needed for intruding into our system.

A DBMS facilitates accessing data in various tables without going through the programs in our application. It provides facilities to read, edit, and delete data items in the database. Apart from that, even the table structures can be modified at will, and the table can even be deleted. This is a big security risk. Even if we prevent intruders from intruding into our system, malicious internal intruders can cause havoc on the data. Of course, we have diligent backup and restore practices, but that would still cause loss of data, however miniscule it may be. Therefore, we should set access levels commensurate with the role of the user at the level of each table for the users accessing the data using the programs designed by us as part of the application. That way, even if any user attempts to access data in the tables by mistake, he or she will be allowed to modify only those items for which his/her role has the access permissions.

When connecting to the database for data manipulation, we usually use the user id and password of the database administrator so that our programming effort is minimized. It is better to use the user id and password appropriate to the user role using the functionality. We can design a script that sets up these roles in the database, which can be used at the time of installation to set up user ids and passwords as needed. Of course, we can include the opening database routine with all the options as a common routine, include it in the common routine DLL, and call it with the role as a parameter along with others like the table name and so forth.

If there is highly classified and critical data in our database, it is advisable to use encryption/decryption mechanisms to store the data in tables. That way, those who gain access to data in the table using the facilities of the DBMS are prevented from locating the required data. Of course, all passwords stored inside tables like those of the users defined by the application will be encrypted by the application itself. Using the encryption mechanism provided by the DBMS is not suggested, as it can be decrypted using the decryption mechanism provided by the same DBMS. So, we must design and specify the data items to be encrypted before storing and decrypted before subjecting them to processing or giving outputs.

Flat File Security

It is better to encrypt flat files when storing data and decrypt them when accessing them through the application programs. Then, we should set the access rights to "read only" for all users except the administrator who is vested with the responsibility of maintaining these files. In most cases, we should not modify the contents of a flat file as we do in the case of database tables. So, we need to archive the flat files whenever we need to update them and replace them with newer versions. We need to retain all the archived flat files for assisting the investigators in the event of a security breach taking place. Of course, the operations team will have a policy regarding the period of storage for archived files.

Other Important Aspects of Security in Design

Most of the applications designed need demonstration of the features of the application to prospective users. This is needed to train new users in using the application, before the rollout, and for a presale demonstration of the software. There could be other needs to fulfill by using the software in an unfettered manner. It is needed not only before the rollout but also later on during production usage of the data. This need is especially relevant in SaaS applications. We cannot allow the demonstration to affect the production data. Therefore, we need to provide for the application to be used in an unconstrained manner without affecting production data. To achieve this, we need to design the following:

1. A copy of the database with a slightly different name that can be used by guest users. This isolates the production database from being accessed by the guest users. I have seen instances where the guest users are allowed to access the main database. The database administrator (DBA) periodically deletes all the demo data. This has a couple of issues associated with such a design.

    a. The demo data is usually retained for longer periods in the hope the prospective users will become real customers. Sometimes, the guests try the application for longer periods of time to gain confidence. So, the production database will unnecessarily hold a lot of what is probably junk data. Junk data is always a risk.

    b. To maintain impeccable data integrity, the data in the production database should never be accessed in raw mode. It should be accessed only using the software built for handling data. Human beings are prone to error, and they may accidentally delete production data, which can cause significant damage.

2. It is a better practice to design a separate login page for guest users. We can also use the same login page for guest users, but we need to verify at the login stage to see if the user is a production user or a guest user, then navigate the guest users to connect to the guest database. But it is risky and a guest user with a rare combination of credentials can access the production database and damage the integrity of production data.

3. We need to place database connection credentials at one place only, and then the application should place the appropriate connection (to the production database or the demo database) in the session variables and use it throughout the application.

4. It is essential to keep the login ids of guest users in the demo database so that even if guest users access the main login page, they should not be allowed to log in and access the production database.

Additionally, we ought to design and specify the following security features during the design phase of application development:

1. *Physical security*: Physical security refers to those aspects of operations in which the main computing assets like the servers are isolated from general access and only persons with proper authorization are allowed to physically access the critical computing assets. This is really a concern of the operations team and part of the operations process; it is better that we specify this in the operations manual we prepare for operation.

2. *Software-enforced security*: We have discussed the security enforced by the software in the preceding sections.

3. *Security from internal attacks*: Internal attacks on our application and data emanate from internal sources, namely the employees. These could be system administrators who already have access to passwords or others who somehow obtain one or more passwords. When such a thing happens, we need to build in these actions:

   a. Block the user id that has hacked the application. Of course, this is an operational issue.

   b. Provide a facility in the software to conduct a trace of all the actions performed by the user id in the last few days to determine the extent of damage caused.

   c. Provide facilities to repair the damage by presenting the data to an entity authorized to repair data and allow corrections.

   d. Make a report for investigators for implementing the necessary preventive actions in the operations.

4. *Check for login credentials before loading any page*: We need to include this code in every page as the first action in the page load event and load the page only when the login credentials are present in the session variables and the user has permission to access the requested page. If the login credentials are absent in the session variables, we need to redirect the user to the login page. If the user does not have permission to access the requested page, we need to display a decline message and send a message to the system administrator about the event. This way, we will prevent application access if the user did not login successfully.

5. *Check for the integrity of the program before loading any program*: Before loading any page or program, we need to check the modification date of the artifact and compare

it with that of the configuration register. If they differ, we need to assume that the artifact was modified without authorization and raise an alert to the system administrator to correct the situation.

6. *Check for the integrity of the cookies, if used*: Internet applications use cookies, and if our application is using them, we need to verify them for integrity by maintaining a configuration register for cookies and verify the date of modification to ensure that they did not undergo unauthorized modification.

We have to build our application in such a way that we check and recheck the users, perhaps unobtrusively, to ensure that only authorized users are allowed to enter and utilize our application and manipulate data using our programs and that unwelcome intruders are kept out.

Security is an aspect that is completely defined and designed by software designers. It is not something that users can define in their requirements. Of course, we can take the assistance of domain experts to understand how the application can be misused or fraud can be perpetrated, but we need to draw up the specifications ourselves and fulfill them through our designs.

Safety

Now, security is for the application and its data. It is about keeping unauthorized persons from accessing our application and manipulating data. Safety is about protecting the users' interests. How can software that is invisible and has no physical presence cause injury to users? Early car designers also thought this way. They expected that the automobile could cause damage to property and the lives of other road users but not the driver. After automobiles were on the road for a significant period of time and after a significant number of driver deaths, it dawned upon them that the driver, too, needs protection from the automobile. Then they designed seat belts, air bags, and a crumpling hood that absorbs the impact of the crash to protect the driver and the person in the front seat. They designed a few more safety features that protect the passengers of the automobile.

We have to do the same while designing software applications. Let us consider the ways in which a software application can injure a legitimate user:

1. *Financial loss*: Now we are performing financial transactions on the Internet using our computers and software applications. Users can click on a button that authorizes payment and initiate a financial transaction. Of course, right from the beginning of online financial transactions, we have been building a feature to ask the user to click another button before proceeding with the transaction. Now that bots have come onto the scene with the express intention of profiting financially from unsuspecting users, we have to be much more careful. Malicious bots would like to work in the shadows (in the background) like ordinary thieves. So, we have to build in features that prevent background processing of critical parts of the application.

2. *Release of vital data*: It is not a laughing matter when I say that, except in very poor countries that are so underdeveloped that computers are unheard of, the complete

information about every individual right from the newborn baby to the very old person is on some server in the country or perhaps the world. Governments, credit card companies, banks, hospitals, healthcare providers, social media sites, email sites, dating sites, and others that are too many to enumerate, all collect a lot of information from individuals and store it. We cannot say that all those servers are well guarded and the software applications that govern the stored data are well built with security features of the highest quality. Worse still, I can state with confidence that the quality assurance practices followed in the software development industry are not mature and fail to provide a quality of software that can make me sleep peacefully without any concern as to the safety of my data. I know some sites sell and share my information, and I am not sure all sites are robust enough to prevent hackers from stealing my information. This is one area in which bots are extensively used to steal our data.

3. *Identity theft*: In the days of BC (Before Computers), to assume the identity of another person, we had to physically alter our appearance and physically be present. We also had to master the art of forgery to be successful at assuming the personality of another person and profit from it. As early as 1953, a film called *Stolen Identity* was made and was followed by many other films in almost every language with similar themes! A best-selling novel, *Second Lady*, was written by Irving Wallace, dealing with the replacement of the wife of an American president with a Russian spy! Of course, the world of espionage used this technique to obtain information about enemies. But physically trying to assume the identity of another person and being physically present at the scene of offence is very risky. The imposter can be apprehended or worse, shot to death. With computers stepping in, the need to alter one's physical appearance and be present at the scene of offense are obsolete. The impostor may be sitting miles away, perhaps in another state or even country, to assume your identity and profit from it before you can even realize what is happening. This aspect of identity theft is experienced by many people, and I do not think it is necessary to elaborate any further.

Now, as software designers, it is not our concern how to deal with identity thieves, but it is our concern that they exist and cannot be eliminated in the near future. So, we must design software features that make it very difficult for prospective identity thieves to hack into our system, and collect data that can be used by the investigators to locate and apprehend the thief. Let us now discuss the measures that we need to include in the design of software applications.

Safety Measures to Be Included in the Application

We need to provide in our application the following measures to ensure user safety and prevent mistakes committed unintentionally.

1. *Authorizations*: We need to ensure that the user trying to perform a transaction has the authority to perform that activity and that the user's credentials are verified. We usually do this. Another way to ensure safety is to ask for authorizations in

special conditions. In financial matters, we can provide for authorization by another higher-level executive to authorize the transaction before proceeding with it. When transactions are handled manually, it is common practice to use authorizations in most high-value transactions. In cases like releasing a purchase order, we can split the activity into two transactions. The first one is preparation of the purchase order by a purchase executive, and the next is authorization by a purchase manager. If necessary, we can add a third level in which a finance manager approves the value of the purchase order. We need to study the situation and build multiple levels of authorization before a risky transaction is executed by our application.

2. *Duplicating the entry*: This is especially important when dealing with huge sums of money. We can define a sum of money as the threshold limit for making the user enter the amount once again to be sure. Often, users forget to place the decimal point, and this may cause the amount to be more than what was intended. We give the user a chance to correct the mistake, if any. Alternatively, we can display a message and ask the user to click a button that indicates that the amount is verified.

3. *Asking for confirmation*: This is the most commonly used mechanism in handling financial transactions. We display the details on the screen once again and ask the user to verify the details and confirm by clicking on a button before proceeding with the transaction. This will give the user another chance to verify what was entered and then make corrections if necessary.

4. *Freezing the data after authorization*: In transactions like raising an invoice or making a payment, we need to take precautions to freeze the transaction data and not allow any modifications after the transaction is committed. We can provide viewing facilities for the completed transaction but not allow modifications. If we allow modifications, somebody may alter vital data, leading to loss of data integrity and loss to the user. For example, a purchase order was authorized and placed. Now if the data is changed, the organization may end up paying more than what was originally committed.

5. *No background processing*: Sometimes, we use background processing so the user is relieved of waiting and can attend to some other activity. While developing software for important high-value transactions, it is better not to use background processing. By processing high-value transactions in the foreground, we keep the attention of the user on the transaction at hand so the user can intervene if necessary. Also, we prevent a foreground activity from interfering with the background activity. In multiuser applications when the users could be at geographically distant locations from one another, we really are not able to see what all the people logged in to the application do.

6. *Locking the transaction*: When important high-value transactions are being handled, it is better to lock the other users from accessing the same functionality using the same data. Two users may accidentally simultaneously try to make payments for the same business transaction. We need to programmatically prevent such occurrences.

7. *Concurrency control*: We generate some reports that use data with the desired data extracted programmatically, and then we connect to the report generator and produce the report. Now, if we allow multiple people to generate the same report simultaneously, the report may not be accurate. In such cases, it is better to lock the transaction and allow only one user to produce the report. We need to allow

another user only after the first user has finished the task. Alternatively, all such cases are allowed only for one user role, such as the system administrator.

8. *Ticket-booking dilemma*: This is a very common occurrence in most ticket-booking scenarios. There happens to be only one available ticket, and two users bid for it. If one user is successful, the other user would be denied. Now, our program may first allocate the ticket and then collect money. This may lead to allocation and not receiving the money. This leaves us with an unsold ticket and dissatisfied users. The second method is to collect the money first and then allocate the ticket. In this case, we may end up collecting the money from both (or, for that matter, multiple users) and not allocate the tickets. This leaves us with upset users who paid money but did not get the tickets. How should we handle this? There are many methods, and you should select the one appropriate for your situation. One way is to lock the transactions until one user completes the transaction, and put the others in a queue. You could message the other waiting users appropriately to indicate a transaction is in progress and waiting is inevitable, or a similar message.

Security and safety are vital overheads to software applications, and we need to expend considerable effort and time in ensuring both in our applications. The time taken to design software applications becomes significantly greater to ensure security and safety, but they are effort and time well spent.

10

Input Design

Introduction

Any computer-based data-processing application needs inputs to process and deliver outputs. The inputs can be data inputs or control inputs. Data inputs are the data that gets processed to deliver the desired outputs. Control inputs trigger the computer to perform some action. The action may be to receive the inputs from the screen and store them in a database table or initiate some processing action such as generating a report, sending a signal to some machine, or performing some other programmed action. Inputs can come into our application from a number of sources, such as:

1. Flat files containing data
2. Database tables
3. Another computer
4. Another program on the same computer
5. A program on a different computer
6. A machine, including airplanes and rockets
7. The keyboard
8. Any input device connected to the computer
9. The Internet
10. Any other source

Whatever the input device, the input data is received under the control of a program in our application that asks for the input using an input statement like Read, Scanf, Input, and so on. Sometimes the data is received without being asked for by a program in our application. For example, in the swiping of a credit card in a credit card machine, swiping an id card on a swiping device located on the door to gain entry, or other such scenarios, the data is sent by a different application. We need to design our application for both scenarios as applicable. Most applications receive program-controlled inputs. Most machine control applications receive input sent by other devices that are not under the control of our application. We need to design inputs as necessitated by our application.

Garbage In Garbage Out Phenomenon and Data Validation

"To err is human, but to make a real mess, you need a computer," or so goes the joke about data errors in the information obtained from the computers. Before we go on to discussing the design of inputs, we need to consider the GIGO phenomenon. This term is used to signify the fact that the computer is just a data processor and the quality of outputs depends on the quality of inputs. If we input garbage or erroneous data, we are sure to receive erroneous outputs. This term was used to explain errors in the outputs generated by the computer, especially in the earlier days of batch processing when the preparation of data was offline.

In the past, when data preparation was offline, the data was entered by data entry specialists, and each and every item of data was verified by re-entering the data or by manual checking to ensure that the data were as accurate as humanly possible. In those days, the data was accurate to 99.96%, or, for every 10,000 records, 4 records were likely to contain defects. Offline data entry is still used, but not in mainline business applications. Most of the data comes from business transactions handled every day by employees working in organizational business processes. The people entering data are not data entry specialists but functional specialists using computers for record keeping and other purposes. They are not likely to enter every item of data twice to ensure the accuracy of the data entering the computers. Therefore, we need to build in data validation statements to ensure accuracy of data and to prevent as many errors as possible from entering corporate databases.

But now, online end-user computing has arrived and become entrenched firmly in the data-processing world. The person entering the data knows what the data is and will input accurate data. All the same, we need to understand that the knowledgeable end user is, after all, a human being, and human beings are prone to error. They commit errors by oversight, by punching the wrong keys, or by lack of concentration arising out of monotony. Therefore, we need to check every data item received as input before either storing it for future use or initiating the data processing action. We perform the following data validation checks on the input data:

1. *Master lookup*: In this validation, we check whether the input data item exists in a master data file or table. For example, in a payroll-processing scenario, we check whether the employee identification number exists in the employee master data table. In a material management scenario, we check to see that the material code received as input exists in the material master table. In a web-based login scenario, we check to see if the IP address from which the login request originated exists in the table containing allowed IP addresses. We maintain master data tables to minimize the data entry effort as well as to avoid duplication, and use an identification code to connect the master data to our transaction data. Whenever we encounter an identification number, we need to check for its existence in the relevant master data table. This protects the integrity of our data.

2. *Range check*: This validation is used on numerical data items. We check the number to see if it is above a minimum value and below a maximum limit. Of course, we ought to know this range before we can use this validation. In a payroll scenario, we check to see if the amount of payment is within the minimum and maximum pay for the designation of the employee. In a marketing scenario, we check if the price offered to the customer is within the acceptable range. In an HR system, we

check the date of birth to see if it is between the minimum age for employability and the retirement age. In a timesheet application, we see if the entered hours are less than 24 per day, and that is after ensuring that the individual is authorized to work overtime. In this manner, we perform a range check for numeric data items whenever we can determine a range of permissible values. One word of caution here: we should never hardcode these ranges into our programs. It is better to store them in a table and read from that table, as these ranges can change over a period of time.

3. *Suspicious values*: When do we become suspicious? We become suspicious if the person performing an activity is not authorized explicitly or when the transaction is close to some limit. For example, if the height of a person is entered as 7 feet, we become suspicious. While it is possible for a person to be 7 feet tall, it is rare. For some numeric data items, we cannot fix any ranges, for example, if we are capturing data for an item purchased with cash for an emergency. In such cases, there is no quote to verify the value. We may verify the permitted limit to go in for a cash purchase if it exists. Similarly, we usually have acceptable ranges for the hourly rate of employees, but we usually do not have a limit for the maximum salary paid to the individual. Sometimes an extra payment falls due to the employee and his/her salary is more than the usual sum. But we need to become suspicious if the employee is receiving a large sum, say $100,000 in one paycheck, or if the total salary for the period is zero. It may be a legitimate transaction, as the employee is receiving compensation for some major injury. If a person enters 30 children as dependents on an income tax return, we have to become suspicious, as while it is theoretically possible to have 30 children, it is rarely practical. If you ask me how a person can have 30 children, the person may have more than one living wife, as certain countries allow a man to have more than one wife. When a payment to a person/employee/organization goes over the usual value by a certain percentage, we alert the user before processing the data. In credit card and debit card applications, we not only check the limits but also compare the present transaction with all the transactions over the past year to prevent fraudulent use of the card. When we encounter suspicious values, we have to force the individual to verify the data item and re-enter the value as well as raising it to another person for authentication and authorization.

4. *Logical check*: We use certain common-sense logic to see if the entered data is accurate. For example, when the user enters the date as February 29, we check if the year is a leap year or not. In an email address, we expect one "@" character and a dot, and at the end there are certain acceptable words, such as com, edu, org, and so on. In a website address, we expect www and at the end acceptable words like com and org. Certain data items are related to one another. For example, the discount offered in a marketing scenario might depend on the quantity being purchased, the sales commission paid to a salesperson could depend on the amount of sales revenue generated, the length of permitted absence for childbirth may depend on the gender of the employee, and so on. Wherever we can see a logical relationship between data items, we need to verify the value of the entered data item and raise appropriate alerts as necessary. These are a few simple examples, but in every application, there will be many situations like this, and we build in as much logical checking as possible to ensure accuracy of the input data.

5. *Spell check*: We use this validation when entry of free text is allowed. Of course, we need to provide a dictionary and include the code to check the spelling and then provide suggestions for correcting the error.

6. *Unexpected characters*: This has become a big problem in these days of Internet applications. As you perhaps know, HTML is built using tags. If data is entered into the text boxes with an executable string, it can cause havoc. We ensure that such tags are either prevented or prevent their being used as valid HTML statements. This has now become an important aspect of today's programming. Another aspect is while entering data in fields, such as names of personnel, where digits and other nonalphabetic characters should not be entered, we check for those additional characters and eliminate them or alert the user about the erroneous entry.

7. *Integrity check*: When codifying important ids such as social security numbers, employee ids, material codes, order codes, and so on, they are built with some logic. When someone enters such data, the data will be verified against the logic to ensure that accurate data is being received.

8. *Type check*: We also check the data being entered to ensure that right type of data is being entered. Common mistakes are entering an O (the letter "O") in place of zero. This is especially important when accepting numeric data.

9. *Constraint check*: In many cases, we place constraints on the type of data being entered. In numeric cases, there could be only one decimal point. In character strings, there could be a minimum and a maximum length of the string acceptable to the application. In some cases, there needs to be only one word. We check for all such constraints.

10. We check for consistency between parts of the data being entered. If the title was entered as "Mr.", then the gender should be "Male." If a product is selected, then the price and discount should be commensurate with the product. There could be many such consistency checks possible depending on the application, and we check for these aspects.

In this manner, we have to design validations for all the data items being received into the application to ensure that we prevent data errors as much as possible. We have to do our very best to make the GIGO phenomenon as nonfunctional as possible in our application. The usual practice is to include data validation routines as part of common routines and make them available for programmers to call in their input programs.

Receiving Data from Cars, Rockets, Airplanes, and Machines

In designing software applications that control machines like rockets, airplanes, ships, submarines, automobiles, and a host of other machinery used in the world, the data comes from the machines. How is this data gathered and transmitted to the CPU that processes it and returns appropriate instructions back to the machines?

For each machine, be it a rocket, airplane, or car, there are certain parameters that need to be monitored to keep the machine running in a healthy condition and do what is expected of it. These are classified into internal parameters and external parameters. Internal parameters are:

1. Temperature in the engine or wherever heat is generated

2. Pressure inside the places where pressure is generated

3. Velocity/speed of the moving parts of the engine and the machine itself in the case of rockets, airplanes, and cars

4. Vibrations of parts at some critical places, like shafts, enclosures, and panels

5. Various measurements like the voltage, current, electrical resistance, volume of liquids, levels of cooling liquids, temperatures, and so on

6. Other situation-specific parameters internal to the machine

The significant external parameters, especially to moving machines like automobiles, airplanes, ships, submarines, rockets, and so on are:

1. Environmental parameters like wind speed, rain, snow, dust, and so on

2. Any approaching objects

3. The direction and the ground speed

4. The time allowed, elapsed, and remaining

5. The distance to be covered, already covered, and the remaining distance

6. Many more situation-specific parameters

All this data comes from instruments/sensors mounted on the relevant parts of the machines, and they collect the data, which is basically analog in nature. The machine has either built-in or externally mounted analog-to-digital (A2D) converters, which will convert the analog signal from the instrument to a digital signal suitable for a digital computer. Now, this signal is interpreted and processed by the CPU embedded in the machine. As software designers, we are not concerned with how these A2D converters work. We simply assume that the data comes in a digital form readily usable by the CPU and design our applications. Most of the data coming in has to be responded to within a specified time limit, but it need not be stored. Of course, we do store some specific data for later analysis, depending on the situation. In airplanes and rockets, most of the data is stored for analysis of how the trip went and to improve the design of the craft. But the input data has to be responded to first and then stored. In business applications, the inputs rarely need to be responded to in real time, but in machine control applications, the inputs demand immediate response.

In these cases, the responses are programmed based on the specifications provided by the machine designers. While receiving this type of data, we perform range validation. If the item is within range, then the machine is functioning in a healthy condition, and if it is out of range, the machine is not in a healthy state, and we need to initiate actions programmed for out-of-range values.

Data Received over the Internet

When our computer is connected to the Internet, it continuously receives data. The Internet carries data from all over the world to our computer. Of course, the network interface unit (NIU) of our computer handles all such data and rejects all the data that is not addressed to our computer automatically without any need for us to design afresh any program to handle all such junk data. Can we say all the data addressed to our computer is benign in nature and can be passed on for processing? There are malicious software developers out in the free world who release malicious data, including viruses and other malware, onto the

Internet that can deceive our NIU into believing that the data is intended for our computer. If our proposed application receives data over the Internet, we need to design checks and validations in our application to ensure that we prevent all hackers and intruders from damaging our application.

When we receive data over the Internet, it comes via the transmission control protocol/internet protocol (TCP/IP) protocol in packets. Usually, data originates at a client computer using our application. In such cases, the app server (or framework or any other name used by the hosting platform) receives that data, interprets it, and initiates the appropriate programmed action. The appropriate action may be to pass the data on to our application. When our application receives such data, we need to design checks to ensure that the data is benign. We need to verify the string to see if it contains any HTML tags or any other types of tags that can be interpreted as executable statements. Of course, most popular hosting platforms available today do this checking automatically and prevent such data being interpreted as executable statements and convert it into ordinary strings of characters. Still, it pays to check and strip the data of all tags that make the string an executable statement. In email applications, we do pass executable statements with links and names of executable files and so on. We have to design our application to treat strings as strings irrespective of the fact that they contain HTML or other markup tags.

Most of the data received by our application is program-controlled data; that is, a program contained in our application gets the data from some source. Our application reads the data from an input device by following the protocol of that device and using input statements like Read, Input, Scanf, or such other input statements. Sometimes, the data has to be received by our application without being requested by our application. For example, take credit card–processing applications. At some place in the world, someone inserts a credit card in the credit card machine and swipes it. This action sends the data to our application requesting authorization of payment. This action is initiated by the machine located at the user's location. In fact, multiple people across the globe may be swiping credit cards at several locations and asking for authorization. In such cases, the requests are queued up, either in the RAM or in a database table, depending on the design. We normally use interrupt programming to awaken the dormant application to process the received request.

If the number of devices placing such requests is limited to a few and the number is known, we could use the polling technique instead of queuing them up. In either case, the response time depends on the number of requests coming in. By using the polling technique, we need not use interrupt programming. Interrupt programming is not easy and we would need experienced programmers who can call OS primitives. But in cases like credit card processing and banking applications, interrupt programming becomes inevitable. In machine control software applications, interrupt programming is necessary. In such applications, we need to select the queuing or polling method of receiving data and then specify the design so it can be programmed.

Now, let us turn our attention to obtaining data from the keyboard.

Screen Design

Perhaps I should call this section presentation design because we present information asking the user to input the necessary data. In the present day, presentation design has become very important to be able to sell our application and make it popular. In fact, most prospective customers are more influenced by how our data input screens are designed than by the invisible robustness of our application. Therefore, we must spend considerable effort in designing our data input screens.

There are two aspects of screen design: one is the aesthetic aspect and the other is the ease-of-use aspect. These are in addition to the fact that all data has to be received and subjected to validation before passing it on to further processing. Let us now discuss these aspects.

Aesthetic Aspects of Screen Design

One thing about aesthetics is that they keep changing with the times! What is considered aesthetically appealing at one time is considered plain some time later. What was considered ugly at one time is considered beautiful later on. In his novel *Wheels*, first published in 1971, Arthur Hailey coined the phrase "ugly is beautiful." Wearing a suit without a tie was unthinkable in the past, but not anymore! People once always wore hats, but not anymore! If you look at the types of clothes worn by both men and women over a period of time, you will understand the phrase "ugly is beautiful."

Therefore, we have to design our screens to appeal to contemporary tastes. Still, certain things remain constant over time. For example, men wear pants and a shirt, perhaps with slight modifications in their design. Women wear dresses of a variety of designs. The color pink is considered feminine; clothes having flowery designs are not considered masculine; brown-colored shoes are deemed respectable; white is considered pure by Christians; orange is considered sacred by Hindus, Sikhs, and Buddhists; and green is considered sacred by Muslims. We need to keep these in mind while designing our screens.

All this is well recognized by the software development industry, which employs people specializing in graphic design for developing a few screens with aesthetic appeal. These people prepare a screen design with links, other pictures, logos, and so on, leaving adequate space to place the controls to get input data. They utilize 10–20% of the space of the screen to make it aesthetically appealing and leave the rest of the space for placing our controls to achieve the functionality expected of the screen. How many such template screens should we get these people to design? While there are no fixed rules, here are a few guidelines to consider:

1. It is better to design a template for each of our major modules. For example, in a material management scenario, we can have a template each for master data maintenance, material receipts, material issues, purchase orders, report generation, system administration, and so on. Of course, we can have certain things common to all these screens such as the dominating color, placement of a "home" link, and other such things.

2. One other theme of template design is to have a screen depending on the functions carried out by the executives in the organization. For example, all the business transaction processing screens use one template, the authorization functionality screens use one template, the administration functions use one template, and so on.

3. I have seen some applications use a single template for all the screens in the application. This achieves simplicity and uniformity of look and feel.

4. When we design multiple templates, we need to maintain uniformity in the following aspects:

   a.   All the links must be at one place in all the screens. If we have them on the left side of our screen, all templates must have the same arrangement. If we place links on the bottom of the screen, it should be so on all the templates.

   b.   If we have navigation buttons (Prev, Next, right arrow, left arrow, and so on) they all must be placed at a similar location. For example, if we locate them at the top (or bottom) of the screen on the right (or left) side, they need to be in the same place in all templates.

   c.   If we display confirmatory message for saving data, all Save buttons in the application must generate a similar confirmatory message on clicking it.

Ease-of-Use Aspects of Screen Design

Now, let us look at how to design our screens within the templates. This deals with the placement of controls on the screen, navigation from one control to another, generation of messages, and so on. We need to remember that user convenience and the availability of contemporary technology have to be considered in designing the screen layouts. Any guidelines need to be improved periodically, taking into consideration the new developments taking place all over the world to deliver better designs to our clients.

1. It is always better if we design the screen in such a way that the user need not scroll in either the horizontal or vertical direction. Of course, the user may be working on any size of screen, and this makes it difficult for us to achieve this goal. We need to select a screen size and resolution and design our screen to fit this screen size. The screen size and resolution selected ought to be the most popular size at the moment. It should not be the largest available screen or the maximum screen resolution, nor should it be the smallest of the available range. When we do so and specify the optimum screen size and resolution to use our application, the users will try to adjust their screens if it is possible or learn to live with that.

2. It is not a good idea to pack too many controls on the screen. How many is too many? Each control needs to be associated with a label giving an idea of what is expected in the control. So, each control is actually two: one is the control and the other is its label. We need to ensure that, between two horizontally adjacent controls, there must be adequate space so the user can clearly and unambiguously distinguish between them. Similarly, between two vertically adjacent controls, we need to provide some space so they do not appear cramped. The idea is to see that the screen appears pleasant and the user does not have to spend too much time or effort to locate the desired control.

3. If the screen has to provide too many controls, it is better to split it into more than one screen. Now, the number of controls we can pack into one screen without necessitating scrolling either horizontally or vertically depends on the size of each

of the controls we place on the screen. If the size of the controls is small, we may be able to place five controls horizontally and 8 to 10 rows vertically. But if the size of the controls is large, then we may not be able to place more than two horizontally and six vertically. But it really depends on the controls and the data size that needs to be entered. Again, there is no point in splitting a screen into two just to accommodate two more controls. When we need to split the screen, the following guidelines may be followed:

a. Just to accommodate a few more controls, it is better to resort to vertical scrolling than using another screen. It takes time to clear the screen and load the next screen. We also need to save the work carried out so far before taking the user to the next screen. Therefore, we should not split the screen just to accommodate a few more controls. Scrolling is a better option. But scrolling should not be such that two screens are cramped into one.

b. We can use a tabbed screen to split the screen. On each tab, we can place a suitable caption to indicate the nature of the screen. A tabbed screen need not reload the entire screen, at least in some development platforms. This saves time for the user. The user can also switch between the screens very easily. For the developer, the need to place a save button on all the screens is avoided. I would advocate this option to split the screen.

c. We can design multiple screens but place navigation buttons (right and left pointing arrows, Prev and Next buttons, or some other arrangement) on each screen at a suitable location.

4. Arrangement of controls on the screen: We need to place the controls on the screen in a logical manner. The first control needs to be placed on the left-hand-side top corner of the form. Then, the remaining controls need to be placed to the right of that control and then move downward if we need to place more rows of controls. The navigation ought to be from left to right and then top to bottom. Most people in the world follow the left-to-right convention except in Arabic countries. If we have to develop an application for those countries, then we need to place the controls from right to left. But all over the world, the vertical direction is from top to bottom.

5. Navigation: Onscreen navigation involves moving from one control to the other. Of course, using the mouse, the user can move to any of the controls, but to move between controls using the keyboard, we have to set the order. The tab key and arrow keys are the usual keys that are used to move between controls. Some development platforms allow specifying the tab order of controls. In such cases, pressing the tab key moves the cursor in the specified order. Unless there are special circumstances, we have to specify the tab order as moving from left to right and then top to bottom. Arrow keys, pointing left and right, are usually used to move the cursor within a control where it is allowed. The top- and bottom-pointing arrow keys are used to move the cursor up and down the rows of controls. The tab key moves the cursor forward, and Shift+Tab moves the cursor in reverse from one control to the other. We need to follow these design guidelines and arrange the controls on the screen.

6. We should keep the general connotations of colors in mind while designing the screens. Warnings and error messages ought to be in red, confirmatory messages can be in the dominant color of the screen but not in red, a correct answer ought to be in green, and so on.

7. Placing all controls too close to one another clutters up the screen. Grouping related sets of controls into frames provides clarity to the user. For example, in a hospital management application's patient data capture screen, we can group the basic data (name, date of birth, address, etc.) into one group, insurance information into one group, preliminary medical information into one group, and so on to provide clarity and assist the user in capturing the information comprehensively and in a logical manner.

8. We discussed data validation in a previous section of this chapter, but the question of when to carry out this data validation is an important one. The following are methods for data validation:

   a. We carry out the validation of the data in the control as soon as the cursor moves from the present control. This is usually referred to as the LostFocus event. There is a big drawback to this method. The user can keep the cursor in the control but use the mouse to click the Save button. This action will not trigger the LostFocus event, and data validation does not take place. at all.

   b. We can carry out data validation as soon as a key is pressed. We especially use this method for checking if the data being entered in the text box is numeric or not. This method is the most popular in ensuring that the user enters only numeric data into the text box control.

   c. We can place all data validations in the Click event of the Save button and then carry out validation of data in all controls at one go. When we use this, we need to display an error message and also move the cursor to the control containing erroneous data.

   d. Of course, we can validate the data in a control at both times, that is, when the cursor moves out of the control as well as when the Save button is clicked. But this is not only superfluous, it also forces us to duplicate the validation statements in two places. Duplicating the statements can affect the code integrity when the code is corrected for any reason. We may forget to change it in both places. The source code for any action ought to be in one place if we wish to maintain code integrity, especially during the maintenance phase.

9. Labels tell the user what is expected in the control. We need to place the label close to the control and at a distance from the adjacent control on the same row of controls. We generally do not allow any gap except the minimum necessary between the label and the control to which it is related. We place a gap of at least two character spaces between the label and the adjacent control to which it is not related. The objective is to make it obvious to the user which label relates to which control.

10. We need to ensure that the background color and the color of the font have good contrast. If the contrast is poor, it becomes difficult for the user to read. We need to keep in mind that users of our application may not have the best eyesight. It is better to test the contrast if we decide to use colors other than the established colors. For example, a black font over grey has very good contrast, but may appear plain, as many applications use that combination. We may try to jazz up the user experience with different color combinations. In such cases, it is better to test the combination using persons with different vision impairments.

11. Font size: The size of the font used depends on the space available on the screen based on the number of controls placed. For text within the controls, we should use a minimum font size of 8 points. Below that may be visible to people with the best

eyesight, but not to the rest. We need to specify the font size, keeping in mind the demographics of the target group of people who are likely to use our application.

12. Graphics on screen: We use graphics on screens to make the user experience enjoyable. We need to select the graphics such that they are appropriate for the subject at hand and will not offend any social group in our target market in any manner. Different graphics have different connotations, and we need to understand the connotation of a graphic before using it.

13. Messages: We need to display messages to the user for various reasons, such as error messages that tell the user that a mistake was made, error messages that something went wrong while processing the inputs, confirmatory messages that an action was successfully completed, and so on. If the development platform allows, it is better to display a message box with the message and command buttons to specify the next action to be taken. If message boxes are not allowed by the development platform, we have to display invisible messages on the screen. That is, the messages are already on the screen but are normally invisible. We change their invisible property to visible whenever this message is required to be called. But, as hardcoding is not encouraged, we place a label setting it to invisible. When the error message is required, we assign the text to the label and then make it visible.

14. Tool tips: The labels placed beside the control give information to the user as to what is expected to be entered in the control. But the labels need to be cryptic because they cannot be allocated larger space. So, we supplement the information on the label with a tool tip. As we hover the cursor on the control, the tool tip appears, giving the user additional information. It is best to provide a tool tip for every control. It is a must to provide tool tips for icons on toolbars, as the pictures of the icons may not be very meaningful to the users, especially during the initial days of operation. It is also advisable to provide tool tips for the command buttons, as the buttons do not have much space to insert a long, meaningful caption.

15. Persons with disabilities: While designing screens, we need to keep in mind the requirements of people with disabilities and design them so that such persons can use our application. Visual impairment can be of many types. All people cannot see all colors in the same way. Some people cannot see some colors. Some people have aversion to some colors due to their cultural background. So, we must provide a feature to set the color for the background and the foreground as well as the color of the font. Similarly, we need to provide navigation not only through mouse or touch but also through the keyboard. If necessary, we also need to provide voice renderings of the actions to be performed by the user based on the message in the message box or on the label and tool tip of the current control.

In short, we need to design the screen to be aesthetically appealing and easy and comfortable to use by all the expected users of our application.

Making Multilingual Screens

If we propose to sell our application to multiple countries, a country that uses multiple languages, or agencies like the United Nations (UN) or European Union (EU), we have to design it so that our application works satisfactorily without modifying the code. For this purpose, our design ought to put the following in place.

1. We can design our screens with English labels. I say English because it is the most widely used language in the world.
2. Then, design a database table to contain the label texts of other languages equivalent to the English labels used on the screen.
3. We need to provide the label length so it can accommodate the longest label in the above-mentioned database table. Alternatively, we need to shorten the label to fit the space provided for it on the screen.
4. We need to provide an option to be selected at the time of installation or as an option in the system administration functions to select the desired language.
5. At the time of loading the form, based on the selected language, we need to replace the English language label texts with the values read from the database table mentioned above.
6. We need to do the same for the report captions, tool tip texts, and command button captions.
7. It is also necessary to design a database table for all the message texts and then use the message text based on the language selected earlier.
8. If we have any other text on the screen, we need to read it from a table corresponding to the selected language and use it.
9. All in all, we have to avoid hardcoding the texts of all types, read them from one or more database tables corresponding to the selected language, and use them on the screen.

Functional Aspects of Screen Design

The purpose of a screen is to obtain input to our application and sometimes also to deliver an output. We will discuss the aspects of screen design to deliver outputs in our chapter on output design. In this chapter, let us focus on designing the screen for receiving the required inputs into our application. We use the input screen design to perform the following functions:

1. To navigate from one screen to another in the performance of our functions
2. To receive inputs into our application
   a. By entering the required information by typing it out in the specified place
   b. By selecting the right input from the choices provided
3. To instruct the computer to perform the action we specify

We navigate from one screen to another using the menu of options provided on the screen. These options are provided in the form of:

1. Links that are basically HTML text: Clicking the control takes us to another web page. This new page may be displayed on the same window/tab or in a new window/tab. What we need to remember is loading the page in a new window or

tab takes up additional RAM from the computer, and opening too many windows/ tabs has the potential to slow down the computer, as it can run out of RAM and begin thrashing from swapping too many times.

2. Menu options: We are presented a menu of options and are allowed to select one of the available options. We now have facilities to display the options merely by hovering the cursor on the menu or by clicking the menu. I would suggest clickable menus over menus that display the options by hovering the cursor, as accidental hovering also displays the options, which can be annoying to the user. But it is to be selected based on the prospective user and the functionality at hand.

3. Command buttons like the Prev and Next buttons to navigate the user to the next or previous screen depending on the user's choice. This is useful in applications such as libraries, retail sales, ticket booking, dating, and other such sites.

4. We also use page numbers when the information presented to the user is on a large number of pages. Usually, we also place command buttons to navigate the user to the first page, last page, previous page, or next page, along with page numbers so that the user has a number of choices to select from.

5. Toolbars: Toolbars contain buttons with pictures to allow the user to perform actions without going through the menus. Each button can perform some function on the same screen or navigate the user to another page. For example, the Open button on the toolbar allows the user to open another page or application and navigates the user to another page.

We select the appropriate method of navigation based on the function to be performed, and here are some guidelines:

1. For performing business transactions provided in our application, we usually provide menus.

2. To navigate to another web page, such as help pages, we use links.

3. We also use links to navigate the user to another related application desired by the user.

4. We use command buttons like Save or Cancel to complete a business transaction and navigate the user to the next action.

5. We use command buttons like Prev and Next to navigate the user to input a class of data split across multiple screens.

6. We use page numbers when the user is browsing a large amount of data spread across multiple pages.

7. We use buttons on the toolbars to open another page or application.

8. In secure applications, we suppress the back button so that the user is forced to use menus to navigate.

9. We usually load web pages such as help pages in another tab/window. This will allow the user to read the help and continue processing business transactions. But a page navigated to through the menus is loaded on the same tab/window. This prevents the user from processing two business transactions concurrently. It also avoids partly completed transactions.

Design of Controls

We place all the controls on the screen. While placing the controls, we have to consider a few aspects, listed below, so that the user experience is comfortable.

1. *Tabs of the screen*: When necessary, we have to split the screen in such a manner that each tab has a single functionality to achieve. All the controls on tab-l ought to be related logically to each other and form an almost independent part of the total screen. Each tab ought to be captioned appropriately such that the user will have no difficulty in understanding the contents of that tab.

2. *Menu design*: Menus are sets of options presented textually. Each of the options can have a submenu. While theoretically there is no limit on the number of submenus a main menu option can have, it is better to restrict the number of submenus to a maximum of three, that is, a main menu and three submenus. While there is no real restriction on the number of words or characters an option on the menu can have, it is better to limit the number of words to three and the total number of characters to about 25. Of course, these are not set in stone and one can have more or fewer words or characters. The purpose of the option text is to communicate the destination clearly to the user, but we must be as brief as possible without losing clarity.

3. *Toolbars*: Toolbars are a bar of icons, with each icon representing a menu option. Toolbars assist users who have problems reading the textual option of the menus for any reason. The user may not be familiar with the language, the user may have visual issues, or the user could be not literate enough to read the text. An icon is a small picture that conveys the action that can be achieved by clicking it. Some of the icons have gained such significant popularity that one doesn't think of using any other icon. For example, the picture of a floppy disk for saving the work, the picture of a file folder for opening a new screen, and the picture of scissors for cutting are commonly used across most applications. We have to design pictures for the icons such that they convey the action that can be performed by clicking that icon. The actions triggered by clicking the icons on the toolbars are duplicated by other triggers, like selecting menu options. Therefore, it is better to write the code at one place and call that code. Usually, we place the code in the event of selecting a menu option. When the icon is clicked, we need to call the code placed in the event of selecting the menu option. We need to avoid duplicating the code, as code integrity can be damaged during software maintenance if the code is duplicated.

4. *Labels*: Labels are used as headings, captions, titles, and prompts. A form has a title, each frame has a caption, and each control has a prompt that tells the user what action is expected of him/her. While it is easy and tempting to hardcode the text on the label in the program or the properties of the label control, it is better to avoid doing so. It is better to read the text of the label from a database table and assign the caption to the label during the form load event. This practice is used in all applications that are likely to be used by users of multiple languages. We have to ensure that the label can accommodate the longest possible text that may be placed on it. It is not a good practice to extend the length of the label during the form load event, as it can overlap the adjacent control. It is essential to ensure that the label is placed as close to its control as possible. What is the best place to

place the control? On the left side or right side? Left is generally preferred, but, based on client preferences, the labels can be placed on the right-hand side of the control, too. Left or right, it is essential to place them on the same side throughout the application. We should not place the labels on the right-hand side on one screen and left-hand side on another screen. Uniformity is the key aspect of placing the labels by their controls. The headings may be centered across the screen or the frame. But in some countries, they may prefer right-aligning the headings. Here, too, uniformity is the key aspect in determining the place of headers.

5. *Text box design*: A text box is the control that receives user inputs from the keyboard or from the application's database. It can accept either numeric or alphanumeric data. Some provide facilities to restrict the entry to either numeric or alphanumeric data. The text box can present multiple lines. We need to size the text box such that the need to scroll within the box can be avoided. If we cannot extend the length horizontally, we may make the box a multi-line, text-wrapping box. We need to design some common routines to restrict the entry to:

a. Integer numeric data: This data consists of digits 0 to 9 only, and no other character is permitted. We also have to restrict the largest number based on the size of the integer. The use of a short integer (achieved with 2 bytes) is progressively being discontinued. Only the long integer (achieved by allocating 4 bytes for a maximum of 2,147,483,647) is more or less the norm. Sometime back, such large numbers entering our database was unthinkable, but with the spiraling rates of inflation, it is no more unthinkable, especially in the case of some countries having low value currency. So, it pays to incorporate size checking in our application to make it future proof.

b. Floating-point numeric data: Sometime back, this data was referred to as single-precision and double-precision data. In those days, a single-precision number was allocated 4 bytes and double-precision 8 bytes. This is still used by some development platforms. Some development platforms use only one type, and that is 8 bytes. The number achieved by using 8 bytes is still astronomically large. But in scientific and space applications, the data is really and literally astronomical. So, in such applications, single-precision is 8 bytes and double-precision is 16 bytes. There is no point in using the largest number possible for all occurrences. We have to judiciously select the right precision, as otherwise, we are unnecessarily overloading the database. While entering this type of data, we need to ensure that only one decimal point exists in the data besides ensuring the characters being entered are digits and a decimal point. We need to code common routines to do this checking and call them at data entry time.

c. Alphabetic data: These are usually names of people, places, or objects. Usually, only alphabetical characters and blank spaces are used in names. Of course, a period character (.) for suffixes like Jr. is also used. We need to develop a common routine to do this checking and call it every time such data is entered.

d. Alphanumeric data: By alphanumeric data, we generally mean data having any printable character. But now, we have to split this category into another and restrict it to entering alphabets and numbers only. The slash (/) character and the less-than and greater-than characters (<, >) acquired new and special meanings with the advent of HTML and other markup languages. In particular, the slash character (/) is also used in arithmetic formulas, document references, and house numbers in some countries. So, it is better to define links that use tags of markup languages in a separate data item and provide a separate text box to capture such data. Can we afford to ignore checking this data field, and if we do check, what should we check? It is very difficult to answer this question comprehensively. We need some research and development of new methods to detect entry of malicious alphanumeric data into text boxes or develop new controls for capturing link data.

    i. Explicitly assign a separate control for capturing link data and data that may contain executable tags of markup languages.

    ii. Check for the presence of the less-than character (>) at the beginning and the greater-than character (>) at the end of the string being entered. If this is the situation, then it is a string of an executable command of a markup language. So, we need to take some action such as disallowing the string, asking the user to check the string once again, or stripping the string of such characters before storing them in the database. We will never know how many varieties of markup languages exist, what changes they undergo at what time, and so on. So, we have to do as much checking as possible with the current level of knowledge and technology available to us.

  e. Links: We are now capturing email ids, website URLs, and so on in our data input screens. Here, we need to ensure that the email ids and website URLs contain a valid end string such as com, org, edu, info, and so on. We also need to check the string for its validity based on the type of string. In email ids, we need to have one and only one @ character and only one valid end string. In a website URL, we need to have a web site id and a valid end string. Whether we capture the beginning strings of http and www is left to us. These are now added automatically by browsers, so whether we capture these is our option. If we design our application to capture these strings, we need to check for their accuracy.

  f. Date and time: Most development platforms provide date and time controls separately. Still, some applications use a text box to capture the date and time needed by applications. In such cases, we need to ensure that the data input by the user is checked logically for the date, month, and year, as well as the relationship between the month and the date in the case of February and for months having 30/31 days in addition to the data being numeric.

  g. We also, especially in the case of receiving long strings of data, need to design the text box to be able to display the entire string without the need of scrolling. We can provide the length of the text box to be equal to that of the length of the expected string or provide a text box that can receive multiple lines with the wrap facility so that the entire string is visible to the user.

6. *List box design*: A list box is like a combo box, except the list box allows selection of multiple items as opposed to one item in the combo box. The same considerations used in designing a combo box have to be used while designing a list box, too. A better practice that will make the user experience better is to show the selected items in another list box or a list so that the user knows all the items selected by him/her without having to scroll the list box repeatedly.

7. *ListView/grid design*: This control looks like a table or like a spreadsheet, such as Excel, with columns and rows. In some development platforms, this grid can be associated with a table. In such grids, the cells allow modification and all such modifications are automatically effected in the database table. While this feature certainly reduces the effort spent in programming, it may not be a good design, as users are likely to commit errors, especially when the end users who use the screens are not experts in computer science. So, I would advocate that the grid on the screen and the corresponding database table be isolated from each other. It is better to use a Save button and then programmatically make the changes in the database table.

8. *Radio button design*: Radio buttons need to be placed inside a frame. Once placed, only one radio button can be selected. This is used when one choice is to be made among a set of choices. However, we need to note that the total choices available ought to be small, say a maximum of five. If there are more than five choices, we can theoretically use radio buttons, but it will clutter up the screen and occupy a lot of screen space. In such cases, it would be better to use a combo box. When we design radio buttons, we need to maintain uniformity by placing the corresponding labels either on the left- or right-hand side. It is better to maintain uniformity throughout the application, not just on one screen. If one screen has labels on the right-hand side and another has labels on the left-hand side, it will inconvenience users. Whether to place the radio buttons side by side or one below the other is a matter of convenience. It would be better to place them one below the other, as we may not be able to accommodate all the radio buttons in one frame one beside the other. Vertical placement can facilitate maintaining uniformity across all screens.

9. *Checkbox design*: A checkbox captures Yes or No information. It is binary in nature. Checkboxes are mutually exclusive, and each checkbox is a standalone control that captures information for one data item, which is Boolean in nature. Here, too, just like in the case of radio buttons, we need to maintain uniformity in the matter of placing the corresponding label. We need to place the label of a checkbox either on the left-hand side or on the right-hand side but maintain uniformity all through the application.

10. *Command button design*: Command buttons are used to trigger the execution of a program by the application. It can be a Save button to store all the information entered in the controls on the screen, a Cancel button to cancel a contemplated action, a Yes button to indicate agreement with the proposed action, a No button to disagree with the proposed action, and so on. A picture or an icon on a command button is allowed but is not essential. It may help the user, who may not know English very well. Another thing that many people do with command buttons is design a shape of, say, oval command buttons with different color combinations. We can do all of them. The color and the shape need to be designed depending on the scenario and the target group of users expected to use our application. One essential aspect I would like to mention here is that at this point, we need to perform all data validations before we store the information in data capture screens. In other cases, too, we need to perform checks to ensure that the action requested is appropriate for the user and the parameters are are supplied.

11. *Frame design*: We use frames to delineate sets of related controls from each other. This will facilitate users in identifying the desired group of items. For example, on a purchase order generation screen, we have a group of data items about the vendor details; a group of data items about conditions like delivery date, delivery

address, tax rate, and other such conditions; a group of data items about the item details; and so on. By using a frame control to group a related set of data items, we can perform some actions en masse like making the frame visible or invisible, enabling or disabling editing of the items, and so on. We need to caption the frame in a meaningful manner. I suggest that its caption be retrieved from a database table so that we can make our application amenable to multilingual usage.

12. *Picture holders*: We may place picture holder controls on our screen to display a picture relevant to our application when necessary. We have two choices: we may adjust the picture to fit the size of the picture holder or provide scroll bars vertically as well as horizontally. We may also fit the picture to the size of the picture holder control and then provide a facility to show the full-sized picture when the picture holder is clicked. What we ought to do depends on the situation at hand and the probable end user preferences.

13. *Video holders*: Video holders have also became commonplace in the present day. A video holder provides controls to start the video, pause, stop, move forward, reverse, and so on. It usually allows display of the video in the video control provided or full-screen mode. It is a better practice to provide both modes of video operation, unless, of course, our application has no need to display the video in full-screen mode. While designing a video holder control, we need to select the size so that the video is capable of displaying a picture adequate size of picture so that most people would be able to view it without the necessity to enlarging it to full screen. Of course, it depends on the space available on the screen.

14. *Audio control*: Audio control is similar to video control, except that it plays only audio. The design considerations are also as noted above in the bullet on video holders.

15. *Dialog boxes*: We use these to give a message and then get the response of the user. Not all development platforms support these features, and sometimes browsers may block these boxes as popups. Popular boxes are those that come with a message and with a pair of command buttons bearing captions like Yes/No and OK/Cancel. At least one command button, OK, is a minimum for a dialog box. Instead of OK/Cancel, it is better to give meaningful captions like Proceed, Edit, Clear, and so on. Retrieving the message from a database table enables us to make the application multilingual and also allows us to improve the message without changing the code.

16. *Messages*: We can give messages to the user either through a dialog box where it is available or through a message where the facility of a dialog box is not available. We use a label that is normally invisible and make it visible when we need to pass on the message to the user. The usual practice is to give the message in red so it attracts the attention of the user. We have to design a mechanism to make the message invisible again based on the user action. Here, we do not have the facility to use a command button to indicate that the user has taken the necessary action. We can hide the message from view if the cursor is moved to the appropriate control or a similar action occurs.

17. *Help*: However well we design our screens, some users are likely to be confused, especially when they are at the initial stage of using the application. So, we need to provide help to guide the users. Providing context-sensitive help is the best method. But it is not easy to provide this kind of help, as providing links to each control is laborious and takes considerable effort from the help developers.

So, most applications provide a help file that is easily searchable. I would advocate the cause of context-sensitive help because it has the potential to save the efforts of users, which outweighs the effort spent in developing the help files. We need to give examples where necessary inside the help files so that the user will be able to understand the usage of the application and use it to serve the purpose effectively. Should we display the help file occupying less than a full screen to the right side of the screen, as many applications do, or should we occupy the entire screen or the middle? Most applications display help files either to the right-hand side of the screen or at the bottom of the screen. These look appropriate to me. There is no hard-and-fast rule that this is the best practice. You can decide the position and the onscreen size of the help window to suit the target end users of your application.

18. *Engineering drawing elements*: CAD packages use drawing elements. There are many such elements. These include line, circle, ellipse, arc, chamfering, hatching, rectangle, triangle, trapezium, and so on. The design of CAD software packages is a big subject in itself, deserving a book on its own, and a few have already been written on the subject. I am not covering this subject in this book, and interested readers may obtain a good book on that subject to learn about it.

Add and Modify Actions

This is a very common requirement in most applications. It is especially important in maintenance of master data files. In a hospital management application, patient records, rates for various services and procedures, doctor details, facility details, and so on need this functionality. In a material management application, a material master data file, vendor master data file, warehouse details, and so on need this facility. We can enumerate many occasions like these in various applications, but I am sure you get the idea. In earlier days, we provided a selection of either add, modify, or delete and based on the selection, and we provided the details. For modifying an existing record, we received the input of a key value, displayed the details, then asked for confirmation of the action. Now, this is out of favor. Instead, we search the database using the key value entered as soon as the entry is completed, retrieve the details, and display them. We allow the user to make modifications, then save when the save button is clicked. If there is no existing record, we present a screen with blank controls facilitating entry of new details. For the delete option, of course, we still provide a separate functionality, as deletion is a risky event. But adding a new record and modifying an existing record are combined into one screen and perform the action.

Of course, all modifications need to be recorded in the file used for capturing the audit trail for future purposes. We discussed the audit trail in an earlier chapter.

Record Delete Actions

We need to make a special mention of the delete action. This action has the potential to damage data integrity. For example, take a patient record in a hospital management system. If we delete a patient record for which some services and medical procedures were performed, it will leave billable items that cannot be billed because its main master file record is deleted. In a material management system, if we delete an item detail from its master database table that has been used to receive and issue items and stock is still available, the integrity of data is damaged and the inventory valuation will be erroneous. Therefore, whenever we perform a delete action, it is necessary to perform the following checks to ensure that data integrity is not affected:

1. We need to check if the item is used in any other table in which it is not the primary key.
2. We need to check each of these tables and see if an entry for the item under deletion is present in that table.
3. If the item is present in any of the dependent tables, we need to pass an appropriate message to the user and then cancel the delete action.

If the item is not present in any of the dependent tables, then the data integrity will not be affected. Therefore, we can delete the record from the database table. Now, when I say it can be deleted, I mean it can be logically deleted. We should never delete any record physically from the database in almost any application that is used by multiple people. What we need to do is keep a field in the table definition that indicates the record is deleted. It can be a Boolean field. What we are doing is marking the field as deleted. So, whenever we retrieve records from a table, we retrieve records that are not marked as deleted. This way, we can assist investigation of fraud should it become necessary in the future.

Of course, perhaps it is needless to mention that we need to capture the audit trail record in the relevant audit trail file or database table.

Voice Input

Voice recognition software utilities are coming of age, and it is my opinion that the day is not far when we will all be speaking to computers instead of typing our inputs. This is a future that is close at hand. So, we need to learn how to design voice input.

Voice interaction is of two types:

1. To assist visually challenged people in using our application
2. To facilitate data entry for normal people as well as visually challenged people

To assist visually challenged people, we have to provide the following features in our application:

1. Announce the screen caption when any new form is loaded on the screen.
2. A facility to vocally announce the label attached to the control as well as the tool tip of the control when the cursor hovers on the control. This facility is already in use in some applications.
3. It is not practical for a visually challenged person to hover the cursor accurately on any control. So, we need to announce all the data entry controls one by one,

wait for the individual's response, and capture it. If the response is in error, we need to vocally announce the error and ask the person to restate the entry. Once the entry in a control is successfully completed, we need to move the cursor to the next control and announce it to the user.

4. For the normal person, we need to await the input of the user. The user may simply type or elect to speak out the entry. So, we must provide both options and switch automatically. If the user begins typing, we need to select the typing option, perform data validation actions, and capture the entry.

5. If the technology does not move as fast as I expect it to, we need to capture the user option for the input method of typing or speaking and then implement it.

6. We need to provide routines for checking that a microphone is connected to the computer for input and a speaker is connected to announce messages to the user.

Now, it will be very difficult and time consuming to develop the utility for speech recognition and announcement based on the label/tooltip text. Therefore, we need to include speech recognition software in our application.

Input from Instruments

In real-time systems controlling machines, automobiles, airplanes and rockets, software interacts with instruments, which in turn control the machines. At vital parts, there will be sensors for various parameters like temperature, speed, pressure, and a host of other parameters to capture the data. Now, the data will be in analog form, which needs to be converted to digital form. The machine or instrument will contain a A2D converter, which will convert the captured analog signal and pass it on to the software, either through a port like a USB port or a network line. The receiving port of the computer hardware will have the necessary hardware and software to receive the data, assemble the data bits by stripping the address and other control bits from the data packet received, store it in a buffer, then place an interrupt on the CPU. Here is where our software begins work. It needs to:

1. Receive the data and decipher it for what it is. An instrument generates multiple types of data, such as:

   a. A measured value captured by the instrument.

   b. A control value stating exceptions to the measured value.

   c. A blank value indicating that the instrument could not receive any data to be measured.

   d. A control value that the instrument is not working.

   e. The measured value is usually accompanied by the type of variable, such as temperature, pressure, density, level, and so on depending on the instrument and the situation at hand. So, we must design our software to decipher the value and then translate it into what needs to be programmed and deal with it.

2. Pass it on to its corresponding program and initiate processing it.

3. Generate the result and transmit it to the corresponding port.

4. When data is received from an instrument, a response from the computer is usually needed within a prespecified amount of time in real time. We must design our software to provide such a response within such specified time period.

Now, there is usually one port in most cases. Even if there are multiple ports on the computer receiving data, the number of such receiving ports will be much lower than the number of instruments generating data. But, as the CPU has the capability to process millions of instructions per second, there will be no delay in processing the received data. As data is received from multiple ports, it is usually queued up. The program takes up each data set and processes it. Sometimes, a data set has to be processed on priority. In such cases, the data received from the instruments is prioritized based on the instrument from which it is received. This prioritization is sometimes assigned by the instrument and sometimes by our application software.

In such cases, we need to design the software for handling data queues. We also need to handle the prioritization of waiting queue items.

11

Output Design

Introduction

The whole purpose of developing a software application is to produce the outputs needed by the business. All other software artifacts are developed so it is possible to produce those outputs. The inputs are taken to provide data for the outputs. The master files are maintained for processing the transactions that produce the right information to be included in the outputs. In fact, it is the outputs that are specified in detail by the end users, whereas they may not be able to specify many other things about how to take inputs or what data to be included in the master data. The end users and their management personnel can appreciate only the outputs. The software developers engaged in project development, that is, developing software that will be used only in one organization, know that during the acceptance testing conducted by the end users, the only things that get really tested are the outputs! Therefore, we need to design the outputs with utmost care, as the customer judges our application by the outputs generated by our application.

Not all outputs are the same or similar. There are a variety of outputs to screens, a printer, or another device. Then there are different categories of users, each needing different types of information reports and outputs. Let us now look at the classes of users and the outputs they need.

Classes of Users and the Outputs They Need

Basically, users needing information outputs are classified into:

1. *Internal users*: Those who work as employees of the organization running the software application performing business transactions. Internal users are further classified into

   a. Business transaction processors

   b. Support transaction processors

   c. Managerial users

   d. Senior management users

   e. Application administrators

   f. System administrators

g. Network administrators

h. Database administrators

2. *External users*: Those users who are not employees of the organization running the software application but are users of that application from outside the organization. External users are further classified into:

   a. *Individual users*: These are individuals using our application to get some service from our application. This class is further divided into:

      i. *Casual unregistered users*: These users are visitors to our website and browse the free stuff provided there. Web sites like Yahoo, Microsoft, IBM, and most business organizations get unregistered visitors from all over the globe. They search for information freely available on the site. On a ticket-booking website, these users are allowed to view the schedules and vacant positions for any trip, but will not be allowed to book a ticket unless the user is registered. Sometimes, they may take paper outputs, save the page, or print the information available to a printer or a file. They take onscreen outputs, downloads, and printer outputs to the extent allowed.

      ii. *Registered users, which includes:*

         A. *Registered paying users*: Many websites allow customer registration with payment as an option. Paying customers get access to premium services provided by the application. Email providers allow a larger file size for attachments, more methods of emailing, more storage space, freedom from advertising, and so on. Information-providing sites make more content available to view and download. Dating sites allow paying customers to get the contact details of desired profiles, and so on. They need some outputs for which they have paid and have the right to demand accuracy, privacy, ease of use, and other facilities.

         B. *Registered nonpaying users*: Many websites allow customers to register and utilize some of the facilities available on the site. For example, free registered users on dating sites are allowed to browse profiles, but contact details of the displayed profiles are not made available. On such sites, the site prompts the user to become a paying member whenever the user tries to get access to the suppressed information. They need outputs slightly different from the paying users, with a reduced set of information.

   b. *Organizational users*: When our application is not restricted to internal use, we will have external organizational users. For example, a credit card application has merchant organizations. There are bankers through whom we receive and pay money to our customers. In a ticket-booking scenario, there are travel agents and tour operators. There could be airlines if our application facilitates booking of tickets from different airlines. In this manner, there are organizational users whose requirements for outputs are different from those of individual users. We have to design appropriate outputs for them.

   c. *Service provider organizational users*: In applications such as marketplaces providing a platform, such as eBay, for sellers and buyers to get together to transact business, there are many service provider organizations or individuals who sell goods or services on the application. In a material management application, there are vendors supplying goods for our organization and the finance department of our organization making payments against supplies received, sanctioning funds for placing purchase orders, and so on. Their requirements for outputs are unique to suit their specific purposes.

d. *Domestic users*: These are from within our country where the requirements for outputs are more or less homogenous, as the rules and regulations are uniform except for minor differences between different states.

e. *International users*: International users are from different countries. Their requirements are not homogenous. Their requirements depend on the rules and regulations of their countries.

f. *Statutory authorities*: These users can be from our country or from other countries. Their requirements are different based on the set of rules and regulations they need to conform to.

Now, the requirements of internal users can be elicited, gathered, and established more easily, comprehensively, and accurately, as the users are available within our organization. But when it comes to external users, it is not easy to establish the requirements comprehensively and accurately, as the users are outside our organization. It is difficult to reach most of them. We can elicit and gather requirements only from a sample set of external users. We have to really brainstorm the requirements based on the sample requirements collected and extrapolate the requirements to design the outputs provided to those external users. The work of designing the outputs for the external users rests on the shoulders of the software designers.

Now, let us discuss the outputs that need to be designed for internal users. We have classified the internal user in the preceding section, and let us discuss what kind of outputs each class of the users needs.

1. *Business transaction processors*: These users are the first level of application users, and they enter most of the data into the application and take out some outputs. Usually, these people face the customers or perform roles that perform the activities that process business transactions that bring in the revenue or cause expenditure to the organization. They take some paper outputs, such as receipts, acknowledgments, lists of transactions processed by them, details of each transaction, and so on They may also transmit information to their superiors or to other users, internal, external, and so on.

2. *Support transaction processors*: These are similar to business transaction processors, except that the transactions they process do not generate revenue but may cause expenditure. For example, a help desk for other users of the application captures information about trouble tickets and a purchase department receives material procurement requests and generates purchase orders; administration department, HR department, and maintenance department users are also examples of support transaction processors. They also generate some hardcopy outputs and transmit information to other users of the application.

3. *Managerial users*: These users usually do not process any transactions but view details of transactions, take summary reports from the data, perform some statistical analysis, generate exception reports, give instructions to the transaction processors, and transmit information to other users of the application.

4. *Senior management users*: These users are similar to managerial users, except that they filter the information further and take out exception and summary reports. They also transmit information as well as passing on instructions to the transaction processors.

5. *Application administrators*: These people perform administrative functions of the application such as adding users, modifying the access rights of users, deleting users, upgrading the application, adding master data, modifying master data, managing the application change/maintenance requests, performing backup and restore functions, and so on. They need a few hardcopy outputs as well as the facility to transmit information to other users or the software maintenance team.

6. *System administrators*: These people maintain the hardware and the system software of the machines used by the internal users of the application. Strictly speaking, these people are not users of the application. But their needs have to be kept in mind if our application is the system software. In such cases, we need to provide facilities in the software to give necessary troubleshooting information to this class of users. Therefore, we need to design security-related information such as audit trails so they can trace, track, and arrest those responsible for security leaks if any.

7. *Network administrators*: This class of users is also outside the application unless we are designing network management software. In such cases, we need to provide information such as network downtime, exceptions in the network speed, intruder information, and so on.

8. *Database administrators*: These people are also not users of the application. They maintain the database, take periodic backups and perform restores as and when necessary, upgrade the database software, and troubleshoot user problems related to the database. But hackers could attack the database to steal information, and we need to provide exception reports on database usage to these people so they can protect the integrity of the application data.

Now, having understood the users needing reports from our application, let us now discuss the outputs designed by us to facilitate efficient, effective, secure, and safe use of our application.

Types of Outputs

We can classify the outputs into the following classes based on the device they are sent to.

1. Softcopy outputs
   a.   Outputs to the screen
   b.   Outputs to a file
   c.   Outputs onto a network
   d.   Outputs to a machine
2. Hardcopy outputs
   a.   To a printer
   b.   To a plotter

3. Electronic outputs
   a. To the Internet
   b. To a machine

Now, let us discuss the design aspects of each of these outputs.

Softcopy Outputs to Screen

Outputs to a screen must adhere to these principles common to all types of screen outputs.

1. The output must fit the screen. As far as possible, we must avoid the need to scroll the screen either in the horizontal or vertical direction. If we need to scroll, it must be because no other alternative is available. The screen size of the output is different for a mobile phone and for a laptop screen. We have to design the output screen so that it fits the screen available on the target hardware.

2. If our output spans multiple screens, we need to provide a facility to navigate between the screens. Now, the present practice is to provide the facilities to navigate to the next and previous screens as well as the first and last screens. If the number of screens is too high, it is a better practice to provide the page numbers to navigate to. Some applications provide multiple page numbers and some provide a combo box with numbers. My preference is the combo box method of providing a facility to select the page number the user wishes to navigate to.

3. Each line of the output must fit one line. It should not spill over to the next line. It will be an eyesore if the output spills over.

4. If scrolling becomes unavoidable owing to the nature of the data, I suggest letting the screen scroll horizontally rather than vertically.

5. The size of the font should not be less than 8 points. If the target user is expected to be below the age of 45, we can comfortably use 8-point fonts. But if we are targeting our application for users above 45 years of age, we need to use larger fonts of 10 to 12 points. If we are targeting users of all ages, then we need to provide a facility to increase the font size by the user.

6. Contrast and brightness are usually controlled by the hardware. But the colors are controlled by the software designer. To achieve better contrast, we need to use contrasting colors for the background and the font. In the color spectrum (imagine a circle divided into seven segments with each segment representing a color of the rainbow [vibgyor—violet, indigo, blue, green, yellow, orange, and red]. The colors in the adjacent segments have less contrast. The contrast between colors increases as the distance between the segments increases. For example, violet has better contrast with green and yellow than with indigo, blue, red, or orange. Again, there are many shades in each of these colors. So, we need to experiment with colors and provide adequate contrast between the background and font colors so that the user does not have difficulty reading the output on the screen. We can also take advantage of the research carried out by large software developers like IBM, Microsoft, Apple, and Adobe; take cues from their applications; and use them in our application.

7. In tabular reports, we need to ensure that the column headings reflect the data that comes under them. Again, if the output spans multiple screens, each screen must have column headings, page headings, and page footers.

8. When we display bills, receipts, or results of computations on the screen, we need to ensure that the numbers are right or decimal point justified and textual matter is left justified.

9. It is a best practice to provide a facility to print the contents of the screen by providing a button to be clicked in case the user desires to print the output. Similarly, we need to provide a facility to save the information displayed on the screen to a file. We can merge these two facilities into a save facility, and the user can always print the saved file.

10. When we design outputs, especially in the case of large data that spans multiple screens, pages directed at a screen, or a file, we need to design control statistics to be included in the output. Control statistics are those numbers that assist the user in understanding and assessing if the processing was accurate. For example, the number of records processed and the number of records selected for inclusion in the output give the user an idea of how much information was culled from the total information. It also tells the user if all the available records were indeed processed. Usually, the user knows the total number of records in the selected database table or tables. Similarly, the page totals and the grand total will help the user know if the grand total was correct. We need to assess what control statistics are needed by the user to determine the accuracy of processing before the output is delivered. We need to place these control statistics on the last screen or page of the file so the user can print that one page and use it in his or her evaluation of the accuracy of the processing.

While designing outputs to computer screens, we need to keep in mind that they come in various sizes and resolutions. While it is true that browsers handle the display of the output and adjust it to accommodate the designed screen, it becomes difficult when we design for a larger screen and the available screen is smaller, for example, if we designed the output for a computer screen and the user is using a tablet. Of course, the tablet browser adjusts the display to suit the hardware, but it may cause problems occasionally. If we have to let the browser adjust the display, we should refrain from specifying the size of the font and pictures. Then, the browser and hardware take care of adjusting the display to suit the hardware.

Softcopy Outputs to a File

When the output is very large and consists of hundreds of lines of information, it becomes very tedious to view the information on the screen by scrolling umpteen times. In such cases, it is better to send the output to a file so that the user can use software specifically aimed at displaying information, such as a PDF reader or MS Word.

In this case, too, we have to design the output just the way we design screen output. We have to place the column headings, page headings, and page footers with equal diligence. But here, we have to note that a browser has a default font and adjusts the display to fit the screen on the hardware. So, we do not specify the font when directing the output to a screen. But when we directly send the output to a print file, we need to specify the font and picture sizes. We also need to specify the page breaks, page headings, column headings, and page footers. As a best practice, we need to include the page number either at the top or bottom of the page.

But how do we send information into a file? It is easy to create text files programmatically, as most development platforms provide for handling text files. Most development platforms also provide a facility to send information to database tables; therefore, it is easy for programmers to direct information to database tables. But if we need to send information to files of type PDF or .doc, we need to have a software tool that can be called by our programs to format our data to suit the target file type. We need to evaluate the available tool and specify it for use by the programmers. Alternatively, we can use a report writer tool and direct the output to it. Most report writers have a facility to direct the output either to a printer or a file, and they usually have facility to save the output in various popular file types. But, that way, we push the onus of saving onto the user. Some users may not like it.

Softcopy Outputs onto a Network

Oftentimes, we need to transmit the output of our processing to a destination over the Internet or a private network. Examples that readily spring to mind are billing for various services such as medical billing, various payments from a bank or insurance company, and order information to a supplier from marketplace websites such as eBay. Most development platforms provide facilities to transmit information over the Internet, and we can design our application around those facilities. It is enough if we specify the network as the Internet, and the programmers can take over from there and implement the protocols in the programs. But when the network is a private network, we have to specify the protocols used by the receiving network. Usually, these protocols are available publicly or are made available by those organizations either freely or for a fee. We need to obtain the specifications and specify them in our design.

When we transmit information over networks, we need to decide if we wish to encrypt the data or not. Encryption is a set of methodologies to transform the information using some methodology and decrypt it back to its original form at the receiver's end reversing the methodology we used initially to encrypt the data.

Softcopy Outputs to a Machine

Outputs to a machine are for the purpose of driving the machine. Many machines are software driven in the present day, and the number is going to increase in the days to come. The machine may be a part of our network. When it is so, we follow the protocols of the network. In most cases, though, the machine is connected to a port on the computer system. In such cases, we need to implement the communication protocol, such as IEEE 803.1, on the machine. The design of such output is not just formatting the output as necessary for the system but also implementing the protocol. The manufacturer of the machine usually gives a driver software utility for the machine, and we may just need to utilize that. If such a driver is not supplied, we may have to design and develop such a utility and use it in our programs.

Now, let us take a look at designing hardcopy outputs.

Hardcopy Outputs

Until recently, hardcopy outputs meant output onto paper, but not anymore! Now we have 3D printers, which produce solid three-dimensional objects. Considering the outputs onto paper, there are two classes of paper: plain stationery and preprinted stationery. Outputs on paper include:

1. Bulk output on plain paper such as tabular listings of large volumes of data

2. Low-volume output on plain paper such as test reports, transaction reports, receipts, tickets for travel, movies, operas, and so on

3. Bulk output on preprinted stationery such as certificates of various types, checks, receipts, acknowledgments, and so on

Plain stationery comes in a variety of sizes, but the main differentiating factor is whether the paper has perforations on both of its vertical edges. These perforations are used for mounting the stationery on printers such as line printers. This type of stationery moves precisely and enables locating the printing at precisely specified positions. Such stationery is referred to as continuous stationery. Stationery without any perforations on its vertical edges is referred to as sheet stationery. Continuous stationery is usually used for bulk printing, although it can also be used in low-volume printing, too. Continuous stationery usually comes in two sizes based on its width. It usually comes in widths of 15 × 11 inches and 9.5 × 11 inches, but we can order custom widths based on our requirements. Sheet stationery comes in various sizes, such as letter, legal, A4, A3, A2, A1, A0, and so on. We usually use letter, legal and A4 size papers on sheet printers. We use A4, A3, A2, A1, and A0 on plotters to generate engineering drawings. The area of A0 is 1 square meter, A1 is half a square meter, A2 is one-fourth of a square meter, A3 is one-eighth of a square meter, and A4 is one-sixteenth of a square meter.

In some cases, the size of the stationery is given to us, and in some cases, we may have to determine the size of the stationery. In the first case, we need to fit our output to the given size of paper, and in the second case, we need to select the paper size to suit our output. When we need to determine the paper size, we need to consider these aspects:

1. The selected paper needs to accommodate all our data, preferably in one sheet.

2. The specified paper size, as far as possible, needs to be a size that is available off the shelf in the market, as it will cost us the least as well as minimizing our procurement effort. If the data in our output overshoots the standard sizes of the paper, then we need to consider ways of reducing the space requirement for our data by reducing the font size or reducing the margins. We should not specify another sheet of paper just to accommodate a couple of lines.

3. In the case of preprinted stationery, the stationery may exist in some cases. In some cases, we may have to design the stationery. While designing preprinted stationery, we have to keep in mind these aspects:

    a. The spacing between the lines needs to be the same as that on the printer.

    b. The blanks left on the stationery should be adequate to accommodate the full size of the data item to be accommodated in that space.

    c. The font sizes selected need to be visible and easily readable.

    d. The color contrast between the font and its background should be distinct such that the characters are clearly readable.

We send the following outputs onto paper:

1. *Listings on plain stationery*: Tabular listings of data of various types used in organizations. When we are generating listings, which are usually in tabular form, we need to ensure that the column headings and the data that comes underneath those headings are aligned. In this alignment, the textual matter needs to be left justified, and the numerical data is right justified in such a way that the decimal point, if used, is aligned vertically. Here, we need to provide control statistics in our design, as they assist data-processing executives in ensuring the accuracy and completeness of the processing. Control statistics include:

    a. Page totals of numeric data

    b. Counts of records processed, records excluded, and records included

    c. If the report is divided into sections, section totals and section counts

    d. Grand totals and grand counts for the entire report

2. *Low-volume output on plain stationery*: Many organizations use plain stationery to produce low-volume outputs such as receipts, certificates, orders, tickets, and so on. This is useful when the customer-facing workstation produces different outputs depending on the needs of the customer at the workstation. This alleviates the need to mount different preprinted stationery every time a different customer comes to the workstation. In such cases, the stationery usually has the company logo and header and footer with company information. While designing such outputs, we need to keep in mind the usable area on the stationery and fit our output in that space. We also need to specify the size of the paper to minimize the cost. However, while so specifying, we need to use standard sizes available off the shelf in the market, as it is cheaper than custom-produced paper even if smaller in size. What information to be included in these outputs depends on the situation at hand, but we need to include some sort of control information to ensure that the processing is accurate and complete.

3. *High-volume outputs on preprinted stationery*: These may include certificates in bulk, receipts, and orders of various types. In most cases, the size of the stationery is provided by the user organization. In a few cases, we may have to design the output and then determine the size of the stationery that can accommodate the data included in our output. We need to ensure that our design aligns our data perfectly with the preprinted matter. In this case, we need to specify the vertical spacing in number of lines and the horizontal spacing in number of characters.

We also have to define the font size, as a change in font size can skew the appearance and alignment. The font size needs to be same as the font size already existing on the preprinted stationery. Sometimes, it may be necessary to specify different font sizes for different lines to align with the fonts on the preprinted stationery.

4. *Drawings and engineering drawings*: Drawings can refer to any graphic, including engineering drawings and any pictures, but it generally refers to engineering drawings. While ink-jet printers and laser printers are capable of producing small drawings of size A4 and in some cases A3, the results obtained on these printers are not of high quality. For engineering drawing outputs, plotters are used. Plotters use ink pens to draw the lines on a drawing sheet, which can be plain paper of 70 grams per square meter (GSM), tracing paper, Mylar (polyester film), or any other type of medium used in producing engineering drawings. A variety of plotters of different sizes are available and are used. A special kind of plotter referred to as a photo plotter is used to produce photo negatives/positives, especially in the production of printed circuit boards in the electronics manufacturing industry. Photo plotters are also used in the medical field for producing a hardcopy of X-ray results. Usually, the plotter manufacturers supply a driver software utility for their hardware and we call that utility in our programs to send our outputs on to the selected plotter.

Design of Outputs

The design of outputs has two components, namely the formatting of the output and obtaining the data to be included in the output. Formatting the output is easier, and we need to focus on getting the right data for output. So first, let us discuss how we get the data that is needed for the output.

The Source of the Data

The data for the outputs is in three places:

1. In the database tables of the application: most of the data required to generate the output is resident in the tables of the database of the application
2. On websites
3. In the user

Let us discuss each of the classes of data.

Data from the tables of the database: We are presently using an RDBMS in which we can relate a table to another table based on a field that is present in both the tables and treat them as one table to extract the required data. Now, in this relation, we may include all the fields present in both the tables, in which case the relation is called a join. Alternatively, we may select a few fields from each of the tables, in which case the relation is referred to as a view. In some cases, this kind of relation is referred to as logical files. Logical files or views can be treated as tables in themselves, at least for the purposes of extracting data for inclusion in the outputs. The advantage of using views or logical files is that the data is produced on the fly. In multiuser environments, when multiple users may be generating the same outputs concurrently, using physical files or tables may create deadlock scenarios and give rise to concurrency control problems at execution time. I would suggest that, as a designer, you need to be thorough in regard to database technology, especially about forming views (or generating logical files) and how to generate the required data accurately and comprehensively.

It has been my experience that when we try to relate three tables into one view, the results are unpredictable. The exception is when one of the tables is an interface table. Just to remind you, an interface table is one that has only the key values of two tables containing data. When the results are unpredictable, it has serious consequences for the organization, which may include court cases involving huge sums to be paid as damages. So, when a necessity arises for extracting data from more than two tables, I suggest using views and relating them to one another. That is, let one view contain the data from two tables and another view have the data from two tables and then relate those two views. One precaution we need to take is that both these views need to have a common field based on which a new relation can be formed.

Another mechanism provided by DBMS software packages is stored procedures, triggers, or queries. They are basically programs written in PL/SQL that are embedded in the database. They work more efficiently than the routines we develop on our development platform. I would like to go out on a limb and say that we should never write routines in programming languages to extract data from database tables; instead, we should call these PL/SQL routines to extract data from database tables.

I have seen the practice of using report tables. A report table is a physical table that is cleared and filled in at the time of generating a report. In single-user applications, this works very well. But in multiuser applications, it can be disastrous. Assume two users are generating the same report simultaneously. The first user clears the table and begins filling the required data, and the second user comes in and clears the table and begins filling in his/her own data! What could happen? If the application places a lock on the table when the first user begins generation of the report, the second user gets into an error situation. If the application uses only record-level locking, then the data in the table is a mix of data from both users, giving unpredictable results. So, it is better to avoid the practice of using report tables in our multiuser applications. But situations may occur when we have to make use of a report table. In such cases, I suggest placing a security lock over the report. What I mean by this is: give authority of generating this report only to an application administrator. An application will have only one administrator, and when he/she generates the report, no one else is generating the report; therefore, the data integrity of the generated report is assured.

Summarizing the above discussion, we note the following on ensuring integrity of data in the outputs:

1. It is better to use views or logical files while generating reports than to join tables on the fly while generating outputs.

2. When data has to be extracted from more than two tables, it is better to form views and then relate the views.

3. The practice of using report tables should be resorted to only in extreme cases when the number of tables from which data is to be extracted is too large and forming views does not produce predictable results. In such cases, we need to restrict access to the report and provide access only to the administrator of the application so that no two agencies generate the report concurrently.

Formatting the output: We generate outputs either as softcopy or hardcopy. Softcopy may go into a file, onto a screen, to a network, or to a device. Hardcopy output is directed to a printer or a plotter. Formatting of data to a network and a device follows the protocol specific to the network or the device. We have to design such outputs adhering to the programming guides of those devices or networks.

We reproduce the drawing on a plotter. The user formats the output on the screen. Then, when the user saves the drawing to a file, all the formatting is stored along with the data. For storing data of engineering drawings, there are specific formats used across the CAD industry to facilitate exchange of information across different CAD software packages and plotters. These basically consist of the X and Y coordinates and the type of the drawing element such as line, circle, arc, chamfering, and hatching with attributes like the angle of the line and length, radius of the circle, type of arc, radius, angle of the arc, and so on. When sending the output to a plotter, we call the device driver utility supplied, call its routines, and supply our drawing element data. The device driver utility drives the plotter and produces the desired drawing, adhering to the formatting information input by the user while preparing the drawings on the screen.

Now, the outputs of data to a file, screen, or printer need us to focus on properly formatting the data.

Using preprinted stationery: We have to ensure the following in our designs:

1. We should fit the data in the space provided. If the data is longer than the space provided, we need to either reduce the font size if it is larger than 8 points or wrap the text to the next line if space is available. If neither option is available, we may truncate the text: suffix a superscripted number and print the truncated text at the bottom of the page, suffixing the superscripted number. We can also allow our text to run below preprinted text rather than restricting it to the space provided opposite the preprinted text. It is a bad design practice to let the text run over the preprinted matter and will render the generated text unreadable.

2. We need to ensure that the generated text appears on the same line as the preprinted prompting text. Of course, it can be slightly above or below and ought to be less than the size of the font used in the preprinted prompting text. We need to ensure that this is adhered to in all prompted places.

3. The font of the generated text ought to be the same size as in the preprinted text, or just one size above or below the font used in the preprinted text. Unless there are special reasons, we should not deviate from this practice.

Using plain stationery: We need to ensure the following guidelines while designing outputs onto plain stationery:

1. We should leave a margin on all four sides, especially on sheet stationery. Continuous stationery with perforated edges provides for margins on all sides on its own without giving us any problems, but sheet stationery requires us to provide

the margins. We usually leave a margin of 1 inch on all sides. The margin should be half an inch at the minimum. When we need to shrink the margin, we should first shrink the vertical margins. Then, if necessary, we should shrink the right margin. The left margin is usually used for punching holes and filing the paper in a file. So, if we shrink the left margin, information may be lost. If the left margin is 1 inch, then even after filing, the information can be read without taking the paper out of the file.

2. We usually use page headings in voluminous outputs. Should we provide page headings on all pages? We usually include the name of the organization; the name of the division, if any; and the name of the report. The name of the company specifies the owner holding the legal rights to the report. But most organizations preprint the company logo and sometimes the name of the organization in a corner of the stationery or as a watermark. When such preprinted information is present on the stationery, we may avoid the name of the organization in the page heading. It is a better practice to provide the report name or description on each page as page headings. I would suggest printing the name of the organization on every page if we are using plain continuous stationery. We may avoid the name of the organization if the stationery has the name of the organization in some form on the stationery.

3. We need to ensure the following aspects while placing column headings on the stationery:

   a. We need to provide column headings and replicate them on all pages. Of course, we lose a minimum of four lines of data space, but we need to provide the headings, as it will be easier for the users to decipher the data presented in the columns.

   b. Sometimes we may have to place multiple data items in the same column because we do not have horizontal space to provide a different column for each of the data items in the output. When we do so, we need to hammock related data items into one column. For example, we can safely place name and address details in one column. But when we place multiple data items in one column, our column heading must make it explicit for the user without any ambiguity about what is contained in the column. I would suggest placing one header detail per line. In the case of the name and address being placed in one column, I suggest placing "Name" on one line and "Address" on the next line just below the "Name." Those two header details must be left justified.

   c. We usually place one data item per column, but the length of the data item can be longer than the space provided for it. In such cases, if we can wrap the text around to the next line within the same columns, then we may do it. It is possible if the data item consists of multiple words. If that is not the case, we may reduce the font size. It is better if we can reduce the font size for all columns in the output, but we can also reduce the font size for just one column programmatically. By reducing the font size of all data in the output, we achieve uniformity in the output. But the question is: Why should we reduce the font size of all data when just one column has the problem, as it would burden people with poorer eyesight? Of course, from the programmer's standpoint, reducing the font size of all data is easier and reducing the font size of just one column places a little extra overhead on the programmer. This is one of the decisions you, the designer of software, need to make based on the situation at hand. Let me also aver here that we designers are prone to making design decisions from the programmer's standpoint, as most of us have risen from the programmer ranks. But we should always base our design decisions on improving the user experience.

d. In tabular outputs, we need to place the page totals of columns with significant numeric data at the bottom of each page. By significant numeric data, I exclude numeric data like serial numbers, record numbers, identification numbers, and so on.

e. Running totals are totals of all the records delivered on the output up to that point. Sometimes these are demanded by the users to verify the accuracy of the processing. They help the users when they detect an error in the grand totals at the end of the output. They help users find out which page has the error. Running totals on the first page are the same as the page total. From the second page onward, they are the sum of the previous running total plus the total on the current page. I do not advocate using a running total in every output, as it would eat three to five lines of the page space and increase the number of sheets in the output. But if the users demand it, we need to provide it to them.

f. Grand totals are the sum of all significant numeric data of the entire report: These help in ensuring that the output is accurate. We print this as part of the control statistics on a separate page at the end of the output.

4. *Control statistics*: Control statistics help the users in ensuring that the processing has been accurate. They include information such as:

a. *Total number of records processed*: In this count, we take into consideration only the main table and not subsidiary tables. For example, when we generate a funds requirement output based on the purchase orders placed, we take into consideration the number of purchase orders processed. Of course, this takes data from other tables such as material master, vendor master, purchase order item table, and so on. We count the number of purchase orders processed but not the number of items in the purchase orders.

b. *Total number of records included*: This is the count of all records that are included in the output as they meet the filtration criteria set for the output. Again, this is the count from the main table and not from the subsidiary tables.

c. *Total number of records excluded*: This is the count of records not included in the report. It is the count of records filtered out by the criteria set for the output. One practice of programmers is just to subtract the number of records included from the total number of records processed and give out this number. I must say this is a bad practice. Programmers do this to avoid a little more coding as well as to get the right answers. But the very purpose of this count is to help users in ensuring the accuracy of processing. As designers, we must insist that a separate variable be declared and counted inside the processing loop.

Processing to generate output: Of course, we just extract information from the database tables and send it to the output in some cases, but mostly we perform some sort of processing on the retrieved data before we produce the report. The minimum processing that we perform is to filter out the data based on some criteria selected by the user to generate the output.

We need to carefully design the processing portion of output generation, as the heart of any computer-based system is the processing. The computer has the ability to accurately and diligently process large volumes of data. But the quality of the outputs depends on how well we design the systems. We need to ensure the following aspects:

1. In most cases, we filter the data using some criteria selected by the user. Of course, we build in the choices a user can select. When we use one relational expression, the results are very predictable; when we use one logical expression involving two relational expressions, it is still simple; when we use two logical expressions, it is a bit difficult but still manageable. When we use three or more logical expressions, we need to be very careful. We cannot leave it to the programmer to achieve accurate results. It is better that we write out such filters and give them to the programmer to use. Of course, such occasions are not frequent.

2. Arithmetic expressions help us compute the results using mathematical formulas. One of the most common problems in arithmetic expressions is the denominator in a division expression becoming zero. Therefore, we need to specify verifying the denominator before division is performed. You may say that this is a standard programming practice, so should a designer be concerned with it? In most professional organizations, there are programming standards that mention this rule. But I have also seen some professional organizations whose programming standards talk only about naming conventions and code formatting. As designers, we need to ensure that the finer aspects of software development are mentioned in standards or in the product design.

3. In some cases, we need to convert long mathematical formulas into arithmetic expressions. Human brains can understand complex things, but computers do not. Computers follow rules more diligently than human beings. Therefore, we need to use parentheses wherever there is a possibility of misinterpreting the expression. We should use parentheses liberally. As a rule, I would say use parentheses to delineate variables wherever the addition and subtraction operators are next to division or multiplication signs. But nesting too many parentheses would again be very difficult to debug. How many is too many? I would say, up to three parentheses are acceptable, beyond which I would disapprove of nesting parentheses. Of course, exceptions exist everywhere. So, unless there are compelling reasons, we ought to restrict nesting of parentheses to three. Another aspect of writing long arithmetic expressions is that it becomes very difficult to debug when the result is wrong. We can place a break point in the debugger after a statement, but not within a statement. With a long arithmetic expression, we cannot see intermediate results while debugging a program. So, we ought to break up the long arithmetic statement into multiple shorter statements so that we can place breakpoints after each statement, see the intermediate results, and pinpoint the statement that is causing errors in the result. There is another aspect we need to know as to why we need to write shorter expressions. Development platforms mostly use stack operations to resolve arithmetic expressions. The longer the expression, the bigger the stack needs to be. Stack operations are also a program, and we would never know how big a stack is or how well programmed the stack operations are. We had better come to grips with the fact that quality assurance is poor in the software development industry, which includes system software developers, too. I am sure that the programs are tested with minimal data. Therefore, writing shorter

expressions ensures that the results are accurate. How long is a long arithmetic expression? I offer the following guidelines:

a. When nesting of parentheses needs more than three sets of parentheses.

b. When the number of arithmetic operators in the expression goes beyond six and we use a mix of addition, subtracting, multiplication, division, square, square root, and so on. If we use mostly addition, subtraction, and one or two multiplication or division operators in the expression, we can perhaps use more than six operators. The idea is to minimize complexity in the expression.

c. Do not allow the value of a division operator to be generated within the expression. In such cases, break the expression into two, with the first one generating the value for the division operator, then ensure that the denominator is not zero, and then have the expression using that value for division operation.

d. With the capability of using long variable names, even though the expression has fewer operators, the statement may become longer, and we may need to scroll the screen to read it fully. In such cases, break the expression such that each statement containing the expression can be read on the screen without needing to scroll the screen horizontally.

e. One common problem is the precision of the result. Division can produce fractional numbers with too many digits after the decimal point. In many cases, we need to round off the result to a certain number of digits after the decimal point. If we apply the rounding-off operation in every arithmetic expression, the final result can be erroneous. Therefore, we should not use the rounding-off operation in the intermediate results. If rounding off is required, we need to use it only on the final result that goes into the output.

f. Similarly, multiplication can produce numbers larger than the size of the holding variable, especially when both variables used in the multiplication are generated in an arithmetic expression, either the present one or the previous one. Not all developmental platforms point out size errors. In most cases, if the size of the receiving variable is smaller than the number coming into it, the significant digits on the left side of the number are truncated. Therefore, we need to build mechanisms in our designs to detect size errors in multiplication operations.

We have to design the processing necessary so that it is efficient and takes the least possible amount of time to generate the output.

Report Generation Tools

In the present day, to extract information from database tables and present it on screen or on paper, the usage of report generation tools has become commonplace. These tools eliminate our effort in formatting the report by counting the number of characters and testing our output. They provide tools to get that what-you-see-is-what-you-get (WYSIWYG) output. But I have found that their capability to extract data comprehensively when we set a relation between three or more tables is not very reliable. Of course, tool developers improve their tools continuously, and by the time you read this book, they might have eliminated this defect. But it is a better practice to make use of views or logical files when using report generation tools for outputs that need data from three or more tables.

Therefore, when you use report generation tools to extract and present your output, I would suggest that you make use of the views or logical files designed earlier.

I have often heard in the software development industry that the user has not stated "this" or "that" as a requirement and that is the reason the output is not designed or not included or in "that" shape/form. In the blame game that is played out when something goes in an unexpected manner, the designers often blame the business analyst for not defining the requirements accurately/comprehensively/unambiguously. But the software designers have the onus of getting out the right product free from all design defects. Before we embark on designing any artifact, we need to ensure that its requirements are well defined. We need to look at the requirements not just from the standpoint of understanding them but also critically, so critically that we assess them more stringently than a quality assurance person! We have to uncover any shortfalls and bridge the shortfalls either on our own in most cases or by approaching a person knowledgeable in that area. When we design something, it must be as foolproof as humanly possible.

Final Words

All in all, the output ought to be:

1. Appropriate for the class of the users.
2. Appropriate for the type of output.
3. When generating bulky outputs, we need to include control statistics to enable the users to assess the comprehensiveness of selecting the records.
4. The output must be suitable for the medium receiving the output and formatted as necessary for the medium and the user receiving it.
5. We need to use right methodology to filter and extract all the necessary records to generate a comprehensive and accurate output.
6. When we use tools to generate the outputs, we should ensure that those tools are generating accurate and comprehensive outputs.

12

Code Design

Introduction

"What is there in code to design? It just needs to be written!" say many software developers. Even today, talk of software design is often met with snide remarks, sarcasm, and skepticism. If there exists such a skepticism about the topic of software design, what is there to talk about in code design? I can confidently assert that the most neglected activity in software development is the activity of software design. It is more or less delegated to the programmer or graphics designer. More time is spent on ensuring the screen design is aesthetically appealing than ensuring that the product is efficient, effective, defect free, and reliable.

True. Many process-oriented organizations whose software development projects lead to a software product are consciously looking at software design and code design. Many ills of software projects could be cured and failures greatly reduced by focusing on software and code design. The amount of money spent of software maintenance is phenomenal, and most of it can be saved by correct software and code design.

When people prepare engineering drawings in either the construction or manufacturing industry, they follow one cardinal rule: a detail is depicted at one and only one place in the set of drawings pertaining to a project. No detail can be duplicated. This is one principle the software industry has been aiming to emulate for a long time but has not yet completely achieved so far. Code components, functions, code libraries whether static or dynamic, component programming, and object-oriented programming are steps in that direction. Currently, we have the tools to emulate that cardinal principle that is standard practice in engineering drawings in our software development work. But we have not been able to achieve it in software development because we are not focusing enough on the design activity of software development.

We in the software development industry have been reluctant to take the best practices developed in other fields like the construction or manufacturing industry, and we happily continue to be so. This reluctance stems mainly from the fact that computer science is still embedded in the mathematics department rather than being an independent computer/software engineering department at universities.

In this chapter, I wish to discuss what I mean by code design and how to go about doing it. Let me confess right up front that most organizations do not practice all these aspects, but most organizations practice some of these aspects to some extent in their projects.

What Is Code Design?

Unless we define code design coherently, we can never understand it. So, allow me to define code design here.

Code design in the software development field is conceptualizing, engineering, and recording the design of code components so that the resultant code works effectively, delivering the expected results, the code utilizes the system resources optimally, the code produces the expected results in real time, the code is easily maintainable with as little effort as essential, and the necessity to modify code in the code components is minimal.

Let us take a detailed look at this definition. First, let us understand the key terms used in this definition.

Conceptualizing: This includes foreseeing what code components need to be coded to achieve the functionality specified for the proposed product. We work top-down beginning with the overall product functionality, then break the product functionality one level down to the module level, then break the module functionality to the submodule level, and we continue moving downward until we reach the bottom and no further breakdown is possible. Then, all the functionality that cannot further be broken down is the functionality we need to code. As we move up from this level, we will need to develop code to integrate the functionality of the components in the level below the integration level. In this manner, we move up from the bottom and determine the integration code components we need to develop. This activity of determining the functionality for each of the code components is conceptualizing the code design of software products.

We design each of the code components down to its minutest level such that each code component achieves the functionality specified for it after developing the code. Then, we need to understand that engineering does not involve just achieving functionality "somehow, either by hook or by crook." Engineering demands achieving functionality in an optimal manner, achieving the needs of efficiency, effectiveness, maintainability, flexibility, reliability, and response time. All these must be possible with the technology available to us. We cannot engineer a component with the technology available at a remote corner of the earth to which we do not have access. Then again, engineering frowns on duplicating effort. That is, we should not develop code for a specific functionality at more than one place in the product. We should develop it once and call it from other places when it is needed. Therefore, we need to foresee the code components that will be needed at more than one place in the product. This can be accomplished by understanding the functionality of the proposed product and then consolidating the functions that are required more than once in the product. For example, the function of checking if the current user is logged in is needed whenever a new form is loaded in the browser. Similarly, we need to foresee what functions will be needed by the functionality specified for the proposed software product. Then, we engineer each of the code components and record it in such a way that developing the code does not require the programmer to use imagination and develop the code quickly. When we engineer the product well, then the integration of the components into submodules, then submodules into modules, and, finally, modules into the software product works without a hitch, smoothly and without errors. That is engineering. Proper engineering reduces the effort spent on quality control and assurance of the product to the minimum and restricts it to confirming that the product is working as specified. When defects are uncovered in the integrated product, engineering should be embarrassed, not the programmers.

Recording: Recording refers to capturing the details of the result of the conceptualization and engineering that was carried out so that others can understand and implement the design to realize the product without any necessity of handholding by the designer. There are many methodologies being used across the software development industry. These methodologies began with SSADM in the late 1960s and include object oriented methodologies (OOMs), UML, P-Language, and the latest fad, agile methodology, which itself is a composite of many methodologies. Each has its die-hard adherents and critics. I would dare say that these methodologies have not truly served their purpose. They cannot be passed on to others less educated than the designer for implementation. Therefore, the roles of the designer and the programmer were rolled into one, which resulted in neglecting the design aspect. Often, people jump into coding without spending an adequate amount of time on design. Other productive endeavors rely on engineering drawings that enable the separation of the implementer role from that of the designer. Most software developers confuse drawings with architectural drawings used in building construction or workshop drawings used in fabrication and manufacturing. The reality is not so. I will deal with this aspect in a separate chapter in which I will introduce the real use of drawings. Whatever methodology you select, the results of your engineering need to be recorded, if not for passing on to someone else for implementation, for future reference during the phase of software maintenance.

Code component: I am using the phrase not in the sense it is used in programming languages such as Python, component object model (COM), or distributed component object model (DCOM) methodologies. A code component is a set of program statements that perform a set of functions, and the set can just be one. Preferably, each code component ought to achieve one unique functionality. If the component performs multiple functions, then it is better if those functions are closely related to each other in some manner. A code component is not part of another program. It is a complete program in itself but not so independent that it can be installed and executed on a computer on its own. While the code component would be capable of being used in standalone mode, it must be callable from within another program by receiving parameters from the calling program and returning results of processing back to the calling program. A code component can be part of a software project, a form, a library. A code component needs to be embedded in something bigger. Of course, a code component may call another code component. Code components are assembled together using a form by tying the code components to the controls placed on the form. Where we do not make use of forms, like in real-time machine control software, all the components are part of independent executable programs. I am discussing the design of code components in this chapter, and we will go into more detail later on.

Working effectively: This is delivering the expected results comprehensively and accurately. While users expect only the results, we need to provide the auxiliary results, too. These includes information with which the user can assure himself or herself and any others that the processing has been comprehensive and all relevant data has been included in the processing and is accurate. The code we design must deliver all of this.

Optimal resource utilization: Software in execution utilizes system resources. Maximum utilization of resources calls for utilizing a resource at its maximum capacity all the time the resource is available. For any hardware resource, its capacity can be rated in three modes: the rated capacity, the maximum capacity, and the minimum capacity. The maximum capacity is the capability of the resource at which it can carry the maximum load. For example, let us take an automobile. We usually run it at the permitted speed, which may be 55–75 miles per hour (MPH). We can of course run it at 120 MPH if the situation calls for it. Each car has a minimum speed at which it has to run at all. It may be between 1 to 5 MPH. If we try to run it below its minimum rated speed, the engine usually stalls, and if we try to run it continuously at such a low speed, the engine is damaged. The maximum capacity and minimum capacity are used only in rare circumstances for limited periods of time for each occurrence. If we continuously try to run the car either at the maximum speed or the minimum speed, disastrous consequences may result. The car may completely break down. We use a resource at its normal capacity, which is designed to run the resource continuously. We have to design software in such a manner that it utilizes the system resources optimally. Optimal refers to running a resource at a capacity that is less than its maximum and more than its minimum capability. The car is a single-user model in the sense that it has only one driver at any given time, but our computers are multiuser, and multiple users will be utilizing them concurrently at any given time. It may also happen that, at times, the maximum number of users is using our software. When maximum number of users is logged into our software, there is stress on the hardware resources, especially for other users. Therefore, we must take these aspects into consideration in our code design and ensure that our software utilizes the resources optimally, allowing others to share the system resources as well.

Produce the results in real time: Some of the outputs we design are offline, meaning that a user is not waiting for the output at a remote location in front of a computer screen. They are produced by the system administrators. But the majority of outputs we design are for users who may be at a distant location and eagerly awaiting the generation of the desired output. Therefore, we need to design our software such that the outputs are produced within such a time that the user is not exasperated waiting for them. Most outputs are produced by gathering the relevant records from a mass of data based on a set of conditions. The computer takes proportionately more time as the number of records to be searched increases. Of course, database technology and modern hardware facilitates quickly reach the desired records, and we should use all such technology to produce the results in real time. Similarly, the amount of processing also has an impact on the response time. So, if there is a process that can take an inordinately long time, we need to otherwise engage the user. We usually make such outputs offline so that the user can put in a requisition to the system administrator. We also can push the processing into the background and free the user to do something else. While (s)he is otherwise engaged, we produce the output in a file and give him/her a message in a suitable manner to view and use it to serve the desired purpose. All this has to be designed into the code and implemented so that the software works, producing the results in real time.

Easily maintainable with minimum effort: Usually, in the software product life cycle, the software spends approximately 50% of its life in maintenance. In some cases, it is much more. In some cases, the software is never replaced, spending more than 30 years only in maintenance. One aspect of software maintenance is to locate the code component that needs to be modified. By avoiding the need for long programs running into thousands of lines of code, we can make it easier to locate the desired piece of code. We have to consciously design our code components such that each is smaller. We need to make most of the code components self sufficient so that the code maintenance programmer need not go in and out of the dependent code components. While we may not be able to avoid this aspect completely, we need to minimize it. That way, we can facilitate software maintenance later with a minimum of effort.

Minimal necessity to modify the code: Of course, one of the prime objectives of code design is to avoid code modification completely, but we have to allow for the possibility of the necessity to modify the code later on. Of course, the organizational coding standards take care of this aspect for the most part. But we software designers also have a role. If we consolidate the code components that may necessitate maintenance into DLLs or something similar, we simplify the process of software maintenance. The system administrators only need to replace components rather than modify code on the production system. Web-based systems facilitate replacement of components, and we should make use of those facilities to minimize code modification, especially on the production system.

With this definition of code design, we can now move forward on the topic of code deign.

Identifying the Common Code Components

Now, looking at code design, the first activity to be performed is to identify the common code components. What.are common code components? Common code components are those that arc used more than once in the project at hand. How do we do this? I would not say that this is easy, but then the job of a designer in any field is never easy! One requires expert knowledge of software development to be able to do this effectively. Some common components are easy to identify. For example, in any web-based application, we need to verify the login credentials of the user before loading any new form. In multilingual software, we have to set labels based on the selected language at the time of loading a new form. This is required for every form. So, we can create it as a common code component. Similarly, in reports, we set the report headings, such as the name of the organization, which can be assigned to a code component that can be used in all the report programs.

Obviously, these can be separated and developed as common components and made part of a DLL so that developers of forms and reports can simply call them as required. Similarly, we can identify common components based on the domain. For example, in a CRM system, the details of the customer are needed by many functions. This could be a common component. In a payroll application, the employee details are required by many functions and are a common component. In a supply chain management (SCM) system, the component details, warehouse details, or vendor details are used by many functions and can be split off as common components.

Another opportunity for identifying repeating pieces of code is during the detailed design or engineering of the software product. As we develop the design specifications for each individual code component, we will come across instances where a functionality is required a second time. Whenever a functionality repeats, we have to consolidate that functionality into a common component pool and give its reference at all places where that functionality is required. Sometimes, it may happen that the activity of engineering the software is allocated to multiple engineers. In such cases, we may miss repeating functionalities, as they are developed by different engineers. In those missing cases, we can identify them during the peer review activity.

Another method for identifying repeating code components is to maintain a register, which can be softcopy such as a spreadsheet giving the list of common code components along with the details of their functionality. All the engineers working on the engineering of the software product would refer to that list and use them as needed. They will develop specifications for a new code component only when that functionality is not found in the common code components list.

Summarizing the discussion, we have four methods for identifying common code components. These are:

1. Foreseeing the necessity of common code components using our expertise in the domain and the development platform
2. During the detailed design or engineering in which program or code component level specifications are drawn up by consolidating the repeating code components
3. During the review of design specifications of the detailed design specifications of code components, consolidate all the code components with same functionality
4. By maintaining a detailed list of common code components at a central place and making it available to all the design engineers, who are encouraged to refer to this list and design a new code component only when it is not found in the pool of common code components

Some of the most frequently used common code components are:

1. Checking for only digits in the inputs for all input controls while receiving numeric input from the user and data files created offline.
2. *Checking for floating-point numbers*: We need to check the inputs for accuracy of floating-point numbers. In some countries, they use a comma instead of the period character to separate the fractional portion from the main number. A floating-point number should contain only one floating-point character. We should ensure these aspects while receiving inputs either directly from the end user or in the data files created offline.
3. *Checking for names*: Names ought to contain only alphabet characters. They may contain blank spaces when all parts of the name like first name, last name, and middle name are received using only one input control on the screen. Names may also contain a period character in certain cases, like the initial of the middle name and when the names are suffixed with Sr. or Jr. Our code needs to have facilities for ensuring that only these characters exist and that no numbers or other characters are allowed in the online input data or the offline input data.
4. *Checking for alphanumeric data*: This consists of letters, numbers, and other printable characters and avoidance of HTML tags. We need to check alphanumeric data to ensure that it contains only printable characters. In some cases, HTML and other markup language characters need to be avoided. Based on the situation at hand, we need to ensure that alphanumeric data contains only permitted characters.
5. *Checking for HTML tags and markup languages*: When our platform permits receiving HTML and other markup language tags, we need to check the appropriateness of those tags using the syntax rules of the specific markup language.
6. *Label loading*: If our product is intended to be used by people who speak different languages or to be sold as a COTS product, we need to provide a facility to load different labels on the screen and reports at run time. For this, we provide a code component to set the labels during the form-load event. As this is needed for all screens and reports, we can have a common code component and call it during the load event of forms or reports.

7. *Link checking*: Often, we receive URLs of websites and email ids in our inputs. We need to ensure that these are as accurate as possible. For example, the end of the link, such as .com, .net, or .org, exists and appears only once. We need to have a code component that checks and ensures that these links are accurately entered and obey their syntax rules. Of course, we cannot programmatically ensure that the links are accurate! We can only ensure that they follow the syntax rules, and we should do that.

8. *Date and time checking*: Unless we use a date and time control for receiving date and time inputs, we need to check the received date and time for their accuracy. This is essential, especially in the data files created offline. We need to check the combination of month and date for appropriateness. For example, a date of 30 is incompatible with the month of February, and a date of 31 for April is not compatible. We need to have a common component in our code for this type of checking.

9. *Checking login credentials*: In the web applications of the present day, it is possible for the user to access any web page of the application, directly bypassing the login page. Therefore, we need to check the login credentials every time we load a new page of the application. Therefore, we need to have a common component to check and return the login credentials to the calling program.

10. *Error handling*: Of course, we perform data validation while receiving inputs, but faults can surface during runtime for a variety of reasons, including viruses, OS malfunction, hardware malfunction, or the software generating unexpected values. For example, the denominator could become zero where we have no tool to check the value of the denominator before allowing division in arithmetic statements. The network may be down and the software may not be able to connect to the database. This will cause a fault. So, we need a code component to trap errors in almost all places where we use arithmetic statements, database connections, and so on so that we can avoid program aborts and provide the user a facility to smoothly transition to other functionality or to exit the system.

11. *Database connection*: We need to connect to the database multiple times in the product. It is tempting to connect to the database at the time of launching the product, but we need to remember that each such connection occupies some amount of memory on the database server, and too many connections will degrade the response times. So, we connect and disconnect the database from our product multiple times only when needed. Thus, it becomes advantageous to have a common code component to perform this task that can be called by any code component in the product.

In addition to these common components, we need to assess the need for common components for the domain at hand. For example, in a CRM application, we need to verify the customer details all through the application. It is better to split it off as a common component. In an SCM application, the item details also can be split off as a common component. We have to thoroughly analyze our domain, identify all such common components, and then design them appropriately so that duplicating those components is avoided to reduce the load on the programmers as well as making it easier for code maintenance later on. It also protects the integrity of the application during maintenance.

Identifying common components does away with the necessity of developing the same code by multiple programmers multiple times. Another more important advantage is safeguarding the integrity across the application. Whenever we upgrade the component, the upgraded functionality becomes available to all the components using the upgraded component automatically.

Reusable Code Components

By reusable code components, I mean code components that have already been developed and exist in our organization from other projects or products. If the organization we work for is a professional software development organization or develops and maintains multiple products, we will have multiple code components that perhaps are suitable for the present software product, too. However, if we have to reuse code components that were already developed, we need to have the proper infrastructure in place. This includes:

1. A well-maintained library of reusable code components.
    a. Each code component is stored carefully, in such a way that it can be called from within another code component by passing parameters and receiving the results.
    b. Each component is fully described in terms of the functionality and the parameters it needs, including the type and size of the parameters.
    c. The results returned by the component, including the type and size.
2. A process for locating the required reusable code components in the project management process.
3. A process for checking in the code components after a through quality assurance process to ensure that the component being checked in has the potential to be reused and to prevent frivolous checking in of every component that is submitted to the library.
4. A well-designed search engine to locate the desired code component easily, quickly, and with the least amount of effort.

With such an infrastructure in place, code components can be reused. The main advantage in reusing code components is the massive savings in designing, coding, and testing of the code. The more we use reusable code components, the less effort is spent on designing, coding, and quality assurance thereof. But the onus for enabling reuse of code components rests on the shoulders of the organizational management, as the development and maintenance of a reusable code component library costs money and consumes effort of human resources. Most organizations look at this expense as unnecessary overhead and do not allocate resources to this vital activity any more than paying lip service. The onus also rests with the designers to design code components in such a manner that facilitates reuse later on instead of designing them just for the use of the present project.

Packaging the Common Code Components

Identifying common components is just the first step in code design. Now, the next question would logically be: How do we package the identified common code components? Once we identify and list the common components for the project at hand, we need to first check the reusable code component library of the organization to see if it contains any of the common components identified for the project. If available, we can import them from the organizational library into our project. Sometimes, the code components in the organizational library may be standalone components, and sometimes, they may be part of a DLL. If they are part of a DLL, we copy the DLL into our project portfolio of code components and include that DLL in our project DLLs. If it is a standalone code component, we import that into our common code components library.

We have two alternatives for packaging common code components. The first is to store them in a separate folder and make calls to them from within the forms as and when necessary. This would call for all the components to be packaged in the executable file and thus increase the required space on the disk as well as the RAM. A second disadvantage of this method is that whenever we modify the code of a code component, we have to replace the executable file. As far as possible, we should retain the original .exe file so that it need not be tested again. Whenever we try to modify the code in the main executable file, we run the risk of accidentally changing some other stabilized functionality.

The better alternative is to package all the common code components into a DLL. Building a new DLL may cause a little more work initially, but it saves a lot of time when the software product begins functioning in its target production environment. Surely we will have to modify the code of a code component sometime in the future for a variety of reasons, and when we need to do so, we just need to update the code component and replace it in the DLL package. The greater advantage would be to achieve newer functionality in the production environment by just replacing the DLL in the production configuration. Another major advantage of a DLL is that it is mainly on the disk and is called into the RAM only when it is required and pushed back once its calling program closes. This facilitates efficient utilization of RAM, which is finite. It reduces the need for frequent swapping and reduces the problem of thrashing. This improves response times for all users of the computer system. For those of you not familiar with the term "thrashing," it is excessive swapping of pages from RAM to disk and vice versa. Thrashing degrades system performance and slows down the response times significantly.

In making a DLL, we need to make a decision about making a new DLL just for the project or upgrading the DLLs that already exist in the organizational common code components library. While making DLLs for the organization, it is a better practice to package code components that deliver similar functionality. For example, the login validation may differ from project to project depending on the unique requirements of the specific customer's production configuration. Now, if we develop a new login validation program, it is better to include it in the DLL that already exists in the organizational common code components library. We need to make a decision for each of the identified common code components about upgrading the organizational DLL or making it part of the project DLL.

Now the next logical question is: Should we have just one project DLL or have multiple DLLs for our project? Here, we need to remember that a DLL is loaded entirely when it is called by the project in execution. If we make one single DLL that is too large, then it occupies a significant amount of RAM when loaded and could cause performance degradation. If we have a single project DLL, it stays resident in the RAM, as some component of the product in execution will be calling it more or less all the time. This wastes our objective of efficient utilization of RAM. Another disadvantage of a large single DLL is that we have to replace the entire DLL whenever we upgrade it. It will be well-nigh impossible to upgrade the DLL while the product is in execution. If we have multiple DLLs, each of which is small, we can make our product an efficient user of RAM and we can easily replace the DLL in the production environment even while the product is perhaps in execution. So, my vote goes for multiple small DLLs for a project.

Code Design

The design of code is making a few decisions about the code to be written; then, documenting these decisions along with the design of each code component concludes code design. The first decision is about the division of code to be written by the programmer between various artifacts available. After consolidating all the common code components, there remains the code to be written in forms to achieve the functionality specified for the project. Now, this code could go into the controls on the form in numerous ways. We can place the code at these places:

1. *On the web page embedded in the HTML code*: We have to note one thing about the web pages: whatever code we write on the web page is visible to users on almost all the browsers. I am saying "almost all" because I admit that I have not seen all the browsers available on all machines. What is the harm if the users see the code, you may ask. When the code is visible to users, they can copy the code and use it. While it is illegal to copy code and paste it into their programs, it is very difficult, if not impossible, to track and sue each and every code pirate around the world. And, God forbid, if there are errors or defects in that code, we may get sued, too! Of course, I have seen many instances where code is placed on the web page, but I advocate hiding all the code from the users' view. The code that I saw on the web pages is to validate the user input and give error messages for user mistakes. This may be deemed harmless, but still, it is a better practice to hide all the code from the users.

2. *In the database as triggers, stored procedures, or queries*: We have the option of coding the data manipulation code components either in the program or in the database itself. If we place all the code, including the data manipulation, within the program itself, we need not engage database specialists. The flip side of this argument is that the SQL language code components placed in the database function better and respond faster than SQL calls from the program because the DBMS is optimized for SQL code components in the database. SQL code components placed in the DBMS itself work faster and more efficiently, enabling faster response times due to this optimization. The programming languages are geared more toward efficient processing of data than to store, modify, or extract data in a database table. Calling SQL uses multiple steps in data manipulation. That includes interpreting the statement and separating the SQL statements, then passing them on to DBMS, which in turn validates the statements, then passes the commands to its execution module, which then processes

the statements and produces the results. The DBMS then passes the results back to the program, the program verifies the results and then uses them for the next set of statements. In a loop, the interaction between the DBMS and the program is there for each iteration of the loop. If we place the SQL code components in the DBMS, all the program does is call that SQL program, passing the parameters; hand over the control to the DBMS; and receive the results for the next statement. In a loop, the interaction between the DBMS and the program is minimized. The DBMS will be ready with the data without being called once again.

3. *Setting parameters on the form for the controls*: In the modern-day Graphical User Interface (GUI), interactive development environments (IDEs) provide facilities for setting parameters for all the controls placed on the form. These parameters are too numerous to enumerate here. They include the name of the database, the name of the table, the field name, the length of the field, visible or invisible, and so on. By setting these parameters, we need not write statements inside the code. Of course, many parameters do not need to be changed inside the program, but some do. In particular, parameters such as the database name, table name, and field require changes inside the program because the environment changes from the development system to the production system. So it is better to set all those parameters that depend on the environment inside the program rather than on the form itself. We need to carefully evaluate each of the parameters and decide which to set on the form. In case of doubt, set the parameter inside the program rather than on the form itself. I have seen runtime errors cropping up because the parameters for a control were set on the form and that parameter did not work as the environment changed. We need to avoid all such actions that can give rise to faults during runtime.

4. *Code written on the form as subprograms for the events of the controls*: We write most of the code for the product inside the code components attached to the controls. Each control on the form has many events, like click, double click, key-press, got-focus, lost-focus, change, mouse-over, and so on. Each of these events is associated with a code component that may be referred to as a subroutine, a method, a function, an agent, or something else. We write the code for each of these events to achieve functionality that is designed for that event. These code components achieve the core functionality of the product. We have to write this code carefully. There will be the temptation to make the code component self-sufficient and standalone, but it is better to keep this code short and precise. We can make calls to other code components, either to the DLLs supplied as part of the development platform, the project-specific DLLs, the DLLs with the reusable code components developed earlier in our organization, or the DLLs purchased from component suppliers.

5. *Code for reports*: It has become common practice to use specialized report generators for producing output reports, as they make our life easier by taking care of pagination, running totals, setting column headings, and so on. These report writers need queries or views to extract relevant data from the database tables. We may be able to define simple relations interactively using the tools provided, but we need to write code to write complex relations. We may need to write some code for calculating values to be placed on the report. Of course, this is simple code compared to the code written for the events of the controls on a form. We need to design this type of code carefully so the results produced are accurate and have the necessary precision in the case of numeric data.

Having understood where we place the code of the software product, let us now look at general principles for designing the code.

The first principle of code design is: *One code component achieves one functionality.* In the past, we wrote one program that achieved all the functionalities set for the product. Programs used to run into thousands of lines of code, and maintaining them was a nightmare. Some of these programs are still running even today. Those days belonged to batch processing of bulk data rather than the end-user computing of today. The data was entered offline, and reports were produced periodically on predefined dates. In the present day, a lot of the data entry is immediately followed by production of reports. Data entry and output production are carried out in many cases by the end users. Now with GUIs, this is made simpler. GUIs also facilitated many events to be programmed. Each event usually achieves one functionality. In some cases, such as when we click the command button either to save the inputs received or to generate an output, we may have to include multiple functionalities in the code component triggered by the click event of the command button. It is tempting for programmers and designers to stuff all that functionality into one code component. Experience has shown us that this results in a debugging and maintenance nightmare. Structured programming was introduced to avoid this practice of writing long programs that are difficult to debug and maintain. Structured programming has the main program calling multiple subprograms and each of the subprograms achieving one functionality. We have to make use of this philosophy while designing long programs and make them shorter by splitting code off into multiple code components. In so doing, we need to design in such a way that each code component achieves one and only one functionality. This kind of design keeps each code component to its minimum length, making the activities of debugging during initial development and then maintaining the code later on easier.

We need to clarify one thing here, and that is what constitutes one single functionality. We have to consider the designer viewpoint here. We should not consider the user viewpoint here. One user functionality breaks down into multiple design functionalities. Let us say the issuance of material from a warehouse to its user is one functionality for an end user. But this involves designing multiple independent functionalities such as looking up the stock and retrieving the instances of the desired material in the stock, presenting them to the issuer, allowing him/her to select the instances, then allowing the issuer to enter details of the material issued to the user into the system, updating the stock to reflect the changes, and computing the stock value and any other values as required by the end user. All these actions ought not to be packaged as one functionality. We have to view them as separate and multiple functionalities. Presently, many view the user viewpoint and designer view as the same. This is far from the reality. The duty of the designer is to design the product to deliver all the user functionality efficiently, effectively, accurately, and within the expected time. So, we have to understand the user's needs and design principles to deliver great code.

The second principle of code design is: *Each code component ought to be kept short in length.* How short is short? There is no universally accepted specification for this question. Programmers usually consider a screen as one functionality. This could be misleading. Let us consider a small screen, say, a report generation screen. It could have just one combo box listing all the available reports and a go button to initiate report generation activity. If there are 20 reports available and all those reports are packed onto one screen, the program could become significantly longer. Instead, if we have a case statement with 20 options, with each option calling a code component to generate the selected report, all the programs would be short. That is, each screen can have one main program calling various code components and code components that are not available elsewhere in the product. This enables detecting and fixing errors easily and quickly. One of the frequent issues encountered in software maintenance is injecting new defects while fixing other defects, which happens mainly because the program is too long. Now that programs are short, the probability of introducing new defects significantly diminishes and completely eliminates introducing new defects in other functionalities. Now, the event-oriented programming facilitated by the GUI greatly aids implementation of this principle, and in those few cases where long programs are likely to creep in, we need to keep this principle in mind and keep all the programs as short as possible.

The third principle of code design is: *Each code component ought to be as standalone as possible*. What I mean by standalone is that it can receive parameters, but it should not call any other code components. We ought to design code in such a way that the main program does all the calling. Each called code component is designed to perform one function and return the result back to the calling main program. When we design code components in this manner, the code components need not be recoded in other projects and code reusability can be promoted.

The fourth principle of code design is: *Each code component ought to use the system resources optimally*. The most common reason behind poor response times and throughput is the misuse of the available RAM. RAM in any computer system is finite. It gets used up pretty quickly. As fast as the hardware industry is increasing the size of RAM in computer systems, the software industry is gobbling it up even faster. OS developers use the swapping technique to handle situations when the processes need more RAM than is physically available. But when there are multiple processes competing for RAM, the system goes into thrashing. We waste RAM by declaring unnecessary variables, declaring variables of larger sizes than are actually required, declaring global (or static) variables where local (or dynamic) variables suffice, and other such actions that lock up RAM for the entire duration of the program execution. We ought to design our code components such that RAM wastage is eliminated. Similarly, other resources such as bandwidth, disk space, CPU time, and database connections need to be used efficiently by our software. All these have to be designed and engineered to be efficiently used. We have to consciously design these aspects in our code design, and we should not it leave to the wisdom of the programmers.

The fifth principle of code design is: *Each code component ought to deliver results effectively*. Effective delivery includes adhering to the specified response time, accuracy, and reliability. The response time has to be appropriate to the situation and needs to be the shortest possible. In some cases, it takes a longer time than the user can tolerate, and we need to indicate the progress by placing a progress bar or displaying a count/percentage of the progress on the screen so that the customer does not become restive. Accuracy includes not just the correct result but also the precision of the result. The result needs to have the precision, that is, the number of digits after the decimal point in numeric results and the length in the case of alphanumeric results, necessary for the result. Reliability includes delivering the same performance every time, even when used continuously without any interruption or with any number of interruptions. It is recorded that in the war Desert Storm, the system firing the Patriot missiles, after firing continuously for 100 hours at a stretch, shifted by one hundredth of a second, which resulted in missing a SCUD missile, causing deaths of soldiers. We have to build in measures to correct any shifts in the accurate delivery of results introduced by continuous operation of the software.

The sixth principle of code design is: *Each code component ought to be defect free*. This surely is a matter for coding and not a matter for design! Coding just implements design, and we need to remember this always. *If it is not designed, it will not be implemented*. As part of implementing this principle, we need to design error-handling code components as part of common code components as well as creating a database table with appropriate error messages and referring to them in each of the code components. Coders use this combination to trap errors and hand over control to these code components at appropriate places in their code components. We need to identify all those places that can give rise to faults and indicate the actions necessary to plug those holes appropriately so that the code components are defect free. The following are a few of the places in the code that can give rise to faults during runtime:

1. Opening database tables, during which time the database might not have been connected, the table may be absent, or the table may return zero records based on the filter applied.
2. Arithmetic operations in which the size of the receiving variable may be smaller than the size of the result of the arithmetic operation.
3. The denominator of a division operation may become zero.
4. Saving information into a database table.
5. The network connection can be disconnected at any time, so each code component ought to have a facility to trap these errors.

The seventh principle of code design is: *Each code component ought to be flexible in its achievement of functionality*. By this, I mean that the code component ought to be flexible enough to allow the user to achieve variants in the processing carried out by the code component. For example, most rules for payment processing like income tax, medical billing, tax rates payable on materials, and so on keep changing from time to time. Every time such a rule changes, it should not be necessary to modify the code. We should be able to change the data or rules outside the code. We can achieve this by splitting off the rules into a rules database or including all possible combinations of rules within the code component itself. Most of the time, it is not possible to foresee all possible combinations at the time of initial software design. While I do not dispute that it is possible to include all combinations inside the code component, I would say such a possibility is minimal. The best course is to place the rules in a database or a specialized rules database.

The eighth principle of code design is: *No code component contains hardcoding*. Hardcoding is one of the prime causes of the need for software maintenance activity. Hardcoding is placing some numeric values inside the code component as constants. It is better to place all such values in a data file or database table and read them when the code component is called into execution during runtime. That way, when any of the constant values change while the software is in production, we can just change the data, and the need to change the code is completely eliminated. Changing and testing the changed data is quicker and easier than changing the code and ensuring its quality.

The above are principles of code design, and we must not confuse them with writing the code. Code writing has many more "rules," not just principles. Each of these principles evolves into multiple rules for writing code. Code design has a bit of a creative element, whereas code writing has a minimal creative element. Based on these principles, each organization has to develop its own standards of code design based on its development platform and programming language.

13

Process Design

Introduction

What is a process, especially in the context of software design? It is a pertinent question to ask here. The computer hardware processes the data using the instructions contained in the software. The term *process* has multiple connotations. The one that is apt for us is about conversion from one state to another. Merriam-Webster's dictionary defines the word *process*, thus: "a series of actions or operations conducing to an end; *especially*: a continuous operation or treatment especially in manufacture." The word *manufacture* can be changed to *software development* to make sense in our context. The SEI, in their CMMI® for Development, version 1.3 (CMMI-Dev, V1.3) defined *process*, thus: "a set of interrelated activities, which transform inputs into outputs, to achieve a given purpose." The IEEE, in their *Standard Glossary of Software Engineering Terminology* (IEEE Std. 610.12 of 1990) defined *process* as: "a sequence of steps performed for a given purpose."

I am not using the other connotations of the word *process* here. The other important connotation is the process of accomplishing something, like the process of management or the software development process in the present chapter. In the present context of software design, I like to define process as "the steps designed to convert the inputs into outputs effectively and efficiently."

So far, we have not delved deeply into the nitty-gritty of software design. We have discussed the major areas of software design. Now, let us dig deeper and see what software design is all about. Software design is about *how we design each of the steps in the process of a business or scientific system for information processing and deliver the desired results accurately, quickly, effectively, efficiently, and economically.* In a computerized system, we have the following major processes,

1. Input process
2. Output process
3. Storage process
4. Conversion process

We discussed the first three processes in the preceding chapters. Now, in this chapter, let us discuss the conversion process.

Conversion Process

By the conversion process, I mean the entire process, beginning with how the application is launched until the application is closed, and all the intermediate processes. As software designers, we develop software programs that process and convert data into useful information. Every program performs some conversion process. But a computerized software system performs a business or scientific process that will have multiple process steps in achieving the purpose for which the system was proposed. Therefore, we have to shift our focus from the program level to the system level when we are designing the software system.

Now, the conversion process has these subprocesses:

1. Application launch
2. Application closure
3. Application to user communication
4. Navigation from one subsystem to another
5. Data conversion process
6. Installation process
7. Rollout process

Let us discuss the design aspects of each of these processes in greater detail.

Application Launch

Application launch can be achieved in a number of ways. The following are the methods we currently use for launching the application:

1. In a single-user application, this is the simplest. We click and select the application from a menu of applications available or click or double-click an icon on the screen representing the desired application.
2. In a machine control software system, we usually launch the application when the machine starts or when the machine places an interrupt on the CPU.
3. In a machine that is completely controlled by the software, when the power is turned on, we launch the software first, which in turn starts the machine, and from then on, each software process is triggered by a machine event or by an interrupt placed by the machine on the CPU.
4. In an organization-wide web application, we use a two-step launch. The first step is to launch the application on the server, usually by the administrators of the application. The second step is initiated by the end users to launch the part of application that is allowed to them by the security rules in force.
5. In large-scale web applications, we have many levels. A web application can be one organization wide but accessed from different geographical locations within one state or one country to another that is accessed globally without restrictions on a

24 × 7 basis. In such applications, we may never be able to close the application once it is launched. But as reality forces us to close the application at one time or another, we maintain local servers and switch the application from one server to another. In such cases, launching the application is achieved using multiple steps based on the system configuration and the hardware setup. This has a minimum of three steps, namely the launch of the application on the main server, the launch of the application on the local server, and, finally, the launch by the end user on his/her machine.

Process of Application Launch

How do we launch the application? Here, I am referring to launching in two places, namely at the server end and at the end-user end. What features do we need to design for a smooth and effective launch at both ends? I try to answer these questions in this section.

Let us first discuss launching the application at the server end. We need to design the following features for application launch at the server end.

The application launch at the server end ought to be restricted to as few steps as possible. We have to build in scripts to perform the actions when the administrator initiates the application. It may not always be possible to restrict the launch steps to one, but we ought to strive to minimize these steps as much as possible. We expect the application launch steps to be a minimum of four:

1. Launch the database server so that it is ready to supply and receive data from users.
2. Launch the app server or the application framework so that our application can begin to serve the end users.
3. Launch the web server so that web services can begin receiving and responding to end user requests online.
4. Launch our application so it is ready to process the end user requests.

While the first three steps are independent of each other, the fourth step depends on the other three steps. We should design the launch of our application to ensure that the other three were launched and are running in healthy states. As the database server, the app server, and the web server are usually bought-out products, we have no control over their design. Therefore, we need to design the following first steps to be performed as soon as the application is launched:

1. Check that the hardware on which our application is hosted is in working condition and that all peripherals connected to the system are responding appropriately.
2. Check the connectivity to the internet to ensure that it exists and is providing us the contracted bandwidth and speed.
3. Check that the database server is up and running and that the required databases are live. We should also design the application to check that all the tables are available and their integrity is impeccable. By checking the integrity of the tables, we will know if hackers intruded into our system and modified our data.

4. Check that all the flat files and parameter files are available and their configuration information is as expected.

5. Check that the app server and web server are working properly.

6. Check all the application components against the configuration register and ensure that the configuration in terms of the modification date and time as well as the file sizes are as expected.

When all these checks are performed and passed, we can launch our application. We need to trap errors in each check and pass appropriate error messages to the application administrator. Now, one question is: What should our application be designed to do when it encounters an error in these initial checks? One common method is to display an error message and then abort the application. This is inefficient, as the administrator needs to relaunch the application after rectifying the trapped error. Instead, the better alternative is to design a method that checks all it is designed to check, passes on appropriate error messages, allows the correction, and then rechecks the rectified error, all without the need to close and relaunch the application. Now, we have the developmental tools to build such a system. Another alternative is to do the checks one by one, display the error message, wait for the prompt to receive the rectification information, and then move on to the next check. All this can be done while the application launch is running.

Once our application is launched, we usually cannot close the application without causing disruption to our business operations. In business-critical systems, we usually maintain mirroring systems to take over in case we need to close our application on one system. In this type of system, we have a main server that serves the end users and a standby system that takes over in case the main server either fails, is brought down for preventive maintenance, or is being upgraded. Once the main server is up, it will take over the service of end users. So, during launch, we launch the application on the main server first and then on the standby server. In some fail-safe systems, we may have multiple main servers serving the end users concurrently. Each request is routed to the server with the least load to be serviced. In such cases, we can bring down one server without disrupting the performance for the end users. In these cases, we need to launch our application on all the servers before throwing them open to the end users.

In some cases, the system is so large that it may be distributed geographically. Each geographical region may have entire system of hardware and software set up to better serve the end users of that region. In such cases, we may have to launch the application at all the distributed sites. Of course, it is rare to set up all those sites at the same time. It is usually the practice to set up the main server at one place initially and then set up another site in a region and split off the traffic emanating from that region to the new server. In that manner, new servers are set up and launched. In these cases, we continue to serve the end users from the main server until the application is successfully launched at the regional server and then make configuration changes to divert relevant traffic to the new server.

We have to note that the application launch is invisible to the end users. It is carried out at the server end by the application administrators, who may or may not be sitting near the server. They may be launching the application remotely. Therefore, the onus is on us, the designers of the software system, to make the process of launching our application as painless and smooth as humanly possible.

The application launch at the user's end: When we design the application to be launched from the user's end, we design it in such a way that the user types a web address and we take him or her to the login page or our home page, which gives the user some useful information and allows him or her to log in as a prelude to accessing the restricted content. We have to design the following aspects while launching the application at the user end:

1. *We have to design a landing page*: When the user types the IP address, which can be a name, we need to present a landing page to the user. This page ought to have a login facility or a link to allow the user to authenticate credentials and access the restricted content. It is possible that unauthenticated users can also visit our application website. We can use this visit to advertise our services and products. So, we need to design the landing page to inform the visitor about our organization, products, and services, as well as a host of other things like career opportunities, contact information, our mission and vision, and so on. We need to design an aesthetically appealing landing page so that even casual visitors are motivated to learn about our organization and tempted to use our products or services. Of course, the information need not be restricted to one page. We can provide links to other web pages with more information. Even authentic users may surf the pages, and when they wish to log in, they either should be able to come back to the login screen with one click or, even better, have the link to log in right on every information page.

2. *We have to ensure that the user logs in before being allowed to access the restricted content*: These days, it has become possible to access any application page directly without going through the main menu of the application by directly entering the web page URL into a browser. Therefore, we need to design all our pages such that the first action performed by the page is to check the login credentials. If the user has not been authenticated, we need to design our application so that the user is redirected to the login page. This can be with a message to the user to the effect that he/she is not logged in and is hence being redirected to the login page. Alternatively, we can directly present the login page. Which of these alternatives is better? My vote goes for the second one, even though I have seen the first alternative being used widely. It is perhaps the designer's choice. But here is the second and the important part. After the user logs in, we need to present the page originally requested. Some applications force the user to go to the main menu page. This would irritate the user in my opinion, as the user needs to navigate through the application to the desired page. Of course, in some cases, the user needs to enter some vital information before accessing the desired page. In such cases, we need to present the first page in the set of pages desired by the user.

3. *We need to perform diagnostics*: The diagnostics that are necessary at the user's end are limited to checking if the internet connection is available. Of course, if the internet connection is not available, the user will not be able to access the application website. In a few cases, we may store application access information in cookies on the user's computer. In such cases, we need to check the integrity of the cookies.

4. *We need to verify and ensure, to the extent possible, that the login is authentic*: I discussed the login action in Chapter 9 on security design. We need to design all actions discussed in that chapter. We need to correlate the IP address from which the login request arrived and the expected login for those login credentials to see if the login is indeed authentic.

5. *We need to set the access rights appropriate to the logged-in user*: We need to retrieve the security access rights of the user trying to log in and set those rights before

presenting the initial page to the user. Where do we keep these access rights? We can do it in a table on the server or in a cookie on the user's computer. My vote goes to keeping the information on the server. We can keep the information on the server safe, as it is under our control. The cookie on the user's computer is not under our control.

6. *We have to present initial content appropriate to the security clearance of the logged-in user*: In our application, there are different users with different levels of access rights. When the login is authenticated, what do we present to the user initially? Some designers present the same page to all users, suppressing the information that is not allowed to be accessed by the logged-in user. Some designers present different pages commensurate with the access rights allowed to the logged-in user. In the first alternative, if there are programming errors, the user gets access to pages that he or she is not supposed to access. The second alternative requires more programming effort. But, in either case, we need to design a common routine and call it whenever giving initial access to the user.

We need to design all these features in the launch of the application from the user's end.

Launching of application in machine control systems: Machine control systems are closed-loop systems receiving inputs from a machine and giving most of the outputs to the same machine, and the rest may be directed to a server at a remote location using wireless communication if that was built in. The power-up action of the machine launches our software. In these applications, we do not have two ends, namely the server and user ends. If there is a remote server or control system, as in the case of rockets or aerial vehicles, then the first step for our application has to be to ensure that communication with the remote application is established and is working flawlessly. Then, the next step is to verify that all the hardware our application controls is in working condition and responding to the commands of our application appropriately. Once these two steps are completed, only then do we need to load the remaining software and declare the machine ready for use.

Application Closure

Applications will have to be closed one time or another. In some applications, such as ticket booking, we do not close the application at the server end as far as possible. But even such applications need to close occasionally for reasons such as migration and periodic maintenance. While we close the application at server side very infrequently, there is a need to close the application at the user side frequently. At the user end, we close the application initiated either by the user or by the application. When the application initiates the closure of the application at the user's end, it will be a forced closure. The application has to initiate closure of the application at the user's end if the session is idle for a long time. How long is really long? It depends on the sensitivity of the information being processed by the user. If the user happens to be some sort of administrator, we can't allow the session to be idle for more than five minutes, and it could be shorter in more sensitive cases. Similarly, if the user is a normal user, we may close the session when it is idle for five or more minutes. We have to decide the time of permitted idleness based on the likely user profile and the sensitivity of the data.

While the time of permitted idleness of the session is one critical decision, the other major design decision is how to close the session. One method is to direct the user to the login page when the machine is woken up from the sleep state or when the user attempts to use the application. The other is to close the application completely for the user. In the first method, we design the following steps.

1. Every time the user begins a new action, that is, a click of the mouse or the press of a key, we compute the time lag between the present action and the previous action.
2. If the time lag is within the permitted limit, then we allow the action, but if it exceeds the permitted time limit, we direct the user to the login page.
3. Once the user logs in, we revert to the earlier page, keeping all the work performed thus far intact.
4. The session is kept alive.

In the second method of application closure, we design the following actions:

1. Every time the user begins a new action, that is, a click of the mouse or the press of a key, we compute the time lag between the present action and the previous action.
2. If the time lag is within the permitted limit, then we allow the action, but if it exceeds the permitted time limit, we close the session and flush all the session variables.
3. The user will be forced to launch the application all over again.

In practice, we use both methods. We set two time limits for application closure at the user's end. One lower time limit is to force the user to log in again to renew working on his or her session. The second and higher time limit is to close the application completely, forcing the user to initiate the application all over again. Why do we use this two-step method of application closure? We do it for the following reasons:

1. It is possible that the user is making some sort of reference to complete the action that was initiated, or the user might have left the workstation temporarily to fetch coffee or visit the toilet. For such cases, it would be hard on the user to relaunch the application. So, to protect the integrity of the data and application, we require the user to re-login. This time limit is usually less than five minutes.
2. If the session is idle for longer times, that is, the session is idle for the lower time limit and continues to be idle, we wait until the idle time crosses the second and higher time limit and then completely close the session. The user is not only logged out, but the session is also closed. Now the user will have to relaunch the application to continue the work.
3. Assuming the lower time limit to be five minutes and the higher time limit to be 20 minutes for the purpose of illustrating the method, the application would be designed to behave in this manner:
    a. If the first time limit is exceeded but the second time limit is not yet reached, the session is locked, and the user has to log in again to unlock the session.
    b. Once the session idle time exceeds the 20-minute time limit, we close the session entirely. The user has to relaunch the application to work again.

How does the relaunch of the application work? It would be enough for the user to refresh the browser. Alternatively, the user can close the browser, reopen it, and invoke our application again. The above method of using two steps to protect the session from being accessed by unauthorized users protects the integrity of the data and transactions being carried out in our application. Of course, the designer is always free to come up with more innovative alternatives to protect the application integrity caused by idleness at the user workstation.

Steps in application closure at the user's end: We design the following steps in closing of the application at the user's end:

1. We must first ensure that the closure action is truly initiated by the user and not by accident. So, we ought to display a warning message and obtain confirmation from the user before initiating the application closure.

2. We mark the login information as logged out, logging the time of logout. We need to update the login information table with the details of the logout time as well as how the logout was performed. That is, whether the session was closed by user-initiated logout or the system initiated logout needs to be captured. If the logout was initiated by the application, then we need to capture the reason the application had to initiate the logout.

3. We close the session and release all session variables, and then release all the system variables and other allocated RAM back to the OS.

4. We terminate connections to the database and any other connections made from the session. We need to design specific actions to close all database tables and database connections. Before doing so, we need to ensure that all updates to the open tables are written back into the tables.

5. We release any other work spaces allotted to the user in the session. If there are any other workspaces allocated to the session, then all such workspaces need to be released for use by other applications.

After designing all the above actions, then we need to design the actions needed to close the application at the user's end. Should we close the browser on the user's system when we close our application? In most cases, we leave the browser open but display a screen giving some sort of "Thank you for using our application" message. Some simply close the browser, too. Perhaps it is better to close the browser window to prevent any attempt by the user to use the back button and look at the contents of the previous screens. It may be the genuine user or someone accessing the system to phish out information. So, if our application is security sensitive, I would suggest closing the browser window when the application is closed at the user's end.

Application-to-User Communication

What is system-to-user communication? It is the information passed on to the user by the system. We pass many messages, including error messages, confirmatory messages, and informational messages, to the user. All these come under system-to-user communication. This communication is sometimes unidirectional and sometimes bidirectional. We pass error messages to the user that the user action was unexpected and cannot be handled by the application. In such cases, we take an acknowledgement of the message and then lead the user to rectify the mistake. Sometimes we may enter into a dialogue with the user using a series of questions and receive the answers. We may pose all the questions in one or more screens and receive all the answers at a time or pose the questions one by one and receive answers one at a time. The decision to pose all questions at a time or pose them one by one is to be made depending on the situation at hand.

It has been the practice in the software development industry to leave application-to-user communication to the programmers. We have to understand that the programmers are the juniormost in the software development hierarchy. They are ill equipped to perform this very important activity. Most applications fail not because they process information any less effectively than successful ones but because the application-to-user communication is poorer. Therefore, I would prefer that this aspect be designed rather than leaving it to the programmers.

Once the user initiates the application, the application takes over and holds the user's hand, guiding him/her all the way to facilitate business transactions. This is achieved by communication. The application performs the communication mostly through messages and sound in some cases and through images in other cases. Communication using sounds is by playing a music file or a beep to indicate the success or failure of the user action. Usually, a beep indicates failure of a user action and a piece of music indicates success of the user action. In communication applications permitting oral communication, various sounds, including telephone ring tones, are used. We use images on toolbars and icons to guide the user to select the desired option.

We carry out the bulk of our application-to-user communication using text. We use the following forms of textual communication:

1. Menu options
2. Captions
3. Error messages

Menu options: A menu is a list of choices available to the user to select and perform business transactions. Modern applications are a bundle of facilities to process various business transactions. We group the available facilities into logical groups and subgroups. Generally, we have the following hierarchy of menus:

1. *Product-level menu*: This menu is presented when the user launches the application at his/her end. The menu that is presented to the user is based on the security permissions granted to the specific user. Usually, we present an aesthetically designed page with some information on which the menu is placed at a convenient location. The positions at the top or on the left-hand side of the screen are generally preferred. In some cases, the menu is split into two or three menus and placed at the top, bottom, and left-hand side of the screen. The number of choices that need to be presented to the user determines the number of menus that need to be accommodated on the screen and where to place them. When the user clicks on an item in a menu, we need to take the user to the next functionality. If there are modules in the application, then we take the user to the selected module menu page. If there are no modules in the product, we take the user to the selected functionality. We use submenus only when the main menu has many items to be accommodated on a single menu.

2. *Module-level menu*: This is more or less similar to the product-level menu. However, usually modules do not have sublevels like the product. Large applications can have submodules, too. In such cases, we provide module menus with options to navigate to submodules.

3. *Submodule-level menu*: Submodule-level menus usually provide facilities that navigate the user to business transaction processing screens. Here, the menus can have cascading submenus. When we have cascading submenus, we usually restrict them to two more levels in addition to the menu of main options. That is, we have a total of three levels of menus. In cascading menus, selection of higher-level menu items leads to display of the next level of menu items. Selection of the menu item in the bottommost menu takes the user to the business transaction processing screen.

Menu design: Menus are the main means of communicating with the user to guide the user to achieve the desired business transactions.

1. *The caption*: We use short phrases as captions, with a maximum of three words to inform the user what to expect in the menu. Of course, there is no hard and fast rule about the number of words that can be used in a caption, but we do have limited space and we need to use that limited space to communicate the contents of that caption meaningfully. It has become the common practice to use just one-word captions in the top-level menu. The words File, Insert, Edit, View, Reports, Help, and so on have become common in the top-level menu. The exact caption we use depends on our application. Another important consideration in selecting the caption is to draw them from the jargon commonly used by the end users. That way, it becomes easy for the end users to understand the meaning of the caption. The overriding consideration is to avoid unnecessary work for the user, such as having to click on help just to understand the caption. The subsidiary menus can have more than one word for the caption. However, we need to minimize the number of words in the caption, but not at the cost of clarity.

2. *Positioning the menu*: The second design consideration in the menu design is where to position it. We can place a menu horizontally or vertically. If we arrange the top-level menu horizontally, we have the alternatives of placing it either at the top of the page or the bottom of the page. If we are vertically positioning the top-level menu, we have the alternatives of positioning it either on the left-hand side or right-hand side of the screen. While it is better to place all top-level menus at one location, it has become common practice in the industry to split the top-level menus into two, the important core functionality top-level menus at the top of the page and the ancillary functionality top-level menus at the bottom of the page. The items that are usually included in the menu at the bottom of the page are Contact Us, Support, Locations, and so on. Of course, there are no hard and fast rules about these, either.

3. *Number of levels of submenus*: When an item in the top-level menu is clicked, it can take the user to another web page, or it can open a submenu. When the user selects an option in the submenu, it may either take the user to another web page or open another submenu. What is the suggested number of levels of cascading of menus we should design? There is no standard defined on this aspect, but in my humble opinion, it is better to limit the cascading to a maximum of three levels, that is, one

item of top-level menu can have two lower-level menus. Assuming four options at each level, we would be able to provide 64 ($4 \times 4 \times 4$) options to the user.

4. *Number of items per menu*: We cannot set a limit to the number of items in any menu. It depends purely on the application domain. However, we have to design carefully such that all the items in a menu logically fit the caption in the immediately upper-level menu. The overriding design consideration is that the list should fit the vertical space available for displaying the list. If the list is so long that it needs two rows to display all the menu items, we better redesign the menu and break it up into further submenus.

5. *Toolbars*: Toolbars are part of the menus for those who cannot read the menu options because of visual impairment or a language barrier. Toolbars contain buttons, and each button has a small picture called an icon. The icon gives a fairly good idea of what happens when the button is clicked. Usually, each button is associated with a tooltip. When we hover the cursor on the button, tooltip text appears, describing the action to be performed by clicking the button. The critical aspect of designing a toolbar lies in the selection of the right pictures for the buttons. Some pictures have become de-facto standard for use as icons. For example, the picture of a floppy disk came to be associated with saving the content, and the picture of an envelope has come to be associated with opening an existing item. We can use other pictures, too, but we need to ensure that the pictures convey the intended action without ambiguity. Toolbars are used in applications that are likely to be used worldwide or by people belonging to various language groups that are not likely to understand the textual menu options. In most computer applications, toolbars are used to supplement the menus, but in applications for mobile phones and tablets, the roles are reversed.

6. *Tooltips*: Tooltips are textual explanations of the action to be performed by clicking the buttons on the toolbars. Tooltips need to be brief yet provide full information. They are akin to headlines in a newspaper. In multilingual applications, we can place all the tooltip texts in a database table and call them while loading the form or when the cursor hovers over the button and then display the tooltip text. The real concern in designing tooltips is in balancing brevity and clarity.

7. *Keyboard alternatives*: Experts are mouse-averse. They are so fast on the keyboard, they find it a drag to switch between keyboard and the mouse. Therefore, we need to provide a keyboard alternative for every clickable button. Pressing the Alt key is more or less standardized for activating clickable menus. We can make use of this to activate clickable menus. But the important aspect is that we design keyboard alternatives to the options we designed in the menus and toolbars.

8. *Activation of menu options*: We need to break down the click action into multiple subactions. The click action needs to be addressed as "mouse down," mouse up," "hover in," "hover out," and "click" actions. The "hover in" action occurs when the cursor is positioned on the selected option or button. It needs to activate the display tooltip action and highlight the selected option. The "hover out" action is when the cursor is moved away from the selected option or button. It needs to deselect the highlighted option. The "mouse down" action is when the user clicks the left button of the mouse but does not release it. When this action happens, we need to just highlight the menu option, the button on the toolbar, or wherever the cursor happens to be at that moment, indicating that the option is selected. The "mouse

down" action should not activate the selected menu option. The "mouse up" action is when the left button on the mouse is released when the "mouse down" action was already performed. We need to design the "mouse up" action in such a way that the action is performed based on the position of the cursor at the time when the "mouse up" action is performed. The "click" action is when the "mouse down" and "mouse up" actions are performed in quick succession and a "hover out" action was not performed between these two actions. This action should activate the action assigned to the menu option or the button.

Labels: Labels are placed by the side of controls on the screen or as headers on reports. Labels need to be brief yet meaningful. We do not have unlimited space on the screen. Even though modern-day computer screens are considerably larger than older screens, space is always finite and we try to accommodate as many controls as possible. Similarly, tablet and smart phone screens are larger than older phones, but space is always limited, even though we can cram in more characters than earlier. When we design multilingual applications, we need to design the labels such that the label texts are of same or similar length in all the languages for which we are designing the application. Label texts need to be placed in a database table along with the texts for other languages and called dynamically while loading the form. The overriding aspect of label design is balancing between brevity and meaningfulness. One cannot be sacrificed for the other.

Error messages: Error messages are an important aspect of application-to-user communication. Therefore, we should not leave the coder the responsibility of defining the error messages. Stupid error messages are the result of leaving the definition of error messages to the junior coder. I am pretty certain the most ridiculed error message, "Wrong command or file not found," was defined by a coder and not by a designer! It should be done at a higher level and that is the level of the designer. Every error message needs to communicate the fault that took place precisely so the user can take appropriate action to correct the situation. Even today, I come across error messages that convey nothing more than the occurrence of a fault. We must design error messages appropriately and put them in a table to be accessed by the coders to use them. While defining the error message, we ought to give more importance to describing the fault than brevity.

Navigation from one subsystem to another: As noted in the preceding sections, menus are used to allow the user to select the desired option to navigate from one set of functionalities to another. But nothing happens automatically inside applications unless it was so designed and built. Nothing would be built unless it was designed consciously. The following steps have to be designed into the application for navigation to happen smoothly and efficiently. One aspect we need to consciously design in navigating the user from one functionality to another is to close the open connections and tables and release the unnecessary variables held in the RAM, as well as releasing any resources held by the present function before navigating to the next functionality.

1. *The application launch*: This is the first step in the execution of the application by selecting the option from the menu presented by the operating system. The process of launching an application is described in a previous sections of this chapter. Once the application is launched, the first web page or screen is presented to the user. We have to note one thing here: the same screen may not be presented to all users. We have the option of presenting the same opening screen to all users and then making the options that are not allowed for the user invisible. Alternatively, we may present disparate screens to users based on the

security permissions allowed for the logged-in user. When the application is highly security sensitive, we design disparate screens appropriate to the level of the logged-in user proportionate to the security level of the specific user. Should we have a separately designed screen for each class of users, or should we build the screen on the fly? It is better to build the screen on the fly. It takes more programming effort but takes up much less space on the disk and in RAM. We need to make this decision based on the technology available and the competence of the coders in our organization. Whatever alternative we take, it makes no difference for the user, but it makes a difference in the matter of efficient use of the computer resources.

2. *Presentation of the first page/screen*: When we design this page, we need to consider whether to make this a transient page or an anchor page. When I say transient page, I mean that this page vanishes when the user navigates away from this page to another functionality. Alternatively, we can make this an anchor page, by which I mean the user is returned to this page when the user completes the action to which he/she navigated. An anchor page contains facilities/links for navigation to other functionalities. The other pages are functionality pages that close after the user completes the intended action, returning the user to the anchor page. The main advantage of the anchor page is that all the links are on one page and the code for those links is called from this one page. This protects the integrity of the application, and modification of that code needs to be tested from only one page. If we place all the links on all pages, when the code is modified, it needs to be tested from each of those pages that use the common code. The testing effort increases during software maintenance. As designers, it is also our duty to consider software maintenance and make it as effortless and easy as possible.

3. *Selection of the option by the user*: What is there so special about designing a process for selection of an option by the user? He or she would just point to the option and click the button, right? Yes, to a large extent. But, small or big, we designers are concerned with all processes irrespective of their size or importance. Technology has improved. Earlier, we had to click on an option to open its submenu or launch the functionality. Not anymore. Mere hovering of the cursor highlights and selects the option, and clicking the mouse button when the cursor is on the option launches the functionality triggered by the option. Now, we may even tap on the option with our finger. We have to use the latest technology and design accordingly. Voice-activated commands are coming up fast, and we need to utilize that technology, too, in the near future. By the time this book hits the stands, it may already be the norm!

4. *Navigation to the selected action*: This refers to the steps needed from opening the application to the launch of the desired functionality. When the application is launched, we need to display a home page appropriate for the user. We should not design our application to launch the same home page for all types of users. That is passé. The main tenet of design is to spend more effort in designing and producing the product so the effort spent by the end user is minimized. We have to design a unique page for every class of user. This is a challenging task, maybe, but it is doable. We can achieve this by designing separate physical pages or designing separate logical pages. In this variety, we design one landing page, but we display the options relevant to the class of user and hide the rest. This can

be achieved by placing a program in the form-load event of the landing page. By having only one page, we can protect the integrity of the programs because all functionality is built in one form and we do not have to change multiple pages. One major design tenet is that one program/artifact has to be built at one and only one location in the product. All other artifacts must make a reference to this during execution and in no case shall a piece of code be duplicated. Once we display a relevant landing page appropriate for the user, we have to design the menus and submenus in such a way that it is easy for the user to understand the path to his/her desired destination and navigate the way by clicking through the menu options.

5. *User completes the action*: When a user completes the desired transaction and achieves the desired results, what next? The main question a designer in this situation has to answer is: Should we take the user back to the previous page, display the present page with blank fields, or send the user to another new page? There is no single right answer. We can use the following guidelines.

a. When the functionality is spread across multiple pages, obviously, the navigation ought to be to the next logical page.

b. When the functionality is accommodated on one single page or it is the last page of multipage functionality, the navigation can be to the previous functionality or to the next page. Let us split this answer:

   i. If it is a data-entry screen such as entering a new entity in a master data table, we present the same screen with blank fields. In such cases, we need to provide an option on the screen so the user can exit this functionality and go to another functionality or close the application.

   ii. If it is a one-time end-user functionality such as ticket booking, we need to navigate the user to a screen that offers some value to the user. It could be new information about our services, a new class of items to be purchased, information about becoming a member so the user can take advantage of some special privileges, or similar pages.

   iii. In some cases, such as a manager reviewing and approving transactions, we need to take the user back to the anchor page or control station. The control station or anchor page is the landing page appropriate for the user from which he or she navigates to other pages based on the need and comes back as soon as the functionality designed for the navigated page is completed.

   iv. In certain cases, like surveys, I have seen a blank page with just a "Thank You" splashed on the screen. In my humble opinion, this is not very elegant. Even if there is nothing for the user to do, it may be better to navigate the user to an information page.

6. *Closure of the application*: In browser-based applications, the user may close the application at any time by clicking the close button in the right-hand-side top corner of the window. We should navigate the action to proper closing of application discussed in previous chapters. This ensures that all files are closed properly, all connections are properly disconnected, and all temporary variables are flushed as designed. We should never leave any close-window button to perform a default action.

User-to-Application Communication

The user communicates with the application to perform desired transactions. The user communication mostly consists of:

1. *Data entry for providing inputs to the application*: We ought to make it as easy and comfortable as possible for the user to enter inputs to the application. This topic was discussed in greater detail in Chapter 10 on input design.

2. *Selecting various options to navigate through the application to arrive at the desired functionality*: This is achieved through a set of well-designed menus and navigation design. This topic was discussed in the preceding sections.

3. *Generation of various reports available in the application*: We need to design meaningful reports and easy-to-use menus. These topics were discussed in the preceding sections and the chapter on output design.

4. *Seeking help from the application in effectively using the application*: The help facility built into the application ought to provide assistance to the user in effectively and efficiently using our application. We will discuss the designing the help facility in Chapter 14.

5. *Acknowledging messages from the application*: Most of the messages displayed by the application to the user are error messages or notification messages. An error message can be pointing out mistakes of commission or omission by the user or faults developed by the operating system while the application is in use. Some messages need no more action from the user than just acknowledging the message. Some messages need the user to correct the mistake committed earlier. Some messages may need the user to close the application and restart it. Some messages may need the user to report the problem to the concerned administrator of the application, the system, the network, or the database. We have to design these messages in such a manner that the user can easily grasp the import of the message and do the needful specified by the message.

Inter-Process Communication

Inter-process communication is used to exchange information between two programs under execution concurrently. It may be necessary sometimes to design inter-process communication. A process is a program in execution in the context of inter-process communication. This inter-process communication is not a frequent necessity in application programming. The operating system builds partitions around the RAM allocated to the program such that one program cannot access and modify the contents of the RAM allocated to another process. For this purpose, the operating system provides the facility referred to as shared memory. It may be called by different names in different operating systems. Shared memory is a chunk of RAM declared by one program as shared. When a program declares some amount of RAM as shared, then other programs can access it, read its contents, and modify its contents. How exactly to achieve this inter-process communication needs to be learned from the advanced sections of the operating system. Some operating systems provide for multiple programs to attach to the shared memory concurrently, and some allow only one process to attach to the shared memory at any given point in time. In any case, it is better to design shared memory usage assuming that only one program can use it at any point in time. Assume this shared memory is like a bathroom in home: a household bathroom is used by multiple people living in the house, but one at a time. A second person can use the bathroom once the one using exits.

In this manner, we can design inter-process communication.

Navigation from One Subsystem to Another

Navigation from one system to another is concerned with how the system is coupled. A system in an application consists of multiple subsystems. One way of coupling them is tight coupling. In this coupling, all the systems are accessible only from the main system. If you are using one subsystem and desire to move to another subsystem, you need to close the subsystem in use and then go back to the main system and access the next desired subsystem. This was possible in applications that were not web based. Those executable files were generated by the compiler from source code and linked to the libraries. But the present web-based applications work by interpreting the source code. That is, the source statements are compiled on the fly during execution. Still, we can make the subsystems accessible only from the main system.

In the first case, when access to subsystems is allowed only from the main system, we do not have to check if the user is logged in or not whenever a new form is loaded. But, what if the user directly gives a reference to the desired subsystem in the browser? Then we need to check from where the request came and deny it if the request did not originate from the main system.

Therefore, either way, we need to do some checking for the authenticity of the request before loading any new form. So, both methods are acceptable designs in navigating from one subsystem to another. We can select either method for navigation from one subsystem to another.

Data Conversion Process

The main purpose of the application is to convert input data to output information. All input data coupled with master data forms part of the output at one time or another. The input data is subjected to some sort of processing including mathematical treatment, ordering, classifying, or formatting. Most of our software code is aimed at doing this work. Now, while doing so, we need to achieve the following objectives.

1. *Achievement of core functionality*: We have to ensure that the core functionality specified for the program is achieved. This must be achieved with the precision specified for the results and in the least possible amount of time and use of system resources.

2. *Achievement of ancillary functionality*: We have to ensure that all the ancillary functionality set for the software is achieved. This must be achieved with in the least possible amount of time and resources used.

3. *Defect free*: For the program to be defect free, the design must be flawless and the code should not give any opportunity to give rise to faults during execution. Our design must ensure that all aspects are covered to ensure a defect-free product.

4. *Defect prevention*: Even when our product is defect-free, there may still exist room for the user to inject defects into the product by inputting wrong data. By building in extensive data validation routines, and then making use of them in all input screens, we can prevent defect injection by the users during the production runs of our application.

5. *Error trapping*: We discussed this topic extensively in the earlier chapters. This is to be mainly achieved by enforcing implementation of the error-trapping guidelines portion of the coding guidelines during the construction phase of software development. Still, at the design stage, we need to identify the places where errors can raise their ugly heads and point them out in our designs so the programmers can use error-trapping routines and trap all errors successfully.

6. *Efficiency*: We should ensure that the computer resources are utilized efficiently. The programmers have a key role in this, but our designs also have to ensure that resources are not gobbled up without a specific purpose. At the cost of repeating, the resources were/are never in excess of the requirements.

7. *Concurrency control*: This aspect is to be tackled at the design stage. This cannot be achieved at the coding stage. The designer is the only one who can see the possibility of resources getting deadlocked in the case of dedicated resources and getting garbage in/out of sharable resources. We have to then design appropriately so that that concurrent operations are properly controlled and the integrity of the data and the transactions is protected.

8. *Failure response*: In spite of defect prevention and error trapping we build in, failures are still a reality. They may occur because of a fault in the operating system, an external attack, malfunction of an intermediate layer, or malfunction of a hardware resource, but failures do occur. When the failure is not due to faults in our application, what can we do? We have to design our system such that unexpected failures do not hurt the integrity of our application and its data. This is usually addressed in the coding guidelines, but at design stage, too, we can detect locations in our applications where the integrity of the application could be affected and point them out to the programmers in our designs so the programmers can implement coding guidelines that will eliminate or minimize the probable damage to our application due to unforeseeable failures.

Installation Process

Is installation of software a part of the application that designers have to focus on? Not really, but the software that is designed by the designers ultimately needs to be installed on some target computer system. Our applications may be a single PC-based application or a multiserver, web-based solution, still it has to be installed on some target machine.

When the software is installed on a single machine, we need to design a package containing the directories and all the software artifacts that need to be installed on the target machine. It should contain the executable files, DLLs, pictures, any master data files, help files, and other artifacts. All these artifacts need to be compressed into a packed file for easy handling. Then for creating all the database tables, we need to prepare a table creation script that needs to be run from within a database. We may also have to prepare a script to authenticate the CD and create necessary tables on our server containing information about the CDs being shipped. Then, we need to prepare an installation script that performs the following actions:

1. Locates the system directory or folder in which new applications are generally installed

2. Creates necessary directories that are needed in the system directory

3. Loads the DLLs in the system library, directory, or folder if such a folder exists

4. Registers the application with the registry, which is searched for information about applications

5. Performs any other actions needed by the specific system at hand

6. Deletes all temporary files or directories created in the installation process

Then, we also need to prepare a document containing information about the installation process. We can also prepare a script, if possible, to run the installation automatically upon insertion of the CD/DVD in the drive. Then, all these have to be built into one package that can be copied onto a CD/DVD. We designers have to design all these tasks. One thing we need to keep in mind is that the process of installation needs to be as automatic as possible. Of course, we need to take user input when needed, but other than that, we need to run the installation process without any need for manual intervention. In earlier days, we received a product key from the user, but with the widespread use of the Internet, we can authenticate the CD using the Internet. One precaution we need to take while making the package is to ensure that all the DLLs referred to by the application must be packaged along with the other artifacts of the application. When we do this, the uninstaller does not delete the common DLLs in system directories when our application is uninstalled. We should not design our installation script in such a manner that we replace any of the common artifacts already existing in the computer with our artifacts. We also need to include an uninstall script along with our application that can be used to uninstall our application should the need arise. If we use the default uninstaller provided by the operating system, it may accidentally delete some common DLLs of the operating system and affect the functioning of the computer. Then, the build can actually be built by the programmers and handed over to the production people for producing the necessary number of CDs/DVDs.

Presently, we also use the Internet for installation of software. The user clicks a link on our website after making a payment to trigger the installation process. Usually, we allow a small executable file to be downloaded that performs the directory creation, and then it downloads all other artifacts into the concerned directories created by it. In this method, instead of inserting a CD/DVD in the drive, the user clicks a link on our website.

In web-based applications, the installation is not like on the PC, where we insert a CD or DVD in the drive. We need to take possession of the servers and then carry out the installation tasks ourselves. Of course, we can automate as many tasks of installation as possible, but we may need to handle the bulk of the installation process manually. In a multiserver web application, we need to install our software on the app server and database on the database server. We need to locate the directory or folder that responds to requests that come from the Internet. That is where we need to install the home page. Then, once the user lands on our home page, we can navigate the user to the desired page from there. The software artifacts are loaded on the server that contains the framework or the app server that runs our application. We may have to build multiple packages to load the artifacts on the right server machine. While the actual number of packages that need to be built depends on the configuration of the website, the below is a typical list of packages that need to be built:

1. Software artifacts, including programs, DLLs, help files, parameter files, pictures, and so on, that are needed to run the application. If the software has large modules that can be loaded on multiple servers, then we have to make main packages to load on multiple servers if the need arises.
2. Database table creation script and any associated artifacts.
3. Home page and other associated static web pages.
4. If our application has special software for ensuring safety and security, we need to make separate packages of such software.
5. Any other situation-specific packages as necessary.

We need to design the installation packages and installation scripts as necessary so that programmers can implement our design on the target machines efficiently and effectively.

Rollout Process

Rollout of the software is an implementation issue handled by the programmers and the installation team. The following activities are performed during the rollout:

1. Installation of the software and testing it to ensure that it is working as expected. This testing is not elaborate but cursory in nature.
2. Creation of all parameter files and testing the data for accuracy.
3. Creating the database, filling the master data tables with data, and testing them for accuracy of the data.
4. System testing to ensure that all components of the system are working as expected.
5. Fix any glitches found in the testing and make the system ready for operation.
6. Train the users to perform their transactions using our application. This activity can be carried out in parallel to other activities enumerated above.
7. Subject the system to beta testing, that is, the users experiment with the system to process some transactions as well as to familiarize themselves with the methods of performing transactions and learn the facilities available in the new system.
8. Train the administrators, system, database, network, and application, in administering the system and troubleshooting when necessary.
9. Train the managerial users at an appropriate time on how to use the new system to manage results expected of their responsibilities.

10. Clean up the system when all the experimentation is completed and all the users are ready to use the system with real-life data and transactions.

11. Roll out the system to production use.

12. Provide handholding assistance to users for the warranty period accepted by marketing and specified in the order.

Now, software designers are not expected to play a major role in this process. All the same, designers are expected to provide instruction manuals, user manuals, operating manuals, and training materials to the installation and commissioning team. It may become necessary for the designers to intervene in the installation process to troubleshoot any problem that proves tough for the installation team. Sometimes, the training of end users and managerial users may be required to be carried out by the designers, as they are the best people to explain the ways of getting things done using the application.

14

Help Design

Introduction

Here, the term *help* refers to the help facility the application provides to the users of the application software. The guidance and assistance made available to the users online without requiring the users to leave what they have been doing has come to be referred to as the help facility. Now, we can't think of software without a built-in help facility except in real-time software and other such software. This has become so common, the bulky manuals for users, administration, and troubleshooting have become more or less extinct. In their place, the use of function key F1 has become the default action to summon help from the system. If provided at all, softcopies of these manuals are provided on the supplier website for download. In the days of the character user interface (CUI) and command-line prompt, one could not even give a command properly without studying the user manual. Now, it is point and click on the GUI, so the need to study the manuals has been rendered obsolete.

But this has placed a further onus on software designers and developers to include this feature in every software product. This is an additional task for the designers. Quite a few organizations assign this task to the technical writers and spare the software designers. Usually, the technical writers or documentation specialists prepare the help text, generate a help file, and give it to the developers, who integrate it with the software. While help compilers provide a feature to summon pertinent help, it is often not used, as the help file allows for searching the help document for the required information when we either click the help option provided on the screen or press the F1 key. The whole help document is displayed in a new window on the application screen. This has become the common practice in most application software packages.

But is this the only way to provide usage assistance to software users? Not really! We designers can do better than that. In this chapter, let us discuss how we provide usage assistance to the software user efficiently and effectively. Now, let us discuss how we can design the best help feature for our users.

Providing the Help Users Look For

Users look for the help provided by the application only when they are not able to understand what is expected of them to process a business transaction. This is how we can ensure that the users are not required to search for the help feature and provide the best help when the user looks for it:

1. Screen descriptions
2. Onscreen help for using the system without the necessity of reading the help pages
   a. Labels
   b. Tooltips
   c. Hover messages
   d. Error messages
   e. Notification messages
3. Help pages

Let us discuss how we can design these aspects in such a manner that we can delight the users who use our application.

Screen Descriptions

It is not very common to provide a description of the functionality provided by the screen in present-day application software. We provide a screen header, which we try to make as informative as possible, but the page header is usually in a large font and is limited to one line. So, we will not be able to make it more informative than the name of the screen. Unless we pack the screen with too many controls, we have space for three lines. We should use this space to briefly describe the functionality that can be achieved by the screen. Of course, we need to keep the text as brief as possible. We should note that this brevity should not be at the cost of the needed explanation. We can achieve a page description by following these guidelines while designing the screen pages:

1. We can describe more fully the functionality of the page to offer more guidance to the user and eliminate or minimize the need to refer to the user manuals.
2. We ought not to use unnecessary poetic language just to beautify the sentences. We need to focus on communicating the information and desist from making the description an ad copy.
3. Depending on the space available, we may take a minimum of two lines to a maximum of five lines. More than five lines is usually not required to describe the functionality of a screen page.
4. If we have multiple tabs, we need to have a separate description that is appropriate for the tab.
5. The language used ought to be crisp and focused on describing the functionality. We should not be tempted to use flowery or poetic language, which obscures the meaning and is counterproductive.
6. In case we are not able to accommodate the description in the available space, it is advisable to provide a link to another page that fully describes the functionality. We may name the link with a tag like "See more," "Continue reading...," or something like that.

This description alleviates the need to refer the user manual to a large extent. Of course, I agree that we cannot totally eliminate all the need to refer the user manual. We need to aim at minimizing the need to refer the user manual, at least for normal usage. For users of the advanced features of our application, it is necessary to refer to the user manual.

We need to provide onscreen help for using the system without a need to read the help pages. We provide this help using the following means:

Labels: With every control we use on the screen, we provide a prompt that explains the contents of that control. We use labels to provide this prompt. We place this label close to the control, either at the top of the control or to the left-hand side of the control. Only in rare cases when we have no space on these two sides do we use the bottom of the control or to the right-hand side of the control. Unless we have too few controls on the screen, it is not possible to provide too much space for these labels. So, these labels have to be short. Usually, these prompts are limited to a maximum of three or four words. Therefore, we cannot rely completely on the labels to supply all the information That is the reason we need to supplement the labels with other means of information.

Tooltips: Tooltips are a facility normally provided in all programming languages. A tooltip is text that becomes visible when the cursor hovers over the control and disappears when the cursor moves out. Tooltips are a great facility to provide additional information to the user in addition to the label prompt of the control. We can have longer text in the tooltip than on the label. We need to design a tooltip as a mandatory feature for every control on the screen.

Hover messages: It is possible that all programming languages may not provide a tooltip facility for all the controls available, or we may be using a custom-developed control. In such cases, we may use the "hover" or "gotfocus" method to display the necessary text to supplement the text on the label prompt of the control.

Error messages: Error messages are displayed when the user commits an error. In non-internet–based applications, development platforms allowed message boxes or dialog boxes to display error and other messages, which helped us display long and meaningful messages to the user. But now, in the age of internet-based applications, message boxes are not provided by most of the development platforms. So, we place the messages right on the screen close to the control, but hide them from view and set them to visible only when we are required to display error messages. This presents us a challenge. Using a label to contain the error message and then making it visible or invisible makes it difficult for us to display a long and meaningful message. Some applications use the status bar at the bottom of the screen to display error messages, and this allows us one line of space for our error message. We can demarcate an area, preferably at the bottom of the screen, and then provide a longer and more meaningful message in that area. To allow the user to know to which control the error message pertains can be achieved by highlighting the prompt of that control in red. Whatever solution we use, we need to ensure that the error messages are as meaningful as possible. Of course, it is a fight between brevity and the need to be meaningful, and we need to win the fight to provide an easy-to-use application to the users.

While notification messages have a purpose different from that of error messages, they are similar from the standpoint of software design and pose identical challenges. We need to solve those challenges, as we discussed in the above section on error messages.

Links: Links to other web pages are not part of the help feature in the strict view of help design. But, in my humble opinion, we can use this feature to provide better onscreen help to the users. When we do not have the feature of message boxes in the selected development platform and need to pass a long, meaningful message, we can provide a short message and a link to another full-fledged web page of help, which gives fuller information. We can caption this link as "see more…" or "read more…" so that the user understands that he/she can get the information if necessary without leaving the transaction screen. However, we need to ensure that the link, when clicked, opens the help page in another tab without disturbing the present page.

Often, the work of devising the onscreen help is left to the programmer. It is not a very good practice. It is better that we design these messages and subject them to editing by an editor. Then, the finalized messages need to be entered into a database table, and a reference is provided in our design artifacts so that the programmer can retrieve the appropriate message and use it in the programs.

Help Pages

Help pages are to be designed to provide comprehensive help to the user. The content should be edited by professional editors even though it has to be originally drafted by the software designers. While designing the help pages, we need to keep in mind the fact that the user is not a software professional. We need to develop help pages for three roles, namely:

1. Users
2. System administrators
3. Security administrations

Each set of help pages is divided into sections and subsections as follows:

1. A title page and a table of contents: In a book, these two items would be on two different pages, but not so in help pages. Both can be on the same page.
2. Each item in the table of contents may go up to four levels; that is:
    a. *Section*: This gives a title indicating the contents of the section. It is not necessary that every section have subsections. This contains an overview of the topic. Then, each of the subtopics is split off as a subsection. If there is no need for subsections, then all the content is included here.
    b. *Subsection*: It is a part of the section, but a significant one, and by putting a heading, we direct the user to the desired content. It is not necessary for each subsection to have sub-subsections. When we use subsections, we should have a minimum of two subsections in a section. Each subsection has a portion of the contents of the topic denoted by the section.
    c. *Sub-subsection*: Use of sub-subsections is infrequent. We use them only when there is a need to show a paragraph as a significant part so the user can jump to it directly should he/she desire. When we use sub-subsections, we should have a minimum of two sub-subsections in the subsection. Each sub-subsection has a paragraph or more of the contents of the topic denoted by the subsection.
    d. *Sub-sub-subsection*: Usage of sub-sub-subsections is very rare. Only when the sub-subsection needs to have sublevel matter do we resort to the usage of sub-sub-subsections. We need to show its significance if we use this heading to help

the user to go the desired information. When we use sub-sub-subsections, we should have a minimum of two sub-sub-subsections. Each sub-sub-subsection has a paragraph or more of the contents of the topic denoted in the subsection.

Let us now see what the help pages need to contain.

The User Help Pages

The user performs business transitions using our application software. The user may be an ordinary user performing business transactions or a supervisor user extracting information from the transaction for decision making or to authorize business transactions where necessary. In these help pages, we need to cover the following aspects:

1. An overview section containing:
   a. An overview of the functionality provided by our application software. We cover all major functionalities of the application in one section. We enumerate all the modules in the software, giving a brief description of each module.
   b. A brief introduction to all the modules in our application software. Here, we need to enumerate all the submodules in each of the modules enumerated in the overview section. We also give explanation about the navigation to the desired module and the security rights set for each of these modules.
2. A section each for all the modules. This gives all the functionalities provided in each of the modules. We also explain the sequence of achieving the desired functionality and relationship between the functionalities in the module, if any, as well as the prerequisites to be in place for performing transactions in the module.
3. A section for each of the transactions containing:
   a. An overview of how the transaction is achieved. Here, we need to specify the sequence of actions to complete each of the transactions properly: the prerequisites that need to be in place before we can initiate the transaction, as well as the mopping-up actions that have to be performed to properly close the transaction and other applicable information. Let us take the functionality of raising a material procurement requisition in a material management application. This consists of filling out a form with the item code for the material, the quantity, the date of requirement, the approximate cost, and the details of the person raising the request. The next step is authorization by an authorized executive. Then, it is routed to finance to ensure that the budget provides for procuring this item. If there is the budget, then the item is routed to the procurement department. If the budget has no provision for this item, it may be routed back to the originator of the request, who then has to arrange a budget provision for it and redo the process. We need to explain this here in a more elaborate manner. Here, we would have three subsections: for raising the request, for authorizing it, and then for allocating the budget or rejecting the request. If the controls are few on the screen and a writeup is not very long, then we can accommodate all of the text here.

b. A help page (or pages) for each of the screens covering each of the controls on the screen. In this subsection, we describe how to use each of the controls, like selecting the item from a list, entering information, the type of information to be entered, the maximum length, and any other rules pertaining to the entry.

c. A help page (or pages) for each of the outputs that can be generated from the transaction. This needs to include the types of outputs, the information included on each of them, what we need to ensure is in place before we generate the output, how to ensure the accuracy of the information presented in the output before we pass it on to the entity that requisitioned it, and any other relevant information

d. Troubleshooting information when things do not go as expected, including what to check, who to contact, and what to do. When the actual results are at variance with the expected results, then we know that there is trouble and something went wrong. In this section, we need to include all the information that we can foresee and the remedial actions that can be taken to get the expected results accurately. We may also include a checklist of information here so that the user can check the actions leading up to the generation of the output and rectify any of the previous errors.

There could be situation-specific requirements for these help pages, and we need to include all such information. Here, we need to ensure that no IT jargon is included, as the users are not expected to be IT professionals. Users are using computers with our software to perform business transactions and produce the results expected of them.

System Administrator Help Pages

Multiuser web-based applications need dedicated system administrators to keep the application software functioning smoothly, delivering the expected results, and servicing the users round the clock. This functionality generally does not allow access by ordinary users performing business transactions. System administrators are usually IT people proficient in IT terminology using the system with minimal help. The help pages for this group need not be as elaborate as in the case of ordinary users. We can use IT jargon to precisely explain the issues.

1. An overview section containing explanations of:

    a. *A brief description about system administration*: It should explain the facilities provided in the system administration module and how to go about utilizing those facilities to administer the system efficiently.

    b. *A brief introduction to all the modules in our application software*: In this section, all the functionalities provided in the system administration need to be enumerated, with a brief explanation of what can be achieved using that functionality.

2. Detailed explanations of each of the system administration functions:

    a. *User management*: We need to provide a detailed explanation of how to add/ delete users and modify the user privileges. We need to explain each function, giving examples where necessary.

b. *Security privilege management*: In systems where security privileges are granted to each user, this module is needed. We have to give detailed explanation of each of the privileges, along with the precautions to be taken while allocating privileges to the user and the consequences of misusing that privilege. We also need to explain how to assign or remove the privileges granted to a user. Then, before assigning any privilege, there should be certain prerequisites in place. Such prerequisites include authorizations from the user department as well as the IT department. All these have to be explained in detail in this subsection.

c. *Exception report generation*: The security module has facilities for generating exception reports about unusual activities, security incidents, disasters, and so on. How to generate these reports needs to be explained in detail in this subsection.

d. *Batch reports generation*: Certain reports need to be generated at the organizational level, as these reports have sensitive information or are so bulky that ordinary users cannot generate them. These reports are periodic in nature and may have to be generated daily, weekly, monthly, quarterly, half yearly, and yearly. Then there are reports that need to be generated based on a trigger incident. We need to explain in detail what those reports are and what prerequisites need to be in place before generating them.

e. *Configuration management and changing software artifacts*: Configuration management activities on the production system include changing software artifacts. These activities cannot be performed while users are logged in and are performing business transactions. Therefore, these are typically performed on a weekend day at midnight. As no employee would like to stay until midnight to perform these activities, the configuration management software usually automates these activities. But the system administrator needs to make the system ready by uploading new artifacts into the specified folders/directories so the system can pick them up and replace the existing artifacts with these new artifacts. We need to explain in detail all these aspects in this subsection.

f. *Trouble ticket management*: If our application software provides for handling help requests from the users, we need to include this subsection and explain in detail how to enter a help request into the system, track it, resolve it, and close the request. This section also needs to include details about generating periodic reports to measure the efficiency of the troubleshooting activities.

g. *Help desk management*: The help desk is a facility to help the users resolve the problems they face in using the application. It could range from a single person to a full-fledged call center. They need a subset of the system administrator functions through which they are able to see the details of users without the ability to modify anything. When this functionality is included in our application software, we need to develop help pages to help the help desk personnel use the system efficiently so they can render effective help to the users.

h. *Application parameter management*: Large applications need a host of parameters to run the application. These need changes occasionally, triggered by some environmental changes. These data items affect the entire application. Therefore, we usually change these offline and upload the files to the production server using the configuration management system. We need to include all the details of how to change the parameters and upload the new parameter files to the production server.

i. *Periodic maintenance*: We need to provide information about periodicity for preventive maintenance of the data to be captured from the maintenance activities performed, the reports to be generated, and how to perform all these activities in this subsection.

j. *Reporting about system administration activities*: We usually include functions to cull information on the activities performed by the system administrator and generate reports to forward to management for evaluation of the performance of the system administrator. In this help page, we need to include a detailed explanation of how to use those functions.

k. *Any other facility available in the system*: If any other functionality is included in the system administrator functionality, then we need to include help pages for those functionalities, too, and provide detailed explanations for all such functionalities.

It is to be noted that not all these functionalities exist in every piece of application software. Some of the system administration functionality may be achieved using specialized tools. Configuration management, help desk management, and trouble ticketing systems are usually handled using specialized tools. But if we include those functionalities in our application, we need to explain them in the help pages.

One precaution—these pages need to be accessible only to those who have access to the system administration functionality. These pages should not be bundled along with the normal user help pages. That would be a security risk—a big one!

Security Administrator Help Pages

We need to include the following in these help pages. One precaution—these pages should not be accessible by all users. They need to be available only to those who have access privileges to security administration functionality.

1. Detailed explanation of each of the security administration functions:

    a. *A brief note about security administration*: Here, we have to explain the details about how to go about ensuring security to the application data and software artifacts. We have to explain physical security, security provided by the application software, and protection of database(s) that can be accessed bypassing the application software.

    b. *A brief note about security provided by our application software*: Here, we have to explain the philosophy of the security system implemented in our application software. We also need to include details about the various security roles built into our software. We have to enumerate the security functions performed by each of the security roles. This subsection should give all the facilities provided by our application software.

2. Detailed explanation of each of the security administration functions: In this section, we give the micro details of all the security functions built into our application software. In the subsections of this section, we have to enumerate the

security roles that can access and perform the functions detailed in the subsection, along with the details of how to achieve the assigned functionality.

a. Monitoring the security of the application, including the application data and software artifacts, is ensured both by preventing and blocking attacks as well as tracking the security incident which took place. In this subsection, we describe in detail how the security system monitors the data and the software artifacts. We also have to describe how the persons performing the security roles need to go about monitoring the data and the software artifacts. If an attack takes place, the monitoring system raises alerts as designed, and we need to explain in detail the alerts built into our system and the actions that have to be taken by the system security personnel.

b. *Security incident management*: When a security incident has taken place, we need to take some actions to track the impact of the incident and then produce audit trails so that investigators can locate the perpetrator of the attack and bring that person to justice. In this subsection, we need to explain the facilities provided in our software for these actions as well as how to generate the information necessary to determine the impact of the incident and supporting information to track the perpetrator.

c. *Disaster backup management*: A disaster goes beyond a security incident. It is when the system, including hardware and/or software, is damaged beyond repair and we need to build everything from scratch. For this purpose, we take periodic backups of the application data as well as the software artifacts and keep a set away from our facility at a different physical/geographical location altogether. These activities are handled by different tools. The database provides for a backup and restore utility, and the software artifacts are backed up using a system utility. But if our software provides for these facilities, we need to explain them in this section. We also need to explain how to utilize those functionalities and achieve the desired protection. If our software does not provide these facilities, we need to explain the importance of disaster management and recovery and emphasize it.

d. *Reporting about the security administration activities*: We have to provide reports at regular intervals of time about various activities performed by the security system, exception reports about security incident handling, and disaster management activities performed. Our application may provide for these facilities. We need to explain in this subsection all those facilities and how to implement those functionalities and achieve the desired results.

All in all, our help pages are aimed at providing exhaustive guidance to users without the necessity of taking specialized training to use our application software. We need to cover every single functionality and its complete details in a lucid manner. This is what we need to design in these help pages.

Context-Sensitive Help

All users would like to have context-sensitive help rather than looking at the first page of the help manual with options to search based on a phrase or parsing through an ill-written table of contents. Most of the tools that assist in the development of help pages provide for tagging the sections of screens and controls on the screen. Of course, I admit it is a tedious task to make the connections between the screen/controls with the sections in the help pages. This tedium is a frequent cause for not seeing context-sensitive help in many applications. I would like to offer these suggestions for your consideration so that some amount of context sensitivity can be built into the help system.

1. All development platforms provide a facility to recognize the active screen.
2. All development platforms provide a facility to locate the position of the cursor on the screen.
3. Now, collect the names of the screens and controls where the cursor is positioned and pass these as parameters to the help pages display tool.
4. Usually, we can pass parameters to the language construct that causes help pages to be displayed on the screen.
5. Using the parameters received, the help pages are searched, and the relevant content is located and displayed on the screen.

But the best way is to connect the sections of the help pages to the controls on the screen to get real context-sensitive help. One alternative is to connect all the help sections of one set of functionality to the screen, achieving that functionality. This would limit the effort required of the user to searching within that small amount of content, which is easier than searching the whole help manual.

15

Establishing the Software Design

Introduction

Once we make decisions regarding the selection of the alternatives appropriate for our product, we need to establish the design. It is needed so others can use the designs in the coding and testing of the software product. This involves documenting the design, subjecting the design artifacts to quality control activities, then obtaining approval for the design documents and releasing them. In this chapter, let us discuss the activities carried out as part of the establishment of software design.

Objectives of Establishing the Software Design

One question we often come across in the software development industry is, "Is it necessary to document the software designs? In the time we take to establish the designs, we can as easily develop the software!" We aim to achieve these objectives by the establishment of software designs.

1. By documenting the design, we bring predictability to the product even before it is built.
2. By documenting the software design, we make it amenable for another person to review the design and ensure that everything is in order.
3. By documenting the design, it becomes feasible to carry out quality control activities that ensure a defect-free product. As design is one level above constructing the product, we prevent design defects percolating downward and getting magnified in intensity. A design defect is much more severe than the coding defect and that much harder to fix. The cost of fixing a design defect is much more costly, and subjecting the design artifacts to quality-control activities minimizes the design defects creeping to downstream activities.
4. By documenting the design, we provide a basis for future projects and a knowledge base to be used by future projects.
5. By documenting the design, the productivity of the programmer increases multifold, reducing the cost of the project.

6. By documenting the design, the propensity for committing errors comes down drastically because the design considered all the alternatives and selected the most appropriate one.

7. By documenting the design, we can relieve the programmer of making crucial decisions regarding algorithms. Thus, the programmer can implement methods and other aspects of good programming, leading to a robust and reliable product.

8. By documenting the design, we can use relatively less costly programmers to implement the design, yet deliver a high-quality software product.

Therefore, it makes sense to document the design and establish it. Now, what do I mean by establishing the design? Here are the activities of establishing the design:

1. Document the design using the methodology adopted by the organization.

2. Arrange for quality assurance activities to be performed on the design artifacts.

3. Rectify the defects uncovered and arrange for the closure of the defects.

4. Arrange for managerial review and close the defects, if any, uncovered.

5. Arrange for approval of the design artifacts and release them for implementation.

Methodologies for Documenting the Design

The software development industry has been using several methods for establishing software designs. The important among them are:

1. Flowcharts for system and program

2. SSADM

3. OOM

4. UML

Agile methodologies do not place an emphasis on establishing software design. Agile philosophy frowns on documentation in general. Agile methodologies have their place in the scheme of software development. But when you come to building large-scale or mission critical applications, it would be of great advantage to document the design, and the merits were discussed in the preceding section. Let us briefly examine each of these methodologies here.

Flowcharts

Flowcharts are pictorial representation of the logic and flow of information or program execution. They use a set of symbols that are connected by arrows. Flowcharts are drawn from top to bottom or left to right. Table 15.1 shows the popular flowcharting symbols.

TABLE 15.1

Flowcharting Symbols

Symbol	Explanation	Symbol	Explanation
	Terminal—either the start or the end		Pre-defined process
	Process step		Punched cards reader or punch
	Decision or a relational operation		Magnetic tape drive
	Input or output		Set of process steps
	Connector to connect flowcharts continued on other pages		Display
	Indicates output on to paper		Manual input
	Indicates magnetic disk for either input or output		Manual operation

There are many more symbols used in flowcharting. But this method is more or less outdated and is not being used extensively, even though, to clarify a point, we do use flowcharts even today. Interested readers may obtain a book on flowcharting and read it to completely learn about and understand flowcharting. A sample flowchart is shown in Figure 15.1.

SSADM

SSADM was originally developed for the Office of Government Commerce (then it was Central Computer and Telecommunications Agency) of the United Kingdom for use in procurement of software for governmental use. It has been in use since the 1980s and has been implemented in many organizations across the world, each adding its own flavor to the methodology. SSADM uses the waterfall method as the software development life cycle. Figure 15.2 depicts the waterfall model pictorially. The waterfall model originally had five phases, namely Requirements, Design, Implementation, Verification, and Maintenance. But, since the original definition, organizations have made many modifications to this model, and many variants are found in the organizations. SSADM lays emphasis on rigorous documentation as the basis for software development. This emphasis, in fact, has originated in the manufacturing model used in the project type of manufacturing organizations.

Below are the stages used popularly in the industry:

1. Feasibility study
2. Requirements analysis and specification

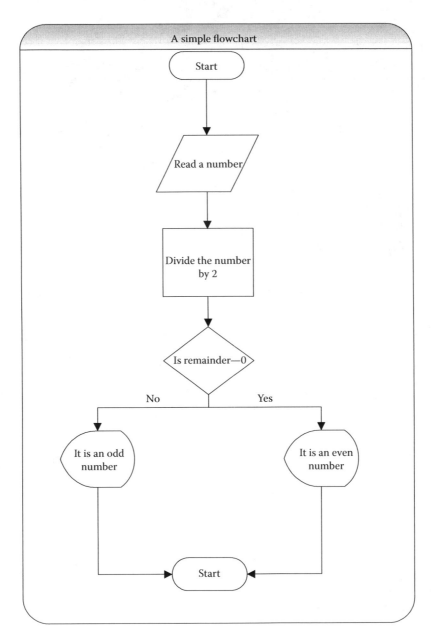

FIGURE 15.1
A sample flowchart.

3. High-level design
4. Low-level design
5. Construction
6. Testing
7. Delivery and implementation
8. Software maintenance

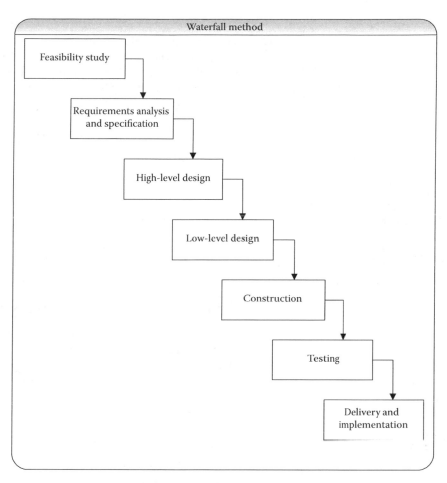

FIGURE 15.2
Waterfall model.

I am not delving deeply into the phases of SSADM because it is not the focus of the book. Its usage in the industry has significantly dwindled. SSADM also devised a set of tools and techniques for modeling and documenting requirements and design. These are:

1. *Logical data modeling*: The logical data model was proposed during the days of hierarchical DBMSs (database management systems) and network DBMSs. With the onset of relational DBMSs, entity relationship (ER) modeling was developed from logical data modeling.

2. *Dataflow modeling*: As computerized systems process data, the system processes revolve around the data. Each process transforms a part of the system data in some way. All the processes, when executed, transform all the system data as desired. The data flows from one process to another until information is extracted and presented as output of the system. This model is currently referred to as process modeling.

3. *Entity behavior modeling*: This is modeling the sequence of operations in the system. Events in the processes impact and transform the entities. We model each event, the behavior of the impacted entities, and the sequence of events in a process from the first input to the final output diagrammatically in this model.

SSADM, from the day it was implemented, held its place among various other software development methodologies. The original model was modified by many organizations and researchers. I would go to the extent of saying that all other methodologies that emerged later on still contained a streak of SSADM in them. In the spiral model and the iterative model, each increment/iteration is still a waterfall model. The logical data modeling that later transformed into the ERD is the only way to model system data even today. Process standards like ISO 9000 and CMM® implement the philosophy of SSADM. The IEEE also followed the SSADM model in defining the software engineering standards when they released the first set. Agile methods denounce the heavy reliance of SSADM on documentation but still implement the waterfall model in each of the iterations. In outsourced development, SSADM is still significantly utilized to drive software development contracts.

Entity Relationship Diagrams

Data modeling deals with establishing the relationships between various data entities in the system. In any information transaction, data is transmitted between entities. Let us take a simplified purchase transaction:

1. An item is to be purchased in an organization. So a purchase order is raised on a vendor.
2. The vendor supplies the item to the inventory.
3. The vendor raises an invoice to the organization for payment.
4. The organization makes the payment.

From this transaction, we could establish relationships:

1. There is a relationship between the purchase order and the vendor.
2. There is a relationship between the vendor and the inventory.
3. There is a relationship between the vendor and the invoice.
4. There is a relationship between the invoice and the payments.

Modeling relationships of this type is referred to as data modeling.

An entity is a place, person, or thing and is described by its attributes. For example, an employee in a payroll system is an entity. A purchase order is an entity in a material management system. ERDs pictorially represent the relationships between various entities in the system.

The entity is represented by a rectangular box in ERDs. The relationship between entities is represented by a line. The ends of the line represent the type of relationship between entities. There are three types of relationships:

1. *One-to-one relationship*: An item is in one purchase order. This is represented in the ERD by a straight line with normal end.
2. *One-to-many relationship*: A purchase order could contain many items. This is represented in the ERD by a straight line with crow's feet at the end of the line, having a "many" relationship.
3. *Many-to-many relationship*: A vendor can receive multiple purchase orders and supply multiple materials. This is represented in the ERD by a straight line with crow's feet at both ends of the line.

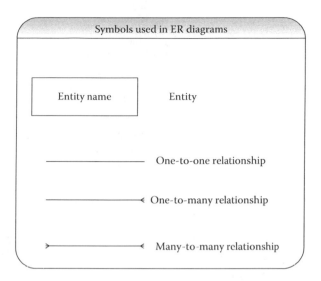

FIGURE 15.3
Symbols used in ERDs.

Symbols used in ERDs and the relationships are shown in Figure 15.3.

Figure 15.4 depicts a simple ERD modeling the purchasing transaction detailed above. The purchase order entity is placed on the vendor, and the vendor entity may receive multiple purchase orders, as depicted in the figure. The vendor supplies items to the warehouse inventory. The vendor could supply multiple items to the warehouse against multiple purchase orders. The vendor raises invoices for materials supplied. The warehouse requests purchase of items that have fallen below the reordering level set for the items.

Of course, real-life ERDs are much more elaborate and complex, as there are many entities in a system and they have complex relationships with each other. Real-life ERDs span multiple sheets. Many software tools are available for modeling entity relationships,

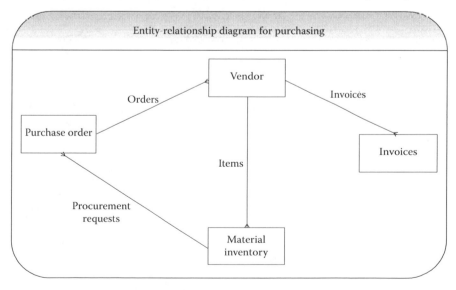

FIGURE 15.4
Example of an ERD.

and some of them could use different types of notations, especially in representing the relationships between entities.

Data Flow Diagrams

Data flow diagrams are used to model the process of transforming the data by the system. In software design, we model the proposed system. The symbols used in DFDs are shown in Figure 15.5. The symbol for the process has many variants. I depict two of those variants.

Now, let us model a purchase order transaction using a DFD. Let us first enumerate the steps in the process that we can model pictorially. Here is the simplified process:

1. An executive from the production department or warehouse raises a procurement requisition on the purchase department for purchase of an item or items.
2. The purchase department receives the requisition and files it (stores it).
3. The purchase department raises inquiries on vendors, asking for price quotations.
4. The vendors receive the inquiry and store it.
5. The vendors transmit price quotes to the purchase department.
6. The purchase department receives the quotes and stores them.

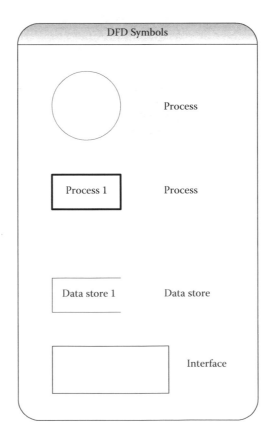

FIGURE 15.5
Symbols used in DFDs.

7. The purchase department transmits the quotes to the executive who originated the procurement requisition.
8. The executive selects the vendor and sends the recommendation to the purchase department.
9. The purchase department stores the recommendation.
10. The purchase department raises a purchase order on the selected vendor.

Let us model this process in a DFD. Figure 15.6 depicts this process pictorially.

DFDs for real-life systems span multiple sheets. To make a large system comprehensible, it is normally divided into multiple levels. The top-level DFD is normally called a context diagram, described in the next section. Then, for each subsequent level, a DFD is prepared. The lowest-level DFD is for a software unit. If a totally granular DFD set is prepared, it can almost supplement a design document. But, more often than not, DFDs are not prepared to the lowest unit level. Each organization decides at what level of granularity the DFDs stop in its projects.

Context Diagram

Context diagrams are used to show the context in which the proposed system operates. They also show the context of the modules within the system. In context diagrams, circles are used to represent entities, and arrows show the relationship, with the arrowhead pointing the direction of the flow of information. An arrowhead at only one of the ends depicts a unidirectional flow. A line with arrowheads at both ends depicts a bidirectional flow.

Figure 15.7 depicts the context of the material management system in an organization.

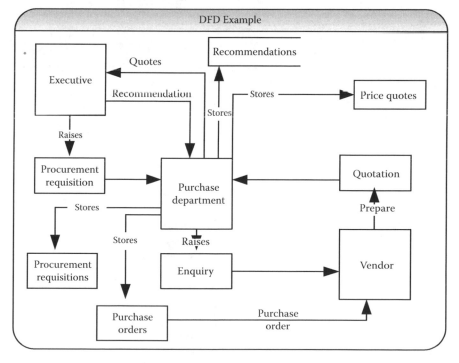

FIGURE 15.6
DFD for a purchase order process.

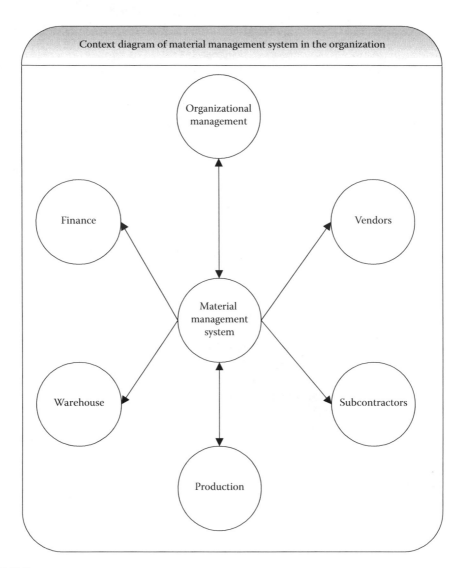

FIGURE 15.7
Context diagram of material management system in the organization.

Structure Chart

A structure chart is used to depict the hierarchy of the functionality in the system. It uses rectangular boxes to depict entities in the system, and lines with arrowheads show the flow of information between entities. Figure 15.8 depicts a structure chart pictorially.

There could be many variants of the model and the diagrams described above. SSADM is one of the most used and improved models of software engineering methodologies. Many researchers modified SSADM with their own improvements and authored books about their models. Organizations, too, have customized the model and implemented it in their own ways. It is not an exaggeration to say that SSADM has not been implemented in its original form anywhere except in the beginning and that too in the United Kingdom.

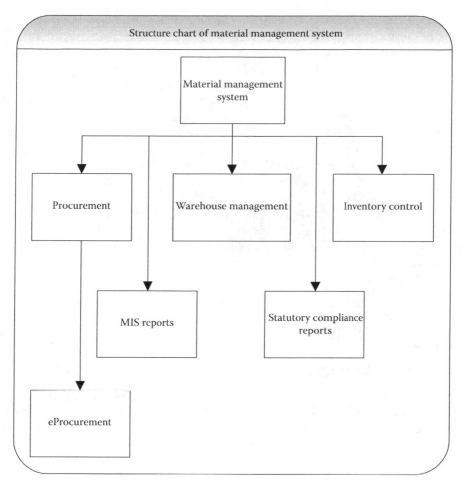

FIGURE 15.8
Structure chart of material management system.

So, I do not claim that the model I described here is the "right" SSADM, but what I described is the one I observed in multiple organizations.

Institute of Electrical and Electronics Engineers Software Engineering Standards

The IEEE is an association of engineers from all over the world. Its membership, about 400,000, includes engineers with a minimum of graduate-level qualifications in the electrical, electronics, computer, and telecommunications engineering branches, or engineers working in these fields. The IEEE has a standards wing that develops standards for the industry collaboratively with engineers drawn from the industry and academia. The individuals involved in the development of these standards need not necessarily be members of the IEEE. The volunteers work without any compensation. All the standards developed by the

IEEE are subject to peer review and voting before they are released. All the standards are periodically reviewed, and the revised versions are periodically released. IEEE standards are highly respected by the industry as well as governments and are implemented in products and interfaces all over the world.

The IEEE released the first set of software engineering standards in 1988. Some of these were revised and rereleased in 1997–1998. The process model Capability Maturity Model (CMM®) released by the Software Engineering Institute of University (SEI) of Carnegie Mellon University in 1998 emphasized IEEE standards in its model document, even though this emphasis was dropped in its later versions of CMM Integration (CMMI®).

IEEE standards advocate a methodical and process-driven approach. One important aspect to be noted here is that implementing IEEE standards has not failed any organization so far!

Table 15.2 gives a list of software engineering standards released so far.

All these standards promote methodical working and implementation of industry best practices. They focus on large-scale projects but allow tailoring to suit smaller projects. Implementing IEEE standards in the organization is one of the best practices in software development in general.

Object Oriented Methodology

Object-oriented programming brought real-world thinking into software development. In the real world, there are objects that have characteristics and functions. How objects perform using the characteristics to produce results is not of concern to the outside world. Therefore, programs were modified to resemble real-world objects.

Object-oriented methodology is a software development methodology that views software development as the development of objects (instead of programs) that can be assembled into a software product. Each object is not a complete standalone unit but is a component that can be picked up and used along with other objects to assemble a software product. Each object has data structures built into it, along with the methods (small programs or functions or subprograms) that utilize those data structures. The object encapsulates (conceals) the methods and the data structure from outside view. That is, the user need not be concerned with the "how" of the object. The user can view the object as a black box that receives inputs and delivers expected outputs. Since each object is self-contained, they can be easily reused. Thus, object-oriented methodology avoids the need for reprogramming the same functionality.

The following terminology is associated with OOM. This explanation is given in brief to introduce the reader to the concepts underlying OOM, and the reader is advised to refer to other material for full coverage of the subject, if necessary.

Object: An object is a combination of methods (a piece of code, functions/subprograms/small programs) and data structures that are used by the methods. Each of the methods performs one action and achieves a predefined functionality, affecting the data defined in the data structures.

Class: A class is a model of the real world from which an object can be created. A class is abstract, and an object is its implementation. Class is a "super object" in that every object is an instance of a class.

TABLE 15.2

List of Software Engineering Standards

Standard Number	Brief description of the Standards
610	IEEE Standard Glossary of Software Engineering Terminology
730	IEEE Guide for Software Quality Assurance Plans
828	IEEE Standard for Software Configuration Management Plans
829	IEEE Standard for Software Test Documentation
830	IEEE Recommended Practice for Software Requirements Specifications
982	IEEE Guide for the use of IEEE Standard Dictionary of Measures to Produce Reliable Software
1008	IEEE Standard for Software Unit Testing
1012	IEEE Standard for Software Verification and Validation
1016	IEEE Recommended Practice for Software Design Descriptions
1028	IEEE Standard for Software Reviews
1044	IEEE Guide to Classification for Software Anomalies
1045	IEEE Standard for Software Productivity Metrics
1058	IEEE Standard for Software Project Management Plans
1061	IEEE Standard for a Software Quality Metrics Methodology
1062	IEEE Recommended Practice for Software Acquisition
1063	IEEE Standard for Software User Documentation
1074	IEEE standard for Developing Software Life Cycle Processes
1175	IEEE Trial-Use Standard Reference Model for Computing System Tool Interconnections
1219	IEEE Standard for Software Maintenance
1220	IEEE Standard for Application and Management of the Systems Engineering Process
1228	IEEE Standard for Software Safety Plans
1233	IEEE Guide for Developing System Requirements Specifications
1320	IEEE Standard for Conceptual Modeling Language and Syntax and Semantics for IDEF
1348	IEEE Recommended Practice for the adoption of Computer-Aided Software Engineering (CASE) Tools
1362	IEEE Guide for Information Technology—System Definition Concept of Operations (ConOps) Document
1420	IEEE Standard for Information Technology—Software Reuse—Data Model for Reuse Library Interoperability—Basic Interoperability Data Model
1430	IEEE Guide for Information Technology—Software Reuse—Concept of Operation for Interoperating Reuse Libraries
1471	IEEE Recommended Practice for Architectural Description of Software-Intensive Systems
1517	IEEE Standard for Information Technology—Software Life Cycle Processes—Reuse Process
12119	IEEE Application of International Standard ISO/IEC 12119—Information Technology—Software Packages—Quality Requirements and Testing
12207	IEEE/EIA Guide—Industry Implementation of International Standard ISO/IEC 12207—Standard fr Information Technology—Software Life Cycle Processes-Implementation Considerations
14143	Implementation Note for IEEE adoption of ISO/IEC 14143 Information Technology-Software Measurement-Functional Size Measurement
P1805	Guide for Requirements Capture Language

Message: A message is the input to the object that invokes a method contained inside the object and triggers that method to process and produce a response to the message received. This response is again conveyed as a message back to the originator.

Abstraction: This is the action of analyzing the real-world objects and forming classes based on the similarity of characteristics of the real-world objects so that they can be understood, analyzed, designed, and implemented to produce the desired software product. Abstraction is at a high level. It does not consider the implementation details.

Encapsulation: In object-oriented methodology, the data is hidden from the sight of the users. The data is accessed through the methods contained inside the object. This aspect of preventing direct access to the data of the objects is referred to as encapsulation.

Polymorphism: This is the ability of objects to be implemented differently to achieve multiple functionalities. When the objects are similar but perform differently, the same message can be used to communicate with different objects and obtain different results. The ability to obtain different results using the same message by sending it to different objects is referred to as polymorphism.

Inheritance: Inheritance is the ability of an object to inherit the characteristics of the class from which it is instantiated. When we instantiate an object from a class, the object inherits all the methods and data structures of the class. In addition, the object can have some more methods and data structures.

OOM focuses more on the engineering side of software development. The software product is assembled using the objects instantiated from the classes. The product is then tested and deployed.

Unified Modeling Language

UML is used for modeling requirements and design of software systems. It began in the object-oriented methodology but is currently used in all types of software development projects. UML was created and is maintained by the Object Management Group (OMG). Ivar Jacobson, James Rumbaugh, and Grady Booch are credited with creating UML at Rational Software (now a part of IBM).

One aspect to remember is that UML is not a software development methodology but is meant to model computer applications. It is more like a language to describe the system. UML uses the following diagrams to model the software system:

1. Class diagrams
2. Use cases
3. Sequence diagrams
4. State charts
5. Activity diagrams
6. Component diagrams
7. Deployment diagrams

We will discuss each of them in a little greater detail in the following sections.

Class Diagrams

Class diagrams are used to depict the classes in a model. Class diagrams are used to model high-level design (roughly equivalent to SRS). User requirements are analyzed and classes are abstracted and then modeled using class diagrams. Each class has attributes (data), methods, and relationships with other classes. Figure 15.9 depicts the symbols used in class diagrams. Using these symbols, class diagrams are prepared to model classes in the system. Figure 15.10 depicts a very simplified class diagram for a procurement system.

Use Cases

A use case (a case in the use of the system) pictorially depicts a "unit of functionality" of the proposed system. Usually, a use case has two elements, namely the use case diagram and a use case description.

Use case diagrams use the symbols depicted in Figure 15.10. In use case diagrams, an ellipse represents the use case. It is usually accompanied by the name of the use case and optionally a use case ID. The actor is depicted by a symbol of a stickman. The stickman is usually identified by a name. The actor could be a human being interacting with the system using a GUI or another system interacting with the system using a machine interface or a protocol. The interaction between the actors and the use case is represented by lines. The system boundary is represented by a rectangle. The actor is usually outside the system. Figure 15.11 depicts the symbols used in use case methodology.

The description that accompanies a use case diagram can be a free-flowing scenario description, but a structured description is preferable. In whatever form the organization

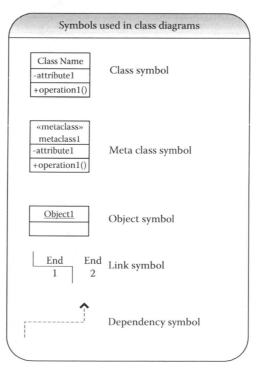

FIGURE 15.9
Symbols used in class diagrams.

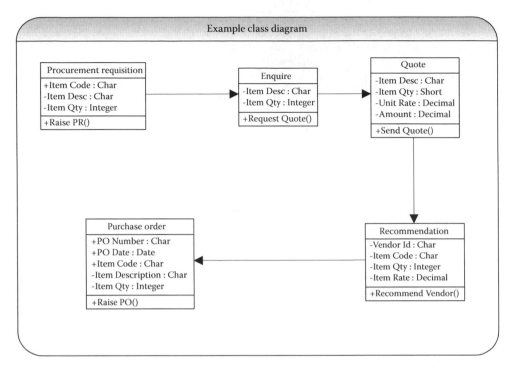

FIGURE 15.10
Example of a simple class diagram.

desires to document the description, it is better to include the following features in the use case description:

1. Use case name and optionally use case id
2. Primary actor
3. Other actors
4. Objective of the use case
5. Precondition
6. Trigger—the event that triggers this use case
7. Exit condition (the definition of completion or success of the use case)
8. Use case description
9. Workflow
10. Alternative workflows

An example description of the use case depicted in Figure 15.12 is given in Table 15.3.

In this manner, we describe each of the use cases in the use case diagram. Now, as you can perhaps see, some vital information is missing from the above description. The data description is more or less absent. For each of the data items, the details of data type (numeric, character, date, currency, etc.), the field width, their constraints, and so on are absent. In some cases, these are described in the use case description or a separate entry is used to describe this information. In some cases, designers attach formats currently being

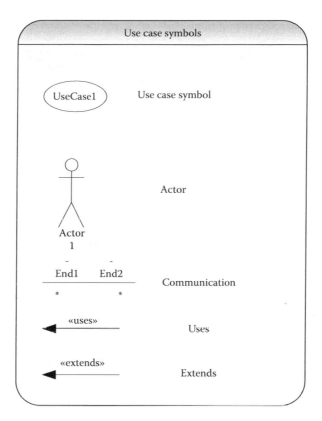

FIGURE 15.11
Symbols used in use case diagrams.

used in the organization. Sometimes, these are elicited from the users by the designers and are used for software design.

Use cases have become very popular tools for capturing project requirements in recent times due to their simplicity and clarity of presentation. Use case diagrams are very easy to draw and even easier to comprehend.

The data description is absent, and it needs to be obtained and documented using other means. Use case diagrams are indeed simple, but it is difficult to represent the complicated logic in large complex software systems.

In Table 15.3, I have not included the description for all the use cases included in Figure 15.12. Only one use case is described as an example. Using the format given in Table 15.3, other use cases can be described.

Use case diagrams coupled with use case descriptions are used to capture the design for projects by many organizations.

Sequence Diagrams

Sequence diagrams depict the sequence of operations between classes or objects. Sequence diagrams are used more to model requirements but can also be used to model designs. Sequence diagrams depict the classes/objects included in the scenario and the interactions between them, along with the sequence.

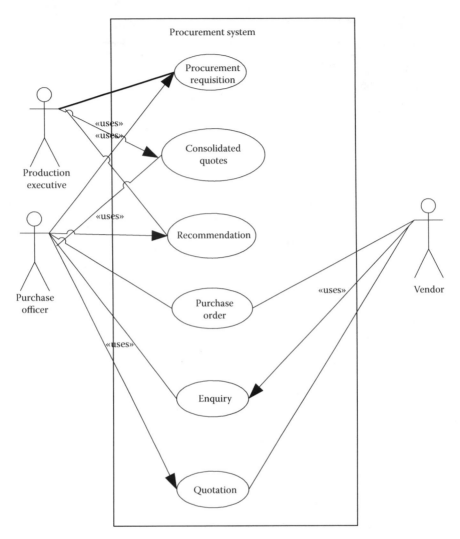

FIGURE 15.12
Use case diagram example.

Objects are depicted using rectangles, the actors are depicted using the stickman, and the messages are depicted using solid or dotted lines. Figure 15.13 depicts a sample sequence diagram for the procurement system.

State Charts

State charts are used to model the behavior of the entities in the system. Usually, state charts are more often used to model the design of the system, but they could also be used to model the behavior of the use cases.

A very simple state chart is depicted in Figure 15.14. In this state chart, the requirement for material is recognized, and at the event of a production executive raising a procurement request, the state of the material requirement transitions to procurement requisition. Now, the event of the purchase officer raising an inquiry on the prospective vendor transitions the state to inquiry (Figure 15.14).

TABLE 15.3

Description of the Use Case (Procurement Requisition) Depicted in Figure 15.12

Project Id	
Use Case Name	Procurement Requisition
Primary Actor	Production Executive
Other Actors	Purchase Officer, uses this use case to raise enquiries of prospective vendors
Objective of the use case	1. To capture the material requirement of the production executive 2. To obtain full information of the items to facilitate raising enquiries
Precondition	There should be a production order against which the expenditure can be booked
Trigger	The BOM (Bill of Material) should have been prepared and approved
Exit condition	1. Procurement requisition is filled in by the production executive 2. Email is sent to purchase officer that a procurement requisition is awaiting for next step
Use Case Description	After a purchase order is received from a customer by the marketing department, it will be passed on to the engineering department. The engineering department would prepare engineering drawings for manufacturing the product and releases them to the production planning. Production planning raises production orders to various production shops authorizing them to initiate production. Production shops assess the material stock and raise procurement requisitions on purchase department for procurement of materials that are in short supply. This requisition triggers procurement action. This requisition would contain information about the item code, item description, the required quantity, the date by which the item is required and the estimated cost of the item being procured, along with references to the production order and the project id. The requisition is computer based and need to be accessible from the production shop's PC.
Workflow	1. Production order is received by the production shop 2. Material stock in the warehouse is assessed and material shortages are enumerated by the production executive 3. Production executive raises the procurement requisition using the computerized procurement system 4. The requisition is sent for authorization of concerned authority automatically by the computer 5. The authorization is granted by the concerned executive 6. An email is sent to the purchase office that a procurement requisition is awaiting action
Alternate workflow	Sometimes, the system itself has to raise the procurement requisition especially in the matter of standard items such as hardware items like nuts and bolts, stationary, cleaning materials and so on. This has to be based on re-order level, ordering quantity, and safety stock decided for each of the standard items in the stock

State charts are definitely useful in capturing the design, especially the transition in the state of the entities.

Activity Diagrams

Activity diagrams model the procedural flow of actions that are part of a use case or a set of use cases. Activity diagrams are normally used to depict the sequence of execution in a system. Activity diagrams use similar notation to state charts.

A sample activity diagram is depicted in Figure 15.15 for the procurement system in a simplified manner.

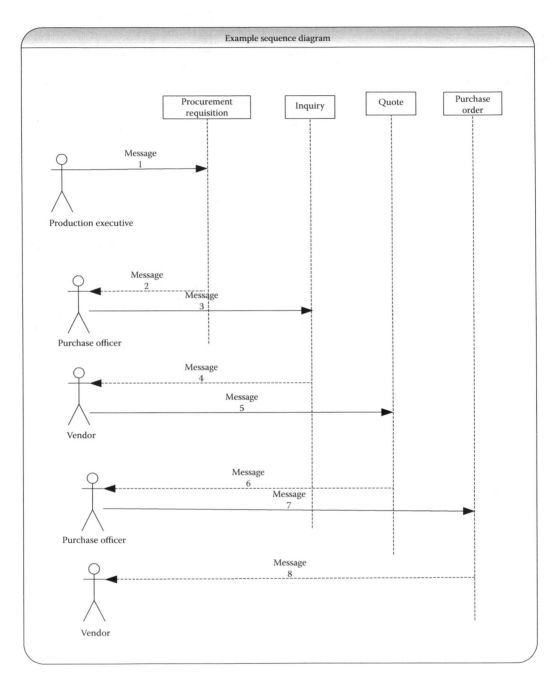

FIGURE 15.13
Sequence diagram example.

Component Diagrams

Component diagrams model the relationship between the components of a software system. Component diagrams are used to model the design of a software product rather than to capture the requirements of a proposed project.

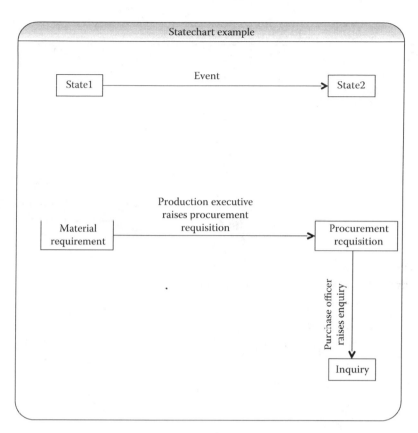

FIGURE 15.14
Example of a simple state chart.

Deployment Diagrams

Deployment diagrams are used to depict the physical deployment of system artifacts, including hardware artifacts, system software artifacts, and application artifacts of a facility. They deal with the facility management and system design that include hardware rather than with either project requirements or software design.

UML has become very popular, and use cases have been particularly popular because of their simplicity and ease of use. Use cases along with use case descriptions are being used to describe project requirements and software design. Of the other diagrams, class diagrams and sequence diagrams are also used extensively. Others are being used, but not on the same scale as the use cases.

Agile Methods

Agile methods do not use any formal methods for modeling systems either for capturing project requirements or the proposed system design. If at all, they use the UML modeling techniques described above for either capturing project requirements or the software design of the proposed system.

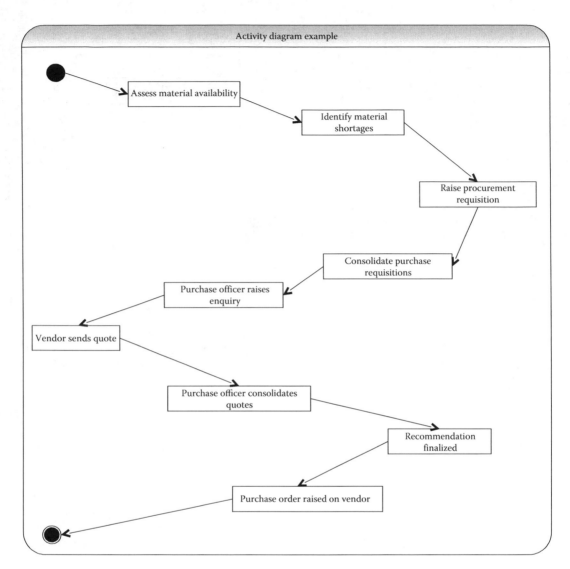

FIGURE 15.15
Activity diagram example.

Planguage

Planguage was developed by Professor Tom Gilb (https://www.gilb.com) for describing requirements as well as software design. It is a set of language constructs that are precisely defined. They are to be used in design documents (as well as requirements documents) in place of plain ordinary English. When an expert in Planguage prepares a design document, it can be easily understood by any other person proficient in Planguage. It was presented in book form in 2005 as *Competitive Engineering: A Handbook for Systems Engineering, Requirements Engineering, and Software Engineering Using Planguage*, authored by Professor Tom Gilb and published by Elsevier Butterworth-Heinemann, USA. Interested readers may acquire that book for details on the strengths of Planguage.

My Understanding of the Present Set of Tools for Capturing Software Design

All the tools and techniques described above, more or less, do aid in capturing the software design. Now, let us address the question: Which tool or technique is best suited to a given scenario? I confess that there is no single right answer to this question. All the tools and techniques discussed in this chapter help us in modeling the system and capturing it so that we can build the "right" software product for our clients. Another important point I would like to stress here is that the techniques described above are by no means comprehensive. There are a plethora of models and diagrams available in software engineering literature. Just to record all the models and diagrams available would take a full book in itself.

One tool that is used across the board for modeling data and assisting us in the design of the database is ER diagrams. I have not seen any other technique being used to model data as much as ER diagrams are used.

Engineering Drawings

So far, no organization like the IEEE, SEI, or any other organization engaged in streamlining the software development process has, to my knowledge, tried using engineering drawings in software engineering. Also true is the fact that, to my knowledge, no software development organization has tried using engineering drawings for capturing either software requirements or software design for their products. In my *humble opinion*, this is because the domain of software development originated in the departments of mathematics at universities and remains there. Mathematicians are not initiated into using engineering drawings. In the case of all other branches of engineering, drawings are used for capturing designs. Discoveries and inventions were made in the scientific laboratories of universities or other research institutions, and engineers take over production using the engineering tools, within which drawings have the primary spot. Industries have formed associations, developed standards, and streamlined the process of production. But, in the case of software development, industries have not formed such associations to streamline the process of code production. The initiatives in this arena emanated from mathematics departments. I have come from manufacturing into IT after spending 15 years in production engineering and have a strong grounding in the manufacturing processes. When I spoke of learning from manufacturing, most software people talked of mass or flow process production systems.

Here is a brief introduction to production systems, which are of five types.

1. *Mass production*: This is the type of production system that most people understand. The facility continues to produce the same product over and over again and again. Currently, except perhaps for matchboxes or cigarettes, no other facility utilizes this type of production system. This type of system is used when the demand exceeds the capacity to produce. In this system, one set of drawings per product is prepared and used continuously. The drawings are updated only when the design is changed.

2. *Flow process production*: This is more or less an automated type of production used in the manufacture of chemicals, cosmetics, metals like steel, cement, pharmaceuticals, soft drinks, fertilizers, and so on. The process goes on with minimal human intervention. We input raw materials at one end and collect the products at the other end. Coca Cola and Pepsi are good examples of this type of production system. In this type of production system, the production does not need product drawings. Drawings are needed only for the maintenance of the equipment and are supplied by the equipment suppliers.

3. *Batch production*: This production system is most prevalent in the present day, such as for electronics products, automobiles, and other such products. The manufacturers make mostly similar yet dissimilar products in the facility. They make televisions one month, laptops another, DVD players another, and so on. In automobiles, they make one brand of car for a quarter or so and another brand another quarter. This system is used when the rate of production exceeds the rate of demand. Drawings are prepared for each of the batches put into production.

4. *Job-order production or tailor-made production*: This type of production system is used when the production of the product begins only when a customer orders it. For example, ships and airplanes are not manufactured unless an order is received along with an advance payment. There are many types of equipment that follow this type of production system. Heavy equipment like heavy electrical equipment, earth-moving equipment, control systems, and so on use this type of production system. This type of production system matches code production in our software development activity almost exactly. There is a lot to learn for software developers from this type of production system. This type of production needs requirements analysis, design, and a set of drawings for each order. The preproduction process is almost identical to that of the precoding process in software development. In this type of production system, the preparation of drawings may take as much or even more time than the actual production itself! So, when software developers complain that it takes a lot of time for preparation of design artifacts, they can take solace in the fact that even manufacturers do spend that kind of time in preparing design artifacts.

5. *Project production*: This system has a facility that produces components using the job-order type of production system, and the final assembly takes place at the site. This is used in the construction of flow process production facilities like fertilizer factories, chemical factories, bridges, atomic reactors, and so on.

It is a fact that the production systems of mass flow process and batch production are vastly different from the process of software development. But the process of job-order production systems is almost identical to the process of software development.

I can certainly say with confidence that the present set of software engineering tools has nowhere near the granularity or the precision that other engineering disciplines have in engineering drawings. They say that "drawing is the language of engineers." But it is not so for software engineers. Therefore, I recommend using engineering drawings to capture and document the software design.

16

Quality Assurance in Software Design

Introduction to Quality

Undetectable errors are infinite in variety in contrast to detectable errors, which by definition are limited.

Gilb's third law of uncertainty

While it is not my intention to deal extensively on the vast subject of quality assurance in this book, which focuses primarily on software design, I feel it is essential for software designers to understand the basics of the subject of quality. It is my humble opinion that an understanding of the concepts of quality will enable software designers to deliver better-quality designs and prevent product defects attributable to design. That is the reason I included a chapter dealing with the basics of quality in this book, which will barely scratch the surface of the subject of quality. I suggest readers interested in learning comprehensively about software quality acquire and read my book *Software Quality Assurance: Best Practices, Tools and Techniques for Software Developers*, published by J. Ross Publishing of the United States.

The term *quality* is often used as a standalone term without any adjectives attached to it. People do not normally use the term *good quality* to express their satisfaction with the products or services they use. To say that a certain product is a *quality product* implies that the product is of good quality. But people certainly use the term *poor/bad quality* to express their dissatisfaction with a product or a service. Therefore, the adjective *good* is prefixed implicitly to the word *quality* in the minds of most people, and the word *quality* connotes *good quality* to most people, including technical professionals.

1. For a customer or end user of a product, quality connotes defect-free functioning, reliability, ease of use, acceptable levels of fault tolerance during use, and safety from injury to person or property.

2. For a producer of goods, quality connotes conformance of the product to specifications, which might be defined by a government body, an industry association or standards body, or the producer's own organization.

3. For governments, quality connotes safety for its citizens and protection of consumers from fraud.

4. For an industry association or a standards body, quality connotes the safeguarding of the industry's reputation, protecting it from fraud and lawsuits, and addressing the concerns of the government, consumers, and the industry itself.

What Is Quality?

First, the word *quality* needs to be defined in a manner that addresses all the connotations noted above.

ISO 9000 (second edition, 2000) defines the word *quality* as the degree to which a set of inherent characteristics fulfills requirements. The term *quality* can be used with such adjectives as poor, good, or excellent. *Inherent*—as opposed to *assigned*—means existing inside something, a permanent characteristic.

This definition uses three key terms: requirements, characteristics, and degree. *Requirements* can be stated by a customer in a made-to-order scenario or by product specifications in a commercial off-the-shelf product scenario. *Characteristics* refers to the capability of the deliverable or the robustness (fitness) of the product. *Degree* implies that quality is a continuum, beginning with zero and moving toward, perhaps, infinity. But this inference is ambiguous and leads to the wrong perception. What is the degree of quality when prefixed with *poor, good,* or *excellent*? More importantly, who is authorized to define the terms *poor, good,* and *excellent*?

Another popular definition of quality, as defined by Joseph Moses Juran, is *fitness for use,* with *fitness* and *use* being crucial to the proper understanding of quality. Unless these two key words are defined, the definition of quality is incomplete. The consumer interpretations and the provider interpretations of these two terms are often at loggerheads.

Specifications

Because *fitness* and *use* are crucial terms, they cannot be left open to interpretation. Organizations often define these two terms in their specifications for the product or service they are providing. Following is a closer look at the attributes of specifications:

1. Specifications can be explicit or implicit. *Explicit* means that the provider selects the specifications and makes them available to customers. *Implicit* means that the specifications are not defined but are understood to be necessary, such as safety, security, and fault tolerance requirements.

2. Specifications can be defined by either the provider or an external body, such as the government, an industry association, or a standards body. They are made available to customers and they are adhered to by the provider.

Oftentimes, providers can resort to unethical definitions of specifications and provide services or products that can be detrimental to customers and perhaps to the industry, too. The possibility of such occurrences has resulted in industry organizations coming together to form associations, such as the NEMA, hotel associations, travel agents' associations, and so on. Such associations define specifications for their particular industry's products or services. Governments also step in and form standards bodies that define specifications for various products and services. Many national defense departments define specifications for the diverse range of products to be used by their armed forces. These specifications stipulate a minimum set of standards to be adhered to by the providers of products or services so that fitness for use is defined and ensured.

Such formally defined specifications become industry standards and are released by industry associations to the general public for a nominal fee that covers the cost of production and distribution of these standards.

Examples of bodies that release standards on a regular basis include the ANSI, British Standards, Joint Services Specifications, Deutsches Institut für Normung, ISO, the International Electrotechnical Commission, the International Telecommunications Union, NEMA, the IEEE, and so on. In recognition of the contributions such standards bodies make to quality and general consumer well-being, a day has been dedicated every year to celebrate such organizations: World Standards Day is on October 14th. Standards specify, at a minimum, the following:

1. Attributes of the components that make up a product, which can include the materials used and the dimensions and methods of testing the product
2. The intended use of the product or service
3. The limitations of the product that need to be conveyed to customers
4. The process by which the components are made
5. The security and safety parameters that need to be built in

Understanding that specifications are at the heart of quality, the word can now be defined in a more cogent manner. Moreover, it is important that the word *quality* be defined from the standpoint of the provider, as it is the provider that builds quality into products or services and it is at the provider's end that quality is ensured.

Definition of Quality from the Standpoint of the Provider

Quality is an attribute of a product or service that is provided to consumers, conforming in toto or exceeding the best of the available specifications for that product or service. It includes making those specifications available to the end user of the product or service. The specifications that form the basis of the product or service being provided might have been defined by a government body, an industry association, or a standards body. Where such a definition is not available, the provider may define such specifications. (Software Quality Assurance: Best Practices, Tools and Techniques for Software Developers, Murali Chemuturi, J. Ross Publishing, 2009).

This definition of quality mandates the provider to

1. Define specifications if they are not already defined by a superior body, such as the government, an industry association, or a standards body
2. Adhere to the *best* of the available definition of specifications
3. Ensuring conformance is 100% or better—no less
4. Make the specifications to which conformance is ensured available to the customer

The result of a product or service meeting the above definition of quality is that the customer is able to enjoy the service fully or use the product effectively for the length of the product's life. This outcome further mandates the provider to be responsible for providing any support required by the customer for his or her continued enjoyment or use of the product or service throughout the life of that product or service.

Any product or service that meets the requirements of this definition is rated as a "quality product" or "quality service." Any product or service that does not meet the requirements of this definition is rated as "poor quality."

Quality and Reliability

Quality and reliability are intertwined and inseparable, but what does reliability mean, especially in terms of a product?

Reliability of a product is the product's capability to function at a defined level of performance for the duration of its life.

Two phrases are critical in the above definition:

1. *Defined level of performance*: Performance level is defined by the specifications of the product or service. It should be 100% or more of the specification, not any less. Continuous use is also defined by the specifications. For example, a car might be capable of reaching a speed of 100 miles per hour, but how long can the car withstand being driven continuously at this speed? Normally, performance is defined at two levels: (1) normal performance and (2) peak performance. Peak performance can be expected for short durations, while normal performance is expected for longer durations.

2. *Duration of its life*: Duration needs to be specified for normal performance as well as for peak performance. Products specifically have two types of life:

   a. First life or initial life, which is the period of time before any repairs to the product become necessary. Initial life is normally specified as the warranty or guarantee period. After expiry of this life, regular maintenance might be required to maintain performance at the specified level for the product.

   b. Operating life, which is the period of time after the warranty expires, with maintenance being carried out. After expiry of this life, it might not be economical to maintain the product to have it operate at the specified level of performance.

In other words, *quality* involves delivering the specified functionality under the specified conditions, whereas *reliability* involves delivering the specified functionality at a specified level of performance over the duration of the product life, even with slight deviations in the specified conditions.

While the initial life of a product is specified by manufacturers as the warranty period, the life after the warranty period is usually not specified. If it is, it is specified with such stipulations as "subject to the condition that the product is maintained and serviced by our own expert technicians" or something similar. If product maintenance is entrusted to the manufacturer or its authorized maintenance shops, the manufacturer specifies two norms: mean time between failures (MTBF) and mean time to repair (MTTR).

MTBF is the average period between two successive failures, assuming that proper maintenance is carried out every time, conforming to the manufacturer's stipulations. MTBF is expressed in the number of *running hours* for the product.

MTTR is the average time it takes to restore the product to its original functionality by carrying out the necessary repairs. MTTR is expressed in the number of *clock hours* it takes to repair the product.

Reliability is gauged by both MTBF and MTTR.

With regard to software, an observation often made is that software has no moving parts that can cause deterioration to the product through wear and tear. Therefore, once a software product functions at its defined level of quality and functionality, there should be no need for maintenance. So, the term "reliability" is not applicable to software, right? This reasoning is true only if the configuration on which the software product runs remains unaltered. If the configuration of the hardware and system software is unchanged, no repairs should be necessary to the software, rendering the attribute of reliability inapplicable. But these days, many other factors play a role in how stable the configuration of hardware and software remains. Here are a number of common situations that can alter the configuration of hardware and software:

1. New versions of the operating systems are released into the market every three years.

2. New web browsers and updates to current web browsers are released regularly.

3. New viruses and spyware are unleashed on unsuspecting internet users without any restraints.

4. Computers are often flooded with a host of new tools, including office suites, antivirus software, and downloaded utilities.

5. Changes are introduced to tiers (middleware) in multitiered architecture software products.

6. Software products can make use of shared libraries that are part of the system software supplied along with an operating system. It is likely that these shared libraries will be updated or modified.

7. Software products can make use of third-party code libraries to achieve specialist functionalities such as rules processing, database independence, and so on. These third-party code libraries are frequently updated or modified.

8. Install and uninstall of utilities on a system can cause changes to or removal of the shared libraries used by the software product.

All of these activities change the configuration of the system on which a software product is running, and this is where the question of software reliability comes into play. A software product is said to be reliable if it can withstand minor patches to the operating system and to the middleware.

Since software quality professionals cannot predict what future upgrades will be made to a system software (that is, an operating system, database, browser, or middleware), they cannot specify the reliability of software in running hours. They are also unable to specify the MTBF of a software product in running hours because a software product does not fail due to use over a number of hours. But it can fail due to a change in the system configuration.

Nonetheless, software quality professionals recognize that the term "reliability" is applicable to the domain of software. Some hints for building reliable software are offered in this book.

Four Dimensions of Quality

Quality of a product or service stands on four pillars, and its quality level depends on the strength and firmness of these four pillars. These are:

1. Quality of the specifications
2. Quality of design
3. Quality of workmanship (development/manufacturing/construction)
4. Quality of conformance

Quality of the specifications: This is the first step in developing a product or a service. Specifications provide details of the capacity, the target market, the materials used, the target application, the facilities to be included, the functionality, and so on. In software development, we use the term *requirements* in place of the term *specifications*. If you take an automobile, Rolls-Royce or Honda Accord are two cars carrying four passengers at the same speed and running in similar conditions but with vastly different price tags. The difference is in the specifications. For some target markets, functionality alone is adequate, whereas for some target markets, aesthetics is equally or more important than mere functionality. In some markets like defense applications, reliability is much more important than other aspects of the products or service. The product is designed to achieve the specifications defined and is built implementing the designs. So, it is vital that we define specifications for the proposed product diligently. This is in the arena of the product managers, marketing, the customer, or management. Designers do not have much of a role in defining the specifications for the proposed product, but they have the role of reviewing the specifications and ensuring that they are achievable. If some specification is not achievable with the current technology or timeline set for the delivery, designers need to raise the issue with the concerned executives and obtain a concession to postpone or drop that specification. Designers willy-nilly become the quality control people for the specifications. The specifications are classified into core functionality requirements and ancillary functionality requirements (*Requirements Engineering and Management for Software Development Projects,* Murali Chemuturi, Springer Science+Business, 2013) in software parlance. Core functionality is that functionality without which the product is useless. Ancillary functionality is that functionality without which the product still functions. For example, in an automobile scenario, transporting the specified number of passengers is core functionality and air-conditioning is ancillary functionality; steering is core functionality, but power in the power steering is ancillary functionality. The ancillary functionality is the differentiator between products offering the same core functionality. A product has to be delivered with both functionalities.

Quality of design: Design implements the specifications and prepares design artifacts that can be used in developing the software as well as testing it. While most of the core functionality comes from specifications or core functionality requirements, most of the ancillary functionality is derived by the product design team. When we come to software design, the safety, security, ease of use, efficiency, customizability, and flexibility aspects come under ancillary functionality requirements. For design purposes, the customer provides the core functionality requirements in full and ancillary functionality requirements to the extent possible in a software development for a specific customer. In a COTS scenario, inputs are received from marketing, the product manager, and organizational management.

How we ensure that quality is built in to our designs is the topic of this chapter, and we will go into detail in the following sections.

Quality of workmanship (development/manufacturing/construction): This is the phase in which the rubber hits the road and the product assumes physical shape. This is the realization of the specifications and the design. In many cases, we can test the product and see if it adheres to the specifications and designs. But in some cases, we simply cannot test to ensure that the product conforms to its specifications and the designs. For example, take a chalk piece: we cannot test at what pressure it breaks, as the item is rendered useless by such testing. Another example is the light bulb. We cannot test how strong the shell is because it breaks when we subject it to the highest specified break resistance. All possible quality-control techniques are used in this phase to ensure that quality is built into the deliverables. In some cases, if the process is not adhered to, the product is rendered useless even if it is finished. For example, if the food item is not prepared adhering to its recipe, it won't be edible, and we cannot rectify the item in most cases. To ensure quality of the product during this phase we use inspections, reviews, audits, and testing.

Quality of conformance: This refers to the seriousness with which we carry out quality-control activities during all the phases of product development/manufacture/construction. The infrastructure built for quality assurance in the organization, the support given by organizational management to QA activities, the diligence with which we carry out QA activities, what we do with the data generated during the QC activities, and the seriousness with which we carry out process improvement to ensure defect prevention form the basis for this activity. This is not an activity that is concurrent to the product development/ manufacture/construction activities. This is a specialist activity that carries out quality assurance activities.

While designers alone do not carry the onus of the quality of a product on their capable shoulders, the bulk of responsibility lies there. Therefore, it is imperative that QA activities be carried out diligently by the designers. If there are defects in design, they will percolate downward and get magnified in the downstream phases. While manufacturing defects get a bad name for the organization, design defects get the organization closed.

Now, let us look at the techniques of QA and then see how to apply them to our design work.

Techniques of Quality Assurance

Quality assurance, or QA, is not just software testing, as understood by many in the software development industry. Quality assurance has two dimensions. The first is to prevent defects, and the second is to trap defects before they are delivered to the customer. The second dimension is familiar to most and is often misunderstood to be quality assurance itself. The defect-prevention portion of quality assurance is achieved by implementing standards, guidelines, checklists, formats, and processes for carrying out work without defects in the organization. The second part of trapping defects and preventing them from being delivered to the customer is referred to as quality control, or QC. QC is achieved by using techniques such as inspection, verification, reviews, testing, and audits. While quality control is used at the execution level, the defect prevention portion of QA is achieved at the organizational level. Let us discuss these two parts here.

Quality control activities are carried out while the work is being carried out in the organization. As soon as an activity is completed, the deliverables of that activity would be subjected to its applicable QC activity. Quality control is achieved by the following techniques:

1. Inspections
2. Reviews
3. Audits
4. Validation

Inspections: Inspections are visual verification of systems. Inspections are carried out against a set of specifications or drawings. In some cases, like repetitive mass production systems, these use the experience and expertise of the inspector, but in almost all cases, there is a reference based on which the inspection is carried out. The deficiencies uncovered are reported in an inspection report. The defects pointed out are rectified by the concerned artisans and resubmitted for inspection. Once the inspector is satisfied, the item is passed on to its next stage. Inspections are one of the main QC techniques in manufacturing and construction. Inspections are used in case of physically tangible items.

Reviews: Reviews are widely used in the cases of documents and drawings, but they can be used in other areas, too. We often hear this word being used in cases such as plan reviews, progress reviews, performance reviews, and so on. This word connotes a periodic activity, but it need not be so. In the software development industry, we use this technique for the quality control of various document artifacts of software, such as requirement documents, design documents, test plans, test cases, test logs, and so on. Reviews used in the software development field are of three kinds:

1. Walkthroughs or peer reviews
2. Managerial reviews
3. Expert reviews

Peer reviews are an activity in which persons other than the author walk through every sentence of the software information artifacts and every line of code for software code artifacts (source code, table scripts, stored procedures, interface routines, etc.). The persons (peers) conducting the walkthrough normally have similar experience and expertise as that of the author. They deliver a report at the end of the walkthrough, known as a review report. A review report contains the following information:

1. The completeness and comprehensiveness of the artifact, including the achievement of the objectives set for the artifact
2. All defects uncovered in the artifact
3. The defects uncovered during the walkthrough that include logical errors; the existence of trash code and malicious code, if any; unused but declared variables and constants; the presence of hardcoding; nonconformance to standards and guidelines; and so on
4. Opportunities for improvement, if any, uncovered during the walkthrough, such as using better constructs, syntax improvements, and so on

5. Suggestions for improvements that might result in more clarity, robustness, or better efficiency of execution, like using reusable components, eliminating redundancy of code in the artifact or the end product of the artifact, and so on

6. Other information, such as the name of the artifact reviewed, date of review, names of the author and the reviewer, information pertaining to closure of defects, and answers to opportunities for improvement as well as suggestions for improvements

There are five types of walkthroughs:

1. Independent walkthroughs
2. Guided walkthroughs
3. Group walkthroughs
4. Expert reviews
5. Managerial reviews

Independent walkthroughs: This type of verification is also sometimes referred to as *postal review*. It is carried out in the following manner:

1. The author of the artifact or the project manager arranges the peer review.
2. The artifact to be reviewed is made available to the reviewer.
3. The reviewer reviews the artifact, prepares the review report, and hands it over to the author or the project manager.
4. The author rectifies the defects uncovered.
5. The reviewer verifies the rectifications and passes the artifact to its next stage when all defects are rectified satisfactorily.

The notable aspect of this review is that the author of the artifact need not be present while the review is being carried out.

Guided walkthroughs are similar to independent walkthroughs except that the author is present along with the reviewer and guides the reviewer through the artifact. This reduces the cycle time of the review.

Group walkthroughs are similar to independent review and guided review, except that instead of one person reviewing the artifact, a group of people reviews the artifact. This technique is usually applied in the case of design artifacts, but can also be used in other scenarios.

Expert reviews: When there are no domain or development platform experts available within the project team, an expert from either within or outside the organization is requested to conduct the review. Experts bring their expertise to bear on the artifact and review its comprehensiveness and its capability to achieve its objectives. Organizations use experts for developing applications as well as for verifying them. These experts can be any of the following:

1. *Domain experts*: People who have long years of experience in a field and who have seen all possibilities.
2. *Subject-matter experts*: People who are experts in a specific subject, such as mathematics, and are normally from academia. These experts might not be

experienced in the field, but they are well versed in the theory and can aid in the development or review of algorithms.

3. *Technology experts*: People who are highly skilled in the development platform. These persons may have long years of experience in the programming language, database, or target platform on which the product functions.

4. *Social experts*: People who have expertise in the areas of social behaviors, market forces, and anthropology fall in this category of experts. They help organizations in product acceptance by the target market as well as in product usability aspects and the possible social impact of the product. These people can assist with such products as games and multimedia applications.

Expert reviews can involve a single expert or a team of experts, depending on the artifact being reviewed. Especially in the case of product specifications, software design, architecture documents in new domains, or new technologies, it is normal to use multiple experts. In other cases, a single expert will suffice. Normally, expert reviews are conducted to supplement peer reviews. A detailed peer review can be conducted in addition to an expert review to ensure that all lurking defects can be uncovered and fixed. The methodology of an expert review is similar to that of an independent walkthrough and a guided walkthrough, except that the reviewer is the selected expert. All other aspects remain the same.

Managerial Reviews

Managerial reviews are performed by the people directly supervising the author of the artifact. This review is the final step before promoting the artifact to the next activity. A managerial review is a cursory review, and it does not delve into the details of the artifact. The objectives of a managerial review include the following:

1. It looks over the artifact to ensure that the right product is built.

2. Using the well-developed hunches of the superior, it specifically looks at possible problem areas and ensures that everything is all right.

3. It ensures that all the essential predecessor activities have been satisfactorily completed before according approval to the artifact or promoting the artifact to the next level.

4. It ensures consistency with other artifacts in the project as well as the organization.

5. It also ensures traceability with both upstream and downstream artifacts, where applicable.

There is no hard-and-fast rule that prohibits superiors from delving deep into the details of the artifact, and sometimes superiors do just that, especially when the reviewer conducting the peer review is slightly inexperienced in the review process. A managerial review starts once the peer review has been conducted and all defects are fixed. A managerial review can take the form of either an independent walkthrough or a guided walkthrough, depending on the size and type of the artifact. Normally, a managerial review does not generate a review report. If defects are uncovered during a managerial review, the work is reassigned either to the same person (or team) who conducted the peer review or to another person to redo the peer review. The managerial review is not expected to uncover any defects, but if defects are found, then another round of peer review is conducted.

Audits

Audits are document verification systems in which documents and records are contrasted with the organization's standards or defined processes. Audits are generally of short duration, with about one to two hours spent on auditing a project or a function. Audits are used as a QC tool, mainly to ensure conformance of the work being carried out to the organization's defined processes. Audits are conducted with the purpose of uncovering nonconformances (NCs), if any, in the artifacts. If the artifacts show deviations from the process described in the organization's defined processes, these deviations are treated as NCs. The output of audits is an NCR. When all the NCs are closed, an audit certificate of compliance is issued.

Audits are conducted by auditors (persons who conduct the audit) on auditees (persons whose project/function is audited). Auditors need to have specialized training in conducting audits. The usual duration of a project audit is one to two hours, but it can extend based on the need. Within this time, the auditor verifies all the artifacts and notes down any NCs found in order to prepare an NCR later. The NCR is handed over to the auditee. The auditee then must take the necessary action specified on the NCR to address the NCs and have them closed by the auditor within the allowed time. Necessary action as specified by the NCR involves the following:

1. Taking corrective action so that the present NC is resolved
2. Putting in place preventive action so that the NC does not repeat in the project again

Audits can be classified in a variety of ways, and these classifications are outlined in the sections that follow.

Conformance Audits and Investigative Audits

Conformance audits focus on the efficacy of implementation of organizational processes during execution. They are conducted to compare and contrast the project artifacts with the organizational processes, uncover NCs, prepare an NCR, and track the NCR to its resolution.

Investigative audits usually focus on finding the causes for a failure situation, but sometimes focus on finding the causes for an extraordinary success situation, too. They carefully verify the artifacts and hold in-depth interviews with the concerned persons to uncover the specific reasons that caused the failure or grand success. These are used in special scenarios only.

Vertical Audits versus Horizontal Audits

Vertical audits are conformance audits conducted across the organization focusing on all aspects of all projects.

Horizontal audits are also conformance audits conducted across the organization, but they focus on only one aspect of all the projects. Configuration management audits are a good example of this kind of audit, and are conducted in most organizations. This audit focuses on the efficacy of implementation of one crucial aspect of project execution in the organization.

Periodic Audits versus Phase-End Audits

Periodic audits are conformance audits that are conducted at organizational level based on calendar duration. Normally, ISO-certified organizations conduct these audits once every two or three calendar months. In each audit, a few of the organization's current projects are covered, and within a one-year period, all projects under execution in the organization are covered. At the end of every cycle of audits, the audit findings are consolidated and presented to management and to the auditees.

Phase-end audits are triggered by project events. When a project execution phase is completed, a phase-end audit is conducted to ensure that all activities in that phase conform to organization's defined processes. Typically, in the software development field, these audits are conducted after the following phases:

- Project initiation
- Software requirements analysis
- Software design
- Software construction
- System testing
- Project closure

Internal Audits versus External Audits

Internal audits can be conformance audits, investigative audits, periodic audits, or phase-end audits, but they are conducted by persons internal to the organization. However, the internal auditors are independent of the project being audited. Internal audits are conducted either to ensure conformance or investigate the occurrence of a special event. An internal audit uses internal process artifacts as the basis for conducting the audit.

External audits are conducted by an external agency specializing in the audit and certification process. Organizations that seek certification for compliance with the ISO 9000 series of standards or any other similar standards use external auditors. Persons who are certified as *lead auditors* can conduct audits for certifying or for ensuring continued compliance to ISO standards. Optionally, an organization can engage external consultants to conduct audits to obtain an unbiased opinion about its process and its implementation in the organization. Sometimes external audits are conducted to ascertain the readiness of the organization for the certification audit. External audits undergo the same process as internal audits, and the NCR is the vehicle to record and report NCs uncovered during the audits as well as for closing the NCs. External audits use national or international standards as reference for conducting audits. External audits are classified as follows:

- *Precertification audits*: These audits are conducted as a prelude to certification audits. A precertification audit also allows the organization to smooth out any rough edges to prepare it for a certification audit.
- *Certification and recertification audits*: These audits culminate in either the awarding or denying of the coveted certificate to the organization. Certification audits are

conducted only once, unless it results in denial of the certificate to the organization. Most quality certification models mandate periodic recertification, such as once every three years. A certification audit is conducted for an organization that has never been certified before. A recertification audit is exactly the same as a certification audit, except that it is conducted for an organization that was already certified.

- *Surveillance audits*: ISO 9000 certification mandates a surveillance audit once every six months to ensure that process implementation is at the same level it was at the time of the certification audit. Usually, the same external agency that originally awarded the certificate conducts these surveillance audits. These audits are scaled down slightly from the certification audits, and a smaller sample of projects is audited.

Audits are very useful tools for effective implementation of organizational processes, and they are used in most software development organizations.

Validation

Validation indicates confirmation or corroboration of a claim. In the context of software development, validation refers to the activities performed on the software product to confirm that all the designed (or required) functionalities are indeed built and are working in adherence with the original specifications (intended use), along with other implicit functions for ensuring safety, security, and usability. The IEEE's standard 610 standard glossary of software engineering terminology defines the term "validation" as "the process of evaluating a system or component during or at the end of the development process to determine whether it satisfies specified requirements." The capability maturity model integration (CMMI®) model document for development (version 1.2, August 2006) defines validation as "confirmation that the product, as provided (or as it will be provided), will fulfill its intended use. In other words, validation ensures that 'you built the right thing'." It also states that "the purpose of validation is to demonstrate that a product or product component fulfills its intended use when placed in its intended environment."

Synonyms for the word "validate" include authenticate, certify, corroborate, confirm, endorse, bear out, substantiate, and support, among others. One definition of validation can be *the act of ensuring that something is valid*. To understand the term "validation" correctly, consider the following scenarios involving validation:

1. You are entering into a contract with somebody. Before you sign the contract, you show it to a lawyer for validation (not verification), and only after he or she certifies that it is valid (that is, valid in law and that it would be valid in a court of law) do you sign it.
2. You are making an affirmation about something in writing. You have a notary authenticate it. Once it is authenticated, your affirmation becomes an affidavit and is valid in law.
3. You are setting out on a journey to the North (or South) Pole. After having studied all the available literature on the subject, you have prepared a plan. You show your plan to an expert who has experience with the North Pole and ask him or her to

"confirm" that your plan is sound. Once the expert confirms your plan is workable, you set out on your adventure.

4. You have authored a spy-thriller novel. Before you publish it, you have a real-life spy read it. Once he or she says, "Yeah, this is okay," you go ahead with publishing the book.

5. An automobile manufacturer claims that its new model car is capable of achieving a fuel consumption rate of 230 miles per gallon. The marketing department demonstrates this fact in front of a select set of journalists, and the journalists substantiate the claim.

Therefore, under this definition, validation is a precaution normally taken before taking risks, especially strategic risks. The previously mentioned scenarios share the following characteristics:

- There is a claim that needs validation
- The originator of the claim arranges for validation.

The validation is not made against the specifications of the originator of the claim. It is made against the specifications that might have been formulated by an external agency:

- In the first scenario, the validation is made against the law of the land.
- In the second scenario, an independent, government-authorized person is validating your affirmation.
- In the third scenario, the person is validating your plan against his or her firsthand experience.
- In the fourth scenario, the spy is authenticating the novel based on his or her firsthand experience.
- In the fifth scenario, the journalists are certifying the claims through firsthand observation.

Validation gives outsiders the confidence to be able to say "yep, this is indeed true" or "yep, it really works." Validation performed in a software-development scenario carries out the same functions listed above. The software development team or organization makes the claim that its software product works without defects. That claim is then substantiated by validation of the software product. To achieve the full value of validation, the following three aspects must be present:

1. Validation is performed by independent persons who are not the same persons as those making the claim.

2. Validation is performed not just against the specifications of the claimant, but also against external specifications.

3. Validation is a planned and coordinated effort performed for the purpose of substantiating a claim and instilling confidence in the stakeholders; it is not performed for self-assurance.

During software development, validation of important software artifacts is carried out. Normally, software designs and software products are validated in a contract development scenario. In a COTS product scenario, product specifications are validated in addition to the software design and the software product itself.

Quality Assurance of Software Design

Defect prevention of software design and trapping the defects in software design are the two activities in the quality assurance of software design. Quality control of software design is achieved mainly by two techniques, namely peer reviews and validation. We discussed peer reviews in the earlier sections of this chapter. These reviews will ensure that the software design is comprehensive and the design artifacts are capable of being used to build the proposed software product. We use the following reviews for ensuring quality in our software designs:

1. Before embarking on preparing software design artifacts. We subject our design approach to a group review. It is a best practice if we include experts not just from software development but also from the domain, security, sociology, and so on, so that all standpoints can be covered and included in the design.
2. Each software design artifact is peer-reviewed by a single peer using either independent review or guided review methodology.
3. Use a group review at each level of integration, preferably including domain experts in the review team.
4. Subject each artifact to managerial review before it is approved.

Validation of Software Designs

Like the adage "the proof of the pudding is in the eating," the proof that the design is robust is in the building of the product and then testing it. How do other industries validate their designs? Where they use the design to produce a large quantity of products, they build a prototype (one sample unit of the product) and subject the prototype to all necessary tests, improving the design based on the results of those tests. This method is often used in the automobile and electronic industries, among others. But what about such industries as shipbuilding and aircraft manufacture? They cannot afford to build a wrong product, even for testing. In such industries, they make a scale model prototype and subject the model to tests. Before building a large ship, for example, shipbuilding companies make a much smaller model of the ship they plan to build and test the prototype in a scaled-down simulated environment. They use the results of the test to validate the design of the proposed ship. Before making a new model of a large aircraft, aircraft manufacturers build a smaller, scaled-down prototype and subject it to tests in a wind tunnel. Based on the results, they improve the design and build the product.

Today, computer models allow testing of designs through computer simulation and making improvements in the designs based on the results of the simulations. Yet software vendors that provide simulation software to test rockets, ships, and aircraft, for example, do not provide simulation software that validates software designs!

A development methodology that uses prototyping methods exists in software development, too. These methods use two types of prototypes: build-and-improve prototypes and use-and-discard prototypes. In *build-and-improve prototypes*, skeletons of the software product, such as screen layouts, report layouts, and simple navigation, are built on the actual development platform. Software developers continue to improve the design based on the results of validation of the prototype. In *use-and-discard prototypes*, a prototype is built on a mockup using drafting tools. The design is validated, and then the actual software product is built on the real development platform.

While the software industry is presently using a prototyping methodology for eliciting user requirements, it is infrequent for validating designs using prototypes. Software designs are validated through group reviews by peers or experts. Only if the members of the group review team are carefully selected does this method become effective for validating software designs. It makes sense to have the review team made up of more external experts, as they would validate the product not just against internal standards, but also against field requirements and field usage. It also makes sense for domain experts who are users of the software products to be included as members of the review team and not have the team made up solely of software designers.

The results of validation would be much more insightful if both prototyping methods mentioned here and group reviews using domain experts were used for validating software designs. This is, in fact, a best practice.

Defect Prevention in Software Design

Defect prevention in software designs is very important because design mistakes are very costly, even to the extent of product failure. It has strategic consequences for the organization. We use the following activities at the organizational level to ensure that the software design activity is carried out diligently and that no defects creep in. This portion of software design QA is organizational responsibility. The individual software designer has the role of implementing the organizational guidelines and suggesting improvements thereof.

1. Define a robust software design process and implement it in the organization. This process is subjected to continuous improvement in a defined manner.

2. Develop various standards and guidelines for software design and implement them in the organization. These standards and guidelines include design of inputs, outputs, processes, database design, error handling, messaging, packaging, installation, rollout, flexibility aspects, maintainability aspects, and so on. These are also subjected to improvement in a defined manner.

3. Develop formats and templates to capture software designs that help capture the design information comprehensively and without missing out on any aspect.

4. Develop various checklists to assist designers to ensure that their designs are comprehensive and robust.

5. Develop a knowledge repository that can be easily used by the designers to keep their knowledge up to date.

6. Support a research and development team to keep scanning the software design horizon, cull the latest developments in the field, and disseminate that knowledge to the software designers in the organization.

7. Support a software design excellence team to come up with better alternatives to existing methods both in the design of the product as well as the building of the product.

8. Recognize software design as a specialist activity, provide resources to that effort, and institute a reward and recognition system in the organization to recognize individuals doing excellent work.

This is the environment that is conducive to achieving good software designs in the organization. While this is primarily the responsibility of the senior management, the individual software designers have the following roles to perform in maintaining this organizational environment at its best.

1. Implement the defined processes effectively in the software designs.
2. Participate wholeheartedly in all the initiatives of the organization concerning software design and contribute their best for the success of the initiative.
3. Participate in defining organizational design processes, including definition of processes, standards, guidelines, formats, templates, and so on, to ensure that the best artifacts are included in the organizational processes.
4. Allocate time to the organization for preparing and reviewing the various standards, guidelines, formats, templates, checklists, and so on.
5. Participate in design reviews as needed by the organization and do their best to ensure a great software design and to eliminate errors attributable to design.
6. Give suggestions for improvement of the process artifacts, giving back the experience gained from designing software products and feedback from the field.
7. Use the organizational knowledge repository extensively for improving the software designs. Also contribute to the knowledge repository as much as possible to keep it up to date and at the state of the art.
8. Make suggestions for improving the software design processes as diligently as possible.
9. Refer software design problems to the organizational research and development team so that new solutions for the old problems can be discovered.

There is a justifiable apprehension in the minds of software designers that processes and standards stifle the creativity of software designers. True, software design is a creative activity. We will deal with the aspect of creativity in one of the appendixes. But, as Thomas Alva Edison said, it is "10% inspiration and 90% perspiration." In any creative endeavor, there is mundane work, and in any mundane work, there certainly is an element of creativity. The standards and processes ensure that the mundane work is carried out comprehensively without any hitch . The processes ensure that "a battle is not lost for want of a nail." They provide the nuts and bolts of software design, while the creative work is carried out by the designers.

Second, any well-defined and successful process provides for exceptions and waivers to cater to special situations. When the design project at hand is at loggerheads with the defined process, all that the designer has to do is raise a waiver request and move on with the design.

We need to remember that organizational processes exist to make the work of individuals in the organization lighter and not to make it tough for people to operate. If organizational processes place a burden on those working, then it is time to revise the processes and redefine them all over again.

Audits of Software Design

Audits are a tool to ensure that the defined processes are being diligently implemented in the organization. Audits are the QC tool to ensure that design work conforms to the defined organizational standards and processes. All design teams are audited periodically, once in three months or so, to ensure conformance of the team to the defined processes of the organizations. Every project is subjected to audits once at the beginning of the design phase and again at the end of the design phase.

The audit at the beginning of the software design work ensures that the team is ready with all the prerequisites that are essential to carrying out the design work in an unhindered manner. The NCs assist the design team in plugging the loopholes that inhibit the smooth flow of the software design work.

The audit at the end of the software design phase ensures that all the design work was performed implementing the organizational processes and standards, all deliverables were subjected to relevant QC activity, and all defects uncovered were fixed. This audit clears after resolving the NCs found by the audit team for the next level of activities to begin.

Quality assurance is a very large subject that deserves a separate book in itself. I authored one. I suggest that you acquire a book (mine is *Software Quality Assurance: Best Practices, Tools and Techniques for Software Developers*, J. Ross Publishing, 2009) and read it to gain comprehensive insight into the subject. It will help you deliver great software designs.

17

Engineering Drawings for Establishing Software Design

Introduction

For those of us in the software industry, the phrase *engineering drawings* connotes plans, elevations, and sectional views. The connotation is true to some extent. When there is a solid item, be it a part, a subassembly, or an assembly, it needs plans, elevations, end views, and sectional views. But drawings are used for a variety of other purposes. The following are the engineering drawings that do not use plans, elevations, end views, or sectional views:

1. *Electrical circuits*: These drawings depict electrical circuits, showing how the electrical currents flow, supplying electricity to various electrical equipment.

2. *Connection wiring diagrams*: These drawings show the connections between various appliances. The appliance is shown as a block with its terminals marked, and the connections are shown between the terminals of the appliance and the source of the electric supply.

3. *Wire harness diagrams*: These are line drawings showing how wires are harnessed to be used in cars, airplanes, rockets, ships, and so on. These drawings help prepare the wire harnesses offline and then used to connect various appliances in the vehicle or other equipment.

4. *Electronic schematics*: Electronic circuits are similar to electrical circuits except that the components are much smaller and the density of these circuits is very high. These are also line drawings.

5. *Landscaping*: Landscaping drawings model the contours of the land so that landscaping can be designed to be implemented by the developers. The development can be a garden, a layout of buildings, or any other purpose.

6. *Printed circuit layouts*: PCBs are used in electronic equipment, including computers. The circuits are etched on a copper-clad base material like epoxy boards or phenolic boards. PCBs can be single layer (only one circuit on one side of the board), double sided (circuits on both sides of the board, interconnected as necessary), and multilayered (multiple circuits on multiple layers of the board. The boards are fused after etching the circuits using special processes). Our computers use multilayered PCBs. These drawings show the circuit as it needs to be etched.

7. *Piping diagrams for water and airflow*: Pipes are used for conveying hot/cold water or air from one piece of equipment to another. The pipes can be routed through multiple floors of a building and in public places, too. These are also line drawings.

8. *Layouts for real estate development*: Real estate developers developing a piece of land into multiple condos use this type of drawing. These are line drawings showing the exact location of condos, roads, common areas like parks, parking areas, and so on.

9. *Facilities layouts*: Facility layout drawings are also line drawings that show the location of various equipment in the given space. The facilities can be restaurants, workshops, assembly shops in factories, hospitals, hotels, software development facilities, and so on.

10. *Material flow diagrams*: This type of drawing is used to analyze the flow of material in a workshop or any other facility to optimize the flow and increase efficiency in the movement of materials and work pieces. It is also heavily used in airports to ensure safe movement of airplanes, buses, baggage, and other vehicles on the tarmac as well as in the halls.

11. *Workflow diagrams*: These drawings are used to chart the flow of work pieces from their initial stage to the final stage in a workshop or other such facility. These are also line drawings.

12. *Process flow drawings*: These are basically used in the design of plants manufacturing chemicals and pharmaceuticals in which the process of conversion of input raw materials into a final product is performed with a minimum of human intervention. These drawings are used to analyze the flow and then design the plant.

13. *Process maps*: These are used in process definition of organizational management and quality processes.

14. *PERT (Program Evaluation and Review Technique) diagrams*: These diagrams are used in project management to plan the execution of projects.

The above are just line drawings. They do not use plans, elevations, end views, or sectional views. The below are textual drawings:

1. Bills of materials/parts lists/materials lists: These are enumerations of materials to be used for manufacturing a part, an assembly, or a product in manufacturing. They are also used in the set of drawings used in the construction industry.

2. An enumeration of labels to be engraved for placing near control instrumentation in control panels and control desks used in the manufacture of chemicals, power plants, mining controls, and so on.

3. Termination lists: These are used for making terminations in electrical wiring and piping drawings. They show a rectangular box of the equipment, and against each terminal, the identity of the other end is shown.

None of the above drawings use plans, elevations, end views, or sectional views. I am not saying the software development industry does not use drawings at all. We use many diagrams, which I described in the preceding sections of this chapter. But we do not use those diagrams with the same rigor and discipline as the engineering disciplines do. I wish to introduce the discipline of engineering drawings for application in recording software designs.

Here are the distinguishing aspects of engineering drawings that we can profitably use.

1. Each sheet of a drawing has a layout. It will consist of:
    a. Title block: The title block is usually placed at the right-hand side at the bottom of the drawing, and it consists of:
        i. Title of the drawing: A brief description, running into a couple of lines if necessary
        ii. Title of the product: Optionally
        iii. The name/signature of the person who prepared it and date
        iv. The name/signature of the person who approved it and date
    b. Revision block to record each of the changes made to the drawing, consisting of:
        i. Location or zone on the drawing
        ii. A brief description of the change effected
        iii. The name/signature of the person who made the change and date
        iv. The name/signature of the person who approved it and date
    c. General notes: General notes are points to be noted when using the drawing aimed at the user of the drawing and other situation-specific notes.
    d. Zones: the drawing is divided into zones by drawing gridlines in a light color so that they do not appear in print. The horizontal rows use the alphabet, and the vertical columns are numbered, so the zones can be referred to as A1, B3, C5, and so on. These zones are used while filling in the revision block under the column captioned "Location or Zone."
    e. Drawing area: This area contains the drawing, which will give information about what is to be achieved.
2. Each drawing is associated with a BOM drawing. The main drawing and the BOM drawing use the same number, except the type of drawing. For example, let us assume that the product assembly drawing is numbered A4-PA-1234. Then, the corresponding BOM would be numbered A4-BM-1234. This helps in identifying the associated BOM easily. The item numbers of the BOM would be used on the corresponding assembly drawing.
3. A detail is shown only once in the set of drawings prepared for a product. No detail is duplicated.
4. Drawings are numbered using a scheme that helps in the easy location of drawings. Generally, the scheme of numbering the drawings is to use the same drawing in different projects and not to tie it up in just one project. These drawing numbers are entered into a database table with all the details based on the drawing title. This greatly reduces the need to redraw the drawings again and again. I will explain the scheme of numbering the drawings later in this chapter.
5. Drawings are made on five sizes of paper, as shown in Table 17.1

A typical blank drawing sheet is shown in Figure 17.1. I recommend sizes A4 (A of USA) and A3 (B of USA) for use in capturing the software designs. Using this blank sheet, I will depict some drawings I used for software designs in my products. In place of a BOM, we need to use a bill of data (BOD) to list the items shown in the drawing. I suggest the use of this code for numbering the drawings used to capture the software design.

The explanation of the drawing numbering scheme is depicted in Figure 17.2.

TABLE 17.1

Drawing Sheet Sizes

Size	ISO Dimensions in Inches	American Size	American Dimensions in Inches
A0 (1 sq. m.)	33.11 × 46.81	E	34.0 × 44.0
A1 (0.5 sq. m.)	23.39 × 33.11	D	22.0 × 34.0
A2 (0.25 sq. m.)	16.34 × 23.39	C	17.0 × 22.0
A3 (0.125 sq. m.)	11.69 × 16.54	B	11.0 × 17.0
A4 (0.0625 sq. m.)	8.27 × 11.69	A	8.5 × 11.0

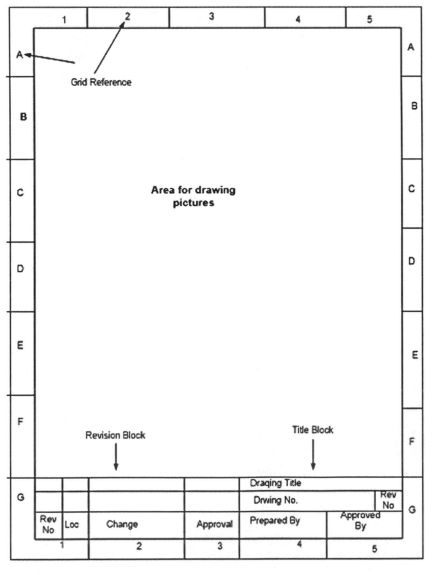

FIGURE 17.1

A typical blank drawing sheet.

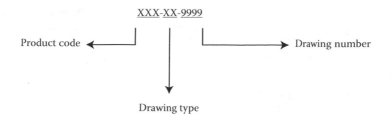

FIGURE 17.2
Drawing numbering scheme.

XXX: The first three characters are used to denote the product for which the drawing is made. For example, MRP denotes the product MRP Pal.

XX: These second set of two characters is used to indicate the type of drawing. Here are the suggested drawing types:

1. *BD*: Bill of data
2. *CC*: Common component
3. *IC*: Icon
4. *MA*: Module assembly
5. *ML*: Menu list
6. *PA*: Product assembly
7. *PG*: Picture graphic
8. *RL*: Report layout
9. *SA*: Subassembly assembly
10. *SL*: Screen layout
11. *SP*: Stored procedure, query, or trigger for a database table
12. *SS*: Style sheet
13. *SU*: Program, component, or unit of software
14. *TB*: Toolbar
15. *TC*: Test case
16. *TP*: Test plan
17. *TS*: Table script

9999: A running serial number for the drawing. We can have a running number for all the drawings in the organization or have a separate set for each of the products. I advocate using a separate set for each of the products. That is, the first drawing in the set of drawings for the product begins with the number 0001, and it is incremented with every new drawing for the product.

Of course, this is the system I suggest. You can have your own method of numbering the drawings. Whatever numbering scheme you use ought to be meaningful to the people in your organization and should assist in easy location of the required drawing with a minimum of effort to locate and retrieve it.

A sample set of drawings prepared for my product MRP Pal is given in Appendix E. Figure E.1 shows the product assembly drawing for my product MRP Pal. The numbers in the circle refer to the items in the corresponding bill of data. The arrows point to the item to which the number in the circle refers. The circles, the numbers, and the arrows clearly establish the relationship between the drawing and its bill of data. As you can see, the title block in the drawing gives the title of the drawing, the name of the person who prepared it, and the name of the person who approved it. Every time the drawing is revised, a row in the revision block is filled up with the relevant details.

Now, look at Figure E.2, which shows the BOD for the product assembly drawing depicted in Figure E.1. As you can see, the numerical part of the BOD has the same number as the product assembly drawing. This convention is used to clearly establish that the BOD belongs to the drawing that has the same number. The item number column refers to the number in the circle in the principal drawing. The column "description" contains a detailed description of the item. It can span multiple lines as required. The column "qty" (quantity) refers to the number of times the item is used in the principal drawing. In this drawing, the quantity is just 1 for all the items. But in screen layout drawings and others, we may need to use an item more than once. For example, the routine that restricts numerical entry into text boxes may have multiple occurrences, and we put the number of times a common routine is used in the principal drawing. Finally, the column "reference" gives the reference for the item. Sometimes, the item may be a bought-out item, in which case we give the model number and manufacturer name. Here, we give the drawing reference to the items. For example, for item 1, that is, the product MRP Pal, I give the reference to the screen layout drawing for the product. For software products, the opening page (home page) or screen is the control center from which the user is navigated to other functionality. For each of the modules, I give their main page (or home page) drawing reference.

Just to make the concept clearer, I also present here a module assembly drawing and its BOD in Figures E.3 and E.4. Figures E.6 and E.7 depict a component drawing and its BOD for material procurement requisition (MPR) functionality. Figure E.5 depicts a sample drawing for the design of a database table.

I strongly recommend the use of engineering drawings to capture, record, and establish software designs. Drawings are pictorial, which makes them easy to understand and interpret. Drawings have facilities to minimize the textual part of the design documents and have the potential to facilitate separating the design from coding, as coders would be easily able to code programs from these design drawings.

Utility of Drawings in Work Execution

Drawings are a great tool in the execution of the project. Here are all the advantages of using engineering drawings during the execution of the software development project:

1. *Ready-made work breakdown structure (WBS)*: With all drawings in place, the WBS is in place. It is nothing but the list of drawings. Each drawing coupled with its BOD is a piece of work that can be allocated to a programmer. This ready-made WBS is a great work simplifier for the project manager.

2. *A supervisor can allot a unit drawing to one programmer*: It becomes very easy for the project manager to allocate work. He or she needs to simply hand over a drawing

and its BOD to the programmer, who can immediately proceed with the work. Instructions and a detailed explanation are rendered unnecessary.

3. *Drawings make it easy to prepare test plans by independent specialists*: Now the project manager can hand over a drawing and its BOD to a testing expert, who can prepare the test plan and test cases without reference to the designer. Drawings contain precise information, and this facilitates testing work being carried out independently.

4. *Drawings make peer review and testing feasible*: Now, peer review is given more lip service than real concern. We abstain from peer review of the code because the reviewer has no credible artifact to review the code and compare it with. The drawing fulfills the need and allows us to conduct effective peer reviews.

5. *Drawings make estimation easy*: Estimation about the quantity of work and the effort required to accomplish it is carried out before the project is acquired for cost purposes and then at the time of allocating the work to the programmers to set targets and to measure performance. Now, in the present day, we may say it is rather guesstimates than credible estimates. Engineering drawings, specifically the BOD, have proven to be credible artifacts in the matter of estimation for both purposes. Thus, engineering drawings facilitate credible estimates for costs as well as target setting.

6. *Improved productivity and morale*: As engineering drawings provide accurate and precise information, the productivity of the programmers improves significantly, as they need not refer back to the designers or project managers for clarification. With credible estimates resulting in credible target setting, which in turn facilitates credible performance measurement, leading to credible reward and recognition management, the employees would be better motivated and the general morale would be high in the organization.

All in all, engineering drawings as a tool to capture software designs not only facilitate precise capturing of the design information but also provide a better mechanism for work execution and improved productivity and morale.

18

Handling Software Design Projects

Introduction

Software design for any sizable software product cannot be achieved by a single designer. Even a small design project needs multiple specialists like graphics and database specialists. When there are multiple people involved in a project, we need management! The design of a software product is a one-time activity. Once designed, the product will be built, tested, released, and put into operation. Then it goes into maintenance. In fact, all product designs are one-time activities. The design team takes up another design project, even in automobile manufacture! So, it is no surprise that our software design also needs to be handled as a project. In this chapter, let us discuss the nature of software design projects and how the industry handles them.

Attributes of a Project

Here are the main attributes of a project:

1. A project is a one-time activity. No project will be repeated. A similar project may be executed again in the organization, but never will an identical project be taken up.
2. A project has a definite beginning and a definite end. Projects are not ongoing operations like a production shop.
3. A project has a sanctioned budget within which it has to deliver results.
4. Projects start with a minimal number of people, increasing the number as the project progresses, and as the project winds down, the number of people is ramped down.
5. An organization specializing in project execution keeps central pools of specialists, allocates them to projects as necessary, and deallocates them as their roles in the project are finished.
6. A project is initiated, planned, executed, controlled, subjected to quality control, delivered, and closed.

Having understood the attributes of a project, let us look at the phases of a project:

1. Project acquisition
2. Project initiation

3. Project planning
4. Project execution
5. Project control
6. Project closure

So, can we really call software design an independent project in itself? Not really! Usually, software design is part of a software development project that is composed of other phases like project acquisition, initiation, planning, requirements analysis, software design, construction, quality assurance, delivery, installation, rollout, and perhaps other phases too. But, sometimes, we may undertake only software design. It is not uncommon to divide a software development project into multiple projects and outsource them to different organizations. However, it is common to group the activities of requirements analysis and software design and treat it as an independent project. For our current purposes, let us consider software design as an independent project and move forward.

Whether as part of a software development project or as an independent project, we need to handle software design as a project. If it happens to be a part of a software development project, certain aspects need not be handled by the chief designer. So, let us discuss the activities of a software design project:

Plan the project: Planning the project involves estimating the resources needed to execute the project at a future date and then scheduling the requirements of those resources. Forecasting the requirements takes estimation skills. The resources are of four types, namely:

1. *People with the required skills*: First and foremost, we need a chief designer who will take charge of the design project and guide/coach/direct the rest of the team. The chief designer, or, as we may call him or her, the design manager, needs to have the experience of completing a minimum of two software design projects and comprehensive knowledge of software development and design. Then we need people with the following skill sets:

    a. *Senior software designers*: These people need to be adept at software design. Each of these persons is expected to take charge of a module and guide the others in carrying out the design work.

    b. *Graphic designers*: They develop the graphics needed for the project as well the web pages. Some people may say that developing the graphics needs to be pushed into the construction stage of the software development project. We can even do that. In my humble opinion, it would be advantageous if the graphics are ready at the time of designing, as these are necessary for screen design. The practice in the industry is to treat this work as part of development and not as design.

    c. *Database specialists*: These people design the databases and the tables thereof

    d. *Code designers*: They design the code components. These people need to be experts in the programming language selected for the project.

2. *Funding for expenses*: We also estimate the total expenses needed to execute the design project. Expenses include salaries for the designers, the cost of any new tools to be acquired, the cost of any new equipment to be procured, and any other resources to be expended during the execution of the project. Should we estimate the cost of power, stationery, and office supplies? In my humble opinion, these are taken as overheads unless they have to be specially spent for the project or are required in bulk.

3. *Equipment, including tools*: To execute the design project, we need computer equipment and software tools. Of course, the organization may already have them, but we need to make an estimate so that the concerned executives can allocate them to the design project team at the time of requirement in adequate numbers.

4. *Time*: We estimate time in two modes, namely the absolute time in person hours and the relative time in calendar days. Person hours assists us in arriving at the number of designers we need to execute the project, and calendar days tells us the date by which we can complete the project. We usually take 8 person hours as one calendar day. But, most of the time, fragmentation occurs. Work usually takes person hours that are not perfectly divisible by 8. We may need 12, 23, or 9 person hours or so for a task. Now, if the task needs 7 person hours, the remaining 1 hour would be lost to the organization. That is, even though the task should take 7 hours to complete, it ends up taking a full day! Therefore, we should not commit the completion date by dividing the total person hours by 8. We need to schedule the project execution taking into account fragmentation losses and then commit the completion date. The techniques of the Program Evaluation and Review Technique/Critical Path Method (PERT/CPM) are the most popularly used techniques for scheduling any project. The software tools that were built based on this technique are MS Project, Primavera, and others that can be used in planning our projects. Coverage of the PERT/CPM technique is beyond the scope of this book. You need to master it once you grow to the level of a design manager!

Execute the Project

The first step in executing the project is the project initiation. During project initiation, we carry out the following activities:

1. Raise, if the following are not already in place, resource requests on:
   a. HR department for human resources
   b. Systems administration department for equipment and software resources
   c. Facilities department for seating space to house the design team
   d. Purchase department for the procurement of any project-specific equipment, software, or tools
2. Set up the facilities for the project team to sit and work.
3. Set up the computer equipment and network facilities.
4. Install the necessary software tools to carry out the work.
5. Finalize the communication protocols and methodologies.
6. Finalize the technical methods, tools, and techniques to be used in the execution of the project.
7. Set up a configuration management system.
8. Document all this in a plan document; subject it to peer, expert, and managerial review; and close all the defects uncovered.
9. Obtain approvals, baseline the document, and bring it under configuration control.

Then we conduct a project kickoff meeting. This meeting aims to obtain support from all the stakeholders and the support department, as well as to inform them about the project, its milestones, and other important information to help plan their activities and schedules considering the requirements of the project. This meeting has a twofold objective, namely to give necessary information for the stakeholders to plan their activities, taking into account the needs of our project, and to obtain their buy-in for the schedules of our project.

Once we conduct the kickoff meeting of the project, we need to begin working. We need to complete some activities before we begin ramping up the resources. These preliminary activities are essential so the resources need not sit idle while we finalize the initial aspects. The initial aspects to be finalized are:

1. Finalize the development platform and the target machine.
2. Study the product specifications/requirements and bridge the gaps, if any.
3. Break the project down into modules.
4. Break down the modules into their submodules and further if necessary.
5. Prepare specifications for the modules and submodules.

All this has to be carried out by the chief designer or the design project manager. This will enable the chief designer to assign work to the senior designers to begin work on the modules. Now, we are ready to ramp up the team by adding the senior designers who will report to the chief designer and take ownership of the design of the modules assigned to them. They will supervise and guide the software designers in carrying out the detailed design of the project. This is also the time to ramp up a database specialist to design the database.

The database specialist will carry out the design of tables to be included in the database of the product and prepare the table scripts. The database specialist will model the data, normalize the data, and divide the data into logical groups, avoiding non-essential data redundancy. Arrange logical data groups into tables and assign names for the tables, which can be used during software design.

One of the senior designers will be assigned the work of identifying the common code components. This designer will study the requirements and identify all the common code components. Of course, more common code components may be identified when the detailed design is carried out by the other designers, and they will be added to the common code components as and when they are identified.

Now, the module designers break the modules into software units. During this work, they will utilize the product specifications/requirements, organizational standards, guidelines, and brainstorming among themselves. Then, each of these senior designers will enumerate the software units that need designing. They prepare specifications for the units. Usually, these specifications are subjected to peer and managerial review to ensure that there are no defects and that they are comprehensive.

Now, we are ready to ramp up the software designers to carry out a detailed design and document the designs in design artifacts approved for use in the organization. They will then subject these designs to the quality control activities of peer review and managerial review.

Now, the designs are ready for release to the coding team to construct the software artifacts.

Configuration Management during Software Design

How are configuration management and configuration control applicable in software design?, you may ask, and you are right to ask this question. The purpose of configuration management in any activity is to ensure that the artifacts are controlled in such a manner that an incomplete or unapproved artifact does not leave the project team. Now, take any design artifact. It is in one of three states, namely the preparation stage, quality control stage, and ready for release stage. Let us take a look at how the artifact changes states during the software design process.

1. The software designer designs the software unit and captures the design in a manner approved for use in the organization.
2. The designer submits the artifact to the senior designer.
3. The senior designer usually maintains four folders/directories/libraries to store these artifacts. They are named "In Process," "Under QC," "Finalized," and "Archive," Of course, these names could differ from organization to organization. When the designer is carrying out the design, the artifact is stored in the folder named "In Process," Once the designer completes the work on the artifact, the senior designer moves the artifact to the folder named "Under QC" after removing it from the "In Process" folder.
4. Then the senior designer arranges for the peer review of the artifact. If the QC activity uncovers any defects, the senior designer moves it back to the "In Process" folder and informs the designer to fix the defects in the artifact.
5. The designer fixes the defects pointed out by QC and informs the senior designer.
6. The senior designer moves the artifact to the "Under QC" folder.
7. Now steps 4 to 6 are iterated until all defects uncovered by the QC activity are closed and the artifact is ready for delivery.
8. Now the senior designer moves the artifact from the "Under QC" folder to the "Finalized" folder.
9. If the artifact needs to be changed for any reason after it was moved to the "Finalized" folder, it is moved back to the "In Process," folder and all the steps beginning with step 1 are repeated.
10. Design artifacts can be released only from the "Finalized" folder.

As you can see, an artifact is at one and only one location. By controlling design artifacts in this manner, we ensure that a semifinished artifact is never released for construction. This is how we carry out configuration management during the software design activity.

Quality Management during Software Design

Software design is a creative activity. Therefore, it is not amenable to quality control. But we divided software design into conceptual design and detailed design or any other two names these two are called. While conceptual design is not at all amenable to quality assurance, detailed design can and ought to be subjected to quality assurance and quality control. We have noted that quality assurance has two parts, namely the defect prevention part and the defect-trapping part. Processes, standards, guidelines, checklists, formats, and templates help us in preventing defects. These are performed at the organizational level, and all software designers are expected to be adept at implementing them. Now, the defect-trapping part of software design is carried out by peer, expert, and managerial reviews. All completed design artifacts ought to be peer-reviewed and passed on to managerial review once all defects uncovered in the peer review are resolved. Managerial review is carried out before approving the artifact. Managerial reviews are not expected to uncover new defects, but sometimes even that happens!

It is the duty of the chief designer or the manager of the software design project team to ensure that all quality-control activities are planned and then implemented before releasing the design artifacts to product construction.

We use expert reviews after freezing our conceptual design and beginning work on the detailed design of the product. This review helps us in taking a second look at our approach to designing the project and help us plug loose ends, if any, in our thinking. This responsibility also rests on the shoulders of the senior designers.

Productivity Management in Software Design

It is not easy to arrive at productivity of software design work precisely. Therefore, we use the PERT model of estimating the duration. For each piece of assigned work, we make three estimate, namely the optimistic or the best-case scenario, the pessimistic or the worst-case scenario, and the most likely or the normal case scenario. The best-case scenario is when everything moves as expected and everything gets finished in its shortest time. The worst-case scenario is when every hurdle is encountered, everything moves at its lowest speed, and everything takes its maximum time. The normal case scenario is between these two scenarios. We compute the average of these three estimates using the formula:

$$\text{Expected time} = (\text{optimistic time} + \text{pessimistic time} + 4 \times \text{most likely time})/6$$

As long as the actual time taken for completing the work is close to the expected time, productivity of the people is acceptable. If the actual time taken is closer to the worst-case scenario, the chief designer needs to take a look at the work and provide assistance to the specific designer by providing expert advice or better tools or removing any hurdles in the performance. We can manage the productivity of the software design project in this manner.

Integrating the Deliverable

Usually, software design or, for that matter, any design project uses the top-down approach. First, we begin at the product level and studiously move downward, breaking the functionality down into lower-level assemblies, subassemblies, and then components, with components at the bottom level. Of course, while breaking down the functionality and designing the lower-level assemblies and components, we may have to modify the design of the higher-level assembles to suit the design of the lower-level components. All such changes have to be formalized and recorded meticulously so that when all the work is completed, the chief designer and the senior designers take stock of all the software design artifacts and ensure that all the necessary details are indeed designed and properly captured in the design artifacts that were prepared and approved.

As a final measure, the complete set of design artifacts needs to be subjected to peer review to uncover any missing aspects and fix these defects. Then it has to be routed through managerial review so that a holistic view can be focused on the product design before approving and releasing the design artifacts for product construction.

Close the Project

The design project cannot be closed until the product is constructed, tested, and delivered to the customer. The proof of the design is in the product. Some of the design defects will surface during the construction phase. The serious design defects will surface only when the product is put to real-life usage, and that will be over a period of time. But we cannot keep the design time hanging around idly until all the design defects are uncovered.

The usual practice is to ramp down the design team as the workload is reduced. After the initial phase, the work of database specialists is finished once all the tables and other activities are completed. So, they are released but are retained on a part-time basis to be available to the software design team on an as-needed basis for consultation or tweaking the database. Similarly, the user interface specialists may also be released when the initial designs are completed. They may be reallocated if necessary. The software designers are released as the work allocated to them is completed and is passed through quality assurance. Usually, the chief designer and the senior designers, who are few in number, are retained on the project until the coding is underway and the confidence level that not many defects could be found in the designs increases. Sometimes, during the final stages of the construction, when the team is confident that no more design defects will surface, the design team is entirely released except one or two persons among the chief designer and the senior designers to provide design support should it become necessary.

The postmortem of the software design project is conducted along with the postmortem of the entire project, but if the project is only for software design and the construction and other subsequent activities are handled outside the organization, the design project postmortem may be conducted immediately after the designs are delivered. But it would be a better practice to hold the design project postmortem after the designs are realized and the product is developed.

Further, it would be still better practice if we could have a review or postmortem of the design project after the product has been in operation for at least six months. This will give us information about all the defects that lurked inside the project and are attributable to software design. But the flip side is that the members of the design team would have been released and be working on other projects. Of course, only the chief designer and the senior designers can be involved in the postmortem. In fact, all members working as software designers need to participate in the postmortem of a software project, including design-only projects.

A project postmortem is led by the project manager or the person who conducted the audit of the completed project. He/she will go through all the issues, including the good and bad aspects. This will give the designers firsthand knowledge of the impact of the designs, and lessons can be learned for future projects. The following are the activities that are performed as part of a project closure:

1. Release of all persons working on the project.
2. The project records are handed over to the organizational knowledge repository.
3. The project manager documents all the best practices, bad practices, and lessons learned during the project execution, and this document is also submitted to the organizational knowledge repository.
4. The project-end performance appraisals are completed for all project members, if such a practice exists in the organization.
5. The project is subjected to the project-end audit and the findings are recorded. This will also be part of the organizational knowledge repository.
6. A project postmortem meeting is conducted. Organizational management, the project manager, the quality assurance team, the members of the project team, and all the senior technical persons in the organization are invited to participate in the meeting.
7. The project manager or the auditor who conducted the project-end audit leads the meeting and presents the project, tracing the execution of the project and highlighting the best practices, the bad practices, the lessons learned, new methods or techniques used, new tools used, and so on to the participants. Any clarifications raised are answered by the concerned persons.
8. The minutes of this meeting are recorded and submitted to the organizational knowledge repository.

The objective of the project postmortem is to learn from the completed project and enhance the knowledge in the organization. The project postmortem meeting concludes the closure of the project.

Appendix A: Creativity and Innovation for Software Designers

Introduction

The word *creativity* connotes producing something that did not exist before. It is the general perception that designers in any field are highly creative people. Of course, this is far from the truth. But designers tend to be creative, and designers benefit from an understanding of the concepts of creativity. Creativity is often referred along with the word *innovation*. There is a misconception that one has to be born with creative traits and that one cannot cultivate creativity. I have also noticed a misconception in the software industry that creativity is for the screen design and is best left to the graphics people. In my humble opinion, creativity is not only for graphics and jazziness on the screen; it is useful in every facet of software design. This appendix intends to give an understanding of the basics of creativity and how to go about cultivating it.

Merriam-Webster's dictionary defines *creativity* as "the ability to create" and defines *create* as "to make or bring into existence something new." Wikipedia defines creativity as "the application" of better solutions that meet new requirements, unarticulated needs, or existing market needs. The created item may be intangible (such as an idea, a scientific theory, a musical composition, or a joke) or a physical object (such as an invention, a literary work, or a painting)." Thus, we can see that the word *creativity* connotes bringing into this world something that was not there earlier. The word was originally used to describe how life began on this earth. Some of the arts like painting, writing (poetry or prose), singing, and dancing began to be called creative arts. Even movie making came to be accepted as a creative work. In fact, today creativity has come to be associated with anything new. Almost all products are claimed to be the result of the creative brain of some scientist. In today's world, the term *creativity* connotes producing some new idea of which nobody thought before. When this idea is realized into a product, it becomes a creative product. Today, creativity connotes coming up with totally new ideas, new ways of doing things, new applications, new ways of combining subassemblies and forming a new product, new uses for an existing product, and so on.

Merriam-Webster's dictionary defines *innovation* as "the introduction of something new, a new idea, method, or device." Wikipedia views innovation as "the application of better solutions that meet new requirements, unarticulated needs, or existing market needs." Creativity and innovation seem like synonyms, and most view them as such. However, when it comes to hair-splitting, there is a subtle difference, as otherwise two words would not exist. The manufacturing industry, where these two terms are extensively used, differentiates between these two words. In the industry, innovation is seen as one or a few steps of improvement over an existing product; the combination of the good aspects of different products to come out with a new product; a change to some aspect of a product with new features to gain a competitive edge; or making a product more productive, safer, more secure, easier to use, more automated, and so on.

I like to think of creativity as *the ability to come up with original ideas* and innovation as *the application of creativity for practical purposes, especially to improve upon the existing products/ systems/mechanisms/applications.*

The industrial revolution began with the invention of the steam engine by James Watt. This, in my humble opinion, is the greatest invention because there was no model to be imitated and improved upon. But when the internal combustion engine was invented, there was the steam engine to imitate and improve upon. Of course, the change was revolutionary in moving the combustion from without to within. While the diode was an invention using the properties of silicon to conduct electricity in one direction, the transistor was an improvement over the diode, and so was the IC chip, which integrated the number of transistors into one component. ICs improved over and over so much that a million transistors are packed into one component. Using electronic components like the transistor to represent numbers, computers were developed. The idea to use the binary numbering system inside a computer was the vital thing that led us to have computers today. Now, in my humble opinion, this is a creative idea, not an improvement over an existing method. The binary numbering system has only two digits, 0 and 1. Digital electronics research produced components to produce electricity, which has only two states, either full voltage or no voltage. Computer scientists combined these two research findings, with the full voltage state to represent the digit 1 and the no voltage state to represent 0. This enabled switching electricity from 0 to 1 to represent digits. Binary numbers could be converted into decimal numbers used by human beings. So, by performing internal arithmetic in binary numbers but receiving inputs and delivering outputs in decimal numbers, automated computing became possible. In this, there is original research in developing the binary numbering system, and digital electronics as well as innovation (or creativity) in combining the two ideas from different fields to develop automated electronic computing. Once a basic computer was developed, a host of innovation was applied on it until we see tablet computers that are more powerful than ENIAC, the first electronic digital computer, which weighed about 30 tons.

Let us look at the automobile. Figure A.1 shows the automobile patented by Carl Benz, and Figure A.2 shows a modern automobile.

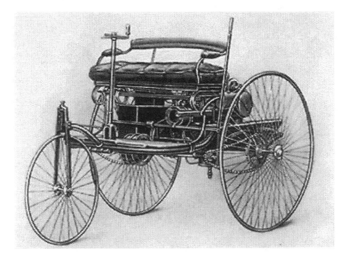

FIGURE A.1
First automobile.

FIGURE A.2
Modern automobile.

As you can see, this is a combination of a tricycle for carrying passengers and an internal combustion engine. The peddler's seat was removed totally, and the handlebars were replaced with a steering wheel. The wheels and spokes, the shaft, the seat, the joining of the front wheel to the back wheels, the fork, and so on were retained from the tricycle. The innovation was the development of an internal combustion engine small enough to fit snugly on the tricycle and powerful enough to transport two people. This car went through a series of innovative steps to be transformed into the present day automobile depicted in Figure A.2.

When we consider the development of airplanes, the impediment for a long time was the misconception that wings and their flapping were essential for achieving levitation as well as forward movement. Lots of people tried flying with wings attached to their hands, and present-day hang gliders are one successful development of that concept. Forward movement without friction between the wheel and the ground was unthinkable. Once it dawned on people that ships moved forward using propellers and the same technique could be used in the air, too, this solved the problem of forward movement. Altering the shape of a large flat wing to a slightly curved wing tilted at an angle created a vacuum above the wing and lifted the airplane, solving the levitation problem. The airplane of the Wright Brothers is shown in Figure A.3, and a modern airplane is shown in Figure A.4.

While the airplane of the Wright brothers did not fly long distances, you can see they borrowed the rudder from ships. It proved that the new concept of the propeller could move the airplane forward by pushing the air back and the slightly curved and tilted wings can achieve levitation without the need to flap. Now, further development was carried out by innovating the application of these two main techniques, producing the modern aircraft carrying about 850 passengers with their luggage over long distances of 5000 miles and more.

Now having discussed creativity and innovation and put both these terms in perspective, let us now discuss the nuts and bolts of these concepts and see if we can cultivate creativity as a way of life for application in software design. Of course, creativity has been and is being regularly applied in software design. Otherwise, we would not have all the wonderful software products available on the market today!

FIGURE A.3
Airplane of the Wright brothers.

FIGURE A.4
Modern aircraft.

Components of Creativity

Creativity has two components: the person and the process. It is the person who produces creative ideas, and the process generates creative ideas in a person. If we understand these two components, we can perhaps use creativity in our endeavors.

Creativity is basically of two types: creativity by serendipity and creativity through a process. Serendipity is finding something good without looking for it. It is also referred to as creativity by accident. While it produces great breakthroughs, we cannot bank on it because we cannot know when such a brilliant idea will strike a person. There are some people who get such brilliant ideas often, but not often enough to justify a big salary. In organizations, we have to have a reliable, albeit less brilliant, process to produce innovative ideas. Many researchers have worked on this problem and developed a process-oriented approach to developing creative ideas by studying creative people. There are many models of the creative process developed by various researchers on the topic. The following steps are found in them.

Preparation: This is common in all models. Preparation is akin to rehearsals practiced in the creative arts. A musician rehearses the proposed compositions before actually performing them. A dancer rehearses the steps before going onstage, but without all the adornments. An actor rehearses all the dialogue and gestures before enacting a scene. Another way of looking at preparation is like a person who encounters a problem situation that arouses curiosity in him/her. Then, that person searches for solutions that are not easily found, forcing the person to look outside the box. That person may then perform brainstorming alone or with like-minded people or conduct research in the library. In short, preparation is recognizing a problem that was not solved and generating a number of alternative probable solutions.

Incubation: This is also common to most models. When the person has completed the preparation and gathered information about the problem space, he/she ruminates on the information and probable solutions in an unconscious manner at the back of the mind, or, as psychologists say, the subconscious. This rumination incubates the ideas, developing some, dropping some, and keeping some without development or dropping. This phase can be looked at as a shortlisting of creative ideas for further evaluation.

Insight/illumination/visualization/imagination/conceptualization: As one keeps ruminating on the ideas and discarding ones that are somehow unsuitable to the situation at hand, an insight is gained or illumination is thrown upon one or two ideas that appear the most suitable for the situation. It is sometimes possible that the person would even visualize the postimplementation scenario, too. A new concept may take form in the person's mind. The key phrase is "keep ruminating." This deep contemplation somehow triggers the innermost layers of the brain, surmounts all known barriers, and throws out a brilliant idea. Of course, it is necessary that we practice this process a number of times before we get such illumination. But the first step is always to begin, and most initial attempts fail.

Evaluation: This is the practical step when the rubber hits the road. The shortlisted ideas are practically tested by building the product or documenting the idea and submitting it for evaluation to the concerned people. One of the techniques that is most useful for evaluation of ideas is the critical examination technique. This is explained in greater detail in the coming sections of this chapter. It is the stage of experimentation with the idea and coming out with the expected results. Other people are involved in this phase and feedback is received. This stage leaves one or two ideas that are really workable.

Elaboration: Now the remaining idea or ideas are elaborated upon. The details of the idea are worked out. It is fully developed. There is nothing left to uncover. This stage develops the idea to its full potential. The solution is fully worked out. Once elaboration is completed, the idea is ready for implementation.

Implementation: This is also common to most models. Implementation is going on the stage and performing. It is the culmination of all rehearsals and the preparatory work. The idea finally comes to fruition. We roll out the solution. Implementation can be on a pilot basis to measure the results to fine-tune the solution.

There could be different process models with different steps. Some people may add a couple more steps or remove a couple of steps from the above model. They can even change the steps. One thing to note here is to maintain the solution after implementation as new forces come into play and a new variety of problems so far unseen raise their ugly heads. The solution has to be retired at some point in time as the circumstances change so much that the solution is no longer workable. But maintenance and retiring are in the domain of people in charge of operations and not creative people.

Creative People

First things first: almost all people are creative, but the degree of creativity differs. I have checked this out and found it to be accurate. I saw the creativity of lazy people in coming up with excuses for not doing the assigned work. I worked in manufacturing organizations and observed the artisans exhibiting creativity in machining a part conforming to an engineering drawing. When the same work is allotted to multiple people, the quality of the deliverables varies. Just observe floors swept by different sweepers and you can check out this statement. And the difference is not because of the difference in skills! All the same, the degree of creativity is not at the same level in all people. Researchers have discovered 32 traits by observing highly creative people. Everyone might not possess all 32 traits, but the more traits a person possesses, the more creative he or she is. These 32 traits are attributed to Dr. Robert Alan Black. Table A.1 depicts the 32 traits that foster creativity in people.

TABLE A.1

Thirty-Two Traits of Highly Creative People

1. Sensitive	9. Question asker	17. Ingenious	25. Curiosity
2. Money is not a motivator	10. Can synthesize correctly, often intuitively	18. Energetic	26. Open-minded
3. Sense of destiny	11. Fastasizing	19. Sense of humor	27. Independent
4. Adaptability	12. Flexible	20. Self-actualizing	28. Severely critical
5. Tolerance to ambiguity	13. Fluency	21. Self-disciplined	29. Non-conforming
6. Observant	14. Imaginative	22. Self- Knowledgeable	30. Confident
7. World is perceived differently	15. Intuitive	23. Specific interests	31. Risk taker
8. Sees possibilities	16. Original	24. Divergent thinker	32. Persistent

I will discuss each of these briefly.

1. *Sensitive*: This word has come to mean the tendency to get injured easily or to be fragile, brittle, and so on. In this context, we need to understand this word as the ability of a person to pick up on even the slightest cue from an event, like a good microphone picks up even a rustling sound. Sensitivity is the ability to pick up meaning from things left unsaid, the ability to read between the lines, to draw inferences from unstated and unrelated sentences. This trait helps creative people draw solutions from other fields or specialities.

2. *Money is not a motivator*: A person who is motivated by money will do only what is essential to earn money. Such people can easily be controlled and made to dance to the tunes of the paymaster. But these people show limited creativity in seeing possibilities to make a fast buck. A really creative person is not motivated by money. But in today's research and development departments, everyone is there mainly to earn money, so I am a bit skeptical about this trait.

3. *Sense of destiny*: The creative person is not satisfied with the present situation whether it concerns him/her or not. He or she usually has a sense of what the situation or method needs to be. This sense of destiny focuses his/her attention on the situation at hand so he/she can ruminate on it and come up with a better solution.

4. *Adaptability*: A quote attributed to George Bernard Shaw states, "90% of the people adapt themselves to the ways of the world, but the remaining 10% want the world to adapt itself to their ways. Therefore, all progress depends on this 10% of people." This trait propels people to look for alternative ways of doing things, come up with different ways of defining something, and look at things differently. We have to understand adaptability as the ability to see the possibility of utilizing seemingly disparate methods to solve a problem at hand. The example quoted earlier is the adaptation of marine propeller to an airplane.

5. *Tolerance to ambiguity*: To really create something new, we need to be tolerant of ambiguity. If there is no ambiguity, it is old hat. In human endeavors, things begin as a paradox before taking shape. Most measures begin in that manner. For example, how much medicine needs to be injected into a person was dependent on the judgment of the doctor, who considers factors like age, health condition, robustness, and so on, and used that information to inject an amount of medicine that was not measured. Slowly, various measures like international units (UIs) were developed, and the dosage can now be precisely specified instead of depending on fallible human judgment. The people who developed the IU recognized the paradox, and, using creativity, they developed a unit of measure that is now used. In the measurement of temperature, it took quite a bit of time before the scales of Celsius and Fahrenheit were developed.

6. *Observant*: A creative person normally does not confine himself/herself to his/her work alone. In addition to minding his/her own business, he/she observes what and how others are doing things, but without poking his/her nose in others' affairs. This observation usually gives information about mistakes or improvements that can be implemented in the way of doing things. This adds to the person's knowledge repository, which can be extracted while focusing on other problem situations.

7. *The world is perceived differently*: Creative people are generally nonconforming. Their perspective on the world differs from others' perspectives. They often have a different perspective on most the things except very obvious ones. Even if you say that the sun rises in the east, they may come up with opinions like, "we need to define east first." The defense of this different perspective causes their creative juices to begin flowing, enabling them to come up with original ideas.

8. *Sees possibilities*: Creative people are not overwhelmed when a challenge confronts them. They can see possibilities where others see only problems. They come up with multiple solutions and possibilities of getting out of tight situations.

9. *Question asker*: They have more doubts than the average person and are not afraid to ask questions and try to get answers. If there is no one to provide the answers, they go out and search for the answers to their questions. This seeking of knowledge enables them to be creative.

10. *Can synthesize correctly, often intuitively*: Synthesis is assembling disparate parts and making a meaningful object or combining seemingly different ideas and developing a new idea or concept. One way of defining knowledge is extracting patterns from disparate events. Synthesis helps in extracting patterns from various concepts, ideas, and information. As you can see, knowledge is essential for creativity and innovation.

11. *Fantasizing*: Creative people tend to be daydreamers. They fantasize, putting themselves in scenarios without ever having the experience. Creative people who are at the peak of creativity are on the edge of hallucinating. But practical creative people fantasize and daydream but do not go to the level of hallucinating. Daydreaming is on the ground level, whereas hallucinating is in the air.

12. *Flexible*: Creative people are generally flexible, and that is the reason they can come up with multiple alternatives. This lack of rigidity coupled with ingenuity and flexibility helps creative people come up with a number of alternatives to any given problem.

13. *Fluency*: In this context, the word fluency refers to the ability to come up with a number of alternatives for a problem. The more alternatives one can generate, the more possible it is to come up with a better solution that fits our specific situation.

14. *Imaginative*: Imagination refers to visualizing things that are not real. Being imaginative involves thinking up things that do not exist. Creative people are capable of imagining situations that did not take place or thinking up objects that do not exist. Until flying became possible, people imagined how flying would be. Until space travel became a reality, people imagined how space travel would be. Imagination helps in creative writing.

15. *Intuitive*: Intuitive people tend to use more of their intuitive skills rather than analytical skills. When a situation presents itself to them, their first reaction is to look at it using their intuition. They try to understand why it took place first before looking for solutions. Even when it comes to solutions, they tend to rely more on intuitive decision-making than analytical decision-making. We have to understand that it is their natural trait, but they can be trained to use analytical skills. We in organizations cannot afford to rely on intuitive solutions not backed by hard data and robust analysis. What we usually do is generate intuitive solutions and subject them to analysis.

16. *Original*: Creative people tend to come up with unheard-of solutions and ideas. They come up with original ideas, original viewpoints on existing ideas, or new ways of applying existing rules or methods. Originality is the distinct trait that separates creative people from the rest.

17. *Ingenious*: Ingenuity includes unusual skills to see possibilities where there are none. People with this trait are excellent at giving excuses for not doing something. And they are the ones who can come up with a solution for apparently unsolvable problems.

18. *Energetic*: Creative people usually have excess energy. They are bubbling with energy and look for opportunities to exert their energy. Of course, without excess energy, the brain cannot divert from vital activities. Excess energy makes the brain work at its full capacity. It goes without saying that we need to take care of our nutritional needs properly to be creative.

19. *Sense of humor*: Creative people have a sense of humor. They are great joke tellers! This allows people to acknowledge their own faults. Humor helps relieve stress in people.

20. *Self-actualizing*: Psychologist Abraham Maslow, whose hierarchy of human needs is very popular, placed self-actualization at the highest level in his hierarchy. He opined that a human would not look at self-actualization unless the other four needs (physiological needs, security needs, belongingness needs, and esteem needs) are fulfilled. For an ordinary human being, fulfillment of these four needs takes a considerable amount of time. It is rare that young people at the beginning of their careers look for self-actualization unless they come from an affluent family with a good record of education and other paraphernalia that would ensure the fulfillment of these four needs. But there is a school of thought that holds that once the bottommost two needs, namely physiological and security needs, are fulfilled, people can begin to look for self-actualization. I, too, subscribe to the idea that one can begin self-actualization even while fulfilling the belongingness and esteem needs. It is also one of the very important traits to cultivate and develop creativity in our personalities.

21. *Self-disciplined*: This seems to be incongruent, as creative people tend to appear like hippies. It is true that most creative people tend not to care about personal appearance. But can you perceive a painter, sculptor, singer, or dancer producing a great piece of art without self-discipline? It is possible that people can come up with great ideas but be unable to bring them to their logical conclusions without self-discipline. When we see a masterpiece of artwork like the Mona Lisa or the statue of Adonis, we can perceive the amount of self-discipline and control the masters exercised. One wrong chipping of the rock would have ruined the statue; one wrong stroke of the brush would have rendered the painting useless. The painting on the roof of the Sistine Chapel required enormous patience and self-discipline from Michelangelo besides his talent and effort for years to finish the painting. It is a misconception that creative people are impatient and undisciplined.

22. *Self-knowledgeable*: It is rare that people are knowledgeable about themselves. Most of us have knowledge about many things but fail to see our strengths and weaknesses objectively. Self-knowledge gives you confidence about what you can achieve and allows for going beyond the usual and coming up with innovative ideas.

23. *Specific interests*: In the preceding sections, I discussed the traits of sensitivity and being observant that suggest that creative people have a wide range of interests. It is true that creative people are observant and sensitive to what is happening around them. They tend not to digress into all those areas, but they use all the information they have culled from the universe to improve and enhance the chosen area of their interest. While they have information and knowledge about a variety of things, they usually concentrate on their specific interests.

24. *Divergent thinker*: If I am asked to name one single trait essential for creativity and innovation, I would name this trait. In my humble opinion, any person who is a divergent thinker is a creative person. The antonym for *divergent* is *convergent*. We are conditioned by schools and most parents to cultivate convergent thinking. We look for one single answer, the best one or the right one. We are asked questions like what is the tallest mountain, longest river, most populous country, who invented the locomotive, which person won independence for our country, and so on, and our textbooks provide one single answer. But reality is not so. George Washington alone was not the person who won independence for the United States. He was assisted by many others at various levels. Our hero-worshipping culture makes us look for one entity to heap our adoration upon. Similarly, given a problem situation, many would converge upon a single best solution, but these single best solutions differ from each other. In most cases, there would be arguments about which is the best instead of seeing the possibilities and merits in the others' solutions. What are the uses of a shoebox? Silly, a shoebox is used to keep shoes! A divergent thinker can come up with more than 25 uses for a shoebox! In order to become more creative, we need to cultivate divergent thinking. Then we can achieve what psychologists call "ideational fluency," which in turn helps us arrive at the optimum solution.

25. *Curiosity*: Curiosity is a desire to know something that really does not concern ourselves. A child has curiosity. As we age, our experiences conditions us to suppress our curiosity. We feel that we know it already, that we do not have the need to know it, or that it does not serve any practical purpose. But creative people have curiosity in large measure. It helps them use the knowledge gained for other purposes.

26. *Open-ended (or minded)*: Open-ended refers to not sticking to one idea or solution. I would prefer to use open-minded in place of open-ended because open-ended connotes one specific situation, whereas open-mindedness refers to a person's conditioning that new ideas would be allowed into the brain. An open-minded person rises above his/her cultural prejudices and value judgments and will be able to learn from others. This ability to learn even from seeming enemies provides for winning ideas. This is another trait I encourage everyone to cultivate in addition to others I have recommended in this list. Closed-minded (or close-ended) people stick to one argument and defend it even to the death.

27. *Independent*: Independent thinkers are not limited by dogma, either of religion or of groups such as unions or associations. They will not blindly follow anything unless they are convinced. This independent spirit propels their thinking toward coming up with original ideas.

28. *Severely critical*: Creative people tend to be critical of almost anything. Except for a few personal faiths, they challenge any idea or rule. This tendency to challenge propels their thought processes to seek loopholes and to plug them with their own version. This gives rise to the creativity of coming up with original ideas, rules, and concepts.

29. *Nonconforming*: Creative people do not conform to even well-established customs and practices. They, of course, do not oppose any and every established custom but are selective and conform when it appeals to them and defy when it does not. Conformance denotes convergent thinking, which inhibits creativity.

30. *Confident*: Confidence is the trigger that spurs all other traits that foster creativity. To accomplish anything in life, confidence is essential, and it is so with creativity, too. So it should not be surprising that being confident is one of the essential traits for creativity. Without confidence in one's own capabilities, one cannot venture out to come up with and suggest new ideas. There is a misconception that confident people are convergent thinkers. But in my humble opinion, without confidence, one cannot ever be creative.

31. *Risk taker*: A risk-averse person can never expose his/her ideas to the public for fear of ridicule.

32. *Persistent*: One has to be persistent to develop something new. An inventor faces hurdles, opposition, and ridicule before people accept the new idea or product. When Nikola Tesla invented alternating current, he faced stiff opposition from his partner and another great inventor, Thomas Edison! However, I tend to think that persistence is necessary to prove the creative idea rather than as a prerequisite for creativity in people.

Having learned briefly about the 32 traits highly creative people possess, the next question is: How many people have all 32 traits? My take is that there are very few people who possess all these traits. The second question is: Can we cultivate these traits by studious effort? My answer would be an emphatic "Yes"! I would go further to say that as software designers, you ought to develop these traits in your personality. However, I recommend these traits as essential for making you a creative person

1. Open-mindedness
2. Divergent thinker
3. Curiosity
4. Independent
5. Original
6. Self-actualizing
7. Fluency
8. Observant
9. Sense of humor
10. Risk taking

In my humble opinion, if you develop these 10 traits, the others will automatically follow. Before we move forward to coming up with original ideas, we ought to know all that is there in the field of our endeavor. If we are not knowledgeable in the subject, then the original idea we come up with may, after all, have already been discovered by someone else. So it is essential that we become masters of the subject that we are trying to improve upon.

Having discussed how a person can be creative, let us now look at some of the techniques we can use to improve our inherent creativity further and use creativity as on ongoing tool to aid our design. They call newspaper writing work "literature-in-haste"; we need to inculcate creativity into our organization as "practical-creativity" like newspaper writing.

Creativity Techniques

There are many techniques, and more techniques are being developed. I discuss a few important and effective techniques that I advocate.

Creative dreaming: By creative dreaming, I am not implying that you sleep during working hours to improve your creativity. The following story is attributed to Elias Howe, Jr., the inventor of the sewing machine. The hand-sewing needle has a sharp point at one end and the eyelet at the other. In this arrangement, the needle drags the thread as it sews. Both ends are free. In a machine, the needle is gripped at one end. This was the major problem faced by Elias. It is said that one day he dreamed he was in a country of savages. As the savages attacked him and escorted him to execution, he noticed that the spears in the hands of the savage warriors had holes near the pointed end. He was jolted out of sleep at 4 a.m. and rushed to his workshop. He had made the needle with a hole near the sharp point by 9 a.m. The rest is history—the history of the sewing machine! There are many other stories about getting solutions in one's sleep. Many poets say that they get ideas in their sleep. Some keep a pen and paper by their bed so they can immediately scribble their thoughts and develop them later on. There is one common thread in all these people: they keep thinking about the problem at hand all the their wakeful time. They are so immersed in that thought that their mind keeps working on the problem, even during sleep! Can we depend on this technique? I am afraid not. Our organizations are now staffed with professionals who do not take any organizational problem as their personal problem. They leave organizational issues once they leave work. Still, if the problem is personally challenging and the employee is motivated to that level, dreaming will help.

Random event: When Archimedes lowered himself into the bathtub, he got an idea about buoyancy and specific gravity. Of course, his mind was fully occupied with the problem of determining the purity of gold in the king's crown without affecting it. Many other people also got solutions at unexpected times, when they were doing something totally unconnected. Some people get solutions when they are jogging or playing a game. Usually, when the person tries to relax the mind, which is deeply occupied with the problem at hand, the solution strikes.

Inner focus: Having inner focus is to delve deeply into the unfathomable inner layers of the mind. Scientists say that we hardly use the power of our brain and that it has capabilities we do not use at all. After assessing the physical attributes of the brains of geniuses and ordinary people, it was discovered that there is no perceivable pattern in the physical brains of geniuses that separates them from ordinary brains. Therefore, it must be how we train or use our brains that develops geniuses. Some techniques are advocated to develop the thinking power of the brain. I tried some of these methods myself and found them to be useful. Here they are:

- *Meditation*: Meditation is a simple technique. One sits at a place where one will not be disturbed for about 15 minutes or more. Usually, a mantra (a word, phrase, or a couple of lines in Sanskrit) is ruminated upon. Then various thoughts come and go through the brain. The meditator is in a semiwakeful state. In that process, some creative thoughts can come to the person. There are many forms of meditation. The critical aspect of meditation is sitting quietly for some time without consciously thinking about anything. The mantra helps you to do that. The mantra need not be in Sanskrit. It can be in your own language, but the important part is it should not be a thought. It could be a word, a short phrase, or a short sentence.

- *Self-awareness*: This is advocated by most religions. It involves becoming detached from the results of one's actions and noncritically analyzing the action in a nonjudgmental manner. This improves the perception of the person and allows the person to rise above himself or herself, see things from a different perspective, and improve creativity.

- *Soft focus*: Soft focus is not to focus on anything specifically. One should not fix the stare or allow the eyes to wander. Sit, let the environment carry on, and allow the inputs to sink into you. This may look as if the person is in a trance or a dazed state, but in reality, it is not so. A person in a trance or a dazed state has fixated on something inwardly in a deep manner and is unaware of his or her surroundings. A person using soft focus is aware of what is happening in the vicinity but without focusing on anything specific. This technique brings in multiple inputs concurrently. This develops the multitasking ability of a person's brain, which leads to improved creativity.

- *Sense of humor or light-heartedness*: A sense of humor allows us to suppress our ego, which is a big barrier to accepting new or different inputs. Ego encourages convergent thinking, preventing us from seeing other alternatives. When you develop a sense of humor, divergent thinking develops. Divergent thinking is an essential trait for creative people.

- *Imitation*: Imitation is the highest form of flattery, as they say. But imitation is the reason for the development of many products. The designers of airplanes imitated birds to design aircraft. If you notice today's aircraft, you can see that the current breed of aircraft looks like sharks or dolphins. The propeller of the airplane imitates the propeller of a ship. You can find a huge amount of imitation in products. So, observing nature, which includes flora and fauna as well as human beings, we can find ways to imitate and improve our solutions. Observation and imitation improve our creativity.

- *Doodling*: Doodling is just scribbling random pictures on paper. It has been found that doodling gives rise to creative thought. When you have a serious problem and you are not finding a workable solution, try doodling and who knows, you may get a brilliant idea.

- *Playing with numbers*: Numbers are magical. When you multiply 9 by any other number, you get 9 when the digits of the product are added together. When you multiply a number containing nine 1s with another number of the same size, you will get all the digits in ascending as well as descending order in the result ($111111111 \times 111111111 = 12345678987654321$). I am sure you know these. Playing with numbers increases creativity. Try this when you have a problem and the creative thought process is triggered.

- *Illusion*: Illusion is not reality. It is a make-believe scenario. Playing with illusions helps creativity. Create an illusion of your problem and solutions and, sometimes, reality jumps out of the illusion and provides a new solution to the problem at hand.

- *Problem reversal*: We recognize that any situation has two versions. We are always looking at only one side, that is, ours. If we stand the problem situation on its head, we see a different perspective altogether. In this technique, we reverse the problem and restate it from the opposite perspective. One example is that when Apple computers entered the computer market, they attempted to produce computers that were not made by any other computer company. Apple produced computers so small that they were called microcomputers. Toyota made smaller cars than US automakers produced. They did the opposite of what the others have been doing. The Sony Corporation came up with small handheld radio receiver sets when the radios were seen as status symbols in the United States and placed on drawing-room tables. General MacArthur used this in WWII while invading Japan by selecting the toughest place to land his troops so the enemy was caught unawares.

- *Discontinuity principle*: When we get used to something for a considerably long time, we fail to see its demerits. In order to stimulate our thinking, we may disrupt the situation and discontinue the existing practice. This stimulates creative thinking and assists us in generating multiple alternative ideas.

- *Prayer*: I wrestled with myself on including this technique. This is my personal technique; I pray whenever I am stuck. It gives me solutions. I do not visit a place of worship to pray as most do. I sit in the northeast corner of my home in the morning hours and pray. The solution comes invariably every time. It is said that it is not important that you understand the text of the prayer. I pray in Sanskrit, of which I understand very little. Perhaps you can pray in Latin or Greek, and it may work for you, too!

Lateral thinking: Lateral thinking deserves a special section on its own. Vertical thinking is considering all aspects of a problem situation. Horizontal thinking is thinking about one aspect of all (or available) similar problem situations. Lateral thinking is neither vertical nor horizontal thinking. Lateral thinking involves different perspectives from stakeholders or nonstakeholders. For example, in a software project, the team may face a problem. The team has two perspectives: that of the team members and that of the team manager. It already has two perspectives. When they are stuck with a seemingly unsolvable problem, they can involve organizational management, the organizational quality assurance department, or the customer representative. That provides some more perspectives on the problem situation that are different from the team perspectives. These new perspectives can provide a new solution to the problem.

Six thinking hats: Edward De Bono invented this technique. Many large organizations use this technique to solve tough problems, with notable success. The six thinking hats are:

1. *White hat thinking*: This method of thinking involves solid reasoning and basing our analysis and inferences on the data of facts and figures.

2. *Red hat thinking*: This thinking is emotional and intuitive thinking. Our thinking is based on hunches and intuition. Facts and figures and logical analysis are not involved in this thinking. This may be thought of as the opposite of white hat thinking.

3. *Black hat thinking*: This is careful, judgmental thinking. Judgments are not decisions. They are based on facts that are based on carefully evaluated solid evidence. This thinking is logical, but used to disprove some hypothesis or solution to a problem situation as unworkable. It is also referred to as logical negative thinking.

4. *Yellow hat thinking*: This thinking is the opposite of black hat thinking. It is also based on solid evidence that is carefully evaluated but used to prove some hypothesis or solution to a problem situation as workable.

5. *Green hat thinking*: This hat connotes creative, original thinking to generate multiple alternative ideas without being critical of any idea.

6. *Blue hat thinking*: Blue hat thinking involves thinking about the process of using green hat thinking. It involves thinking of how green hat thinking is carried out.

Brainstorming: This, in my humble opinion, is the most popular creative thinking technique used in the corporate world to generate many alternative ideas for a problem situation. It is also extensively used for new product specifications. In this technique, a few concerned people or stakeholders in the problem space meet in an informal meeting and give free rein to their imaginations. All ideas aired are captured. During the meeting, no discussion or analysis of the ideas is allowed beyond asking and receiving clarifications. Later on, these ideas are subjected to analysis and the best ideas are picked up for a final round of analysis. In a few rounds, the final solution is determined and applied.

Forced analogy: An analogy is making a comparison between two objects or situations that have something in common. A forced analogy is making a comparison between things that do not have much in common. When you compare two dissimilar things, funny situations develop, and from these funny situations, creativity springs up. Let us say you compare a bazooka to a management system or the customer to an ogre or something like that. If nothing else, we get a good laugh. As we try to try to force similarities between two dissimilar attributes, it may suddenly inspire a creative spark.

Storyboarding: This originated in the Disney studios. During the making of animated movies, drawings were pinned to a wall, and the succession of drawings told the story. Reviewing these drawings, Walt Disney could add or remove drawings from the wall to make the story more meaningful and complete. In our creativity-stimulating exercises, in place of drawings, we put up our ideas in large fonts or drawings. Now, this wall full of ideas is reviewed by the stakeholders, who allow their imaginations to take to wing. This effective visualization of the problem situation helps us arrive at a creative new idea or ideas.

The above are some of the techniques used to generate a number of ideas, some of which could be original in nature, and perhaps arrive at a brilliant solution. I am sure there are some more techniques, and I selected some that, in my humble opinion, are the best. A lot of research is being carried out in this field, and I am sure new and better techniques will emerge in time. If you are curious about creativity and wish to make extensive use of creativity in your designs, I suggest you acquire a recent book on this subject and study it.

Critical Examination Technique

Critical examination is an industrial engineering technique extensively used in work study. This technique draws inspiration from the famous quote by Rudyard Kipling: "I keep six honest serving men/They taught me all I knew/Their names are *What* and *Why* and *When*/ and *How* and *Where* and *Who*" (from *Just So Stories*). While this technique does not fit in the realm of creativity, I am presenting it because it assists in analyzing both the problem space and the solution space.

This technique poses two sets of questions, namely the primary set of questions and the secondary set of questions. Table A.2 depicts these questions.

We elicit the information for five aspects of the situation, namely the purpose, means, place, sequence, and person responsible. Against each of these five aspects, we put the four questions, as shown in Table A.2. The first two questions are primary questions aimed at eliciting information about the problem situation. The last two questions are secondary

TABLE A.2

Critical Examination Technique

Question	Primary Questions		Secondary Questions	
	What	**Why**	**What Else**	**What Should**
Purpose	What is done? Is it necessary?	Why is it done?	What else could be done?	What should be done?
Means	How is it done?	Why this way?	How else could it be done?	How should it be done?
Place	Where done?	Why there?	Where else could it be done?	Where should it be done?
Sequence	When done?	Why then?	When else could it be done?	When should it be done
Person	Who does it?	Why them?	Who else could do it?	Who should do it?

questions aimed at arriving at the solution. The exception is the aspect of purpose, about which there are three primary questions. The extra question, "Is it necessary?", ensures that we are not trying to analyze an unnecessary step. If the answer to this question is "no," then we drop that activity and do not perform any further analysis. These primary questions need to be answered by the person or persons facing the problem and seeking the solution. Once these primary questions are answered, we ask the secondary questions about each of the five aspects of the problem situation. These two questions are aimed at proposing alternatives and selecting the right solution. The answers to the question "What else?" may not come from the stakeholders alone. We may have to involve experts in the problem space, if necessary. The "What else?" question is the one that can bring forth alternatives to the aspect. Before we attempt to answer the "What should?" question, we need to analyze all the alternatives proposed and select the right alternative. We can record the analysis and reasons for selecting the alternative against this question.

In this manner, we critically examine all dimensions of the problem space. Once critical examination is completed, we have the answers for:

1. What we should be doing
2. How we should be doing it
3. Where we should be doing it
4. When we should be doing it
5. Who should be doing it

This is the solution we can implement. I have used this technique extensively and benefitted from it immensely.

Value Engineering

Again, this technique is not a creativity technique. But, in my humble opinion, every designer, regardless of the discipline, ought to be aware of this. Value is a composite of utility and price. In any product, both these aspects are critical. We cannot sacrifice one for the other. Utility is the functionality and price is what the customer pays for it. When we design products, we have multiple alternatives for almost every aspect of the product. The product value depends entirely on the alternatives we select at every step. The purpose of value engineering is to reduce cost or offer better functionality. The philosophy of value engineering is:

1. Same value at a lower price
2. More value at the same price

What is not acceptable is:

1. Less value at the same price
2. Higher price for the same value

We achieve this for the product at every stage of product design and whenever we choose among available alternatives. Value engineering is also referred to as *value analysis*. Value engineering offers a couple of techniques for applying value engineering to situations. I am not going into detail, as it would consume space. Interested readers may acquire a good book on value engineering and study it.

Appendix B: Who Can Be a Software Designer?

Introduction

The person doing the work is vital for the activity to deliver successful results. We may have great tools, methodology, techniques, or processes, but they do not produce great deliverables on their own. All these assist the person in producing a great deliverable. The person has to be an expert in using all these effectively and be motivated to produce a great deliverable. In this appendix, let us discuss the qualifications, attributes, and training that a person needs to possess in order to be a great designer. First, let us look at the activities performed by persons working as software designers.

Activities Performed by Software Designers

Software designers perform multiple activities besides software design. Teachers do not always teach; they set question papers, prepare quizzes, evaluate quizzes and answer scripts, participate in syllabus design, audit each other, prepare assignments for the students as well as evaluating the student projects, and there could be other one-time activities that take their time and effort. So it is in every profession. Software designers also perform various activities as part of their work life. Usually, they perform the following activities.

1. Software design activities
   a. Study the requirements/specifications
   b. Discover gaps in requirements/specifications, interact with the concerned persons, obtain clarifications, and bridge the gaps
   c. Shortlist the requirements/specifications for the first version of the proposed product
   d. Conceptualize the solution
   e. Develop a few alternative solutions; interact with the customer/organizational management and select the right solution for implementation
   f. Work out the details for the design of components, units, modules, and product
   g. Prepare the test plans
   h. Establish all the designs
   i. Subject all the design artifacts to quality assurance activities
   j. Release the designs for development, QC, and implementation of the product
   k. Prepare documentation for product usage, operations, system administration, troubleshooting, installation, and commissioning of the developed product

2. Activities that foster better software design

   a. Develop processes, procedures, formats, templates, and checklists for performing software design

   b. Develop standards and guidelines for implementation in software design

   c. Identify opportunities for improvements in processes and standards

   d. Participate in the evaluation of suggestions for improvements in design processes and standards

   e. Implement the selected suggestions for improvement in the design processes and standards

   f. Subject all the above activities to quality control

   g. Train other software design personnel in processes and standards

   h. Participate in the rollout of standards and processes

3. Activities that assist the organization

   a. Assist the organization in the recruitment of personnel to staff the design department, including developing question papers for conducting written examinations and evaluating them, conducting interviews and induction training for new recruits, and so on

   b. Implement the organizational processes in the work and participate in certification audits to obtain and maintain quality certifications for the organization

   c. Conduct internal audits for peers to assist the quality assurance department in fulfilling the certification requirements

   d. Prepare work progress reports and send them to concerned stakeholders

   e. Participate in progress review and other necessary meetings

   f. Assist the marketing department in project acquisition by preparing cost estimates and participating in technical discussions

   g. Represent the organization in technical matters relating to the products

   h. Any other miscellaneous activities that may be assigned by the management from time to time based on the exigencies of the organization

Software design activities and the activities that foster better software design in the organization are core activities, and the other activities to assist the organization are ancillary activities. In fact, every position in the organization has to perform some form of ancillary activities. Therefore, we need not consider these ancillary activities while discussing the qualities that a software designer ought to possess.

Personality Attributes

What is a personality? Personality is *the integrated organization of all the psychological, intellectual, emotional, and physical characteristics of an individual, especially as they manifest to others.* It is the uniqueness of a person. It is the distinctive or well-marked characteristics of a person. The field of psychology defines "personality" as *a set of response tendencies that are consistent over time.*

Key words associated with this definition of personality include:

Response tendencies: A response is a reaction to a stimulus received. Human beings are not consistent in responding to stimuli. Therefore, we cannot say "consistent responses," but add the word "tendencies" to indicate that, by and large, the responses of human beings tend to be consistent and predictable, provided that the conditions and circumstances surrounding the "stimulus" are similar in nature. Response tendencies include:

1. Emotional responses
2. Motives
3. Beliefs
   a. Ethical
   b. Religious
   c. Social status
4. Interests
5. Fears and threats
6. Desires
7. Attitudes toward
   a. Elders/youngsters
   b. Members of the opposite sex
   c. Society in general
   d. Animals
   e. Work
   f. Authority

Consistent over a period: When we collect empirical data on responses over a period of time of a person to a given stimulus, an individual shows consistency in his or her response. That is, a correlation exists between stimuli and responses.

Personality is subject to change when a change in circumstances occurs over time. A person is born with a personality in line with his or her genetic characteristics. This personality develops as the person matures, influenced by the immediate environment, including the work by which the person earns his or her livelihood and his or her spouse, children, superiors, subordinates and peers, along with world affairs and religious affiliation. The influences that act on the personality and effect change on it include:

1. *Genetic determinants*: These are consistent over the life once physical maturity is attained.
   a. *Physical determinants*
      i. Height
      ii. Weight
      iii. Handicaps, if any
      iv. Intelligence

     v.   Physical strength

     vi. Stamina

    vii. Race and skin color

   viii. Attractive/unattractive

  b. *Psychological determinants*

     i. Cognitive abilities

    ii. Learning abilities

   iii. Resistance to provocative (positive and negative) stimuli (anger management)

   iv. Comprehension abilities

    v. Style of thinking—convergent or divergent

   vi. Creative abilities

  vii. Taboos

2. *Experiential determinants*

  a. Early childhood environment

  b. Education

  c. Scholastic environment

  d. Upbringing

  e. Work environment

  f. Outcomes/consequences of critical decisions

  g. Travel

  h. Group activities

3. *Environmental determinants*

  a. Level of prosperity of the household

  b. Education of parents/guardians

  c. Existence and cohabitation of parents

  d. Single mother/father upbringing

  e. Marital status

  f. Place of work

  g. Status/level in society in general and in the community

Some might also include prenatal determinants in the above list. I consider genetic determinants to include prenatal influences.

While it is impossible for us to ascertain the influences on a person at the time of recruitment, we need to recognize that every person comes with a set of personality traits that may not change just because the work environment changes. Work environment is just one factor that influences a person's personality. There are several other factors that influence the person's personality. Software design is affected by the personality of the designer in addition to his or her qualifications and experience in the field. While it is not my intention to say that attitude is more important than qualifications and experience, I certainly would stress that personality is also important. Rather, the personality is the factor that differentiates between an ordinary designer and a great designer.

Now what are the personality traits that are essential and desirable in a designer? I enumerate these here and discuss them.

1. Creativity traits
    a. Divergent thinking
    b. Fluency
    c. Open-mindedness
    d. Curiosity
    e. Originality
    f. Observant
    g. Sense of humor
2. Personality traits
    a. Quick learner
    b. Fast reader
    c. Perseverance
    d. Patience
    e. Pursuit of excellence

I have discussed the creative traits in the Appendix A. Let us now put the personality traits in perspective.

Quick learner: Design is more or less a continuously improving activity. The product life cycle has become amazingly short. Sometime back, product life was about 10 years. Now, the life of a product is about three years! It has become customary to release a new product or a new version of the product every three years. In the arena of software products, Microsoft began this trend and has been releasing new products or new versions of the product once every three years. What this means is that the designers are at work as the dust settles after releasing the new product working on the next version. This is even before feedback from users on the latest release becomes available. Obviously, they are working on the feedback received on the last release. Now, the whole industry is following this trend which means our SDKs and third-party libraries are updated every three years. The result is by the time we release the product, new development tools and technologies are already in place. We have to learn about the new technologies and tools and begin work on our new version. The more time we take to learn, the less time we have for our new version. Any delay in our learning reduces the time available for us to design our new product. Therefore, we need to learn quickly. I think that slow learners have no place in the field of software design.

Fast reader: Designers have a lot to read. In fact, designers read more than any student preparing for examinations. And they do that every day! They have to read the updated usage manuals for new technologies, technical journals, conference proceedings, technical papers, requirements documents, and so on. They have to read them, understand them, assimilate the content, and then apply it in their designs. This requires the ability to read quickly, and that reading is not just to complete the assignment and forget soon after. Therefore, in my humble opinion, the designer needs to be a fast reader.

Perseverance: Perseverance is persisting with an endeavor in the face of opposition, difficulties, and setbacks. In my humble opinion, this trait is essential in all persons to achieve success in any field of human endeavor. Design is not an easy task. It involves looking into the future and devising something that can be gainfully used by other human beings in the future. While people are quick to criticize, rarely do they come forward with positive suggestions beforehand. It is a fact that designers face more criticism than praise. People oppose good ideas. In fact, the better the idea, the stiffer the opposition. Every criticism, even if it is constructive, is discouraging. But it is perseverance that keeps designers moving forward toward success. Designers have to overcome opposition to persist with the idea, surmount and circumvent difficulties, and recover from setbacks to come out with great products.

Patience: Patience is restraining oneself from expressing anger or resentment at not getting the expected outcomes from a situation. Everything in life takes more time and effort from us than we had originally estimated or expected. Only a few people can afford the expense of expressing their irritation at the delays and extra effort. Designers are not among those who can afford to express annoyance. To bring a great idea to reality takes perseverance and patience in addition to ingenuity. Designers need abundant patience to see their great ideas take shape.

Pursuit of excellence: Excellence is a continuously moving target that can be pursued through actions of integrity, reliability, efficiency, knowledge, commitment, meeting all obligations, continuously learning, and improving in all spheres to meet the moving target. Excellence is a pursuit and not a goal. When you think you have arrived, the goal posts move even before you reach them. If we want to make great designs, we need to be continuously pursuing excellence. This is one essential trait that designers ought to have.

In these personality traits, I did not discuss one essential trait: integrity. I am sure all professional organizations include integrity as an essential requirement for prospective employees. Present-day organizations conduct an aptitude test before conducting interviews as a matter of routine in the recruitment process. Aptitude tests are psychometric tests to ensure that the candidates possess the traits necessary to perform well on the job once inside the organization. Usually, these tests are designed with one grade of employees in mind. For example, an organization is likely to use a different test for people in the worker category, one for professional workers, one for managers, and so on. Of course, in addition to aptitude testing, each candidate is tested for the technical skills expected of the position. In addition to the usual aptitude testing, it would be better if candidates for the position of software designer were subjected to special aptitude testing to ensure that they possess the above-enumerated personality traits.

Educational Qualifications Required for Software Designers

Usually, the industry prescribes a postgraduate qualification for recruitment as a software designer. The idea behind this practice is the belief that higher the level of education, the greater the knowledge the person has on the subject. Of course, this assumption is largely correct. But, I would like to suggest that the qualification be in computer engineering or computer science. In the present day, universities offer a variety of qualifications and certifications in the field of information technology and software development. Here is a sample list:

1. Computer science
2. Computer applications
3. Information technology
4. Software project management

5. Risk management

6. Software measurement

7. Information systems

8. Computer engineering

9. So on and so forth…

There could be other qualifications being offered by other universities. To my limited knowledge, universities are focusing on programming under the umbrella of software development. The topics of software requirements analysis, software quality assurance, software project management, and database management are more prominently covered than software design, if it is covered at all. More than one professor has said, "What is software design separate from programming?" As the current academic scenario is like this, I would like to suggest a postgraduate or graduate qualification that covers these subjects in significant detail:

1. Database management systems

2. Programming theory

3. Software requirements engineering and management

4. Software quality assurance

5. Screen design

6. Report design

7. Program design

8. Software maintenance

9. Software design, if available

There was a time, not so distant in the past, when postgraduates from the computer science stream were not available and the industry recruited from other disciplines. Now there is no shortage of postgraduates from the information technology stream. Therefore, I suggest recruiting postgraduates coming out of universities with majors in computer science or information technology. I am sure that one day, software design will be offered as a major in postgraduate-level course in universities.

Skills Necessary to Be a Successful Software Designer

In addition to educational qualifications and the personality traits described above, software designers need the skills enumerated below. Of course, education ought to have given them these skills, but in these days of varying syllabi adopted at different universities, we cannot know if all universities are imparting these skills.

1. *Excellent communication*: Communication is receiving and giving information. Designers need to communicate with the customers or organizational management to obtain the product specifications or requirements. In most cases, these interactions do not occur as and when we want. We have to understand, assimilate, and be

ready to implement these specifications in as few interactions as possible, as the concerned people have their own duties to be fulfilled and are not likely to allot us as much time as we wish to have. We have to ask focused, briefly worded questions to obtain the maximum amount of information in the minimum time possible. We have to communicate design information during quality assurance activities. As you climb to higher rungs of the organization, your ability to communicate defines your success, and designers are no exception.

2. *Excellent drafting skills*: Designers have to produce an immense variety of documentation. They may take the assistance of editors and technical writers, but the first draft of almost all documents has to be prepared by the designers. Designers prepare documents like the users' manual, operations manual, troubleshooting manual, test plans, training materials, and so on. So, one of the essential skills that a software designer must possess is excellent drafting skills.

3. *Excellent listening skills*: Every professional is expected to understand others' requirements and feedback. We have to assume that the givers of information or feedback lack good communication skills. We have to carefully listen to what is being communicated to us, or we are likely to miss out on something that we may have to regret later on. Listening skills are not very common or less common than speaking skills.

4. *Analytical skills*: Designers ought to possess analytical skills. They need to be adept in mathematical analysis, statistical analysis, and situational analysis. Without these three analysis skills, poor designs result. It is easy to process data and give information, but to give information that is actionable, analysis of data and information is a prerequisite.

5. *Diagramming skills*: A picture is worth a thousand words, goes the saying, and I subscribe to it. To communicate our designs, we need to produce a variety of diagrams. If designers are not adept at diagramming, the documentation and establishment of designs becomes very difficult. We need not have freehand sketching skills, but we ought to be able to produce line diagrams using drawing implements or a diagramming software tool.

Experience

Is it a good idea to recruit fresh talent coming from colleges into the design department to work as software designers? Organizations may be doing just that. I would not advocate that, however meritorious that candidate may be. In my humble opinion, it is better to route them through other departments so that they have a well-rounded idea of software products. I advocate routing them through these departments before they are put on software design work:

1. *Quality assurance*: Working in this department will give them a perspective of seeing the final product from the standpoint of the user. They will come to know what sort of mistakes are perpetrated on the product innocently. The second and more important perspective the prospective designers gain is the ability to criticize

the product. This will help them later on while reviewing their own or others' designs.

2. *Software maintenance*: Working in this department will bring them directly into contact with the end users and the problems faced by them because of bad designs. They will also come to know what impact a fault has on the smooth operation of an organization, as well as the losses suffered by the organization due to bad design. No other method can teach prospective designers the importance of defect prevention and efficient usage of computer resources, as well as how the performance of the application degrades as the load on the computer increases.

However, the stay in each of these departments should not be so long that the prospective designers develop an affinity for those departments. It should not be so short that they do not gain any useful information by working in those departments. If the departments have full load, a stay of six months is adequate in my opinion. That way, the prospective designers stay away from their department for about a year.

There is a practice of inducting people fresh from college into design departments without routing them through the quality assurance and software maintenance departments. Some management gurus have suggested that people must be developed to have one perspective and that is of their department and not of other departments. In their opinion, by routing people through other departments, they develop a sort of affection for those departments and begin showing more concern for the convenience of those departments in their work and neglecting other important aspects of their main work.

If there is a robust design department with a solid framework for achieving great designs in place in the organization, perhaps we can directly induct recruits into the design department as trainees to work with the already experienced designers. Otherwise, my humble suggestion is to route the fresh recruits through the two departments cited above.

Appendix C: Roles and Responsibilities

Introduction

Nothing delivers a great result by accident in organizations. Everything has to be planned meticulously and executed flawlessly. Even then, plans go berserk and execution goes haywire. Software design is no exception. In this chapter, let us see how to ensure that software design activities result in great products each and every time they are attempted. Organizations mainly have two layers, namely the management layer and the execution layer. Unless these two layers perform their responsibilities diligently, we cannot achieve the desired results efficiently and effectively. Let us discuss the roles and responsibilities of these layers in the following sections.

What Is Management?

The term *management* has multiple connotations. The first is a set of people managing the affairs of the organization. We hear people saying, thus, "This company has competent management." The second connotation is that of a body of knowledge. There is a body of knowledge collected on the subject of management, and universities are offering courses in management. The third connotation is of a process. The activities performed by people in the management ranks and the process to which those activities conform constitute the process of management.

Management was generally defined as the "art and science of getting things done." The activities performed by managers are generally accepted as planning, organizing, staffing, coordinating, and leading/directing/controlling. This was the consensus during the 1970s and 1980s when computers had not made extensive inroads into organizations and prior to the introduction of the famed IBM PC, which revolutionized the computing scenario, bringing computers from a central place to all the desktops in the organization. Now almost every employee has a computer as a workstation, and registers and paper exited the organization except for printouts as necessary. Now, powerful software for information management and analysis is available at a very low cost and organizations are using such tools. Now, the definition and activities of management have undergone a metamorphosis. We can no more look at management as getting things done. Now it is defined as "producing expected results." While earlier managers refrained from working with their own hands, present-day managers do work with their own hands. The secretaries, assistants, and such other positions who assisted managers in getting things done simply vanished from the organizations along with the manual typewriting machines.

With the advent of computers, the layers in management have shrunk considerably. Earlier, there were top management, senior management, middle management, and first-line management layers. Now the first-line management and middle management layers have evaporated. Top management, consisting of the board of directors and the senior management, including heads of profit centers and functional departments, remained. The top management sets broad policies and is concerned with appointing and overseeing the functioning of the senior management. It is the senior management who look after the day-to-day functioning of the organization, including facilitation of working. Software designers, as well as all the other employees in the organization, report to this senior management layer.

In this appendix, when we talk of management roles and responsibilities, we mean the senior management.

The Need for a Separate Software Design Department

Nothing great ever emerged by accident. Even those things that were discovered by accident were preceded by unrelenting effort and deep reflection on the problem at hand. When we attempt to accomplish things in an organization, our approach defines the outcome. Organizations in their infancy depend on an ad-hoc approach, but as they grow, they tend to move to a more methodical approach.

In the software development arena, most organizations do not see software design as a separate specialist activity. They usually group it with programming. But things are changing. The activities of database design and graphic design have been recognized as separate specialties apart from programming. Programmers use the deliverables given by the graphic designers to lay out their screens and develop programs connecting to the database designed by the database designers. In the present day, the project leader usually has a team of programmers and shares the services of database designers and graphic designers with other project leaders. Graphic designers and database designers are sharable resources shared among various software development projects reporting to the overall head of all the projects for administrative purposes and resolving scheduling problems. There are hardly any organizations that have independent software design departments. The growing popularity of agile methodologies also discourages specialization and discourages formation of a separate design department in software development organizations.

But to sustain specialist skills in the organization and to recruit, train, and ramp up graduates fresh out of college requires a specialist core group of designers in the organization. Having a separate core group of software designers as a specialist department in the organization has the following advantages:

1. The activity gets recognition as a separate specialty, which fosters pride in the work, leading to achievement of excellence in the deliverables.
2. It becomes easier to attract and recruit talent and train and develop a talented pool of software designers.
3. The junior members of this group have easy access to a more experienced and talented set of people bringing organizational experience to bear on the problem at hand and making it possible to design great products.
4. The people in the department develop an affinity with each other and can put all their heads together to solve difficult design problems.

5. When there is a pool of specialist designers, some can be assigned to research and development for developing new methodologies and technologies.

6. Peaks and troughs of workload are common to any department in any organization. When a trough happens in this department, the spare resources can be used to carry out research and development.

7. When there are peaks in the workload, the stress on one or two projects can be evenly shared among all the people in the department and thus avoid stressing out a few people, which is disastrous to the morale of the involved people.

8. When there is a common pool of designers, attrition due to any reason would not have a major impact on any project as resources can be adjusted among projects and the work can be carried out without any issues.

9. When there is a department, the consolidation of design tools and reusable designs can be gainfully employed. They can be collected at one place and reused as and when an opportunity arises.

10. It becomes easier to develop standards and guidelines, which can bring predictability and a minimum level of quality into the products as well as increasing the productivity of software designers.

11. With a separate department, it becomes feasible to develop processes and methods to infuse uniformity in the work of different people.

We can think of some more advantages of having a separate specialist software design department in a software development organization. I strongly advocate having a separate design department. I also advocate bringing the graphic design and database design activities under the umbrella of software design.

Roles and Responsibilities of Organizational Management

Organizational management is responsible for producing results for the entire organization and not just for the software design department. It has to provide support and facilities for every department. It cannot single out any one department or group of people for special treatment. That would be detrimental to the health of the entire organization. It accomplishes this feat by designing a framework for each department that will ensure that all of them work in tandem with each other, shoulder to shoulder in a close-knit manner. It ought to define a framework for software design to ensure that great designs are developed, resulting in great products. This framework should consist of:

1. A well-defined and continuously improving process: This ensures that work is carried out uniformly by all the employees working in the department. This process should include:

    a. *Design process*: This provides how design work is carried out by the employees carrying out software design across the organization. This is the top-level document in the process, and all other documents in the process are subordinate to this document. It includes how the software design work is initiated, how it is performed, how the quality of the deliverables is ensured, how waivers for any aspect are obtained, how to escalate issues, how to obtain approvals for deliverables, and so on. A simple framework for software design management includes:

    i.   Initiation of software design project

    ii. Executing the software design project

    iii. Quality assurance for the software design

    iv. Release the design

    v. Closure of the software design project

    b. *Procedures* for performing various activities: A procedure is a step-by-step instruction for carrying out a specific activity. There are separate procedures for how to perform software design activities such as screen design, report design, database design, query design, process design, arranging QC of designs, escalation when necessary, planning, and so on.

    c. *Formats and templates* for capturing information comprehensively: Formats are generally used to maintain records, and templates are used for documentation. Of course, sometimes formats are also used for creating documents. These are used to capture the designs as well as other information generated by the software designers.

    d. *Checklists* to ensure completeness of the work flawlessly. Checklists are an enumeration of items that can be checked off as token of having performed that activity or ensuring that the activity was satisfactorily performed. These are used by the performers of an activity as well as by the people ensuring that the activity is performed as expected.

2. *Standards and guidelines* for achieving a minimum level of quality in the activities performed: Standards are prescriptive and guidelines are suggestive, but both are directed at ensuring that a minimum level of quality is ensured in the deliverables. These standards and guidelines include details about selecting various options while carrying out various design activities. They also include details about the look and feel, ease of use, efficient use of resources, accuracy of results, and so on.

3. *Provide funding and resources* for carrying out the assigned work: All activities need funding, without which no employee can be recruited and, as a sequel, no work can be performed. Funding is required for salaries, tools, workstations, subscriptions to journals, participation in relevant seminars and conferences, experimentation when required, and so on. Then, we need human resources of good quality for carrying out the design activities, for advancing knowledge, for documentation, and for other necessary activities. Time is also a resource that needs to be available for doing quality work. In organizations, there are urgencies like time-to-market, beating the competition, idleness in downstream activities, late change requests, and a score of other valid reasons. Urgencies take away valuable time that is needed to achieve great results. Good planning coupled with controlled execution alleviates the necessity for urgencies. Planning is a management responsibility. Management ought to strive to provide adequate time for designers to do their work comfortably and without unnecessary pressures. Pressures are disconcerting and are capable of degrading the quality of work for anyone.

4. *Instituting a reward and recognition system* to recognize outstanding performers. This is described in greater detail in the following section.

5. *Knowledge repository*: Setting up and maintaining a credible knowledge repository is one of the main activities of management. This is a very important topic; therefore, it is detailed separately in Appendix D.

6. *Research and development facilities*: The onus for instituting and sustaining a robust research and development initiative in the organization rests on the shoulders of the organizational management. The temptation to have it only in name and not support it with funding and resources is very seductive. Many organizations take this route, maintain a research and development department only in name, and just pay lip service to it. A robust research and development initiative calls for experimentation on live projects. It can try out new methodologies and technologies and select the ones appropriate for the organization. It can also come into design projects to troubleshoot vexatious problems by providing expert resources. A professional software development organization seriously intent on achieving excellence in software designs and resultant products ought to institute a robust research and development in the organization to aid software designers.

The organizational management has the role described above in the matter of achieving excellent software designs, which will lead to the development of successful software products that work flawlessly and reliably. Now let us discuss the role of recognition and rewards to motivate the designers, which have the potential to elevate the performance from acceptable to excellent.

System for Achieving Excellence

All employees are expected, in theory at least, to perform at their peak capacity, but this expectation is limited to paper. Peak performance is normally delivered at the time of initial entry into the organization and when jobs are threatened. Most other times, employee performance hovers from just above the penalty-avoidance level to the above-average level. During planning and goal setting, only average performance (normal-case scenario) is considered, not peak performance (best-case scenario).

Ergonomic and industrial engineering studies show that peak performance is not sustainable for long periods, but that it is possible to improve performance over a period of time. Professor Elton Mayo's studies at the Hawthorne Works of Western Electric have shown conclusively that human performance can scale unheard-of peaks when the right motivation is provided. While it is not practical to enumerate and discuss the many current theories on motivation here, it is well recognized that a properly designed rewards and recognition system does elevate the commitment of individuals, motivating them to higher levels of performance. Therefore, most organizations use a variety of rewards and recognition systems to motivate employees. For a rewards and recognition system to be effective and result in higher levels of performance, it must feature the following characteristics:

- It must be a formal mechanism that recognizes and rewards efforts to improve the productivity and quality of products, with the rewards handed out regularly.

- It must be based on objective data that is obtained through systematic measurement.

- It must set aside a formal occasion when rewards and recognition are handed out. This occasion should be periodic and held without fail on its appointed day.

- It must allow star performers (those who always stand first for rewards and recognition) to be recognized separately and provide rewards for a wider section of employees. If it turns out that the same person, even with a deserving performance, earns the reward on every occasion, the system demotivates the rest of the employees. The system ought to give hope to all employees so that they aspire to receive the reward and work for it without having to compete with the "heavyweight champion."

- It must recognize an adequate number of employees on every rewards occasion. If only 1 employee out of 1000 is recognized once a year, the other employees will carry no hope of receiving a reward in their career with the organization. The material value of the reward can be reduced and the number of reward earners be increased so that hope remains in the rest of the employees that they will achieve the coveted recognition. Hope propels people to scale higher peaks in performance. It is the recognition that matters, not the material value.

All in all, it is necessary to define a scheme that truly recognizes achievements in the domain of software design and to reward such achievement fairly and regularly. It does not augur well at all if the recognition and rewards for achievements are given only sporadically or only when outstanding efforts manifest.

Roles and Responsibilities of Individual Designers

Individual designers make use of the organizational framework that fosters excellence and carry out software design for products diligently. The important point to note here is that software designers do not work "within the framework," they "make use of the framework." The objective of the organizational framework is not to constrain the software designers but to make their lives easier. The following are the important roles played by the software designers:

- Individual designers carry out software design to the best of their ability with as much diligence as possible to facilitate development of great products.

- Individual designers need to participate in the definition of all process assets, including processes, procedures, formats, templates, and checklists, as well as in rolling them out successfully.

- Diligently implement the approved processes in design projects, but this does not mean that they should stifle their creativity and innovation for the sake of implementing the approved process. They need to raise waivers whenever the need arises and obtain approvals for such waivers.

- Be on the lookout for the opportunities for improvement in the process assets; raise process improvement requests; and follow through on their analysis, approval, and updating the process assets with the approved process improvement requests.

- Continuously update their knowledge relevant to software design using every available avenue. They need to use the organizational knowledge repository, attend seminars or obtain the proceedings and study them, do self-study with books and journals, conduct and participate in knowledge-sharing sessions within the organization, participate in project postmortems to learn about design implementation successes, consciously study the feedback from the maintenance team, study the customer complaints received by the help desk, receive and study market reports of similar products collected by the marketing department, and use whatever other methods are available for updating their knowledge.

- Assist the organization in setting up and maintaining a credible knowledge repository, then make effective use of the same. Raise improvement requests as and when necessary.

- Any other activity that is necessary for improving the products of the organization or fostering an environment conducive to generating better product designs in the organization.

Excellence is an outcome of close, effective, and efficient collaboration between the organization and the individuals working in the organization. The organization is responsible for facilitating (funding, resources, framework, and support) excellence, and the individuals are responsible for using that facilitation and achieving the intended excellence in the deliverables of the organization. In that collaboration, both the organization and the individuals, along with the customers, the industry, the government, and the citizens—all of them—prosper together.

Appendix D: Knowledge Management

Introduction

There is an adage that knowledge is power. Knowledge is information about something, and it is gathered from study of books, structured training or instruction, observation, experimentation, information sharing, and experience. Knowledge is gathered over a period of time with conscious effort. There is one more adage relevant in this context. It goes something like this: "you listen, you forget; you see, you remember; and you do, you know." This implies that if you do/have an experience, you gain knowledge. If you listen or read, you gain theoretical knowledge, and when you observe or do something, you gain practical knowledge. Both theoretical and practical knowledge are important for success in any field.

Coming down from the theoretical level to the practical level, let us try to put knowledge in its proper perspective so that we understand what we need to do to manage knowledge in organizations. When work is carried out in organizations, significant amounts of data are collected and when this data is processed, we get information. When we put this information together and uncover patterns, we gain knowledge. Thus, there are three levels, data at the bottom, information in the middle, and knowledge at the top. If we allow data to come in, pass through, and leave, we do not have information. If we process data and derive information but leave it at that, we do not gain knowledge.

When things happen, the individuals performing and those observing gain knowledge. As long as people in the organization have knowledge, the organization has knowledge, as, after all, the organization is known by the people it employs. But when people leave the organization, the knowledge gained at the expense of the organization walks out with them. People leave an organization for various reasons, including retirement, death, resignation, or dismissal. When new people come in, they begin at the bottom of the knowledge continuum. Therefore, we have a need to put in place systems to gather knowledge, organize it methodically, and make it available to needy individuals within the organization with proper security measures. This will ensure that the knowledge generated in the organization stays in the organization and is put to profitable use for the organization.

Let us first understand what knowledge is:

1. Something that is believed, true, and reliable
2. More than information, the ability to detect patterns
3. Implies repeatability and predictability
4. Information, combined with experience, context, interpretation, and reflection
5. Ability to bridge gaps in information

Knowledge is of two types, namely explicit (rational/lower) knowledge and tacit (intuitive/ higher) knowledge. Explicit knowledge is the one we find in books and other media. It has been articulated and recorded. It is available for anyone for learning and utilization. Tacit knowledge is not amenable to being recorded on some media. It is difficult to explain. For example, diagnosing the malady affecting a patient, even for an experienced doctor, is not easy even with diagnostic tests. It comes with years of practice and interaction with senior doctors. Writing a compelling story, composing a master piece of music, producing a masterpiece of artwork, and so on, are beyond capture. We can teach the notes of music and singing, but it is not possible to teach how to produce a melodious song. You can teach language and grammar, but not how to write a bestseller. You can teach law, but not how to win cases. Often, we feel that we know more than we can articulate. Words are not adequate to express ourselves. That is tacit knowledge. It is not easy, of course, to understand tacit knowledge. But many have endeavored to convert this tacit knowledge into explicit knowledge so that others can learn and master it. That is how doctors are better able to diagnose maladies than ever before and athletes are given training to win events. Some tacit knowledge has been converted into explicit knowledge in the world, but a lot still remains as tacit knowledge.

However, we deal with explicit knowledge in organizations. It is amenable to capturing and management.

Sources of Knowledge

There are two sources of knowledge for an organization, namely internal sources and external sources. Internal sources of knowledge emanate from the operations of the organization and from the employees carrying out the assignments. We design products, and when we market them, we get feedback in the form of customer complaints and commendations about our product. This is knowledge. Similarly, we gain a huge amount of knowledge in all the operations of the organization. The successes tell us how to do well, and the failures tell us what not to do. We gain knowledge from both successes as well as failures.

External sources of knowledge are professional associations like the IEEE, standards bodies like the ANSI, industry associations like the NEMA, consultancy organizations such as Gartner, and so on.

The organization will certainly be a member of an association of organizations conducting similar business. Organizations also sponsor their employees to some professional associations by paying the membership fees. So, the organization has access to the knowledge gathered by these associations. The knowledge gathered by these organizations is in a structured manner and ready to use. But it is the internal knowledge that is in unstructured form and not amenable to immediate use by others. It remains with the individuals until it is analyzed, codified, and recorded.

In knowledge management, we deal primarily with capturing internal knowledge and the knowledge from external sources, analyzing it, codifying it, and recording it in a manner such that it becomes easy for the people who need it to locate and retrieve relevant knowledge quickly. In knowledge management, we have the following activities:

1. Capture knowledge.
2. Analyze the captured knowledge to identify its probable uses and users.

3. Codify the knowledge to classify it into various categories for easy retrieval.

4. Record the knowledge on a suitable medium for long-term storage and easy retrieval.

5. Organize to ensure that the activities are carried out regularly and efficiently without any external intervention.

Let us now discuss these activities in detail.

Capturing knowledge ought to be painless. We should not ask executives or managers to prepare documents for inclusion in the knowledge repository. One of the major causes knowledge management initiative failure is the way knowledge is captured. One fact to note is that we cannot capture knowledge! We can capture information and then derive knowledge. Failure occurs because executives are asked to capture knowledge and then transmit it to the knowledge repository.

We need to collect internal information from the normal organizational documents and information systems and then analyze the information to derive knowledge for the organization. The following internal documents can provide us with information from which we can derive knowledge:

1. Plans and schedules of all types

2. Design documents

3. Proposals or quotes submitted to prospective customers against requests for proposals

4. Proposal status reports from the marketing department

5. Specification documents for product or service

6. Test/inspection reports

7. Progress/status reports of different departments

8. Customer complaints/commendations

9. Interdepartmental complaints

10. Interactions with statutory agencies by exception

11. Best practices, worst practices, and special achievements

12. Any other organization specific documents

We can also draw information from organizational information systems resident on computers, such as:

1. ERP systems

2. CRM systems

3. SCM systems

4. Data warehouse management systems

5. Decision support systems

6. Management information systems

7. Business intelligence systems

8. Any reports commissioned by the top managements for any specific purpose

9. Any other organization-specific information systems

We can capture knowledge from external sources, too. The following are some sources for capturing information external to the organization:

1. Scientific and technical journals and journals published by professional associations
2. Information on websites
3. Seminars and conferences, including their proceedings
4. Standards published by standards bodies
5. Special reports brought out by consultancy organizations, such as Gartner and Forrester Research and research labs in universities and government agencies
6. Reports by statutory agencies that have investigated mishaps, accidents, and disasters

All the captured information either from internal or external sources needs to be stored in a methodical manner. We need to use computers to extract knowledge from information. Extracting knowledge manually is nearly impossible from the mass of information available. A powerful computer is a necessity and, of course, today's desktops have adequate power to do the job. We have to carefully design the data storage to methodically store the information captured; then we can apply our analysis algorithms to the information to cull the knowledge from the mass of information and make it available to our people who need it.

Information Analysis and Derivation of Knowledge

To uncover knowledge, we need to carry out quite a few analyses. If we have to use computers in analysis, the data have to be numeric. Of course, we can perform a limited analysis on alphanumeric data, too, but it is limited to indexing, ordering, and classification. A few analysis techniques are enumerated below, which are by no means exhaustive. We are also not going into the details of how to carry out these analyses, as it would unnecessarily extend this chapter. It would also not be possible to give those details in a comprehensive manner in this book. There are many resources out there in the form of books and internet resources to learn.

1. *Pattern recognition*: Our minds are well equipped naturally to recognize patterns using methods that are yet to be decoded. Fuzzy logic is one technique useful in discovering patterns. Then there are a host of mathematical algorithms, including swarm intelligence. All these can be used to recognize patterns and subject the emerging patterns to manual analysis or used directly.
2. *Relative occurrence*: Percentages, statistical measures of central tendency and dispersion, skewness, and so on are also useful to derive knowledge from a mass of information.
3. *Correlation analysis*: We can perform a correlation between one or more series of numeric data and derive a correlation coefficient. Alternatively, we can also correlate between a set of events and their outcomes to see if there is any relation between them to derive knowledge. An example of this type of correlation is the occurrence

of cold and the season of winter. We can also find the correlation between a random event and its circumstances to see if there is any relation between the circumstances and the event.

4. *Variance analysis*: In organizations, there are estimates and actual achievements, plans and their results, schedules and their realization. We can carry out variance analysis between these values to derive knowledge. It would be better to normalize the values for known causes affecting the values so as to obtain credible results.

5. *Trend analysis*: As we collect data over a period of time, we can carry out trend analyses on the data for chronological trends. This knowledge is useful in a variety of ways to the organization. In addition to chronological trends, we can also derive trends for random events and the circumstances surrounding them.

6. *Critical examination* of successes and failures from various reports generated in the organization. Critical examination is an industrial engineering technique that subjects a specific piece of information, technique, event, or value to a set of primary questions about the purpose, the place, the chronological sequence, the person performing it, and how it is performed. Then we ask a secondary set of questions of "what else" and "what should" for each of the primary questions. The question "what else" begets the alternatives, and the question "what should" gives the best-suited alternative. Subjecting the information to critical examination helps in deriving credible knowledge that can be disseminated to the concerned parties.

Perhaps we can perform more analyses. The purpose is to derive knowledge from the mass of information generated in the organization to make sense of it and to derive knowledge that can be utilized by people in the organization for the benefit of the organization.

Where do we get the data for all these analyses? If we have to get the data separately from people, it will be very difficult and uneconomical. We need to get them from the normal documents generated as part of the work and from information systems. Timesheets filled in by employees can provide information. So can design documents, plans, schedules, progress reports, estimates, and other documents. We may perhaps need to enter these data from the documents either manually or electronically. We can perhaps use software to scan the documents and pick up the data automatically, too.

Once we analyze information, we have derived knowledge, and it can be disseminated to the concerned people. But before we disseminate, it needs to be organized.

We basically have data that are facts and figures of various operations performed in the organization. That data are in the organizational information systems. We derive some information from them and store it separately. Some of the information derived from organizational information systems is just information from which knowledge can be derived on the fly using specially developed software, and some of the derived information can be knowledge itself. Therefore, we need to organize the derived information/knowledge carefully so that it is easy for the concerned people to use effectively.

We usually organize our knowledge repository as a knowledge base and a corporate memory. A knowledge base contains directly actionable knowledge. Corporate memory contains derived information after all abnormal values are removed and the information is credible. Corporate memory consists of information in a database or a document repository containing documents like estimates, plans, schedules, best/worst practices, and so on. We attach an inference engine (software) to this information to derive knowledge on the fly as and when needed.

A knowledge repository is usually associated with discussion boards/databases in which concerned staff members conduct moderated discussions about the contents of the knowledge repository. If the discussions result in a consensus about an aspect, that would be fed back into the knowledge repository.

We also create a database of best and worst practices, which are usually in documents. We create an index that is easily searchable and through which the desired document can easily be accessed.

A very important aspect of organizing a knowledge repository is the system of retrieval by concerned people in the organization. The retrieval should be easy and fast. A knowledge repository is like a library of books, but with all information inside computers. How do we access knowledge? We may need patterns, we may need trends, we may need projections, and we may need documents. Our system should enable retrieval of all these and more depending on the needs of the organization and the contents of the knowledge repository. It should enable key phrase searches, document searches, data analysis, and other tools as necessary.

Creating a Knowledge Repository

A knowledge repository is a set of software tools that has the following components:

1. A set of documents, and this set may have innumerable documents named and organized in carefully captioned folders on one or more servers. The knowledge repository software should have an easily searchable index and facilitate retrieval.

2. A database of knowledge: This contains carefully culled knowledge from the organizational information. The knowledge repository software will have facilities to search and locate the right knowledge for the purpose.

3. The data and information in the information systems of the organization: The knowledge repository software hooks into these data, analyzes and extracts information from the data at current dates, and populates the knowledge repository or just makes it available to the requestor, as the case may be.

4. Setting up discussion databases for focus groups to discuss the issues and find solutions.

5. Mechanisms for knowledge sharing among employees.

6. A set of software tools that facilitate efficient functioning of the knowledge repository.

Creation of a knowledge repository is the responsibility of the top management. It takes a significant amount of resources in terms of money, human resources, and then time of top management. It needs specialists to be brought in to create the repository and to develop software for its usage. Then we need to maintain the repository, which requires human resources and funding for additional hardware and software. That is the reason many organizations pay lip service to knowledge management activities and leave it at that.

The following are the steps in creating a knowledge repository:

1. *Define framework*: This includes the definition of the components of the knowledge repository and the software interfaces needed for it, the hardware and software platforms on which the repository would reside, the strategy to acquire those

resources, the need for human resources for its initial creation and maintenance, and allocation of budgets. There could be other organization-specific issues in the creation of the repository.

2. *Collection and filtering mechanisms*: Maintaining a knowledge repository is a continuous activity, as new knowledge keeps surfacing every day. Therefore, we need to have robust mechanisms for collecting the information from internal as well as external sources of knowledge. It is easy to capture information from internal sources, as it emerges from the operations of the organization and comes in automatically. External information is not so easy to capture. We need to make special efforts to locate relevant knowledge and then capture it. We need to set aside people to do this job. The second aspect is the filtering the information to locate relevant knowledge from all the information that is coming in. We may need to analyze the information to weed out irrelevant or misleading information. For this, we need to allocate people or form committees with people from within the organization on a part-time basis.

3. *Transformation and loading*: We get information from various sources and the information is not in a format that can go straight into our knowledge repository. We need to transform the information from its present format to a format that is suitable for our knowledge repository. The transformation may be in two or three steps. For each source of information, we may need a separate software tool. Fortunately, we have off-the-shelf software tools to transform the incoming data and load them into our repository. All we need to do is to define the formats, and the software takes care of it. These tools will be frequently used, as knowledge collection is a continuous activity.

4. *Establish controls*: Without proper controls in place, the knowledge repository could soon become a dumping ground. We define a process for controlling the knowledge repository activities. We have to establish controls for the activities of:

    a. *Inducting new knowledge into the repository*: Without this control, the repository would become a dumping ground

    b. *Remove obsolete knowledge from the repository*: Knowledge is becoming obsolete due to newer developments and changing circumstances. For example, what is the use of keeping voluminous information about floppy disks in the present day? Locating obsolete knowledge in the repository, the periodicity of reviewing the knowledge projected as obsolete, the decision to remove, and the postremoval actions form part of this control. When we delete information from the knowledge repository, we may keep it in the offline backups, or we may totally trash it, depending on the situation.

Now the knowledge repository is created and ready for use. The first activity is to populate the repository before it can be used by the staff in the organization.

Knowledge Management Activities

While setting up a knowledge repository is a one-time activity, maintaining and using it is a continuous activity. While top management has the onus for creating the knowledge repository and defining a framework for utilizing it, software designers bear the onus of utilizing it effectively and deriving benefits from it. These are the activities of maintaining the repository and utilizing it.

1. Finding knowledge, collecting it for analysis, and capturing it in the repository. This is an ongoing activity, especially for knowledge from external sources. We have to collect it in a state such that it can be put into analysis directly without needing further work on it. This is for every executive to do. Again, it is counterproductive to collect every bit of unusual information, for it can put too much load on analysis and the repository, too. We need to exercise good judgment to sift what is relevant and then collect it.

2. Discussion databases: Discussion boards and databases allow us to focus on issues that have not been solved somewhere, including outside the organization. We put our collective minds together to arrive at an optimum solution. As users, we need to volunteer to moderate discussions and to participate. When we moderate, we have to be quick to approve or disapprove messages so that meaningful discussion can take place. When we participate, we need to ensure that we are contributing meaningfully. There is no point in picking up arguments or picking feathers from an egg. Our aim should be to arrive at an optimum solution to the problem posed rather than to play one-upmanship games.

3. Encourage employees to share knowledge. We need to voluntarily share information with our peers and juniors and encourage others to do so. We also need to accord recognition for the initiatives taken by others in the enhancement of knowledge. Of course, the recognition need not be financial. A simple email recognizing and congratulating the individual would be well received. We can change the culture of the organization to one of striving to create new ideas as well as sharing them.

4. We need to carry out routine chores associated with administering the knowledge repository, including:
   a. Arranging analysis of collected information.
   b. Obtaining approval for inclusion or deletion of information.
   c. Managing the configuration of the system to ensure integrity of the information in the repository.
   d. Regular backups and restores as needed to keep the system running.
   e. Maintenance of the facilities housing the repository.
   f. Coordinating the collection of change requests for modification/enhancements of the software tools used in the repository.
   g. Analyze the change requests received, put up proposals, and obtain technical and financial approvals. Then coordinate the work related to software modification/enhancement as required and roll it out after it has been developed and subjected to quality assurance.
   h. Any other related task.

Some organizations attach the knowledge repository to the library. Perhaps this is right, as the function of library is also to store knowledge and make it available to those who need it and ask for it.

Role of Top Management

The role of top management is, as always, to define an efficient framework that can be utilized by the others to perform and excel. In this activity, building and maintaining the knowledge repository is a crucial activity, and top management has to take ownership of this activity. In these days of stiff competition, fast obsolescence, and globalization, the organization needs to be at the cutting edge of not only technology but also of knowledge. Therefore, it is imperative for the organization and the top management thereof to support knowledge management activities in the organization.

In day-to-day activities of knowledge management, the top management needs to oversee the state of the repository and its utilization, albeit in a cursory manner. It is often the case that there is a knowledge repository in the organization but rarely does anybody use it. The nonusage may have genuine reasons. Therefore, top management needs to monitor its performance and remove hurdles in the usage of the repository. Only then can the money invested in knowledge management yield benefits to the organization.

Role of Software Designers

The role of software designers is to perform all activities needed to make the initiative a success. The creation of the knowledge repository, loading it with knowledge, and then maintaining it need to be performed by the software designers. Maintaining the repository includes capturing the information, analyzing it, loading it into the repository, and attending to its routine chores. Apart from that, they are the people who utilize the repository. They need to make the knowledge repository work for the benefit of the organization.

Software designers also need to ensure that the repository is kept up to date by deleting obsolete information and loading it with state-of-the-art knowledge. They also need to look for opportunities for improvement in the repository and the software tools facilitating its usage. They need to raise modification/enhancement requests for the software tools or add a new section to the repository. To do that, they also need to submit requests to top management and obtain technical and financial approval for the desired modifications and improvements.

When all is said and done, we need to acknowledge that knowledge management is still poorly understood in the industry and still a neglected area in organizations.

Appendix E: Sample Set of Drawings

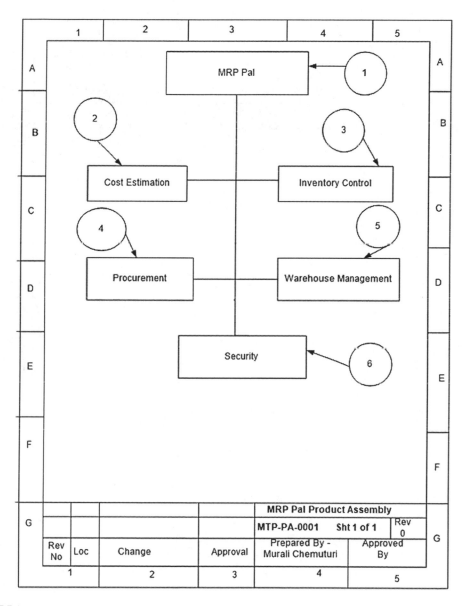

FIGURE E.1
A sample product assembly drawing.

	1	2	3	4	5	
		Bill of Data for MRP Assembly				
A	Item No	Description		Qty	Reference	A
	1	MRP Pal screen layout		1	MRP-SL-0002	
B	2	Cost estimation module screen layout		1	MRP-SL-0003	B
	3	Inventory control screen layout		1	MRP-SL-0004	
	4	Procurement module screen layout		1	MRP-SL-0005	
	5	Warehousing module screen layout		1	MRP-SL-0006	
C	6	Security Module Screen Layout		1	MRP-SL-0007	C
D						D
E						E
F						F
G				Bill of data for MRP Assembly		G
				MRP-BD-0001	Sht 1 of 1	Rev No - 0	
	Rev No	Loc	Change	Approval	Prepared By - Murali Chemuturi	Approved By	
	1		2	3	4	5	

FIGURE E.2
A sample bill of data.

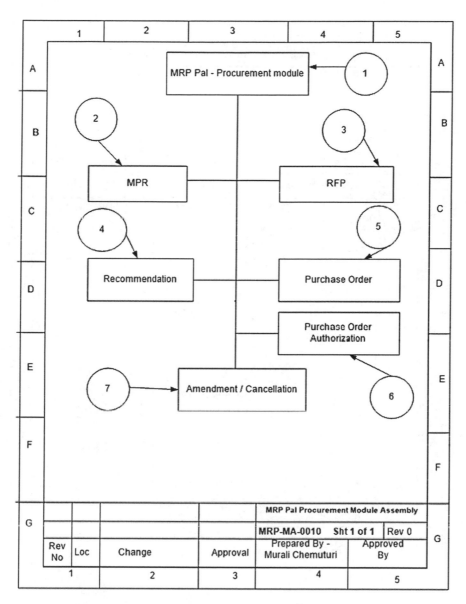

FIGURE E.3
A sample module assembly drawing.

	1	2	3	4	5	
A	**Bill of Data for Procurement Module Assembly**					A
A	Item No	Description		Qty	Reference	A
	1	Procurement module screen layout		1	MRP-SL-0005	
	2	MPR Functionality Screen layout		1	MRP-SL-0010	B
B	3	RFP functionality screen layout		1	MRP-SL-0011	
	4	Recommendation functionality screen layout		1	MRP-SL-0012	
	5	Purchase order functionality screen layout		1	MRP-SL-0013	
C	6	Purchase order authorization functionality screen layout		1	MRP-SL-0014	C
	7	Purchase order amendment/cancellation functionality screen layout		1	MRP-SL-0015	

				Bill of data for Procurement Module Assembly		
G				MRP-BD-0001	Sht 1 of 1	Rev No - 0	G
	Rev No	Loc	Change	Approval	Prepared By - Murali Chemuturi	Approved By	
	1		2	3	4	5	

FIGURE E.4

A sample bill of data for a module assembly.

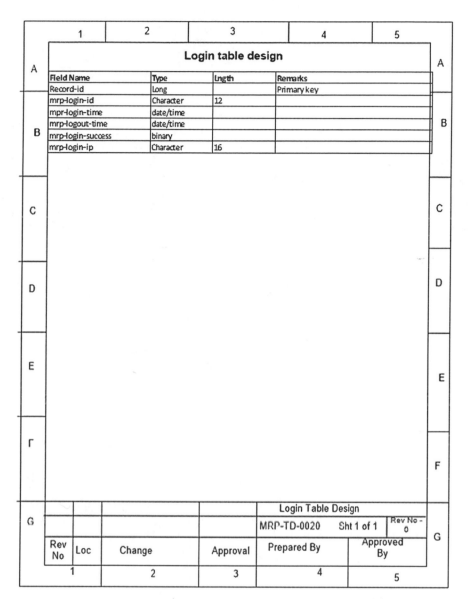

FIGURE E.5
A sample database table design.

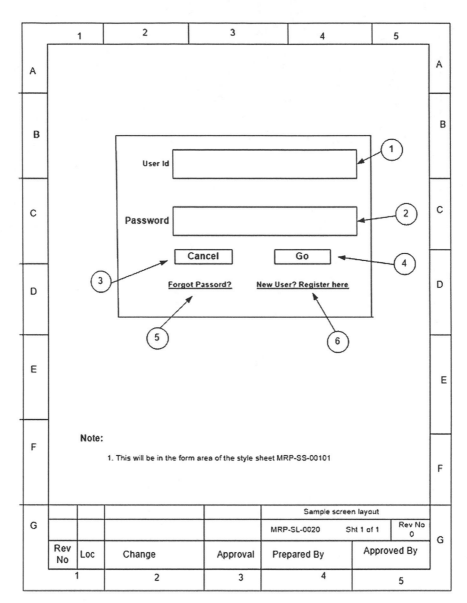

FIGURE E.6
A sample screen layout drawing.

	1	2	3	4	5	
A			**Bill of Data for Login screen**			A

	Item No	Description		Qty	Reference	
A						A
B	1	Text box - mrp-login-userid		1		B
	2	Text box - mrp-login-password		1		
	3	Command Button for save operation		1	MRP-SU-00031	
	4	Command Button for cancel operation		1	MRP-SU-00032	
C	5	Link for Forgot password functionality		1	MRP-SL-00033	C
	6	Link for New User Registration functionality		1	MRP-SL-00034	

Bill of data for MRP Login Screen

MRP BD 0020   Sht 1 of 1   Rev No - 0

Rev No	Loc	Change	Approval	Prepared By - Murali Chemuturi	Approved By
1		2	3	4	5

FIGURE E.7
A bill of data for screen layout drawing shown in Figure E.6.

A.	**General specifications**		
1	Stationery used	15" X 12", perforated,	
2	Report name	Statement of Monthly Material	
3	Database name	DB-MRP- Materials	
		TBL-Matl_Master	
		TBL-Matl-Receipts	
4	Table Names	TBL-Master_-Dtls	
		Rcpt_dt >= beginning date AND	
5	Filter	Fld-Rcpt_dt>= ending date)	
B.	**Page heading – centralized horizontally**		
1	Font	Arial black, 14 point, bold	
2	Line 1	Table name - TBL-Master_-Dtls	
3	Line 2	Report name given in A-2 Field name – FLD-Coname	
C.	**Column heading**		

		Beginning position	Length	Caption
1	Line 1	Dashed line		
2	Line 2 – column			
	Column 1	0	6	Item No
	Column 2	8	10	Item Code
	Column 3	20	80	Item Description
	Column 4	102	10	Item Rate
	Column 5	114	4	Qty
	Column 6	120	12	Amount
3	Line 3	Dashed line		

D.	**Columns**		
Tables 1 - TBL-Matl_Master			
2 - TBL-Matl-Receipts			

	Column number	Beginning position	Length	Contents
1				
	Column 1	0	6	Integer – Auto increment number
	Column 2	8	10	Character - TBL-Matl-Receipts – Fld_item-Code
	Column 3	20	80	Character - TBL-Matl-Receipts – Fld_item-Desc
	Column 4	102	10	Numeric - TBL-Matl-Master – Fld_item-Rate
	Column 5	114	4	Numeric - TBL-Matl-Receipts – Fld_item-Qty
	Column 6	120	12	Numeric – format 999999999.99 – (cplumn 4 X column 5)

Monthly Materials Receipts Report

Drwing No. MRP-RL-0039 Sht 1 of 2			Rev No 0

Rev No	Loc	Change	Approval	Prepared By - MC	Approved By CMK
1		2	3	4	5

FIGURE E.8

A sample report layout—Sheet 1 of 2.

	1	2	3	4	5	
A		**E Page Totals**					**A**
		1 Line 1	Dashed line				
		2 Line 2 - column	Beginning position	Length	Caption		
B		Column 1	0	11	Page Totals		**B**
		Column 2	120	12	Sum of Column 6 of the page only		
		3 Line 3	20	80	Item Description		
		Column 1	0	16	Cumulative total		
C		Column 2	120	4	Sum of Column 6 from the beginning to the present page only		**C**
		4 Line 4	Dashed line				

Note:

1. Grand totals and control statistics would be printed on a separate page after the last page of the data.

2. All positions indicated are in number of characters

			Monthly Materials Receipts Report		
G				Drwing No. MRP-RL-0039 Sht 2 of 2	Rev No 0
	Rev No	Loc	Change	Approval	Prepared By - MC	Approved By CMK
	1	2	3	4	5

FIGURE E.9

A sample report layout—Sheet 2 of 2.

Index